ALSO BY BARRETT TILLMAN

★ ★ ★

America's Fightingest Ship

and the Men Who Helped

Win World War II

★ ★ ★

ENTERPRISE

BARRETT TILLMAN

SIMON & SCHUSTER

NEW YORK   LONDON   TORONTO   SYDNEY   NEW DELHI

Simon & Schuster
1230 Avenue of the Americas
New York, NY 10020

First Simon & Schuster hardcover edition February 2012

SIMON & SCHUSTER and colophon are registered trademarks
of Simon & Schuster, Inc.

For information about special discounts for bulk purchases,
please contact Simon & Schuster Special Sales at
1-866-506-1949 or business@simonandschuster.com.

The Simon & Schuster Speakers Bureau can bring authors
to your live event. For more information or to book an event,
contact the Simon & Schuster Speakers Bureau at
1-866-248-3049 or visit our website at www.simonspeakers.com.

Designed by Ruth Lee-Mui
Maps by Paul J. Pugliese

Manufactured in the United States of America

1   3   5   7   9   10   8   6   4   2

Library of Congress Cataloging-in-Publication Data

Tillman, Barrett.
Enterprise : America's fightingest ship and the men who helped win World War II /
Barrett Tillman.
p.   cm.
Includes bibliographical references and index.
1. Enterprise (Aircraft carrier : CV-6) 2. World War, 1939–1945—Naval operations,
American. 3. World War, 1939–1945—Aerial operations, American. 4. World War,
1939–1945—Campaigns—Pacific Ocean. I. Title.
VA65.E5T65 2012
940.54'5973—dc23   2011039886
ISBN 978-1-4391-9087-6
ISBN 978-1-4391-9089-0 (ebook)

To the carrier aviators, aircrewmen, and sailors of the U.S. Navy who fought and won the Second World War.

Eternal father, strong to save,
Whose arm hath bound the restless wave,
Who bid'st the mighty ocean deep
Its own appointed limits keep;
O hear us when we cry to thee,
For those in peril on the sea.

Lord, guard and guide the men who fly,
Through the great spaces of the sky;
Be with them always in the air,
In dark'ning storm or sunshine fair.
O hear us when we lift our prayer,
For those in peril in the air.

—"THE NAVY HYMN"

CONTENTS

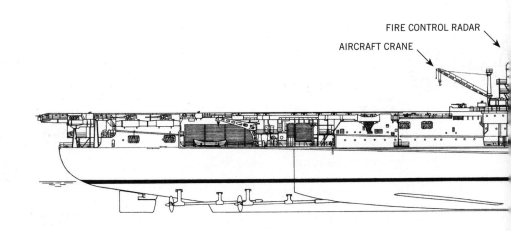

FIRE CONTROL RADAR

AIRCRAFT CRANE

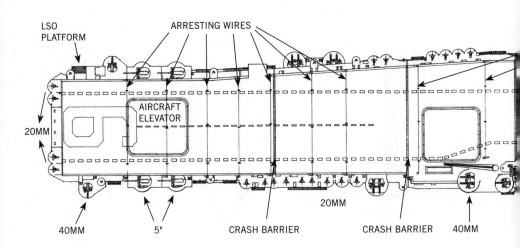

LSO
PLATFORM

ARRESTING WIRES

AIRCRAFT
ELEVATOR

20MM

20MM

40MM   5"   CRASH BARRIER   CRASH BARRIER   40MM

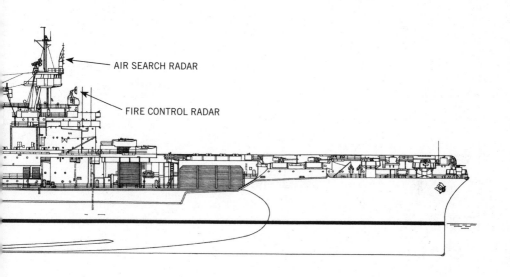

AIR SEARCH RADAR

FIRE CONTROL RADAR

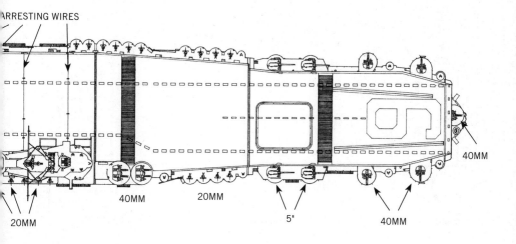

ARRESTING WIRES

40MM

20MM

40MM

20MM

5"

40MM

Aleutian Islands

N
W E
S

PACIFIC OCEAN

□ Midway

International Date Line

□ Marcus

Hawaiian Islands
Pearl Harbor •
Oahu
Hawaii

□ Wake

Kwajalein

Eniwetok □
ine Islands
Marshall
Islands
◙ Truk

Palmyra
Christmas
Line Islands

◪ Tarawa

Gilbert Islands

Equator

aul Bougainville

Solomon
Islands

Georgia

Cook
Islands

Guadalcanal

oral Sea
New
Hebrides
Fiji Islands

New
Caledonia
Noumea •

Pacific Ocean

Islands

Note on Distances and Aircraft Code Names

Though naval usage employs nautical miles (1.15 statute miles), throughout the text distances are rendered in statute miles for a general readership.

Japanese aircraft code names appear throughout the book for the convenience of many readers. "Zeke," "Betty," "Val," and other Allied names were assigned in late 1942 but are employed anachronistically here from Pearl Harbor onward.

ENTERPRISE

PROLOGUE

Kearny, New Jersey, 1958

In the tidal flats of the Hackensack River rested a warship waiting to die. She was the most honored man-o'-war in her nation's history. In the spring of 1958, however, USS *Enterprise* (CV-6) was just one more project in a long line of structures due for dismembering.

Lipsett Incorporated was vastly experienced in demolition. Among its credits were dismantling New York City's Second Avenue and Third Avenue elevated lines, as well as many previous ships.

An obsolete aircraft carrier, *Enterprise* had been stricken from the Navy's register in October 1956 and purchased for scrap. Lipsett reckoned that it could turn the half-million-dollar acquisition into a profit by rendering the ship's components into salvageable materials.

The carrier's distinctive tripod mast had been removed at the Brooklyn Navy Yard, toppling onto the flight deck so she could clear the East River bridges en route to the Kearny, New Jersey, execution site. Propelled by tugs, *Enterprise*'s final journey had taken her past Brooklyn Heights and Governors Island, southwesterly into Upper Bay, thence across to Jersey. Despite the foggy weather, thousands of people and scores of small craft had turned out to witness her dolorous trek.

Now, riding easily alongside Lipsett's pier, *Enterprise* was still intact, her cavernous hangar deck empty of men and aircraft. Only the large scoreboard depicting her wartime tally reminded visitors of what she had been, where she had sailed, and what she had done. She was already thoroughly demilitarized: her last aircraft gone since 1945; her antiaircraft batteries removed; her communications and radar equipment stripped away.

In her ready rooms, the chairs for pilots and aircrewmen stood empty, facing large blackboards still bearing grids for navigation, plane assignments, and weather data.

It was easy to think, *Here there be ghosts.*

Up in flag quarters Vice Admiral William F. Halsey had learned the stunning news of the Sunday surprise at Pearl Harbor on December 7, 1941. He had vowed that before he and *Enterprise* were finished the Japanese language would be spoken only in hell.

On the after part of the flight deck, on February 1, 1942, a machinist's mate had leapt into a parked dive-bomber and grasped a .30 caliber machine gun to shoot at a Japanese bomber bearing down upon the ship. His heroic initiative earned him aircrew status—and after the Battle of Midway, a terrible fate at the hands of his captors.

In a once boisterous ready room, Torpedo Squadron Six had been briefed for its disastrous date with glory on June 4, 1942. Fourteen Douglas Devastators had rumbled off the deck to attack the Japanese fleet threatening Midway: four returned, one so badly shot up that it was pushed overboard.

Portside aft was the landing signal officer's platform where a darkly handsome lieutenant had delivered a virtuoso performance, bringing aboard plane after plane onto the increasingly crowded deck after bomb damage on October 26, 1942.

In the combat information center, specially trained officers and men had conducted the first generation of electronic warfare. Tracking phosphors on radar screens, they had conducted electronic triage, naming various blips as friendlies, bogies, and hostiles, taking appropriate action for each.

In the forward elevator well a Japanese pilot had plunged his Zero on May 14, 1945, killing himself and a dozen sailors and ending the Big E's combat career.

But all that was in the past now, fast disappearing in the memory of a nation bursting with excitement over the dawning space age, hula hoops, and television.

Disposal of the ship—expected to take eighteen months—was placed in the hands of a master executioner. W. Henry Hoffmann was a man of the sea. He had seen combat with the kaiser's navy in the Great War, sailed in the Norwegian merchant marine, had taken himself to America where he demonstrated an intuitive grasp of engineering. Becoming a foreman on the New York subway system, he then returned to his nautical roots by joining Lipsett.

By 1958 Hoffman had dismantled three battleships and the luxury liner *Normandie*. With that extensive background, he brought to the task at hand an appreciation for the history inherent to every ship. His feelings for USS *Enterprise* were evident in the way he documented her destruction: Hoffman carefully recorded the process with 150 photographs, showing the phased reduction from a recognizable warship into 20,000 tons of scrap metal.

In 1959, before the project was finished, Hoffman donated the carrier's stern plate, bearing her name, to the nearby township of River Vale, New Jersey.

Meanwhile, the process continued. The wooden flight deck was smashed to splinters by air hammers, permitting access to the cavernous hangar deck below. After the three aircraft elevators were cut up, work began dismantling the structure. It was a tricky job, as removing eight-by-forty-foot steel slabs affected the ship's balance, and Lipsett devoutly wished to avoid capsizing the hulk. Alternately, large hunks of the bow and stern were severed, working toward the middle. Occasionally partial flooding of the hull preserved *Enterprise*'s trim. Fifty-ton gantry cranes hoisted each slab sliced from the hull as the process continued day by day, month by month.

Where high-powered aircraft engines once had revved up, spinning three-bladed propellers; where antiaircraft guns had chattered and boomed at inbound attackers, another cacophony erupted. The hull was crisscrossed with air lines for pneumatic hammers that raised a din while oxy-acetylene torches gushed and sparked as they bit into tempered steel.

Enterprise's flight deck of Douglas fir was burned. Some profit was realized by stripping out miles of copper wiring and burning off the insulation so the base materials could be recycled.

Each of the four shafts and propellers weighed nearly forty tons, but even with the weight of the superstructure gone, they remained underwater. Divers cut slits in the shafts that weakened their integrity, and when they fell of their own weight, they were lifted out by huge gantries. That was the last major chore; all that remained was the dismembered center hull.

The task was finished in May 1960, when the keel was dragged ashore. There, the Big E's structural spine was severed into manageable pieces and hauled away. Ironically, considering her history, much of the steel was sold to companies in Japan.

Lipsett had purchased *Enterprise* for $561,333. It was a fraction of the $20 million she had cost the American taxpayer twenty years before, but by 1958 that was the value of her 20,000 tons of steel, aluminum, copper, rubber, asbestos, wood, and assorted other materials.

In 1942 she had been priceless.

During the Second World War, the U.S. Navy recognized forty-one Pacific battles or campaigns. *Enterprise* was involved in twenty, a record unmatched by any other ship. The cruiser *San Francisco* (CA-38) finished with seventeen battle stars, and the next most engaged carrier was *Essex* (CV-9) with thirteen. But the Big E's unique record was not merely the number of her engagements: far more important were her specific battles. When the need was greatest, *Enterprise* with her sailors and fliers had been there, from Pearl Harbor almost to VJ Day. She outlived four of the other five Pacific Fleet carriers during 1942, and the vital Midway battle would have been lost without her. Eight months later, at the end of the sanguinary Guadalcanal meat grinder, she was America's only large carrier still steaming in the Pacific.

Because of her battle honors, the Big E was called "the fightingest ship" in the U.S. Navy. A few pretenders—late-coming carriers or surface ships of long service but little combat—tried to usurp the title but they made poor competitors.

Even discounting her record, *Enterprise* proved a highly adaptable lady. She bulked up from her original 25,000 tons loaded weight to 32,000 with more of everything. Wartime requirements called for more men, food, fuel, airplanes, guns, electronics, and just plain stuff than her designers ever anticipated. At the end of the war, the Big E had crammed, wedged, and finagled thirteen pounds into a ten-pound seabag.

Men were the most pliable commodity aboard and, of course, the most important. From her 1938 complement of 2,100 sailors and fliers, her manning grew to nearly 3,000. They lived cheek by jowl with each other for weeks and even months at a time: eager-earnest youngsters of seventeen and world-experienced seadogs in their fifties. *Enterprise* had fifteen captains during her nine-year career (nine were wartime skippers) but few made an impression. Her deck plate leaders were petty officers and chiefs who had been aboard for years and knew their jobs and their men intimately. The most influential officers were two "execs"—also aviators— who bonded with the "whitehat" enlisted men and retained their welfare at heart even after leaving the ship.

Enterprise pioneered the arcane martial art of flying from carriers at night. Her aviators became winged evangelists, preaching the heretical gospel of nocturnal tailhook aviation. In doing so, they stripped away the enemy's advantage of darkness, exposing him to attack twenty-four hours of every violent day.

At the end of the war, the United States possessed nearly 100 carriers of all types and sizes. But the taxpayers who purchased *Enterprise* had come to know her as they knew no other vessel of the conflagration spanning the world's greatest ocean. She was *Enterprise*—the Big E. Thirteen years after the war, Americans still remembered when she had been the last fighting flattop in the Pacific, so they strove to save her from the breaker's yard. When that effort failed, thousands paid her homage as she made her way to the Jersey shore.

Enterprise was America's ship, and there will never be another like her. This is her story.

1

* * *

"I Have Done the State Some Service"

Lucy L. Swanson, wife of the secretary of the navy, christens USS *Enterprise* on October 3, 1936. (Joel Shepherd, Enterprise Assn.)

The Roosevelts long had their hands on the helm of the U.S. Navy. In an unprecedented record, five members of the extended family served as assistant secretary of the navy for half the years between 1897 and 1936. Two made historic contributions.

The first was Theodore, who loved naval history. Following graduation from Harvard in 1882, he published a landmark account of the War of 1812. It was so thorough and well written that it remained in print more than a century later.

Despite his pince-nez glasses and portly physique, young Theodore was no dilettante. He lauded "the fighting races," and his combative juices could boil over. In 1897 he declared, "I should welcome almost any war, for I think this country needs one." When he saw the opportunity, he grasped it with both stout hands.

In 1898 when the battleship *Maine* blew up in Havana Harbor, Teddy was assistant secretary of the navy and, in the secretary's absence, he ordered fleet units to prepare for action before a declaration of war with Spain. Thereupon he resigned to form a volunteer regiment of Eastern socialites and Western broncobusters that rose to glory in Cuba. Nine years later, having inherited the presidency from the martyred William McKinley, Teddy gleefully sent the Great White Fleet on a fourteen-month world cruise, adding an exclamation point to the drubbing that the Yankee navy had inflicted upon a European power.

Teddy's fifth cousin Franklin was assistant secretary from 1913 to 1920, the second-longest tenure ever. Diagnosed with polio in 1921, Roosevelt was paralyzed below the waist—a fact kept from the public for the rest of his life. But he projected a vigorous image that helped propel him to four terms as the nation's commander in chief.

Upon election as president in 1932, the patrician FDR sought to rescue the American Everyman from the grinding grip of the Great Depression. Whether his economic policies helped or hurt remains disputed, but one thing is certain: no chief executive wielded executive power more broadly or enthusiastically than Franklin Delano Roosevelt.

With an ironclad majority in the 73rd Congress, in 1933 the Democrats voted $238 million for public works. On June 16 Roosevelt issued Executive Order 6174, which required some of the public largess to be used for naval construction. Subsequently, funding was channeled to the Works Progress Administration as a job program for the Norfolk area. Those funds included two new aircraft carriers.

ENTER THE AIRCRAFT CARRIER

Between the assistant secretary tenures of Theodore and Franklin Roosevelt, by far the greatest change in naval affairs was aviation. The British Royal Navy had first flown combat aircraft from ships during the Great War, and the world's admiralties took note. America and Japan followed, slowly perfecting the ships, planes, and operating procedures that would fight the Second World War.

By 1934 America had four flattops in commission. The USS *Langley* (CV-1) was an experiment dating from 1922. Upon her short, narrow deck, the first generation of tailhook aviators learned their esoteric trade, occasionally paying their tuition in blood.

Langley was followed by two fighting carriers, the sisters *Lexington* (CV-2) and *Saratoga* (CV-3), in 1927. Converted from battle cruiser hulls in compliance with the Washington Naval Treaty, they were 33,000-ton giants capable of thirty-two knots while launching seventy or more aircraft. "Lex" would die early, in the Coral Sea battle of May 1942, while "Sara" survived torpedoes and kamikazes to perish in a radioactive cloud at Bikini Atoll in 1946.

CV-4 was *Ranger*, the misbegotten result of treaty obligations. Too small and slow to compete in the nautical Darwinism of the Pacific war, she served briefly in European and African waters but spent most of her war days in training status. Clearly, the Navy needed larger, more capable carriers for the future.

Thus emerged the Yorktowns, contracted to Newport News Shipbuilding Company in August 1933. The name ship of the class was CV-5, laid down in May 1934. *Enterprise*'s (CV-6) keel was laid in July, and she was launched on October 3, 1936.

The Yorktown design was expensive. It cost nearly $1,000 per ton, and tonnage was a huge factor when the United States remained bound by naval treaties limiting the size of warships.

A carrier was a giant three-dimensional jigsaw puzzle; a 20,000-ton Rubik's cube. For a given volume, designers had to find room for more than 2,000 men to work, eat, and sleep; for the machinery to power the ship; for seventy or more aircraft; for thousands of tons of fuel oil and aviation gasoline; for bombs and torpedoes and ammunition and food; for communications and staff space.

The Yorktown design was the product of enormous study that would shape not only a ship's configuration but its nautical character. Throughout 1931 the Navy considered fifteen sets of specifications for the next carrier, ranging from 13,800 to 27,000 tons and a hull 730 to 900 feet long. The ninth option, "Scheme I," was selected: tentatively 20,000 tons standard displacement and 770 feet in length, subject to modification.

Considerable foresight was needed in designing the next-generation flattops. In 1932 carrier aircraft were all biplanes, but with commissioning expected in 1937–38, the ships would operate some all-metal monoplanes—faster and heavier than existing aircraft. Naval architects made adjustments, providing larger hangar decks, bigger flight deck elevators, and more powerful catapults to launch airplanes. Heavy armor was installed, especially around bomb and torpedo magazines—a decision that would pay dividends in 1942.

But every ship is a compromise, and something had to give in the Yorktowns. That was underwater protection against torpedoes. Committed to a specific hull shape with only a twenty-four-foot draft, the CV-5 design could not accept a wider midships section without unacceptable increases in power plant and weight. The compromise required that antitorpedo protection ended just four feet above the keel, with little air space between the protective layer and the hull.

The final design naturally affected seakeeping qualities. Because the Yorktowns were "fine-ended," the unusually narrow bows and sterns provided little buoyancy. That meant greater bending stresses at sea, translating engineering data into a ship's physical personality—how she performed when under way. Thus, the carriers' handling and seakeeping qualities were determined long before any of them met saltwater.

Another factor was weight of the flight deck. Steel decks would increase the ship's rolling tendency in heavy seas with a higher center of gravity than wood. The Navy favored Douglas fir, which was resilient enough to withstand repeated impacts of landing aircraft. The new carrier's flight decks—802 by 86 feet—were each an acre and a half of piney product from the Great Northwest.

A NAME FOR CV-6

Three quarters of a century later, it is unknown who suggested the name for CV-6, but certainly *Enterprise* came from a list maintained by the secretary of the navy's office. *Lexington, Saratoga,* and *Yorktown* honored Revolutionary War battles, while *Ranger* had been one of John Paul Jones's ships—all were more recognizable names than *Enterprise.* Six previous vessels dating to the Revolution had borne the name, including a sloop lost to the British at Lake Champlain in 1776; a successful privateer against Britain, France, and Tripoli; and a World War I vessel. None was famous, but CV-6 would permanently affix the name *Enterprise* to the dome of the naval pantheon.

In the Navy's Bureau of Ships, draftsmen's paper was consumed in wholesale lots for delivery to Newport News and conversion into riveters' steel. As the hull was completed by stages, vital equipment was craned into place, including steam turbine engines and fuel oil bunkers as big as houses.

The Yorktowns were smaller than the Lexingtons but still good-sized for their day: 827 feet long and 114 wide, measuring 143 feet from keel to the top of the fire control mast. Fully loaded, a CV-5 ship displaced 25,500 tons of water.

Aircraft handling was an essential feature. The Lexingtons had two aircraft elevators, which proved insufficient because it took over thirty seconds to raise or lower each one. Experience with *Ranger* showed the advantage of three lifts, and that concept continued with CV-5 and -6, and their 1941 relative *Hornet* (CV-8).

Additionally, two hydraulic flight deck catapults and one hangar deck cat were installed, capable of flinging a six-ton airplane into the air. But the latter was rarely used and was removed in 1942.

Defensively, the two new carriers would be armored against the six-inch guns of light cruisers, and because dive-bombing seemingly posed the greatest threat, automatic weapons were provided. Originally the defensive batteries included eight five-inch guns and forty .50 caliber machine guns; the latter proved inadequate.

Yorktown was christened by Eleanor Roosevelt, the president's wife and Teddy's niece, in April 1936. The lead ship of the class raised her commission pennant in September 1937.

CV-6 was launched on Saturday, October 3, 1936, some twenty-seven months after her keel was laid. She was christened by Mrs. Lucy Swanson, wife of Navy Secretary Claude A. Swanson; she chose a passage from Shakespeare for the occasion. Quoting *Othello,* she declared, "May she also say with just pride, 'I have done the State some service.'" Then she swung a netted champagne bottle against the towering gray edifice, christening United States Ship *Enterprise.*

With that task completed, the blocks holding the hull were removed and the nascent aircraft carrier slid down the ways and entered her element, the waters of the world.

Yet much more work was required. Nineteen months would pass before *Enterprise* was commissioned on May 12, 1938: nearly four years from start to finish. The ceremony was endangered when a predawn storm blew in to the Virginia Peninsula, threatening rain. But as an official publication noted, on Thursday morning "the sun broke through auspiciously."

NEWT

Enterprise's commissioning skipper was fifty-seven-year-old Captain Newton H. White, Jr. Reared in rural Tennessee where he had attended a one-room school, he struggled at Annapolis, making the varsity crew and graduating near the bottom of the class of 1907. He served in battleships and cruisers, and after the Great War he was an assistant attaché in Europe. Between sea tours he attended the Naval War College, served in the Office of Naval Intelligence, and was aide to the commander, U.S. Fleet. But White grasped the potential of aircraft. He earned wings of gold in 1919 and was well positioned for advancement in aviation. He was an early executive officer of *Lexington,* commanded the seaplane carrier *Wright,* and served as chief of staff aboard *Yorktown.*

That May morning Captain White read his orders and directed the first watch to be set. At that moment, USS *Enterprise* came alive. Other ships in the harbor rendered honors by whistle blasts, and the 200 guests on the flight deck were treated to a spectacular sight as the combined aircraft squadrons of Carrier Division Two droned overhead, sporting red tails for *Yorktown* and blue for *Enterprise.*

The original ship's complement was 1,529 men plus about 540 in the air group: a total of some 2,070 officers, sailors, and marines. The officer most involved with those men was Commander James C. Monfort. Aboard warships the executive officer handles most personnel matters, and Monfort was no exception. An early aviator (only the thirty-fifth Navy pilot), he had served with White in *Wright* and *Lexington.*

The new carrier's first flight operations were conducted on June 15 when the air officer, Lieutenant Commander Allan P. Flagg, logged the first arrested landing. Commander of Enterprise Air Group was forty-two-year-old Lieutenant Commander Giles E. Short, in charge of seventy-seven aircraft in the four squadrons and a utility detachment. Because the ship was CV-6, her squadrons bore the same number: Fighting Squadron Six; Bombing Squadron Six; Scouting Squadron Six; and Torpedo Squadron Six.

With *Enterprise* joining the Atlantic Fleet, Carrier Division Two was complete. The division commander was Rear Admiral William F. Halsey, Jr., a jut-jawed seadog whom history would know as "Bull." *Enterprise* would see much of him over the next four years.

Captain White immediately set about learning his ship. The engineering spaces contained four Parsons steam turbines with power from nine Babcock & Wilcox boilers, each operating at 400 psi peak pressure. That combination produced 120,000 shaft horsepower, driving *Enterprise* to 33.5 knots during sea trials. She was rated one knot less in service, but still made nearly thirty-eight mph. At an economical sixteen knots she could steam 12,000 miles.

Enterprise was agile: she could reverse her course in 800 yards—less than half the figure for the faster but larger, bulkier Lexingtons. The Yorktown design's turning ability would prove its worth time and again in combat, making her a light heavyweight contender, able to bob and weave, jab and punch against bigger opponents.

Before departing on the shakedown cruise to South America, Captain White began laying plans for an event at sea. He convened a secret meeting with several chief petty officers and a couple of favored enlisted men. One was Seaman First Class Carl Marble, a teenaged veteran of two previous carriers. When summoned to the captain's cabin, Marble wondered, "What'd I do *now*?" The young storekeeper could think of no recent transgressions.

In the meeting, Marble and the co-conspirators learned their mission. White gave them full-time "freedom of the gangway," meaning they could come and go anytime. Their mission: acquire whatever clothes, shoes, and accouterments were deemed necessary for a crossing the equator ceremony. Toward that end, traditional roles were assigned, with Chief Michael Krump taking the lead as Neptunus Rex. A senior machinist, he produced his own crown and those for the nautical court, including the Royal Queen (chief yeoman F. L. Patton) and Royal Princess (seaman Marble). A short, stout second-class electrician became the Royal Baby while the burly master at arms drew the significant role of Davy Jones. The Royal Maid in Waiting (chief storekeeper Charlie Esler) completed the entourage.

Carl Marble explained his selection as the Royal Princess: "I was nineteen years old with the best pair of legs on board." Beyond that, he was already an accomplished mariner, having achieved Golden Shellback status aboard *Lexington* by crossing "zero at 180"—the equator at the International Date Line.

On July 18, escorted by the two-year-old destroyer *Shaw,* the Big E departed Norfolk, with her fighters and torpedo planes on board. The opportunity of taking a new ship on its shakedown cruise was relished by all, old hands and recruits alike. The sea service accords special status to those who place a ship in commission, and forever after the men who took *Enterprise* to the Caribbean relished the title of "plankowner."

Several days later the ships anchored off Puerto Rico's south coast. On July 25 *Enterprise* contributed a 105-man landing force and the ship's band to a parade at Ponce. Governor Blanton Winship decided to observe the fortieth anniversary of U.S. Army landings in the Spanish-American War, complete with a flyover by Fighting Six and Torpedo Six.

The show went unappreciated by Puerto Rican nationalists. *Enterprise* sailors watched incredulously as a touring car sped between the ship's band and the landing force, screeched to a halt, and ejected three men in white suits who began shooting handguns into the crowd.

Since none of the sailors had ammunition for their weapons, they could only scatter or seek cover. A clueless ensign with a movie camera was so focused on filming the parade that he failed to grasp what was happening. Chief C. F. "Jelly" Jones, one of the Big E stalwarts, yelled at the youngster, "They're shooting real bullets!" and shoved him aside.

In the reviewing stand, white-clad officers from *Enterprise* and *Shaw* hit the deck. The would-be assassins fired about fifteen rounds, killing a local military officer and wounding others. Guardia policemen returned fire, felling one assailant and capturing another while the third escaped.

Big E sailors gawked as police picked up the killer's fresh corpse, blood-red splotches visible on the white suit coat, and tossed it into the car "like a sack of wheat."

Newspapers around the world reported upon Governor Winship's coolness. Having been under fire during the Spanish war, he merely remarked, "What damn poor shots they are." Then he delivered his prepared speech.

Upon reassembling, most of the *Enterprise* men adjourned to a nearby Catholic parish for sandwiches and refreshments. Sailors spiked the punch with something atypical of church socials—probably an ultra-potent Caribbean rum. Whatever the beverage, it produced spectacular results. Seamen were laid low from the church down to the pier where whaleboats shuttled inert white forms back to the ship. En route, one sailor held a friend's feet so the man could regurgitate over the side without despoiling shipmates' uniforms.

Marble recalled, "I'd been in the Navy three years and never saw anything like it, before or since. Guys who could barely stand up straight were carrying their buddies up the gangway. There were so many puking drunks that the watch standers didn't even bother to take names. One bunch was hauled aboard in a cargo net—like in the movie *Mister Roberts*."

It had been a hell of a day: a parade, a shootout, and an epic drunk.

Enterprise's institutional identity was partly shaped that July 25, 1938: individuals were being melded into a crew; a crew into a family.

More bonding came three weeks later.

On August 20 the navigator, Lieutenant Commander (future Vice Admiral) Ralph Ofstie, calculated that *Enterprise* crossed the equator at longitude 37 degrees 00 minutes west—about 300 miles north of Fortaleza, Brazil. In a rite whose origins are lost in antiquity, relays of lowly Pollywogs were initiated into the Mysteries of the Deep.

The process began on the hangar deck, with Captain White the honored guest of the royal court: King Neptune, his Queen, Baby, Princess, Maid in Waiting, and Davy Jones himself, all attended by the Royal Guard—those few Shellbacks aboard, outfitted in pirate attire. On the forward elevator the court was raised to the flight deck, then proceeded aft to the island where all manner of nautical nastiness awaited the supplicant Pollywogs.

It was a lengthy process, as *Enterprise* had taken 600 men straight from boot camp. However, under Captain White's liberal reign, the sailors in the front half of the line emerged as Trusty Shellbacks in time to inflict traditional indignities upon their newfound shipmates at the back of the line.

The rigors were many and varied. All Pollywogs had to approach the Royal Baby and kiss "the Royal Ham" in the form of his rotund, exposed belly, lubricated with an odious slime of indeterminate origin. Others, selected at random or because a Shellback just didn't like the cut of a Pollywog's jib, were lowered into the Royal Coffin and subjected to mild electric shocks. Many stole an apprehensive glance at the Royal Guillotine. Others were dunked in the Bear's Den—a large vat filled with malodorous water—or were tossed into mesh cages and sprayed with a high-pressure fire hose. Still more victims were subjected to the Royal Barber, who set up shop near the island and carved whatever pattern took his fancy in a Pollywog's coiffure.

Some ships were notorious for especially rough initiations but Newton White's supervision ensured that nobody got out of hand. Even so, one sailor died. In the excitement a fireman succumbed to an enlarged heart—shipmates thought he should not have been permitted to enlist.

After the initiation the crew anticipated liberty in Rio de Janeiro where, with ample time ashore, *Enterprise* sailors sought the pleasures that sailors seek. The seventeen-to-one exchange rate permitted an American to rent a beach house at Copacabana, furnishings including temporary girlfriend, at $100 for ten days. The other renowned beach was Ipanema, with its spectacular view of the Twin Brothers peaks and more spectacular scenery along the shore—even in those days famed for a lax attitude toward bathing attire. A few men ventured far uphill to view the 130-foot-tall Christ the Redeemer, though far more were content to enjoy life at sea level.

Bearing fond memories, *Enterprise* and *Shaw* departed Rio on September 20, making a mail stop in Cuba before continuing northward.

But while the excitement of Ponce and the glamour of Rio remained uppermost in sailors' minds, the purpose of a shakedown remained undisturbed. The ship, crew, and squadrons needed a full evaluation, each as a separate entity and most importantly as a whole. From M Division running the ship's main engines to E Division electricians, S Division supply, and R Division repair, up to the V Divisions operating aircraft, each day brought CV-6 closer to the goal of an integrated, seagoing, potentially war-fighting team.

However, a far greater enemy than any man or nation lay ahead. En route home, *Enterprise* learned of an impending hurricane off the East Coast. Ringing up full speed, Captain White tried to beat the storm into port but lost the race. Off Cape Hatteras, *Enterprise*'s 20,000 tons were battered by mountainous seas of fearful power. Amid cresting waves and shrieking wind, expansion joints opened to the maximum, rendering the flight deck untenable. Not even the hangar deck was safe: one of the metal curtains was blown in, and a spare airplane lashed to the overhead fell nose-first, crunching the propeller and engine mount. At that point the captain passed the word: "All hands lay below the main deck." Most of the crew rode out the violent storm in the lower berthing and work spaces.

Upon return to Hampton Roads, *Enterprise* got down to business. The bombing and scouting squadrons "refreshed" their carrier qualifications in Northrop BT monoplane bombers and Curtiss SBC biplane scouts while the flight deck crew learned its esoteric trade. The fighting squadron with biplane Grumman F3Fs and the torpedo outfit flying Douglas TBD monoplanes qualified later. But it was no easy task: two thirds of the plane handlers, catapult, and arresting gear teams were rookies who learned their trades on the job. Those who had served aboard *Lexington* and *Saratoga* appreciated the Big E's faster elevators, permitting shorter cycle times in bringing planes up from the hangar deck, arranging the flight deck for launch, and recovering aircraft.

Professional education was continuous, from engine room to ready rooms. In fairly short order *Enterprise* sailors became a team en route to becoming a crew. Sailors learned one another's strengths and weaknesses: a squared-away seaman might prove a sloppy drunk on liberty while a gold-brick on the job would not hesitate to clobber a shore patrolman harassing a shipmate. Though the Navy rose or fell on the shoulders of the chief petty officers, mentors often emerged among lesser rates: perennial first- or second-class petty officers who couldn't pass a written exam but knew everything about steam, electricity, hydraulics, or aircraft engines.

BALDY

Sometimes ship captains were selected almost on a whim. During a trip to Washington, D.C., Newton White stopped at the Bureau of Aeronautics. He dropped in on Captain Charles A. Pownall, who had been three years behind him at Annapolis. "Charlie, how would you like to take the *Enterprise?*"

Surprised at the offer, Pownall replied, "Why sure." Satisfied with the response, White said, "Then this morning we'll see Admiral Joe." With that, the friends called upon Rear Admiral J. O. Richardson, personnel chief and future commander of the Pacific Fleet.

Enterprise's first change of command ceremony occurred four days before Christmas 1938. With officers and men arrayed in white-clad ranks, the Big E's crew heard Captain Pownall read his orders. He then turned to Newton White and said, "I relieve you, sir." Newt White, the benevolent old-timer, acknowledged his successor's orders, packed his sea chest, and walked off the ship. Four months later White retired to Mitchellville, Maryland, where he built a mansion adjoining Prince George's Country Club at 2708 Enterprise Road.

In nearly eight months White had wrung out most of the Big E's wrinkles, human and mechanical. He set the stage for the ship to begin the strenuous task of preparing for war, and when he turned over command, his successor inherited a ship and air group capable of more than either realized at the time.

The ship's in-port period during the holidays was not very happy. The new captain recalled, "Norfolk Navy Yard was having trouble. The first day after I got aboard, the catapult blew up. . . . An explosive had been put there purposely. The clues were cold. But the next thing . . . we found some of the arresting gear was cut through with a hacksaw."

No foreign agents were involved in sabotaging America's newest warship. As Pownall explained it, "The workmen were hard up, and the *Enterprise* was their breadbasket." Realizing that the civilian workers were trying to extend the ship's repair time, Pownall and the navy yard commandant decided to move her to the operating base. "With the ship's force and a few helpers we finished the ship."

1939

Charles Alan Pownall was called "Baldy" at Annapolis, where he graduated in the lower half of the class of 1910. He came late to aviation, earning his wings in 1927 at age thirty-nine. Though pleasant and affable, he was widely considered too polite to wield authority, and later displayed a seeming distaste for combat that some attributed to his Quaker origins. However, others discounted the religious aspect, concluding that Pownall simply was too gentle a soul to deal with casualties.

Plankowners such as Carl Marble recall, "Captain Pownall was 100 percent on training." Unlike some senior officers, he recognized that an aircraft carrier was more than a ship that embarked four squadrons, and worked his V-1 Division in efficient handling of planes on the flight and hangar decks.

Aircrews learned that there was no such thing as "routine peacetime operations." For example, from 1939 through 1941 Torpedo Squadron Six lost five planes and sent one back for rebuild. Predictably, most of the accidents occurred at sea. An experienced enlisted pilot stalled his big Douglas on launch from the ship; an ensign stalled taking a wave-off on landing; and engine trouble put a chief naval aviation pilot into the water off Oahu. The squadron's only fatalities occurred in April 1941 when Ensign Edgar Rowley apparently neglected to complete his checklist before takeoff at San Diego. The port wing folded during climb-out, plummeting the aircraft 150 feet into the water, killing the pilot and both crewmen, H. J. Roy and W. L. Rose.

Whatever his faults, Baldy Pownall was appreciated by the crew, which generally considered him a stern but understanding CO who demanded perfection—and usually got it. Under his tenure the communications department won the coveted "C" for excellence; M Division won an engineering "E"; and three efficiency "Es" appeared on the five-inch gun mounts. All indicated that the departments met specific high standards or outpaced their counterparts in other carriers.

Additionally, under Pownall the Big E's baseball, basketball, softball, and rowing teams all were competitive for fleet honors. The teams were paced by stellar athletes including baseball players Chief Quartermaster C. J. "Bing" Miller and Chief Boilerman C. F. "Jelly" Jones, plus the boxing champ, Chief Watertender H. N. Sobeloff. Success in athletics built upon confidence and competence in military matters. Throughout her career, morale was seldom a problem in CV-6.

In early 1939, while America enjoyed oceanic separation from European tensions, *Enterprise* and *Yorktown* joined annual exercises in the Atlantic and Caribbean. Carriers had participated in fleet problems since 1923, but with the arrival of CarDiv Two, more options were explored. In Fleet Problem XX the Black Force defended the East Coast and environs against a White Force deploying from Europe. (At the time, only Britain remotely possessed such a capability.) It was one of the few times that *Yorktown* and *Enterprise* operated together. With identical silhouettes, from overhead the only way to tell the sisters apart was the yellow YKTN and EN on the flight decks.

Despite the European-oriented scenario of Fleet Problem XX, the eight previous exercises had been held in Pacific waters, from the West Coast to Hawaii and the Aleutians. Clearly the concern was the Imperial Japanese Navy rather than Hitler's Kriegsmarine. Consequently, in April came a major shakeup as CarDiv Two was ordered to join the Pacific Fleet. "Hot dope" from rumormongers held that the Japanese were planning to blow up the Panama Canal, hence the hasty move to the Pacific. In any case, the carriers eased their eighty-three-foot-wide hulls through the canal's locks, with about twelve feet to spare on each side. Exiting into the Pacific, they proceeded to San Diego on May 2. Two months later *Enterprise* led the carriers visiting the Golden Gate International Exposition at San Francisco's Treasure Island.

During the exposition several Navy ships competed in the regatta, and the Big E's crew caught the racing bug. A first-class fireman, O. E. Kelley, who had raced for the battleship *California,* approached the skipper. "Sir, I've sounded out the crew, and we want a race boat." In fact, the sailors were willing to turn in their liberty cards so they could practice rowing more often. Pownall was impressed. "If the crew wants a race boat, the captain does too."

With only four carriers available, flattop sailors competed against heavy cruisers, which had similar-sized crews. "Old Kelley" proved his worth that July as his oarsmen bested entries from *Pensacola, Yorktown, Chicago, Indianapolis, Louisville, Lexington,* and *Saratoga.* The winning crew received a large trophy, but better yet, each rower received a twenty-dollar gold piece from the city of San Francisco. The Big E continued racing that year, including sailing events in Seattle and Guantánamo Bay, Cuba. Ship's morale, already high, climbed higher.

That summer sixteen newly minted ensigns, fresh out of Annapolis, reported aboard in San Diego Bay. *Enterprise* shone as the new officers gaped at the brightwork: gleaming stainless steel, polished brass, and fresh-swabbed tile. She resembled a high-tone cruise liner more than a warship. To James D. Ramage of Waterloo, Iowa, "She was a beauty . . . the biggest thing I had ever seen."

Properly decked out in dress uniforms and swords, the ensigns reported to Captain Pownall. He greeted the youngsters, then asked how many had requested *Enterprise.* Only Ramage and his Annapolis roommate, Grant Rogers, raised their hands; the others were indifferent or had been reassigned from the incomplete carrier *Wasp.* Next Pownall asked about the attitude toward aviation at the academy. One youngster admitted that they had been advised against going to carriers. Absorbing that information, Baldy Pownall assured them, "None of you ensigns will ever regret coming to this ship."

In October 1939, following summer exercises off southern California, *Enterprise* (minus *Yorktown*) steamed west to join the Hawaiian Detachment, Pacific Fleet. Subsequently Vice Admiral Halsey rotated in and out of Carrier Division Two, temporarily shifting to CarDiv One aboard *Saratoga* in San Diego.

Bill Halsey had come late to aviation. A destroyer man and former naval attaché to Berlin, he received his wings of gold in 1934 at age fifty-two because so few senior aviators were available for command. Upon return to *Enterprise,* he resumed command of CarDiv Two. His chief of staff was Captain John H. Hoover, sardonically called "Genial John." (It was an Annapolis affectation: reputedly the ugliest midshipman in the class of 1918 was called "Beauty" for the rest of his life.) Hoover had graduated well up in the class of '07, but to say that he was unpopular was akin to stating that Eliot Ness disapproved of crime.

Though equal in rank to Pownall, Hoover lorded it over the captain.

Because Halsey had been promoted to vice admiral in 1940, subordinates said that Hoover wore his boss's third star in dealing with Pownall, and often it was true. Junior officers were astonished when Genial John began giving course corrections over the voice tube, not even being on the bridge. Pownall was far too easygoing to resist Hoover, and Halsey seemingly approved of the situation. The icy relationship still existed when Pownall departed in 1941.

Other pecking-order feuds occurred at even higher echelons. Upon arrival at Pearl Harbor, *Enterprise* became flagship of the fleet's Hawaiian Detachment under stout, fleshy Rear Admiral Adolphus Andrews, whom aviators considered "a real Lord Plushbottom."

Andrews was a sixty-year-old battleship man who resented aircraft carriers' irritating tendency to operate aircraft. Said one Big E junior officer, then Ensign Jig Dog Ramage, "We didn't particularly like the staff because they didn't like aviators." Andrews further irritated the pilots because he prohibited flying during the noon hour, lest his lunch be interrupted by airplane noise.

Andrews's attitude was not unusual, as the doctrine that would transform a flattop from a naval vessel into a man-o'-war was still evolving. Yet current naval terminology still reflects the 1930s argot: blackshoe versus brownshoe. When wearing khakis, surface officers and submariners wore black shoes whereas aviators sported brown shoes—nearly as much a badge as wings of gold.

"There was a tremendous animosity against aviation at the time," explained Jig Dog Ramage. The blackshoes kept the ship's wood flight deck scrupulously scrubbed of oil stains that drip-prone aircraft engines typically deposited, courtesy of brownshoe airmen.

Sailors also felt the discrimination. Later, Radioman Ron Graetz of Torpedo Squadron Six said, "It was obvious through peacetime months and until the first time we had action where airplanes proved themselves that a great many of the old 'sea dogs' not connected to aviation thought we were kind of unnecessary gear. It was not real uncommon to hear them refer to us, occasionally, as 'damn airdales,' and the aviation personnel were all fed at a different chow line from the rest of the crew."

1940

Following Andrews aboard was Admiral James O. Richardson, newly appointed commander in chief, U.S. Pacific Fleet. Two years previously he had approved Pownall as Newton White's successor. In 1940 Richardson brought his considerable staff to the Big E for a week's orientation in Hawaii, and to *Enterprise* men "It was hate at first sight." Finding room for sixty or more staffers was a nontrivial function aboard ship, where space was always at a premium. The staff "immediately took over everything" so something had to give, and that meant the junior officers. Jig Dog Ramage said, "We got along like cats and dogs; there wasn't anything about it that was pleasant." Richardson's people behaved as Congress intended for officers and gentlemen, whereas aviators often did not ("We were kind of dirty and noisy").

When the blessed day arrived that Richardson's retinue returned to the battleship *Pennsylvania,* the admiral's flag lieutenant left an envelope with payment for the food consumed during the staff's durance vile. Thereupon a reservist, Ensign Bill Himmel, seized a rare opportunity for mischief. Gaining access to the envelope, he inserted the contents of a "liberty kit," including a condom and a prophylactic salve that sailors called "Marine toothpaste."

The mess treasurer, Ensign Joe Roper, opened the envelope and saw what he saw. Being Annapolis-raised, he made the logical assumption. Thereupon he took himself and the offending items to the executive officer.

Commander Felix Budwell Stump was a popular Virginian known for his low boiling point, but even so the liberty kit was simply too much. "Those goddam blackshoes!" he exclaimed. "They're insulting the *Enterprise!*"

Stump took Roper to report the offense to Captain Pownall. Even Baldy's gentlemanly nature was piqued, and satisfaction was required. Once upon a time it could have meant cutlasses at dawn or pistols at twenty paces. In the twentieth century nothing would do but a face-to-face confrontation: the captain's gig sortied with Pownall, Stump, and the very junior Mr. Roper, crossing the bay to the flagship *Pennsylvania.*

The visitors were suitably impressed. "Pennsy" was a showboat. One officer said, "The deck was so clean that you wouldn't dare step on it."

Working their way up the nautical food chain, Pownall and company arrived in the presence of the CinC himself. Once the carrier officers pled their case, Admiral Richardson offered a gentlemanly apology, and the pleaders returned to their casually dirty, cheerfully noisy home, having gained satisfaction.

A week or so later, Bill Himmel asked Roper, "Did you get that little thing I sent you?"

Joe Roper was nonplussed. Whereupon Himmel explained about "that little item" in the staff's envelope.

There ensued an "Oh my God!" moment as Ensign Roper, who had graduated in the top 15 percent of the class of '39, pondered his career prospects. However, he could only present himself to Commander Stump, who presented himself to Captain Pownall, who repeated the trio's trek to USS *Pennsylvania*, presenting themselves to the commander in chief.

Genuflection is rarely a military posture, but Admiral Richardson's thick carpet must have offered a suitable cushion for the supplicants, as all was forgiven.

Richardson's willingness to hear the details of so minor a case spoke well for his consideration of subordinates, whatever his staff's attitude. Certainly the admiral had greater matters in mind. Franklin Roosevelt was considering moving the Pacific Fleet from California to Hawaii, presumably as a deterrent against Japan's increasing ambition. Tokyo's aggression in China—dating from 1931 and continuous since 1937—seemed to call for sterner measures than diplomatic maneuvering. Subsequently Richardson told Roosevelt that moving the fleet to Pearl Harbor would only tempt the Japanese into attacking; he was fired for his advice in February 1941.

The reality of duty in Hawaii did not always match the brochure.

In those prewar days, recruiters sometimes portrayed the islands as near idyllic. Certainly there were benefits for some: Commander Edward P. Stafford wrote, "the big outriggers and surfboards crowded the breakers and the Kanaka beach boys pretty much took their choice of the lush young flesh that covered the sand."

However, many ordinary sailors and GIs considered Honolulu overrated. The two hotels—the Royal Hawaiian and the Moana—were inevitably crowded. Consequently, servicemen frequently took themselves to Hotel Street in Chinatown, where they found cheap food, diluted liquor, and professional companionship. Some ships required an enlisted man to present a written invitation to a civilian home in order to get liberty. Many crewmen abandoned the effort: one sailor was granted only two liberties in nearly two years.

Meanwhile, the Big E shuttled between Hawaii and the West Coast, ferrying equipment from San Diego or undergoing modifications at Bremerton, Washington. Relatively little aviation training was accomplished—a situation that did not fit well with Commander Edward C. Ewen, commander of Enterprise Air Group.

CEAG Ewen featured prominently in an episode that fall when Navy Secretary Frank Knox came aboard. The new secretary was shown to the flight deck to view the aircraft: monoplane Douglas TBD torpedo planes and Northrop BT dive-bombers with semi-retractable landing gear, plus biplane Grumman F3F fighters and Curtiss SBC scouts with fully retracting wheels. There Ewen took up the tour.

Frank Knox had been around. One of Teddy Roosevelt's Rough Riders, he became a journalist and prominent Republican newspaper publisher who had run for vice president in 1936. Nevertheless, he supported the administration's foreign policy and accepted FDR's offer as SecNav in July 1940.

Surveying the gleaming, blue-tailed airplanes, Knox remarked that they looked impressive. Eddie Ewen could have tossed off a casual remark, but he did not. Tall and well built, the former football and lacrosse player replied, "Mr. Secretary, these planes are not fit to die in."

Knox probably did not expect such candor, but Ewen pressed ahead. He seized the opportunity to educate the secretary on the aeronautical facts of life, explaining that Mr. Knox's navy lagged well behind other countries in aviation. Standing to one side, Ensign Jig Dog Ramage overheard the discussion. Long after he said, "I considered that a lesson in leadership."

The Christmas season of 1940 included release of an MGM film, *Flight Command,* starring Robert Taylor and Ruth Hussey—and USS *Enterprise.* Director Frank Borzage was a thorough pro: in 1929 he won the first Oscar for best director.

The Navy Department had assigned Fighting Six to support the film, and production began at North Island, San Diego, in June. When the ship was recalled to Hawaii in August, a Marine squadron had to fill in for *Enterprise*'s planes. Though there was little carrier footage, the F3Fs appeared incognito as the fictional Hell Cats squadron: "the best, the nerviest, the most loyal outfit that ever climbed into one of Uncle Sam's planes and took it into the blue of God's heaven." It proved one of the best recruiting films of the period.

1941

In April 1941 CarDiv Two was split, with *Yorktown* returning to the East Coast for Franklin Roosevelt's ill-named "neutrality patrol," watching for

European combatants approaching American waters. In truth, the patrol was directed against Germany. *Enterprise* sailors would not see their teammate again for several months, and then in far different circumstances.

That spring *Enterprise* was back in San Diego, where she appeared in another splashy film, *Dive Bomber,* starring Errol Flynn and Fred MacMurray. The script was written by former Commander Frank "Spig" Wead, a medically retired aviator who became the subject of a postwar John Wayne film. *Dive Bomber* was directed by the tyrannical, talented Michael Curtiz, who three years later won the Oscar for *Casablanca.* His collaborations with Flynn included the 1939 historical drama *The Private Lives of Elizabeth and Essex.*

Errol Flynn was in his prime. His swashbuckling reputation from *Captain Blood, The Sea Hawk,* and *The Adventures of Robin Hood* was only enhanced by a string of offscreen dalliances and scandals that kept the tabloids rolling. If any movie actor defined "glamorous," it was Flynn.

Bill Halsey disliked him on sight.

Warner Brothers committed an exceptional $1.7 million budget to *Dive Bomber,* the same as for *The Sea Hawk* and only slightly less than for *Robin Hood.* Despite a tense international situation, about 1,000 Navy personnel were allotted to the production at San Diego and Los Angeles.

Principal filming began in March on a tight schedule, as *Dive Bomber* was slated for summer release. Curtiz's cameramen spent a week on board *Enterprise* filming flight deck operations. Halsey was perennially cranky because filming interfered with training, yet he had no choice but to cooperate. Nevertheless, Wild Bill made his displeasure known frequently and loudly. Witnesses reported that the day shooting wrapped, he leaned over the bridge railing and yelled downward, "Now get the hell off my ship!" Reportedly Errol Flynn turned, rendered honors with a single-digit salute, and dived off the flight deck into San Diego Bay. The film crew roared in approval.

Fred MacMurray was known as "a regular guy" who, before departing, used one of the officer's heads. In honor of the occasion, the crew hung a sign saying, "Fred MacMurray pissed here!"

Dive Bomber was released in August 1941. Though *Enterprise's* airplanes were portrayed in glorious Technicolor, they were hopelessly obsolete by European standards. Nevertheless, optimism reigned. Among *Dive Bomber's* cast was Regis Toomey, later interviewed by film historian James H. Farmer. "Toomey said the fliers were talking about the forthcoming war," Farmer recalls, "insisting they would make a quick victory over the Japanese, believing all the stories about near-sightedness and copied, second-rate aircraft designs."

Fortunately, by premiere time Fighting Six was learning how to fly and maintain monoplane Grumman F4Fs while the scouts and bombers were receiving Douglas SBDs. That fall the new machines were named Wildcats and Dauntlesses while the four-year-old TBDs became Devastators. They were the aircraft that the Big E would take to war.

A DIFFERENT KIND OF SKIPPER

Enterprise received her third captain in March 1941. When Pownall was relieved on the 21st, he had been in command for twenty-seven months. Nobody else came close to that record, before or after, and he left the *Enterprise* a going concern. For the rest of his life he considered her "a wonderful ship with a wonderful crew and wonderful officers."

The new skipper proved a totally different breed of naval cat from Baldy Pownall. George Dominic Murray was a natty Bostonian out of the Annapolis class of 1911. He was passionate about deep-sea fishing and flying: the Navy's twenty-second pilot, he had won his wings in 1915.

High among Murray's priorities was sorting out the relationship with Halsey's staff. Knowing of the tension between Pownall and Hoover, Murray bided his time, awaiting the best opportunity to confront Genial John.

The chance came late one afternoon when Murray was showering in his cabin. The officer of the deck (OOD) received a course change order from Hoover and astutely did two things: he said, "Aye, aye, sir," and dispatched a messenger to the captain's cabin. Minutes later a moist Murray materialized on the bridge. "Young man," he asked the OOD, "what are you doing?"

"I'm coming left to the new course, sir."

Feigning ignorance, the skipper asked, "Why?"

"Sir, I was directed to do so by the chief of staff."

Though short, pleasant, and normally quiet, G. D. Murray nurtured a heavyweight attitude in a welterweight frame. He spun on a squishy heel and stalked up to the flag bridge, where the ensuing dialogue was intense, loud, and brief. The bridge watch exchanged knowing glances, and probably more than a few grins.

Murray reappeared on the bridge. "Young man, who is the captain of this ship?"

"You are, sir!" the OOD exclaimed.

"And don't you ever forget it!"

With that, Commanding Officer, USS *Enterprise,* departed the bridge, and thereafter Genial John Hoover gave no more orders. But the frost on the relationship between staff and ship only grew thicker in coming months. Hoover's replacement as chief of staff did absolutely nothing to improve matters.

Halsey held himself above the squabbles of mere captains, apparently content to remain the grand old man on the flag bridge. The admiral's lax attitude proved an early indication of his inattention to detail—a trait that would rise up and bite him repeatedly in 1944–45.

In the berthing compartments and work spaces—and especially in the messes—the machinations of captains and admirals were largely ignored even when known. Of far more import was food.

Chow aboard *Enterprise* was tops, and to sailors that was a big deal indeed. It featured in the ship's growing reputation within the fleet, with her fabled food becoming a recruiting tool. A plankowner in the communications division told a chief looking for men to re-up, "If you will put it in writing that I can stay aboard the *Enterprise,* I will ship over!"

Most evenings in port *Enterprise* showed movies on the hangar deck, and word got around. At Pearl Harbor sailors from other ships came aboard, not because *Enterprise*'s films were better, but because her cooks and bakers provided a famous spread. After the movie, the galley crew laid out tables full of cookies, cobbler, or pies. Knowing that the visitors would scarf up most of the goodies in the hangar bay, *Enterprise* men went down to the mess deck for coffee and whatever cake was provided that day. Life was good.

OFFICERS AND MEN

Enterprise was not only a ship: she was a thirty-two-knot, 20,000-ton classroom. Officers learned life lessons about command and leadership, often from the keel up. One reason for the Big E's exceptional leadership was uncommon longevity. Chief Yeoman James M. Martin served in the Big E an incredible seven and a half years. He reported aboard as a first class petty officer in M Division (main engines) and finally departed as a chief in November 1945. Three others matched his record.

Those junior officers who paid attention could absorb lessons not taught at Annapolis. As a junior officer in the deck division, Ensign Jig Ramage was mentored by the leading petty officer, Joseph Van Kuren, a plankowner. Bosun's Mate Van Kuren was a genuine old salt, complete with a full-rigged sailing ship tattooed across his chest. Ramage later recalled, "There was never a problem, and I learned very early not to meddle with things that were working right, because he had that division running just like a watch."

The division's chief boatswain was Fred Filbry, who imparted essential knowledge by demonstrated competence. Officers realized that if they listened to him, they learned how to do things. Filbry acted more as an overseer than a hands-on leader, allowing his highly competent petty officers to run the division. His sage advice to ensigns, "Always be around but don't interfere."

Relations between officers and enlisted men remained good throughout *Enterprise*'s career, and were frequently excellent. Some prewar veterans cite Baldy Pownall's attitude as setting the stage, as they appreciated an Academy graduate who was considerate of sailors.

The pro-enlisted atmosphere at the top trickled down to the junior officers. One example was Seaman First Class Ron Graetz, fresh out of radio school in early 1941. Though nominally assigned to the bombing squadron, for six months he bounced between mess duty and the first division's deck force "where I spent a little over a month chipping paint and painting."

Then a shipmate lent a hand. A fellow radioman mentioned Graetz to Ensign Severin Rombach, Torpedo Six's twenty-seven-year-old communications officer. Rombach liked what he heard and requested Seaman Graetz as his radioman-gunner. Almost immediately Graetz found himself flying in the rear cockpit of the Douglas TBD with "T-2" painted on the side: the number two torpedo plane. It was the beginning of an unusual association: "We got along so well, that he wrote his mother in Ohio and gave her the address of my mother in Iowa, and they corresponded regularly."

Amid the work and training, some squadron parties included officers and enlisted men, a rarity in many ships. One dramatic example occurred during a Fighting Six event in Hawaii in November 1939. Joining the party was tall, slender Lieutenant (jg) Jim Gray, twenty-five years old and an Annapolis graduate. He had learned to fly in 1930 when, at sixteen, he became the youngest pilot in America. During the beach festivities Machinist's Mate Frank Malkov had swum out to aid another sailor but was defeated by the undertow and cresting breakers. Gray sprinted into the surf but could not reach Malkov, who drowned. Nevertheless, Gray swam out to Seaman J. E. Dickens and towed him to shore. Then, with another man, the pilot rescued Machinist's Mate Joseph Wisniewski.

A year later Gray received a Navy Department commendation. He would feature prominently in the Big E's future.

Another example of officer-enlisted relations occurred in May 1941 when Lieutenant (jg) Norman J. Kleiss reported to Scouting Six. The Texan was delighted; he considered flying from *Enterprise* "the best of all worlds."

Preparing for his first carrier landings, twenty-six-year-old "Dusty" Kleiss was approached by twenty-one-year-old Aviation Machinist's Mate Bruno Peter Gaido. With nothing to lose but his life, the Wisconsin sailor asked if he could ride along. Kleiss was astonished: "This is my first carrier landing and I'm supposed to have only sandbags in the rear seat."

Undeterred, Gaido irreverently asked, "You got wings, ain't ya?" Then he replaced the bags with his own stout frame. Thus encouraged, Kleiss related, "With that supreme confidence I made a half dozen perfect landings."

That year, aviators arriving in *Enterprise* found a different atmosphere from the early days when flying was barely tolerated. Kleiss said, "The ship's company knew our needs and our limitations. They may have regarded aviators as oddballs, but not as a condescending elite. By then the problem of 'brownshoe' versus 'blackshoe' did not exist. The decisions of Captain Murray and his exec, Commander [Tom] Jeter, regarding actions for discipline and infractions were only exceeded by the Ten Commandments."

From the ready room perspective Kleiss said, "Officers and enlisted men respected each other. The enlisted men respected officers for their knowledge and experience. The officers respected the enlisted men for their skills, perseverance and abilities."

Yet some sailors such as Aviation Ordnanceman Alvin Kernan had another view. "Few enlisted men knew an officer as a person, which meant that the deaths of the pilots when they came were not felt very personally. We felt them as fans feel the loss of a game by their football team. There was always a lot of tension between the enlisted men and the officers, largely based on the enlisted men's real fear of officers, who looked down on them, and the officers' reciprocal fear that their orders would not be obeyed by men they never quite trusted."

Judging by the comments of most *Enterprise* sailors, Kernan's impression, while shared by some, remained the minority view. More held to the opinion of scout pilot Dusty Kleiss: "We were a family."

Bill Halsey could be surprisingly friendly toward enlisted men, especially unusual in an era when admirals reputedly conversed with the Supreme Being. Electrician's Mate John J. Kellejian's battle station on the flag bridge often put him beside the task force commander. During a general quarters emergency drill there was little to do in flag country, prompting Halsey to ask Kellejian if he played cribbage. The youngster had never heard of it so the admiral exclaimed, "Don't worry about it, son. I'll teach you."

After a tutorial, Halsey declared the electrician ready to play, the stakes being a nickel a round. "I lost my ass," Kellejian said, losing more than fifty games, but since sailors never had much money, the admiral seemed to forget the debt.

Following Halsey's death in 1959, Kellejian—long out of the Navy—received a summons from the admiral's estate, demanding payment of a debt of $2.80. Kellejian phoned Halsey's sister, who explained that Wild Bill had carried the amount as a joke to share with friends. The debt was forgiven, but John Kellejian kept the summons as a souvenir of his costly lessons at the knee of Admiral William F. Halsey.

With food and board provided, enlisted men (called "whitehats" for their "Dixie cup" caps) and chiefs could build a reserve if they were frugal. In 1942 a chief petty officer with a permanent appointment earned $138 per month (about $1,800 in 2010). That was grandiose compared to the starting $54 a seaman second class received. For each three years of service, pay increased 5 percent to a maximum 50 percent above base pay, so longevity counted for penny-pinchers.

Parsimonious as wartime pay might seem today, the figures alone lack context. In 1940 a motorist could fill his new $850 car with 15-cents-per-gallon gasoline. But that typical automobile represented nearly half the average annual income—quite a stretch when a new house cost $4,000 to $6,500.

OMENS

During 1940 events in Asia convinced many American military men that war with Japan was inevitable. In retaliation for Tokyo's aggression in China, the Roosevelt administration imposed increasingly strict embargoes, limiting exports of petroleum and steel to Japan. When Japan signed the

Tripartite Pact with Germany and Italy that fall, war clouds darkened on the geopolitical horizon. During port calls on the West Coast, Bull Halsey cast a leery eye from the flag bridge, watching Japanese ships loading gasoline and tons of scrap metal. War was coming. He could feel it.

Enterprise took note. The Pacific Fleet moved to Hawaii in February 1941 and the Big E began to "strip ship" in April. That meant removal of unnecessary flammable and "splinterable" equipment: wooden boats and furniture; canvas awnings, linoleum, excess rope—and a great deal of paint. In peacetime paint was a preservative, protecting metal from maritime rust. But paint also was highly combustible, a hazard in combat. With hostilities a possibility, the crew set about the onerous, filthy task of chipping it off. Sailors detested the chore.

Recalled one erudite whitehat, "To chip it all off, flake by flake, with a chipping hammer . . . was a labor of the damned. It was hot inside the ship, and the men, stripped to their skivvies, rags around their heads, chipped away—*clink, clink, clink,* sonofabitch! It was maddening work, difficult, endless, seemingly pointless, and when it was finished after many months in which it took up every spare hour, the linoleum ripped off the rusty decks, the compartments with their raw, rust-pitted bulkheads were as depressing as if the ship had been burned out."

A far less onerous requirement was calibrating the carrier's radar. The first CXAM set installed in 1941 was accurate with an aircraft's range but erratic in altitude. Consequently, a series of flight profiles was arranged at precise altitudes, tracked by fighter direction officers in the small radar plotting room inside the island. When a blip became faint or disappeared, fighter direction officers noted the pilots' reported altitude and atmospheric conditions. When contact was reestablished, officers made note of the "nulls" or blind spots. After repeated runs at thousand-foot intervals, it was possible to compile "fade charts" that provided reasonably accurate data for combat use. With its large "bedspring" antenna, the CXAM could detect multi-engine aircraft at 10,000 feet about eighty statute miles away; smaller carrier planes at fifty-five miles.

Detecting aircraft was one thing but identifying and intercepting them quite another. Radio communication between the ship and its defending fighters was an essential component of air defense, as was a doctrine for coordinating all aspects of fighter direction. Many of the problems were still being addressed as fall turned to winter.

Nor were all the problems technical in nature. During November night exercises *Enterprise* barely avoided swapping paint with *Oklahoma*, as the flight deck overhang bent the battleship's stern flagstaff. It was not a unique situation—*Oklahoma* and *Arizona* crunched together in October as did the Big E's old partner *Shaw* and the oiler *Sabine* in November. Even near collisions at sea were potential career killers, but Halsey concluded that Captain Murray should retain command.

In the last months of 1941 the Big E pushed hard to make up for lost training time. With two new aircraft—Wildcat fighters and Dauntless scout-bombers—there was no time to waste. The latter were especially active; pilots logged nearly forty hours per month, sometimes flying three times a day. During October Bombing Six concentrated on bombing, gunnery, tactics, and carrier qualifications. But practice could exact a price: on the 21st Ensign Tommy Ashworth was killed attempting a night landing.

November was busier yet as the air group practiced coordinated attacks, the scouts flying with smoke generators to screen the low, slow approach of the torpedo planes. Aircrews also conducted over-water navigation, and the Dauntless scout-bombers dropped inert bombs on the old battleship *Utah*. That month Lieutenant Richard H. Best of Bombing Six was typical: he logged forty-three hours in twenty-two flights including eight carrier landings, the rest being ashore.

On November 28 *Enterprise* embarked a Marine fighter squadron for delivery to Wake Island. It looked like an easy trip: out and back in nine days. Radioman Ron Graetz's perspective was typical: "I do not recall any talk of the probability of war. Before we sailed for Wake, it was announced to all hands who had their wives out there, that after our return we would be departing on December 13 for return to the States, and they should send their wives back ASAP. All the attitude that I recall was we were going home!"

Christmas in Bremerton: it sounded wonderful.

2

★ ★ ★

"Keep Cool, Keep Your Heads, and Fight"

Her air group arrayed for launch, the Big E is approached by the fleet oiler *Sabine* in the Coral Sea, May 11, 1942. (Joel Shepherd, Enterprise Assn.)

The Sunday flight began with a premonition.

Manning their Dauntless scout-bomber, Lieutenant Clarence E. Dickinson and Radioman William C. Miller settled into their prelaunch routine. But this morning Miller seemed different. Though normally calm and unruffled, he appeared unsettled. "Mr. Dickinson, my four years sea duty ends in a few days and there's something funny about it."

"What's that, Miller?"

In his Carolina drawl the back-seater replied, "Out of the twenty-one of us who went through radio school together, I'm the only one who hasn't crashed in the water. Hope you won't get me wet today, sir!"

Dickinson reminded the twenty-two-year-old radioman that they were about to fly together for the last time. An easy scouting flight to Pearl Harbor, one more landing ashore, and their mutual job was finished. Bill Miller would be on his way out of the Navy if he wished. "Dick" Dickinson, nine years downstream from Annapolis, was in for the long haul.

RUMORS OF WAR

Amid continuing diplomatic tension between Washington and Tokyo, Vice Admiral Bill Halsey was taking no chances. Upon leaving Pearl on November 28 he had issued Battle Order Number One, placing the task force on a wartime footing in case of an encounter with Japanese forces. His philosophy: "If anything gets in my way, we'll shoot first and argue afterwards." He also urged, "when put to the test, all hands keep cool, keep your heads, and FIGHT."

While delivering Marine fighters to Wake Island—less than 2,000 miles from Tokyo—Halsey wanted to be ready. Training ammunition had been exchanged for "service ammo," and pilots were cleared to attack any ship or aircraft they found because no friendlies were expected. Seldom if ever had Americans been authorized to shoot without provocation.

Nevertheless, few men were concerned. Yeoman Bill Norberg said, "We in the captain's office never mentioned impending war. We looked on the Japanese as squint-eyed midgets due to lack of knowledge. Battle Order Number One to us was somewhat comparable to The Second Coming—it'll happen someday but certainly not this week or this month, and come the evening of December 6, we'd be celebrating in Honolulu as we were accustomed to."

On the way back from Wake, heavy weather interfered with refueling the carrier's escorting destroyers. Consequently, *Enterprise* was a day behind her expected return to Pearl on Saturday the 6th. But still Halsey played it safe: he wanted an air search between himself and Oahu.

From 225 miles out, on Sunday morning *Enterprise* launched eighteen Dauntlesses, searching a ninety-degree eastern perimeter ahead of the task force, two planes to a wedge-shaped sector. The scouts would land at Ford Island, Pearl Harbor, where the ship would dock that afternoon.

Riding with air group commander Howard L. Young was Halsey's assistant operations officer, Lieutenant Commander Bromfield Nichol. Seven years previously, then Lieutenant Nichol had taught then Captain Halsey how to fly ("The worse the weather, the better he flew"). "Brom" would deliver a report to fleet headquarters about the trip to Wake.

The fliers saw few ships, none arousing suspicion. Then, reaching the limit of their search sectors, the nine pairs of Dauntlesses turned for Pearl.

Operating under radio silence, some crews used the opportunity to practice radio homing, rear seatmen tuning their sets to stations KGU or KGMB in Honolulu.

Flying in Sector E, which overlapped Oahu, Young (variously nick-named "Brigham" or "Cy") passed Barbers Point with Ensign Perry Teaff on his wing. They spotted aircraft over the Marine Corps base at Ewa and reckoned the Army was up early that morning. It was barely 8:00 A.M.

Then Young noticed antiaircraft bursts over the harbor. Nichol mar-veled that the Army would hold an air defense drill on Sunday.

At that moment Teaff saw a single-engine aircraft flying a pursuit curve on him, closing fast. Nichol also spotted the interloper, whom he reckoned was "one of those fresh, young Army pilots," brashly ignoring regulations.

The intruding pilot was neither Army nor American. He pushed his gunnery run to minimum range—perhaps twenty-five meters—before press-ing his triggers. The fighter's 7.7mm guns chattered, punching holes through the lead SBD's tail.

As Young later reported, "The plane that attacked me appeared to be a low-wing monoplane fighter with retractable landing gear." Such was the U.S. Navy's introduction to the business end of the Mitsubishi Zero.

The Japanese pilot had misjudged his closure and overshot his intended victim. The gray-painted fighter with the rust-red suns on its wings pulled around for another run, giving Teaff's gunner time to respond. Facing aft, his canopy open, Radioman Edgar Jinks stepped on the pedal that opened the spring-loaded doors behind his cockpit, pulled the Browning machine gun up and back, and felt it lock into place. Then he tugged twice on the charging handle, feeding live ammo into the chamber.

The enemy aviator—now he clearly was such—declined to shoot it out with Jinks. Instead, the Zero went for the section leader, pointing its black nose at Brig Young's aircraft. Young pushed forward on his control stick and dived inland, Teaff following close behind.

It was a come-as-you-are war: no warning, no time for thought.

Oahu was the target of six Japanese aircraft carriers—the mobile strik-ing force, called *Kido Butai,* unlike anything previously assembled. In an act of tactical brilliance and strategic suicide, Tokyo sought to neutralize the U.S. Pacific Fleet long enough to secure the resources needed to sustain the empire's ambition. Permanently engaged in China since 1937, Japan now sought the petro-wealth of the East Indies and the geostrategic advantage of the Philippines. Tokyo somehow expected to defeat the world's greatest industrial power with an economy nearly six times its own.

On board *Enterprise,* Halsey was into his second cup of coffee when a staffer announced, "Admiral, there's an air raid on Pearl!"

Even the combative Wild Bill Halsey, who had the task force operating under shoot-first conditions, balked at reality. He leapt to his feet. "They're shooting at my own boys! Tell Kimmel!" Like nearly everyone else on board, he assumed the U.S. Army was doing the shooting. His instinct was to tell Admiral Husband Kimmel, a classmate from Annapolis in 1904, to stop the firing.

Moments later came confirmation from Kimmel himself:

FROM: CINCPAC
  TO: All ships present

AIR RAID PEARL HARBOR X THIS IS NO DRILL.

Shortly a nonregulation addendum came from Lieutenant Earl Gallaher, one of the Big E's scout pilots approaching Oahu 150 miles away. During the outbound flight he had been thinking about going to the club and relaxing with a beer. Now he opened up on his radio, declaring, "Pearl Harbor is under attack by the Japanese. This is no shit!"

On the bridge Lieutenant John Dorsett as officer of the deck ordered general quarters. Just outside the pilothouse Seaman Jim Barnhill, barely nineteen and one of four buglers on board, had just relieved the previous watch stander, his friend Calvin St. Clair. Raising his instrument, Barnhill placed the polished brass bugle near the loudspeaker and blew the call to arms, thirty staccato notes of "Boots and Saddles." At that point Jim Barnhill thought to himself that he was 3,700 miles and a world war away from Cisco, Texas.

Immediately thereafter Bosun Max Lee ("an old guy in his late twenties") called, "General quarters, general quarters. All hands man your battle stations!"

Lee turned to the bridge watch, most of whom knew he had nearly completed his enlistment. He intoned, "We're at war, and I'll never get out of the Navy alive."

Throughout the ship men scrambled to their stations—up and forward to starboard; down and aft to port—leaping through shin-high "knee-knocker" accesses in bulkheads, dogging watertight doors behind them. They pulled on World War I–style doughboy helmets, opened ready-ammunition lockers, manned five-inch, 1.1-inch, and .50 caliber mounts, and wondered what the rest of the day would bring.

Claude Clegg, a Bombing Six radioman, recalled, "When I reached the flight deck the first thing that caught my eye was the biggest American flag I had ever seen, flying at the mast. Over the speakers came, 'This is the captain speaking. Pearl Harbor is being attacked by the Japanese.' From the radio shack we could hear some of the accounts of the attack."

The "size one" colors made an impression on everyone, including the generally undemonstrative Lieutenant Richard H. Best. Looking up at the red, white, and blue of his nation's flag whipping in the wind on the first day of battle, the Bombing Six pilot recalled, "It was the most emotional sight of the war for me."

Bombs, torpedoes, and ammunition were brought up to the hangar and flight decks as ordnance crews scurried to get every plane armed. Bombs were fitted to shackles on Dauntlesses, and red-shirted "ordies" threaded nose and tail fuses into place. Others trundled torpedo dollies bearing one-ton "pickles" beneath Devastators. Still others hoisted heavy .50 caliber ammo cans into place under the Wildcats' square-tipped wings. *Enterprise* was a seagoing beehive of frantic choreography that morning. Men willingly pitched in, forcing themselves to focus on the immediate task while suppressing disbelief: *We're at war? Are we really at war?*

Some had a hard time accepting the sudden reality. Surely, they reasoned, it was a drill of some sort involving the Navy, Marines, and Army. Even the Honolulu radio stations seemed to be participating.

A chief petty officer strode past some Torpedo Six crewmen, waving a hundred-dollar bill while wagering that the excitement was a practice attack. Said Radioman Ron Graetz, "Nobody would call him on the bet because we all believed the same."

In the ship's radio shack, operators listened to mysterious, disconcerting calls on the primary channel. Something about hostile aircraft, an air raid in progress. It made little sense. True, the ship had been operating under wartime conditions for several days, but who would be shooting on a Sunday morning?

More calls crackled over the circuits. Radiomen heard a high-pitched voice, "This is 6-B-3, an American plane! Do not shoot!"

The pleader was Ensign Manuel Gonzalez. Flying the northernmost search sector, he and wingman Ensign Fred Weber were intercepted by six strange aircraft with fixed landing gear. Manny Gonzalez, a Hispanic pilot, and Radioman Leonard Kozalek, his Polish American gunner, were the first *Enterprise* men killed in the Second World War. Meanwhile, Weber dived for the wave tops, and if any Japanese followed him, they abandoned the chase after he scraped them off at twenty-five feet.

While air group commander Brig Young and Perry Teaff squeaked into Ford Island through a thick barrage of automatic weapons fire, others were less fortunate. The wreckage of Ensign John H. Vogt's plane was found near a Zero. Apparently the planes collided. Neither Vogt nor his gunner, Sydney Pierce, survived.

In Sector G, south of Oahu, the two-plane section of Lieutenant "Dicky" Dickinson and Ensign John R. McCarthy neared Barbers Point at 1,500 feet. Clearly something was wrong: flak bursts over Pearl and thick smoke at Ewa.

Worst of all, heavy smoke rose from Battleship Row alongside Ford Island. There the leviathans were being slaughtered at their moorings.

Climbing for a better look, the Dauntlesses were spotted by at least two Imperial Navy fighter pilots, who immediately attacked. Dickinson led the section in a fast descent from 4,000 feet and ran into another bunch of black-nosed killers. They ganged McCarthy, set his plane afire, and forced him over the side. He landed in a tree, breaking a leg in the process. His rear seatman, Mitchell Cohn, went down with the plane.

Fighting for survival, Dick Dickinson faced hopeless odds. He reckoned that he faced at least three assassins, and all he could do was keep turning, trusting his gunner to keep the Mitsubishis off their tail. Bill Miller's single Browning machine gun spat out repeated .30 caliber bursts, though he hollered over the intercom that he was wounded. Nevertheless, shortly he called that he hit a fighter. Then he ran out of ammunition and was wounded a second time.

Dickinson glimpsed a Zero that appeared afire but he had no time to watch it. Another fighter slashed across his nose, and he hosed off a burst of .50 caliber. Then his controls went slack and his port wing caught fire as the plane dropped into a graveyard spin.

At perhaps 1,000 feet, Dickinson unfastened his seat belt, unplugged his radio lead, and called for Miller to jump. Then the pilot heaved himself over the side. He pulled the ripcord, felt the blessed jerk of the canopy opening, and descended into a cane field. Hiking toward the smoke on the horizon, he thumbed a ride to the naval base. Bill Miller hadn't gotten his feet wet, but he was among the first Americans killed that morning.

In Sector F, overlapping southern Oahu, Scouting Six skipper Halstead Hopping took in the spectacle and radioed *Enterprise* a confirming report. He landed around 8:45 A.M., between the two waves of attackers. Hopping began scrounging ordnance while Commanders Young and Nichol reported to Admiral Kimmel. Men like Hopping quickly passed through the emotional twilight zone between peace and war, accepting the awful reality and moving to deal with it. He convinced a warrant officer to deliver bombs to his three Dauntlesses.

Commander Brig Young observed the Japanese second wave with a professional eye. He described the attackers as "low-wing monoplanes, with fixed landing gear. . . . My only criticism of this particular attack was that they all came in from the same direction. . . . However, the ineffectiveness of our AA fire, lack of air opposition and the manner in which they pressed their attacks home in this particular instance combined to make the attack practically perfect." *Enterprise* men would see much more of the Aichi "Val" dive-bomber in the next year.

A few Big E families witnessed the attack, including Jane Dobson, wife of a pilot on the search mission. Having seen her husband's squadron on practice missions, she noted that the Japanese did not dive as steeply as Scouting Six. Later, when she imparted that intelligence, Ensign Cleo Dobson hugged her in appreciation of "a real dive-bomber's wife."

The thirty-six men on the eighteen-plane mission suffered grievous losses. Six died that Sunday, and over the next several months eight more perished while two were captured and one was crippled—a 47 percent casualty rate.

Between combat losses and damage inflicted by Japanese and American ammunition, only half the *Enterprise*'s search planes were available by noon. But "Spike" Hopping led nine Dauntlesses away from Ford Island, deployed in three-plane sections seeking the Japanese task force. They fanned out over a sixty-degree sector: 330 through 030, west-northwest through east-northeast.

They found nothing because Vice Admiral Chuichi Nagumo had long since reversed his helm, taking his six carriers and supporting ships back toward Japan. It was just as well: nine unescorted SBDs against the might of *Kido Butai* would have stood no chance.

*   *   *

Aboard the ship that morning, half of the scout-bombers were unavailable, either ashore or shot down. Therefore, to launch an attack against any Japanese ships, *Enterprise* had to rely upon Lieutenant Eugene Lindsey's eighteen Devastator torpedo planes.

War is the province of confusion, and December 7 was no exception. A bogus report of an enemy force southeast of the carrier prompted launch of Torpedo Six and half a dozen Dauntless dive-bombers with smoke generators. They were expected to lay a smoke screen to mask the Devastators' low, slow approach. Six Wildcat fighters also were assigned, departing into the gathering dusk.

An hour after launch, Gene Lindsey found merely gray-dappled sea, so he began a search pattern. Only later did it become apparent that a scout pilot had misidentified friendly ships and aircraft, generating the false alarm. With darkness setting in, Lindsey led the twenty-four bombers back toward the ship.

Lieutenant (jg) Francis F. Hebel's fighters lost sight of the bombers and torpedo planes, so the tall, blond ex-instructor navigated directly back to the *Enterprise*. Arriving before the bombers, the Wildcats were ordered to land ashore, alleviating crowding on the ship in a rare night recovery. "Fritz" Hebel led the F4Fs toward shore in the gathering dark.

The air group was not fully night-qualified, but her aviators had no option other than to try landing. With her flight deck lights illuminated—a risky necessity in submarine water—the Big E received her homing chicks. Waving them aboard was Lieutenant (jg) Hubert B. Harden, a former scout pilot elevated to landing signal officer. His green wands imparted confidence in the dark, and the pilots did uncommonly well: all but one "trapped" safely. The exception was a TBD that struck a raised barrier, wrenching its one-ton torpedo loose. Sliding up the deck with 400 pounds of explosive in its nose, the "fish" was wrestled into submission by flight deck crewmen. The final braking action was provided by the flight deck officer, long-legged Lieutenant Commander William E. Townsend.

Over Oahu, Fighting Six flew into chaos.

In the dark, Fritz Hebel's pilots saw fires still burning around the harbor, but glimpsed Ford Island's illuminated runway. Entering the traffic pattern at 500 feet, the fighters took their landing intervals with wheels and flaps down. In a normal left-hand pattern, Hebel led his five pilots over the dry dock area and burning, battered, bleeding Battleship Row. There, some ships challenged the "intruders" to give the day's recognition signals, which the aviators lacked. Failure to respond caused antiaircraft officers aboard the battleship *Pennsylvania* to start shooting.

Today, the phrase is "firing contagion." After Pennsy's machine gunners opened up, so did everyone else. Tracers lit up the night as gunners hosed bright streams of bullets at the Wildcats.

Four Grummans were shot down in a few minutes. First to fall was Ensign Herb Menges, whose plane slanted into a beachfront house, which burned to cinders. Thirteen months in the fleet, he was the first Navy fighter pilot to die in World War II.

Seconds later Lieutenant (jg) Eric Allen's plane burst into flames from repeated hits. Desperately low, he went over the side and pulled his rip-cord, but his fall was barely checked as he smashed into the oily water. He sustained serious internal injuries, and was shot by a sailor onshore. Three years out of Annapolis, the twenty-five-year-old pilot found the willpower to swim, and was rescued by a minesweeper. He was whisked to the base dispensary in critical condition.

The other four pilots did the only thing possible: they doused lights, shoved up the power, and began cranking up their wheels to avoid the steady fusillade. Ensign Gayle Hermann's sturdy Pratt & Whitney engine took a five-inch shell that blessedly failed to detonate. Amid more gunfire he dead-sticked into Ford Island, swerving to a stop on the golf course. There he was subjected to more shooting from adrenaline-crazed marines. Seemingly unfazed, Hermann tucked his chute under his arm and began hiking for Fighting Six's hangar. Later he counted eighteen holes in his F4F's tough hide.

Meanwhile, Fritz Hebel abandoned any hope of getting into the naval air station. He reversed helm toward Wheeler Field, seeking a better reception from the Army. But his plane was too badly shot up, and in the tropic darkness he felt his way earthward, settling for a cane field. The Wildcat caught a wingtip, tumbled tail over nose, and disintegrated. Witnesses pulled the unconscious aviator from the wreckage and rushed him to Scho-field Barracks.

December 7 already was the most memorable day of Ensign David Flynn's life (it was also his twenty-seventh birthday). With a dead radio, he was on his own so he headed for the Marine Corps field at Ewa. Four miles shy of the runway his engine died so Flynn abandoned ship, parachuting into the dark. He lit in a field, injuring his back, but soldiers took him to Tripler Hospital.

That left capable, plainspoken Ensign Jim Daniels. He had escaped the worst of the shooting by bending his throttle southwesterly. He was able to contact the Ford Island tower, which convinced him to land at the air station. Flying up the channel at fifty feet, he passed close aboard the beached battleship *Nevada*'s foretop, drawing a blizzard of more gunfire from the sailors and Hickam Field.

"Moments later I touched the runway," he said. "I overshot. There were two crash trucks in front of me at the end of the runway. I slammed on the brakes and spun around in a full circle on the first green of a golf course." Not far from Gayle Hermann's abandoned airplane, Daniels taxied back toward the flight line. Already unimpressed with leathernecks, Daniels noted, "A Marine gunner sprayed the plane with bullets. He just missed my head."

At the officers' quarters, Daniels looked out the window, seeing the remains of USS *Arizona* still blazing. Finding an operable phone, in minutes he was talking to his wife in Pearl City. He summarized, "I was the luckiest man in the Navy on December 7, 1941."

Early the next morning, word arrived that Eric Allen had died of his injuries and Fritz Hebel succumbed to a fractured cranium.

Total *Enterprise* losses that terrible day were eleven fliers and nine aircraft, which had cost the Japanese only the Zero that collided with John Vogt.

SCENES OF WAR

After slow steaming off Oahu most of Monday, low on fuel, *Enterprise* and her escorts headed for Pearl. The Big E nosed into the narrow channel after dusk, and every officer, sailor, and marine who could manage to be topside took in the spectacle. The harbor's oil-scummed waters and the stink of burning fuel were unmistakable.

Even in the gloom, far worse were the sights: the gutted carcasses of familiar ships. There was *Oklahoma*, the battlewagon that *Enterprise* had brushed two months before, capsized off Ford Island. In dry dock rested the shattered remains of destroyer *Shaw*, which had shared the excitement of the Big E's Caribbean shakedown three and a half years before. *Utah*, which Bombing and Scouting Six had practiced upon: blown up. *Arizona*: blown up. The latter was especially hard on Scouting Six's Earl Gallaher; she had been his first ship out of Annapolis. He was "very, very angry."

Many *Enterprise* men felt chills down their spines, realizing that, absent the blessed storm that had delayed their return, the Big E also surely would have been destroyed in port.

Bill Halsey stood silent for a time, then muttered more to himself than anyone else, "Before we're through with 'em, the Japanese language will be spoken only in hell!"

Enterprise already was a solid team, an accomplished guild of professional sailors and fliers. But in 1941 Americans had not been truly united amid the bitter debate about isolationism. Franklin Roosevelt's contradictory neutrality—what he said versus what he did—was only partly appreciated at the time. Secretly he had authorized action against Germany in the North Atlantic and dispatched a group of mercenary airmen to kill Japanese in China. Meanwhile, he maintained normal if strained diplomatic relations with Tokyo and Berlin.

But *Enterprise*'s crew knew little of the geopolitics and generally cared far less. At the visceral level—from deck plate to flight deck to flag bridge—George Murray's and Bill Halsey's men craved payback. It mattered little whether they considered Roosevelt the nation's savior or the antichrist. There were New Deal Democrats who adored him and Southern Democrats with Klan connections who despised him. There were Wall Street Republicans who had cheerfully voted against him three times and a good many others who were too young to vote.

The Big E incurred a blood debt that her men vowed to repay with compounded interest. *Enterprise* was not merely at war—she was in the business of vengeance. Seaman Bobby J. Oglesby, a plankowner, spoke for many shipmates. He said it was "the personal conviction of every man aboard that it was our job to avenge Pearl Harbor. We had come into Pearl on December 8, to find ships still burning and the stench of the dead on the air. Every man was hopping mad to refuel, rearm, get back to sea and kill the enemy. That burning desire to kill the enemy was still in me when I left the *Enterprise* months later, and didn't disappear until long after I returned to the United States."

Without realizing it, Tokyo had turned USS *Enterprise* into one of the worst enemies of the Japanese empire.

THE ENEMY BELOW

Meanwhile, the enemy was still close at hand.

His Imperial Japanese Majesty's submarine *I-70* was a 344-foot-long boat commissioned in 1935. On November 23, 1941, Commander Takeo Sano took her out of Kwajalein Atoll for Hawaiian waters with two sisters. They were deployed south of Oahu, awaiting the morning of December 7.

On the 10th, *I-6* reported a carrier steaming northeast, and Kwajalein ordered the subs to overtake and sink her. But *Enterprise* also was hunting, and that morning at least four pilots attacked hostile submarines, none decisively. Clearly Hawaiian waters were teeming with I-boats.

With multiple sub sightings, Halsey was both concerned and combative. Just before noon he dispatched scout-bombers to the reported locations in hopes of flushing game. Dick Dickinson had lost Bill Miller, his regular gunner, on Sunday morning, but was pleased with Lieutenant Earl Gallaher's back-seater, Radioman Thomas E. Merritt, "an extremely reliable radioman and gunner."

The Dauntlesses began sniffing southward for a scent now more than six hours old. Upon reaching his assigned area, Dickinson began an expanding box search, flying twenty miles south, thirty miles east, and forty north. Visibility was excellent—over twenty miles—with the waves spumed in whitecaps.

Scanning the northern corner of his sector, Dickinson could hardly believe his luck. About fifteen miles to the northeast he beheld "a great big submarine running on the surface." He radioed an immediate contact report and began climbing to attack altitude.

During the climb, Dickinson armed his 500-pound bomb, gauged the wind—almost on his nose—and worked out the geometry of his attack. Foremost in his mind was the dread that his prey would "pull the plug" and dive. "I didn't see how I could stand the disappointment were that Jap to submerge."

Commander Sano had no such intent; he ordered his men to open fire with both deck guns. Their shells burst wide of the mark, though Dickinson reckoned that now he had been shot at twice in four days "and I was a little tired of being on the receiving end."

Meanwhile, Merritt was conscientiously doing his job. "Mr. Dickinson, is the bomb armed?" The back-seater repeated the query until his pilot snapped back, "The bomb is armed. For God's sake, relax!"

During Dickinson's eight-minute approach, the sub barely maneuvered but fired two dozen shells at him. Apparently it had been damaged in previous attacks. However, automatic weapons now chimed in.

Dickinson extended his flaps, throttled back, and nosed over.

"All the way down I could see those heathen still shooting," he later wrote. Then he pulled the bomb release, shoved the throttle forward, and tugged the stick into his belly.

The quarter-ton bomb exploded close aboard, midships. By the time Dickinson circled back, he noted only one gun still firing but the big boat was settling on an even keel. In less than a minute *I-70* was gone from view. She left a residue of foam and oil, followed by "another bubble-like eruption" and unidentifiable debris.

Returning to the Big E, Dickinson keyed the intercom to the backseat. "Glad you didn't let me forget to arm that bomb."

It was the initial entry in *Enterprise*'s accounts payable ledger.

December 10 only whetted *Enterprise*'s appetite for submarines. Ten days later her planes bombed another sub, without Dickinson's accuracy, as the pilots' target was USS *Pompano*. She survived to torpedo five Japanese ships before she disappeared in 1943.

However, sub hunting worked both ways: on January 11 *Saratoga* was torpedoed by an I-boat northwest of Oahu. Sara limped away for repairs and updating that kept her sidelined nearly five months. That left the Pacific Fleet with only two carriers, *Enterprise* and *Lexington,* so *Yorktown* was quickly transferred from the East Coast, arriving in January. *Ranger* and *Wasp* remained committed to Atlantic operations, and *Hornet,* last of the Yorktown class, was still shaking down at Norfolk.

On January 16 a Dauntless crashed on the Big E's flight deck, wrenching off a wheel that struck one of the arresting gear crew. Chief George Lawhon was critically injured. A plankowner, he had been aboard more than three years—a respected professional and an innovator in flight deck equipment. He died the next day, *Enterprise*'s first noncombat fatality of the war.

That same day Chief Machinist Harold F. Dixon launched a search with other Torpedo Six Devastators. Late in the patrol, he realized that he was lost. He radioed the carrier, requesting a bearing, but it was too late. His last transmission said that he was ditching. Nothing more was heard of Dixon with Ordnanceman Anthony J. Pastula and Radioman Gene D. Aldrich.

The crewmen knew they were in big trouble. As another pilot said, "In the first year of the war there was no such thing as air-sea rescue. Every flight was potentially your last."

Dixon put the big Douglas into the water; it bounced twice before splashing to a halt. Crammed into a blessed eight-by-four-foot rubber raft with minimal supplies, the trio faced an unknown fate. One plane passed by without seeing the yellow dot on the immense gray sea. Nevertheless, Dixon remained professionally detached. He recalled, "I was an old head in this business and knew that our admiral could not risk his entire force in a doubtful attempt to rescue three men. After all, we were at war . . . it was only simple, military logic."

The fliers rigged a crude sail from what little clothing they possessed and began an excruciating five-week exercise in survival. They subsisted on occasional fish, birds, seaweed, rainwater—and raw courage. The mental and emotional agony of not knowing what would come of them was a constant companion. Yet they refused to yield to the Pacific.

Finally—dehydrated, starving, naked, and sunburned—the men fetched up at tiny Pukapuka Island, 750 miles and thirty-four days from their ditching position. The gods of sea and storm watched over the *Enterprise* men: the castaways crawled ashore one day ahead of a storm that would have killed them.

OUR TURN TO SHOOT

The Big E sortied again on January 11 with orders from the new Pacific Fleet commander. Admiral Chester Nimitz was a white-haired Texan anxious to take offensive action. Lacking battleships, with his submarines an unknown quantity, he ordered carrier strikes against the Japanese-held Gilbert and Marshall Islands, some 2,000 miles southwest of Hawaii. *Enterprise* would hit three atolls in the Marshalls while *Yorktown* pummeled the Gilberts. Intelligence was scarce; after an hour-long briefing, pilots knew little more than before.

No matter: the raids were set for February 1. Halsey's Task Force 8 headed for Kwajalein, Maloelap, and Wotje atolls, which, unknown to the Americans, hosted thirty Japanese fighters and nine twin-engine bombers. The excitement was palpable: *Enterprise* was about to hit back at a treacherous enemy who had killed Big E shipmates.

On February 1 the ship's executive officer, Commander Tom Jeter, inserted some verse in the plan of the day. He had fenced in the 1924 Olympics, and if his poetry did not match his athleticism, it was nonetheless heartfelt:

An eye for an eye,
A tooth for a tooth.
This Sunday it's our turn to shoot.
Remember Pearl Harbor.

Flight quarters at 3:45 A.M. meant a 3:00 reveille and a battle break-fast. The crowded officers' wardroom was redolent of cooking aromas: hot coffee, toast, bacon. The U.S. Navy ran as much on java as on fuel oil, but there was canned juice for those who shunned caffeine.

The khaki crowd was a study in contrasts. Some men ate quietly; others chattered earnestly or nervously. One or two who lost their appetite abandoned the tables for the nearest head. Some were like Dick Dickinson, who had survived Pearl Harbor and sunk the war's first submarine. Suddenly he was unable to swallow. "That piece of egg seemed to swell and turn into something only slightly smaller than a tennis ball. I crammed my mouth with dry toast and washed it down with water." With that brief breakfast he reported to Scouting Six's ready room.

Meanwhile, the Big E neared Wotje from the north, preparing to launch aircraft while cruisers closed on some of the islands to unlimber six- and eight-inch shells. Air operations would be conducted within 150 miles of the farthest targets to accommodate the limited range of fighters and torpedo planes.

Illuminated by a full moon, *Enterprise*'s flight deck was packed with planes awaiting launch. Pilots and gunners manned aircraft, each observing his private ritual. The devout paused for a brief prayer, the most sincere being the aviator's heartfelt, "Please God, don't let me foul up." (Probably few actually said "foul.") Some Catholics were seen crossing themselves. But most men focused on the routine business of settling into cockpits, neither thinking too much nor too little that they were about to launch with live ordnance, knowing that before they returned men now living would be dead.

A flier's first combat mission represents a landmark: a finite point in time and space when he evolves from a trained airman into an aerial warrior. The Gilberts-Marshalls operation was the first mission for most of the aircrews, excepting those who had been caught on December 7. The rookies tried feigning a studied casualness. Many were like Radioman Ron Graetz of Torpedo Six. He recalled, "I really did not feel that I was nervous at any time. But I used the pee-tube and relieved myself four times on the way out

and five times on the way back. I guess I was more nervous than I had realized!"

A quarter hour before dawn Brig Young was first off; thirty-six Dauntless scout-bombers and nine Devastator torpedo planes followed. So began
an extremely busy day.

Enterprise launched four main strikes: both bombing squadrons against
Kwajalein Atoll, followed by smaller follow-ups against Maloelap and
Wotje atolls. Fighters would cap the airfields, strafing grounded planes
ahead of the bombers.

The first air action resulted in a dandy dogfight. Approaching Taroa
Island at Maloelap, Lieutenant Jim Gray's four-plane Wildcat division
encountered the defenders' dawn patrol: two antiquated Mitsubishi A5M
fighters with open cockpits and fixed landing gear. Eventually they were
code-named "Claude" by the Americans.

The F4Fs carried 100-pound bombs, which Gray's pilots scattered
over the large airfield. Pulling up from his attack, Lieutenant (jg) Wilmer
E. Rawie spotted three Japanese ahead of him, drawing away. Rawie liked
what he saw—meat on the table. He pushed his throttle to overtake the
enemy from below and behind.

It was an execution more than a combat—the preferred method of
aerial fighting. Rawie centered the right-hand wingman in his reflector sight
and pressed the trigger on his stick grip. The four .50 calibers chewed up
the Mitsubishi's light airframe, turning the little fighter into a red gout of
flame vivid against the early sky.

Fighting Six had just scored the first aerial victory by a U.S. Navy
fighter pilot since 1918. Unknown to the Americans, the Japanese flier took
to his parachute.

Having pulled ahead of the other Claudes, Rawie hauled into a hard
reversal to meet them head-on. He squared off with Petty Officer Tomita
Atake; neither pilot had ever had an opportunity to shoot at an aerial target
nose-on. Both pressed ahead in a high-speed aerial game of chicken.

It was a tie.

Rawie felt an impact as his Wildcat's belly scraped across the top of
Atake's wing. But Long Island's sturdy products were rightly called "the
Grumman ironworks." The rugged F4F shook off the collision, only losing
an antenna. The Mitsubishi was far worse off: a wingtip was crunched and
one aileron almost severed. Tomita Atake managed a shaky landing and
lived to fly another day.

Still eager, the combative Rawie descended to shoot up the airfield but his guns malfunctioned. With the third Claude hosing 7.7mm rounds at him, he shoved the power to his Pratt & Whitney engine and set course for home.

Scouting Six skipper Halstead Hopping led the attack on Roi Island, taking his first division down on the airfield. Circling overhead awaiting his turn, Earl Gallaher saw the action: "Hal went into a very shallow dive and I made a complete circle with my second division to come in faster . . . the Japanese had their fighters in the air. I saw them on Hal's tail and saw him go in the water. The enemy plane then started up toward me and we were shooting at each other. I ducked as he pulled up and my rearseat man took a couple of bursts at him."

Gallaher expended his two 100-pound bombs on the airfield but saved his quarter-tonner for ships reported in Kwajalein Harbor. He selected "an antiaircraft cruiser"—she was the 5,800-ton *Katori*—and went after her with a wingman. Executing a figure-eight evasive maneuver in his dive, he straightened out briefly, got a good sight picture, and released his bomb. While pulling out under the oppressive force of gravity, he glimpsed a hit on the stern.

Meanwhile, on the first Devastator mission to Kwajalein, nine planes under Lieutenant Commander Eugene Lindsey dropped fifty-four bombs with marginal results. Before they returned, a false alarm of two carriers in the lagoon prompted a second launch. Therefore the exec, the well-regarded Lieutenant Commander Lance Massey, led nine planes in the first aerial torpedo attack in American history. Boring in low and slow, the "torpeckers" went after a transport and two oilers.

Ensign Severin Rombach's back-seater was Ron Graetz, gripping his machine gun during the run-in to the lagoon. No fighters intervened but Graetz felt the antiaircraft fire beginning to burst. He also sensed his pilot's determination to get a hit: "He must have slowed below 90 knots and was probably only 50 or 60 feet off the water, and instead of making the drop at about 500 yards he must have been more like 250 to 300 yards from target when he made the drop." Graetz felt the one-ton torpedo fall from the TBD's belly as the plane lurched upward.

Denying the Japanese a clear shot at a climbing target, Rombach descended almost to the wave tops. Cutting it close, he flew past the bow below deck level. Graetz said, "I looked up at a gunner on the deck starting to swing his gun around toward us, so I sprayed a good long burst in that direction to discourage him."

At the rendezvous point only five other Devastators joined up. Graetz's heart fell: nine went in, six came out. Sad and subdued, the reduced formation headed back to the ship.

Then came a radio call. The leader of the third section reported he was returning with his three aircraft. Torpedo Six had gotten off clean. The joy of friends' salvation was indescribable.

The Devastator crews claimed four torpedo hits, though only one was confirmed later.

At Kwajalein *Enterprise* aircrews sank the 6,500-ton transport *Bordeaux Maru* and damaged *Katori* plus a submarine and seven other vessels. One of the Dauntless pilots unknowingly scored a coup when he put his bomb through the roof of the atoll headquarters and killed Rear Admiral Yatsushiro Sukeyoshi on his fifty-second birthday, the Imperial Navy's first flag officer fatality of the war.

The Japanese were not idle. That morning they launched eight twin-engine, twin-tailed Mitsubishi bombers under the determined Lieutenant Kazuo Nakai. The "Nells" bombed the cruiser *Chester*, killing eight men, and returned to base for more ordnance.

Enterprise fliers also recycled for more bombs and ammunition. Leading the afternoon strike against Taroa Island was Bombing Six exec Dick Best. His first bomb of the war destroyed a hangar ("a pretty sight"), but as he pulled off-target he was jumped by two Claudes.

Best felt eerily calm. Previously one of the few officers in the legendary "Flying Chiefs" squadron, he had flown the target plane for gun camera practice and knew what a good pass looked like. He outpaced the Mitsubishis, listening to the 7.7mm bullets rattle through his airframe. Back aboard ship he counted some forty holes in his Dauntless but only two were forward where they belonged. "The other forty-plus were all in the tail and port wingtip. Not enough lead," he declared with professional detachment.

Holly Hollingsworth led the bombers' second mission four and a half hours after his first, attacking Taroa airfield at Maloelap Atoll. Diving from 13,000 feet, his nine SBDs put their 500- and 100-pounders across hangars and parked aircraft. The Dauntlesses made a clean getaway.

Throughout the day *Enterprise* maneuvered within sight of Wotje. Figuring he had pushed his luck far enough, Halsey ordered an end to operations and began "hauling out." But he reckoned without the aggressive

Lieutenant Nakai. Early that afternoon Nakai was back with five twin-engine Nells, dodging in and out of clouds, avoiding most of the prowling fighters. Lieutenant (jg) Frank Quady and Ensign Norman Hodson shot up Nakai's plane, then he was gone in a fast, slanting descent toward the *Enterprise*. It was her first time under fire.

The attackers became visible beneath the undercast, drawing a barrage of flak as Lieutenant Commander Elias B. Mott called "Action starboard!" and his gunners opened up. Meanwhile, Captain Murray alternated between the helm and glancing out the wing of the bridge, once even grasping the wheel in his enthusiasm. The carrier pounded along at thirty knots, weaving port and then starboard to throw off the bombers' aim.

Nakai's men bombed from 3,000 feet, the ordnance mostly striking to starboard. However, one hit to port, starting a small fire that was quickly extinguished.

As the Japanese raced away one plane turned back, trailing smoke. It was Nakai. Badly damaged by the fighters and AA fire, his bomber could not make it home, and he was determined to die as his emperor and his nation expected. He pressed in from astern. *Enterprise* sailors gawked at the spectacle: a large bomber, visibly doomed and obviously bent on suicide.

Every gun mount that could bear opened up. It didn't matter; the Nell came on in, both engines now streaming flame, aiming for the carrier's deck crowded with aircraft.

Reportedly Captain Murray himself took the wheel to swing the rudder hard over. The deck canted to port in the starboard turn, and the bomber couldn't cut the corner. By that moment Nakai might have been dead.

In the rear seat of Dauntless S-5, parked on the flight deck, Machinist's Mate Bruno Gaido unlimbered the Browning and opened fire, adding .30 caliber rounds to the .50 caliber and 1.1-inch barrage. The blazing Mitsubishi banked sharply, swerving across the flight deck from port as its right wing slashed through Gaido's plane just ahead of the tail.

The bomber's severed wing slewed into the catwalk, spewing high-test gasoline across the deck. The rest of the Nell lurched into the ocean.

Bruno Gaido looked back at the wreckage, his gun still warm. Nakai's wing had struck the Dauntless about ten feet from where he sat.

But *Enterprise* had not seen the last of Nakai's men. Over two hours after their leader had died so valiantly, two more bombers closed on the task force. Deterred by neither fighters nor flak, they pushed through a pockmarked afternoon sky to release their 550-pounders over the Yankee carrier. Now well practiced, George Murray gauged the geometry nicely and ordered hard-a-port, escaping the bombs' ballistic parabola.

Heading outbound, the Japanese encountered Fighting Six. Skipper Wade McClusky, Roger Mehle, and Jim Daniels jumped the pair and began shooting. They scored hits but neither Nell fell. Then Daniels throttled within range and triggered several bursts. The bomber gushed flames and dropped into a death spiral, prompting a joyous "Bingo! I got one!" For Jimmy Daniels, who had survived American gunfire on December 7, "it was both wonderful and terrifying."

At Wotje both sides displayed courage and determination. It was going to be a long war.

In fourteen hours of operations *Enterprise* launched 158 sorties—more than two per pilot with some logging multiple flights. The flight deck crew worked unceasingly as the ship turned into the wind twenty-two times to launch or land aircraft. For the first time in her career the Big E's fast elevators paid for themselves, permitting rapid cycling of planes from flight to hangar deck and back again.

Despite the contemporary claims, Enterprise Air Group had sunk one ship and damaged eight, plus a submarine. But the cost was steep: seven Dauntlesses plus a pilot drowned in his crashed Wildcat and a Devastator that went in the water, crew saved.

Four days later the Big E returned to a joyous reception at Pearl. Flying her largest flag, with the crew manning the rail in whites, she moved up-channel as bystanders gave a rousing welcome. Ships blasted tributes, other sailors cheered, and people ashore waved towels, rifles, even mops. In truth, the Gilberts-Marshalls hadn't been much of a victory, but it was a win just the same, when wins were few.

Time in port was brief, and the wartime curfew limited the hours of opportunity. Even operating under "three dollars for three minutes," long lines spilled outside the bordellos onto sidewalks and into the streets. But gripers were met with the universal, "Don't ya know there's a war on?" Some fortunate men established relations with members of the Women's Air Raid Defense organization, whose WARD acronym reputedly meant "We Are Ready Daddy."

During the ship's ten days in Hawaii, Admiral Nimitz acknowledged Halsey's recent efforts with award of the Distinguished Service Medal. At the time it ranked second only to the Navy Medal of Honor, though months later it was rated below the Navy Cross; some recipients described the DSM as the senior officer's good conduct award.

That evening Halsey attended the usual movie on the hangar deck, his presence attended by the scraping of chairs and repeated calls of "Atten-*hut*!" The admiral directed the men to take their seats but he remained standing. The audience sensed that the old man had something to say.

Facing the young studs and old-timers he had led in battle, Bill Halsey held aloft his DSM. In his loud, gruff voice he announced, "I want to make a little speech. I just want to say that I've never been so damn proud of anyone as I am of you!"

Then he sat down before he started to blubber.

UNFINISHED BUSINESS

The Big E had unfinished business at Wake. She had delivered Marine fighters there in late November, and was returning to Pearl on December 7. The leathernecks had displayed exceptional resourcefulness, keeping a handful of Wildcats flying against insurmountable odds before the island was seized December 23. Now payback was on the morning menu of February 24 as three dozen carrier bombers plus cruisers and destroyers were going to paste the place.

Scouting Six's Earl Gallaher was usually the first SBD pilot off the deck, but that day he did not relish the honor. Sitting in his Dauntless with the canopy speckled by a misty predawn rain, he was nearly blind. His whirling propeller combined with engine exhaust to create an eerie effect—"a rolling fire going around in a halo."

Nevertheless, operations had priorities. The launch officer waved him off, so Gallaher advanced the throttle, nudged right rudder to offset the torque, and tracked down the deck though "I couldn't see a thing." Somehow he made the first and possibly only instrument takeoff from an aircraft carrier—a near miraculous achievement.

Second off was Perry Teaff, another December 7 veteran. But in the halo-glimmered gloom he lost orientation, struck a gun mount, and went over the side. The water impact flung him into his sight—there were no shoulder harnesses yet—and he barely recovered from the sharp blow. His gunner, Radioman Edgar Jinks, was lost. A destroyer rescued Teaff, whose flying career ended that morning with loss of an eye. Nevertheless, by VJ Day he was a lieutenant commander.

Gallaher orbited overhead while the launch was delayed. With improving conditions fifty other aircraft rolled down the moist deck, slowly forming up for Wake. The mission achieved reasonable results as the Americans bombed fuel storage tanks and buildings, but Ensign Percy Forman and his gunner were shot down and captured—it seemed that Scouting Six always took the heaviest losses.

A bomber pilot, Ensign Delbert Halsey, took a good deal of kidding about his surname. He wasn't related to the admiral, but he was a motivated young aviator. Searching for enemy ships, he spied a flying boat east of the island and turned to pursue. However, the big Kawanishi was too fast and pulled away, leaving Halsey to holler for help. Patrolling nearby, Wade McClusky radioed, "We'll take him."

With speed gained in a descent from 15,000 feet, the F4Fs overhauled the four-engine snooper. McClusky and his wingman, enlisted pilot Ed Bayers, set two engines alight, then his second section leader pressed in. Lieutenant (jg) Roger Mehle already had two kills, and was known for aggressiveness. Lower classmen from Annapolis recalled him as a dark presence at the end of the hall, but he knew his way around a fighter. He flew through the smoke before firing, and the target blew up in his face. Back on deck he found a souvenir embedded in a wing, a fitting stamped "1938."

Most of the little damage inflicted on Wake was owed to Admiral Halsey's two cruisers and two destroyers.

TO JAPAN'S DOORSTEP

The next operation came eight days later—a quick swipe at Marcus Island on March 4. It was a nervy caper: the target bore less than 1,000 miles southeast of Japan. Owing to the distance, Halsey took only the cruisers to Marcus, leaving his short-legged destroyers with their oiler.

Recalling the operation, Earl Gallaher said, "We launched a long way out. The surprise was that we would hit the island so close to Japan for psychological reasons."

Again the Big E launched beneath a full tropic moon, the attackers departing in darkness compounded by clouds, 145 miles from the target. By far the greatest challenge was basic airmanship as Brig Young led thirty-seven other planes into the cumulus curtain that rose from 4,000 feet to an unknown height. Pilots in their red-lit cockpits focused intensely on their instruments—artificial horizon, turn-and-bank indicator, and airspeed. Climbing slowly, their main concern was avoiding collision.

They broke out "on top," the aircrews sucking bottled oxygen at

15,000 feet, seemingly afloat above a moonlit cloud deck. Unable to see the ocean, until very recently they would have to rely upon dead reckoning—basic time and distance navigation.

Enterprise had a trick up her sleeve.

In radar plot, Lieutenant John Baumeister kept radio contact with Young. Baumeister was an astute Floridian who had graduated well up in the Annapolis class of 1936. There he was deemed "a clear, deep thinker," and so he was, developing an innovative procedure not previously used in combat. He traced a grease-pencil line on his scope showing the track to Marcus. When the radar blips representing the strike group drifted left, he sent a Morse code correction received by Young's radioman-gunner.

It worked. At 6:30 that morning the clouds parted enough to see Marcus's shoreline where breakers turned white against the dark surface.

Even so, the formation had become scattered. "We had a hell of a time getting planes together," said Earl Gallaher. He waited for Bombing Six to attack, then followed with several of his scouts in an approach that took him in and out of the clouds' gray-white tendrils. When he broke clear he was too low for a steep diving attack so he executed a glide-bomb run on the still dim island.

Everybody got away but one. Machine gun fire tagged the SBD flown by the popular Lieutenant (jg) Dale Hilton. Now with his plane afire, he made a water landing offshore and deployed the rubber raft with Radioman Jack Leaming, a plankowner. They watched their shipmates winging home, then awaited rescue with all the trepidation of Americans falling into Japanese hands. Later, Leaming described most of his captors as "a swell lot of fellows." But that solicitude did not continue once the prisoners reached Japan.

After return to Hawaii on March 10, torpedo exec Lance Massey was reassigned, assuming command of *Saratoga*'s Devastator squadron. Sara got a plum—probably the Navy's most experienced combat torpedo pilot. A sailor from childhood, at Annapolis he battled math and "Dago" (foreign languages) but finished well in the class of 1930.

Later that month Wade McClusky, the senior squadron CO, succeeded Howard Young as air group commander. McClusky recommended Lieutenant Jim Gray as the new fighter skipper—a bold move considering that Gray only had graduated from Annapolis in 1936, but the nomination was confirmed.

Another change also occurred in Fighting Six. The stiff wing F4F-3s were replaced with folding wing "dash four" models with six guns instead of four. The space saving permitted twenty-seven fighters instead of eighteen, but few pilots liked the new Grumman, which was 500 pounds heavier with no increase in horsepower. Nevertheless, the F4F-4 would remain the standard carrier fighter until well into 1943.

DESTINATION UNKNOWN

Enterprise's scouts had taken some serious hits lately, so Earl Gallaher's squadron was beached for the next sortie while *Saratoga*'s temporarily orphaned Bombing Three moved to the Big E. Lieutenant Commander Max Leslie's aircrews were solid—they had ample experience and only lacked the opportunity to show their stuff.

Enterprise left Pearl April 8, escorted by cruisers *Northampton* and *Salt Lake City* plus four destroyers and an oiler under the calm, capable command of Rear Admiral Raymond A. Spruance. It was a gloomy atmosphere: that day the last American and Filipino forces in the Philippines surrendered on Bataan.

For more than three days outbound from Pearl, scuttlebutt ran its course with typical speculation and informed rumor as to the next target. None proved accurate. But the situation clarified north of Midway on the 12th, when *Enterprise* beheld an image of herself—her sister *Hornet,* fresh from the States. She was the third and last of the Yorktown class, and the Big E had never seen her before. *Hornet*'s escorts matched *Enterprise*'s, raising the force's total to four cruisers, eight destroyers, and two oilers.

But the mirror image was skewed: in place of gray SBDs, TBDs, and F4Fs on her flight deck, *Hornet* held sixteen olive-drab twin-engine aircraft. Army B-25 bombers. Apparently she was delivering them someplace, but where?

The mystery was revealed later that day when Halsey announced, "This task force is bound for Tokyo."

Pandemonium erupted in USS *Enterprise*. Sharp male barks yipped throughout the ship. Hitting outlying bases may be satisfying—but *Tokyo*!

Leading the B-25s was America's hottest pilot—Lieutenant Colonel Jimmy Doolittle. He was an icon to the generation that had grown up between the wars: a record-setting racer, superb stick-and-rudder man, and aeronautical engineer. His crews were going to deliver payback for Pearl

Harbor by bombing Tokyo and other Japanese cities. They planned to take off nearly 500 miles from Japan, hit their targets, and proceed to China, where they would land.

After topping off from the oilers on the 17th the two carriers with their cruisers began their run-in to the launch point. That day the Big E paused to observe a landmark event as an enlisted fighter pilot, Chief Howell Sumrall, logged the ship's 20,000th arrested landing since commissioning in 1938. But the jubilation was short-lived: between wave action and a howling wind, LSO Bert Harden needed somebody standing behind to steady him on the platform. Consequently, flight operations were canceled owing to swirling seas driven by raw, forty-knot winds.

Any military plan is merely the starting point for improvisation. So it was with the First Special Aviation Project. About 3:00 A.M. on the 18th *Enterprise*'s radar watch reported two surface contacts ten nautical miles southwest. Bugles and alarms sounded, sending men to GQ. Halsey turned the force to starboard, tracking north to avoid whatever was out there. An hour later the Americans returned to their westerly heading, apparently without being spotted.

About three hours after the radar contact, Bombing Three's Lieutenant Osborne "Obie" Wiseman returned from the morning search. Flying low across the deck, his rear seatman tossed out a weighted message bag: a Japanese picket vessel was plotted some forty miles ahead, and Osborne thought he had been seen.

Determined to reach his launch point unseen, Halsey pressed ahead at twenty-three knots, his ships bucking heavy seas with waves cresting over the bows.

Halsey's luck couldn't last. At 7:38 *Hornet*'s lookouts glimpsed masts above the horizon—another seagoing sentinel. Moments later task force radiomen monitored Japanese-language transmissions.

The Americans were busted.

Halsey directed *Nashville* to destroy the picket ship. There was no option but to launch the bombers earlier than planned—a long 750 statute miles out.

Enterprise signaled *Hornet:*

> To Colonel Doolittle and his gallant command.
> Good luck and God bless you. Halsey.

To cover the vulnerable *Hornet* during the launch, *Enterprise* sent off eight fighters and three of Max Leslie's Dauntlesses.

Being carrier men, the Big E's sailors took a special interest in *Hornet*'s operation. They gaped as Jimmy Doolittle hauled the first B-25 off the deck in a nose-high attitude that seemed perilously close to a stall. The sailors had no way of knowing the extensive training the Army pilots had received in short-field takeoffs. With a howling wind and the carrier's forward motion, there was ample lift to raise the fourteen-ton bomber into the air.

Doolittle circled once, then set course for Tokyo. The fifteen other bombers trailed him at four-to-five-minute intervals. They bombed targets in six Japanese cities and got away clean. However, because of the premature launch, every B-25 ran out of fuel. One force-landed in Russia but the others crashed along the China coast. Despite the loss of sixteen bombers, the raid worked marvels for American morale and forced Japan to find a way to destroy American aircraft carriers.

Meanwhile, attention returned to the Japanese picket ships.

Enterprise men with a topside view were fascinated as *Nashville* opened fire from her five triple-gun turrets so rapidly that it sounded automatic. Many like Radioman Ron Graetz had never seen a warship unlimber its main battery: "That was the first time I ever saw all turrets on a ship fire, then start over again at the forward gun, like shoving a typewriter carriage back to start the next line. I was really intrigued by that."

Nashville closed the distance to the picket—a ninety-ton whale catcher—and Captain Francis Craven's gunners slammed six-inch shells at the vessel, but all hope of surprise was lost. Aviators trolling nearby saw the gunfire and were drawn to the scene. Dauntlesses and Wildcats made nearly a dozen passes, little different from a stateside gunnery drill. The Brownings chopped large pieces out of the second modified whaler, which stubbornly remained afloat, though she slowly settled.

With ammo remaining, Roger Mehle's "bloodthirsty bunch of bastards" returned to the first contact and shot it full of half-inch holes. *Number 23 Nitto Maru* was a tough little tub: she absorbed the F4F's remaining ammunition while *Nashville* expended hundreds of six-inch rounds before destroying her.

With the sixteenth B-25 safely away, *Hornet* spotted the deck with her own planes to launch combat air patrol and scouting flights. The rest of the day was full of wartime routine: ship and aircraft sightings both real and imagined. None threatened the task force but occasionally one of the numerous enemy vessels put up a fight. A sharpshooting Japanese seaman put enough machine gun rounds into a Bombing Six SBD that Lieutenant Lloyd A. Smith was forced to ditch; he was rescued with his gunner. In return, at least five picket boats were sunk. Halsey's force turned for home, every ship unscratched. The downside: nobody was allowed to tell what the force had just done.

Task Force 16—*Enterprise* and *Hornet*—got under way again on April 30, bound for the South Seas. The Big E again embarked a Marine Wildcat squadron and steamed for Efate in the New Hebrides. Additionally, the sister carriers would make themselves known to Japanese in the area by steaming within 350 miles of the eastern Solomon Islands. Meanwhile, the *Lexington* and *Yorktown* task forces would strike enemy bases at obscure places in the Solomons and New Guinea. It was geostrategic chess played on a giant oceanic board with squares defined by degrees of latitude and longitude.

An enduring complaint among sailors is that they seldom know what's happening until it occurs. Partly due to perceived security needs, but more often due to indifference, captains seldom told their crews much about events beyond the ship. If a sailor wanted to know the score, he made friends with radiomen. So it was the first week of May. Gradually word got out: *Lexington* and *Yorktown* had tangled with Japanese carriers in the Coral Sea on the 7th and 8th, derailing Tokyo's plan to seize Port Moresby, New Guinea.

The Coral Sea battle represented the naval millennium. For the first time in history, two fleets had exchanged blows without sighting each other. The seemingly impossible event represented the norm in the unprecedented realm of carrier warfare.

In the world's first flattop duel, Lex and Yorky had sunk the small Japanese carrier *Shoho* on the first day. But on the 8th the American heavyweights met two scrappy counterparts in the form of the new *Shokaku* and *Zuikaku*, veterans of Pearl Harbor. Both sides got hurt: *Lexington* succumbed and *Yorktown* limped away with bomb damage. It wouldn't be known for months, but *Shokaku* was badly hit and her sister's air group was mauled. Strategically, Coral Sea was an American victory since it averted the Moresby landing. But in tonnage, little *Shoho* was a poor trade for big, capable *Lexington*.

In the Big E, aviators and whitehats wondered how former shipmates fared. Of special interest was *Lexington*'s group commander, Bill Ault, who had led Torpedo Six in that long-ago peacetime world of 1938. He had radioed that he scored a bomb hit on a carrier, then disappeared into the vast reaches of the world's greatest ocean.

In the Coral Sea down-and-back, Enterprise Air Group lost ten aircraft in nineteen days. The fighters were especially hard hit, with five Wildcats destroyed or badly damaged in the violence of routine carrier operations. Two Dauntlesses also were lost, including a VB-3 crew that found safety on an island. The other was Bombing Six's extroverted, popular Bucky Walters with his back-seater, veteran Radioman Parham Johnson. Walters was another survivor of the Sunday surprise at Pearl, never seen again.

Delivering the flying leathernecks to swampy, fevered Efate in the New Hebrides on May 11, *Enterprise*'s mission was partly done. But then it was time to act upon Nimitz's excellent intelligence, which had sniffed out Japanese plans to occupy the Ocean-Nauru islands nearly 600 miles northeast of Guadalcanal. If nothing else, the Pacific war became a giant geography lesson, increasingly focused upon places that most Americans had never heard of.

A dozen Japanese ships were aimed at Ocean and Nauru when they crossed the bow of an American submarine, which torpedoed a destroyer. Another Japanese vessel also was ambushed, which was bad enough. But then on the 15th a Japanese patrol plane from Tulagi near Guadalcanal radioed an astonishing report: two American carriers with escorts, 450 miles east. Halsey had been seen, as intended. Faced with such unexpected opposition, the enemy invasion force reversed course.

So did Task Force 16. Having served their deceptive purpose, Halsey's ships shaped course for Pearl Harbor.

Something urgent was brewing up Hawaii way.

3

★ ★ ★

"Revenge, Sweet Revenge"

A damaged Dauntless of *Enterprise*'s Bombing Squadron Six on the deck of USS *Yorktown*, June 4, 1942. The bomber was flown by Ens. G. H. Goldsmith and ARM3c J. W. Patterson, Jr., during the morning strike against the Japanese carrier *Akagi*. (National Museum of Naval Aviation)

The message flashed out from Admiral Nimitz to Task Force 16 in the Coral Sea: "Expedite return."

That was navalese for "Get back here, fast." Halsey bent on the knots, aiming to return *Enterprise* and *Hornet* back to Pearl soonest.

The Big E had barely docked on May 26 before provisioning began with a manic intensity never seen before. Everything essential was brought aboard: food, fuel, ordnance. The word quickly spread: the ship would only be in port one day before leaving again, destination unknown.

While supplies were carried aboard and stowed below, a vivid contrast appeared on the flight deck. White-clad officers and men stood in ranks, arrayed by squadrons and divisions, while a full admiral's four-star flag rose on the halyard, catching the Hawaiian breeze. The flight deck loudspeaker came alive with the bosun's whistle and the traditional announcement, "Pacific Fleet, arriving."

Chester Nimitz stepped on board as the ship's band struck up the ruffles and flourishes due an admiral. In quick order the award ceremony was conducted as Nimitz presented medals to men who had spilled Japanese blood at Pearl, Wake, Marcus, and the Gilberts. After pinning the Distinguished Flying Cross on Roger Mehle, CinCPac leaned close and confided that Fighting Six would have an opportunity to carve more notches within days.

Wherever the Big E was bound, it would be without Bill Halsey. After the ceremony he left the ship, underweight and fatigued, grumpily acknowledging the departing salutes. Incredible though it seemed, *Enterprise* was headed for the greatest battle of the war to date while Halsey remained behind, beached with severe dermatitis. Years later the memory was so painful that he only managed a short paragraph in his memoir.

The question demanded an immediate answer: who would replace Wild Bill at the helm of Task Force 16? Nimitz had asked Halsey, who immediately replied, "Ray Spruance."

Rear Admiral Raymond A. Spruance was respected as one of the brightest officers in the Navy. He had graduated near the top of the Annapolis class of '07 and established himself as that rare combination: a thinker and a doer. Commanding Halsey's escorting cruisers since before Pearl Harbor, he had gained the respect of even die-hard aviators. Yet therein lay the problem. As a blackshoe, Spruance had no aviation qualification other than Halsey's and Nimitz's confidence.

There was precedence. *Yorktown*'s Task Force 17 had been well run by Frank Jack Fletcher, another nonaviator, who had led the unit through the war's most rigorous deployment: 101 days at sea with frequent combat from February to May. Now Yorky lay in dry dock, having her Coral Sea bomb damage hastily repaired by swarms of navy yard workers. Nimitz, wearing waders, had inspected her hull and asked the engineers how long it would take to complete repairs. When they said six weeks, he replied, "We must have this ship back in three days." He got her.

THE MIDWAY PLAN

The strategic axle upon which the upcoming battle would turn was American-owned Midway Atoll, 1,300 statute miles northwest of Oahu. The two small islands could support long-range aircraft and submarines—a potential stepping-stone to Oahu. Tokyo wanted them and assigned massive sea power to the task under Admiral Isoroku Yamamoto, commanding the Combined Fleet.

However, Chester Nimitz possessed the priceless asset of knowledge of enemy plans. His code breakers had reached into the atmosphere and plucked down enough information to give CinCPac a look over Yamamoto's shoulder at the strategic card table. The Japanese admiral, a formidable gambler, unwittingly showed enough of his hand for Nimitz to double down and call him. Vice Admiral Chuichi Nagumo's carrier striking force, with four of the December 7 perpetrators, would support an amphibious attack on Midway. Seizing an American air and naval base so close to Pearl Harbor would force the remainder of the U.S. Pacific Fleet into decisive battle.

The odds were overwhelming. Excluding forces assigned to the simultaneous attack on the Aleutians up in dank, misty Alaskan waters, Nagumo's carrier was directly escorted by two battleships, three cruisers, and eleven destroyers. Dozens of other warships, transports, and auxiliaries comprised the Midway invasion and support forces.

Trailing Nagumo with the Japanese main body was Yamamoto with eighteen ships including three battlewagons and a light carrier. But the Imperial Navy fumbled badly owing to its institutional insistence upon dispersion. Had Tokyo committed two more carriers to Midway, the battle probably would have been unwinnable for the Americans. But the two missing heavyweights—*Shokaku* and *Zuikaku*—were recuperating from their Coral Sea casualties.

Midway would be the only time that all three Yorktowns operated together, with *Enterprise* and *Hornet* in Task Force 16 and *Yorktown* in Task Force 17. Escorting the carriers were eight cruisers and fifteen destroyers.

Despite Japan's huge advantage in surface firepower, the odds were far closer in airpower. Nagumo owned about 250 carrier planes to 230 American plus 130 Navy, Marine, and Army aircraft on Midway. Of the latter, however, nearly fifty were mainly useful for reconnaissance.

Nimitz possessed the edge. If his plan worked, the two U.S. Navy task forces would be positioned to strike the Japanese before they realized the Americans were anywhere near Midway. Like the Pearl Harbor attack, the outcome of the battle depended heavily upon surprise.

Fletcher, as senior admiral, had overall command but the weak link in Spruance's force was *Hornet*. She was still new, having been commissioned in October and in the Pacific only since April. The Doolittle raid had deprived her of vitally needed training time, and her captain further limited opportunities for training. Many of her aviators had never dropped a live bomb from a Dauntless, and only a handful of her Devastator pilots had ever launched a torpedo. Captain Marc Mitscher and air group commander Stanhope Ring would not even permit dry practice dives by scout pilots returning from routine patrols.

Fortunately, *Enterprise* was "an all-up round" with an experienced team comprising the ship and air group. *Yorktown* embarked most of *Saratoga*'s temporarily orphaned squadrons, which were sharp, and her air department was perhaps the best in the business.

The SBD-3 Dauntless dive-bomber already was a proven ship killer, the main sinew of American carrier aviation, and the new F4F-4 Wildcat fighter was tough and durable. Consequently, the main concern was the TBD-1 Devastator, already obsolescent and more importantly, armed with marginal torpedoes that often ran erratically or failed to explode.

Those concerns bore heavily upon *Enterprise*'s torpedo squadron skipper, Lieutenant Commander Eugene Lindsey, who hailed from everywhere. As a child he lived in four states, attended six high schools, and graduated from two. At Annapolis he excelled in diving and gymnastics. He struggled with his studies though his classmates noted, "His brow is unfurrowed from worry over academics." As a midshipman he proved a crafty tactician, allegedly missing daunting classes by resorting to sick call. Even so, he graduated in the middle of the class of 1930.

Lindsey was almost thirty-seven. He had led Torpedo Six nearly two years, and the squadron had a depth of experience. Of the fourteen pilots slated to fly the first mission, ten had been aboard since 1940 or before, including two plankowners. Only one had joined in 1942. The radiomen-gunners also included a high percentage of old hands.

What Torpedo Six lacked was blue-water combat. Since February the squadron had logged twenty-seven action sorties, mainly with bombs. Only nine torpedoes had been dropped, at Kwajalein. The Navy's prewar lapses—equal parts bureaucratic arrogance and economic parsimony—had deprived the Devastator squadrons of the opportunity to test the Mark 13 torpedo realistically. Consequently, it took months of combat failures to begin to appreciate the weapon's multiple shortcomings.

Whatever the problems, on May 28 Task Force 16 departed Pearl Harbor: the Big E, *Hornet,* and fifteen escorts. That afternoon, as the air group flew out from Oahu, Torpedo Six led the squadrons overhead the ship. Gene Lindsey was first into the traffic pattern, driving up the wake in his big, stable Devastator. But he got slow, and not even the thick Douglas wing could sustain enough lift for nearly four tons of airframe, fuel, and crew. The aircraft stalled, following the propeller's torque to the left, and smacked the water off the port quarter. The Devastator rode nose-low in the waves long enough for the three-man crew to vacate the plane, permitting the standby destroyer to retrieve them.

However, Gene Lindsey was another victim of the Navy's lack of shoulder harnesses, suffering injuries to the face and torso. He could move, but his back pained him. It was uncertain when he could fly again.

Intelligence indicated that Nagumo would strike Midway on June 4. That gave Ray Spruance perhaps a week to learn the trade of carrier admiral. He proved a diligent student and a quick study: he wore out relays of officers in his daily walks up and down the flight deck, absorbing the collective wisdom of subordinates.

Spruance had to rely upon Halsey's staff, very much a mixed blessing. The group of some seventeen officers and men was experienced, having worked together since before Pearl Harbor. But Halsey had paid no more attention to selecting a new chief of staff than he had to the meddlesome Genial John Hoover of prewar memory. Captain Miles R. Browning had finished well up in the class of 1917, and possessed a wealth of experience in battleships, cruisers, and destroyers. He won his wings in 1924, ultimately commanding the *Yorktown* Air Group in 1941. He was smart, abrasive, and convinced of his own infallibility.

Just before noon on June 2, northeast of Midway, two *Yorktown* SBDs overflew *Enterprise*. One dropped a message from Fletcher directing Spruance to rendezvous at the position northeast of Midway optimistically designated Point Luck. In hours the American forces were joined, ready for battle.

Unlike most admirals, Spruance told his entire command as much as he could. With air operations largely canceled in the cold, drizzly region northeast of Midway, he inserted an addendum in the plan of the day: "If presence of Task Forces 16 and 17 remains unknown to enemy we should be able to make surprise flank attacks on enemy carriers."

Some officers knew more. One was Clarence Dickinson of Scouting Six, privy to some high-level intelligence but not the source. He recalled, "I was one of the few individuals that had access to those dispatches because I was the operations officer for the dive bombers and scouts. So I was well aware of the numbers, and I think in general the information was available to the air group as to what was there. We knew what ships we were up against so I don't think there were any illusions."

Despite the Navy's fetish for security, some sailors knew more than any admirals suspected. Among them was Ordnanceman Alvin Kernan. He recalled that before *Enterprise* reached Pearl Harbor, scuttlebutt contained some astonishing detail: "The Japanese fleet, it was said, was about to attack Midway Island, with a diversionary move on the Aleutians, and we, having broken their code, were going to lie off Midway and surprise them."

WEDNESDAY, JUNE 3

On the evening of the 3rd, everybody was busy. Ordnancemen, aerial gunners, and even pilots inspected every .30 and .50 caliber round loaded into ammo trays. Firing circuits were checked and double-checked—some fighter pilots had lost certain kills when systems failed in the ephemeral moment that one's sight was dead-on on a "meatball," as gunners called the rising sun emblem. Losing a victory was bad enough: unnecessarily losing a friend was intolerable.

Plane captains with a few moments to spare applied some extra wax to their aircraft, optimistically seeking more speed. Pilots cleaned their plotting boards to receive updated navigation data in the morning.

Most men turned in tired, but some were restless and slept erratically if at all. In the Big E a few like Bombing Six skipper Dick Best were nerveless. A thirty-one-year-old professional, he loved his work. Tall and spare, he had blue eyes and spoke in a rapid New Jersey accent. Best was absolutely dedicated to the war, exactly where he wanted to be, doing exactly what he wanted to do. After Pearl Harbor he had sent his wife and daughter stateside, expecting to remain in the Pacific for the duration. He said, "I thought it was a great war and I intended to stay until it was over."

Best intended to be the best dive-bomber in the Pacific Fleet, and admirers said that if dive-bombing were made an Olympic sport, their money was on Dick for the gold. He was also confident of his squadron. "At that time the fleet bombing average was about 12 percent hits. I promised 20 percent but Spruance's chief of staff demanded 100 percent!"

The Germans have a concept—*schussfest*—which translates as

"bulletproof." It connotes more of a mystical certitude, a profound assurance, that no harm can befall one. Whatever it was called, Dick Best had it. That night he "slept like a baby."

Scouting Six CO Earl Gallaher had a similar attitude: "More than any kind of fear, I think we felt the anticipation of the fact that we were really going to have a chance to pay them back for Pearl Harbor. That was my feeling and I know it was the feeling of many pilots. I had no trouble whatsoever going to sleep that night."

THURSDAY, JUNE 4

The Battle of Midway began far too early for most men. By 1:30 A.M. Chief Steward J. Reddell Collins, Jr., arranged an *Enterprise* favorite breakfast. He had been aboard almost three years and knew about the care and feeding of aircrews. Coordinating with the supply officer, Commander Charles Fox, Collins served the "one-eye special," a slice of toast carved to accept an egg, fried in butter until the egg was over medium and the bread golden brown. Fighter skipper Jim Gray admitted, "If one of our wives could do the 'one eye' as well, we never identified her."

Torpedo skipper Gene Lindsey stiffly eased himself into a seat. One of his pilots, Lieutenant P. J. "Pablo" Riley, asked how he was doing after the crash on the 28th. Rather than answer directly, Lindsey said, "This is the real thing today, the thing we've trained for, and I'll take my squadron in."

All was ready: Torpedo Six had fourteen planes and crews. With four spare crews, some men were necessarily left behind. One was Radioman Ron Graetz. "It was scary sitting on the hangar deck with no duties. My friend Dick Butler and I went to the squadron office and tried to get flights rescheduled so we could fly but the skipper refused to mess with any changes."

Before launch, Lindsey huddled with Gray to coordinate fighter cover for the TBDs. Based on Coral Sea reports, the dive-bombers were the most vulnerable so the fighters would stay high with them. However, the torpedo squadron could call for help if needed. Dispensing with radio call signs, the two COs agreed to use first names. If Torpedo Six encountered Japanese fighters, which seemed likely, Lindsey would holler, "Come on down, Jim."

Other than combat air patrols, *Enterprise*'s Captain George Murray and the air staff intended to launch the entire air group once enemy carriers were located. The eighteen Dauntless scouts were armed with 500-pounders to lighten the takeoff load for the short deck run, twelve also carried

100-pound incendiary bombs beneath each wing. Best's fifteen Dauntless bombers each packed half-tonners.

After two false starts, the word came down just before 7:00. Midway-based patrol planes had spotted at least two Japanese carriers almost 200 miles southwest of the task force. Spruance's instinct was to launch immediately but his chief of staff, Captain Miles Browning, urged him to close the range. Since *Yorktown* was re-covering Task Force 17's morning search, Fletcher as the senior commander on the *Yorktown* released Spruance on the *Enterprise* to act independently, which he did.

The prevailing breeze was only five or six knots from the southeast— away from the target—so Captain Murray rang up more speed and the Big E responded, working up to twenty-eight knots. With adequate wind over the deck, the aircraft could safely get off with full loads.

Bombing Six skipper Dick Best's gunner was James F. Murray, the squadron's leading chief petty officer, who had been in the Navy fifteen years, serving in aviation and submarines. Much later Murray recalled, "As he climbed aboard 6-B-1, [Best] said, 'Murray, this is it,' just like the movies!"

Among Best's new aviators was Ensign Lew Hopkins, who had never launched with a 1,000-pound bomb. Additionally, he was making his first high-altitude flight with sustained use of his oxygen mask.

Scouting Six began takeoff at 7:06 A.M., including air group commander Wade McClusky's three-plane section, followed by Best's fifteen bombers. While the thirty-three Dauntlesses bored holes in the sky, the deck crew positioned fourteen Devastators and ten Wildcats. It was a maddeningly slow process, and after nearly forty minutes Spruance exhausted his patience. He ordered the signalmen to flash a message to McClusky, "Proceed on mission assigned." Seven minutes later, with his two Dauntless squadrons well in hand, McClusky turned southwesterly: course 231, estimated distance to target 165 miles.

Still, there were problems. Lieutenant Frank Patriarca's engine had refused to start, and another plane returned with supercharger trouble. That left McClusky with thirty-one scout-bombers to continue the mission.

The air group opted for a procedure called "deferred departure." It was a time-consuming process in which all four squadrons launched, formed up near the task force, and set course as a unit. It had the advantage of retaining cohesion but at the expense of fuel, the most precious commodity in aviation. In contrast, *Yorktown*'s battle-wise air group used a "running rendezvous," with the fighters overtaking the slower bombers, the squadrons joining up en route to the target—the optimal arrangement.

McClusky's two squadrons climbed to altitude for the hunt. It was beautiful hunting weather: unlimited visibility with scattered clouds at 1,500 to 2,500 feet with a slight breeze out of the southeast.

While McClusky's Dauntlesses headed outbound, Gray's ten Wildcat fighters lost track of them. He expected to remain close to the bombers but missed the order directing them to leave without him. Consequently, he made a logical assumption: he thought the torpedo squadron below him was Lindsey's Torpedo Six, and Gray tacked onto it. Even cruise-climbing, the Wildcats outpaced the Devastators and had to weave overhead to keep them in sight beneath breaks in the clouds.

Actually, the TBDs were Torpedo Eight from *Hornet;* Lindsey's squadron did not depart until 8:00, nearly an hour after the launch began.

TORPEDO SIX

Gene Lindsey, still gimpy from his crash a week before, was determined to take his squadron into the Japanese fleet. He had limped to the lead Devastator and painfully eased his way into the cockpit, helped by a mechanic. Lindsey's gunner, Chief Radioman Charles T. Grenat, settled in behind the newly installed twin .30 calibers.

The seven planes of the squadron's second division were led by an Annapolis "trade-school boy," Lieutenant Arthur V. Ely, a Pennsylvanian out of the class of '35. Known as "Brother Eli" and "Doc," he was short, dark, and smiling, a gymnast and cross-country man. Well experienced, Ely had been in the squadron since 1938.

As Torpedo Six launched, Ron Graetz stood in the catwalk, watching as each TBD took off. T-2 was flown by his usual pilot, Severin Rombach, with Radioman Wilburn Glenn facing aft. Like a victorious boxer, Glenn clasped hands over his head all the way up the deck. It was the last Graetz saw of either man.

Lindsey took course 240 degrees southwest, cruising at 2,000 feet to read the whitecaps and compensate for the wind. Departing later than the scout-bombers, Lindsey flew nearly straight to the target. Around 9:30 he saw smoke on the northwest horizon—it had to be the Japanese fleet. He turned that way, knowing that he faced the short end of very long odds.

Meanwhile, *Hornet's* forty-nine dive-bombers and fighters had climbed almost due west, following Commander Stanhope Ring and entering Midway lore as "the flight to nowhere." None of them found the enemy; many splashed with dry tanks trying to return to their carrier.

Unknown to either torpedo outfit keeping radio silence, orbiting four miles over the Japanese fleet was Jim Gray with his ten Wildcats, awaiting the "Come on down" call from Lindsey. Gray circled for about thirty minutes before turning for home.

"We were at about 20,000 feet," he later wrote. "I looked at my gas gauge, and expecting to see I had about a quarter of a tank gone. Actually I had about a quarter of a tank left. . . . Only an idiot runs out of gas in an airplane. We lost the Torpedo Eight people under the overcast, and that was the last I heard of them. . . . We went back, and we lived to fight another day. We were up at altitude, and we ran ourselves out of gas getting up there. Sorry about that."

Gray's explanation is unconvincing. It strains credulity that a squadron commander who insisted that only an idiot runs out of gas belatedly noticed that he had one quarter of his fuel remaining. His actions left a bitter residue. Five decades later Dick Best, a former fighter pilot, insisted, "The fighter's job is to die getting the bombers to the target."

Meanwhile, Torpedo Six faced a nightmare scenario: an unescorted daylight attack on an alerted enemy fleet bristling with flak and fighters. Prewar doctrine called for a smoke screen, a coordinated attack with dive-bombers, and friendly fighters running interference. Lindsey's men had none of that. What they did have was obsolescent aircraft and damnably erratic torpedoes from service politicians who prohibited testing the weapons. It didn't matter: Torpedo Six never flinched because it possessed courage, professionalism—and just plain guts.

Ten minutes after sighting smoke, the Devastators began their approach to Admiral Nagumo, whose carriers were screened by battleships, cruisers, and destroyers on fifteen- and six-mile circles. Lindsey sent Art Ely's second division in a sweeping turn to port, hoping to set up an "anvil" attack on the nearest carrier—two formations conducting a pincer from each bow. She was *Kaga,* pounding along at twenty-six knots or more.

Seamen say that a stern chase is a long chase, and so it was as *Kaga* turned away northward. About that time the Devastators drew the first antiaircraft fire—initially more a threat indicator than effective defense. Other ships took note and gun crews swiveled their mounts outboard: 25mm automatics and five-inch explosive rounds.

It could only go one way. During the next quarter hour, constantly subjected to AA fire, Torpedo Six began taking losses. Japanese fighter pilots saw the flak bursts, knew their meaning, and swept in. A few aircrewmen heard Ely's call to Jim Gray to "Come on down" but apparently the Wildcats never heard the plea. The fourteen Devastators were on their own, facing nearly thirty interceptors with a 200-mph advantage. The Zeros' 20mm cannon were lethally potent, chopping hunks of aluminum from the airframes, severing spars, sending the big TBDs tumbling into the water.

At least one Zero got careless. Lieutenant (jg) Robert Laub's gunner got a clear shot as one fighter pressed too close, and Radioman W. C. Humphrey used his twin .30 caliber mount to good effect. The Japanese went down, but his partners continued executing the slow, unescorted Devastators.

Probably no Torpedo Six pilot got better than a seventy-degree angle off *Kaga*'s bow—below preferred parameters—and no closer than 800 yards. Five or six torpedoes were aimed at the 36,000-ton carrier, churning the water in their twelve-foot-deep runs, but none scored.

Five TBDs cleared the boiling, flak-speckled sky around the enemy fleet but Machinist Albert Winchell splashed into a water landing. Bob Laub, the senior survivor, led the other three home. When they reached the Big E's briefed position they found empty sea. Stretching their gas to the limit, with fuel mixtures leaned for maximum efficiency, they found Task Force 16 forty miles from "point option," the expected location.

Robin Lindsey, who had relieved Bert Harden as senior landing signal officer, waved four Devastators aboard. But Machinist Stephen B. Smith's plane was so badly shot up that deckhands quickly pushed it overboard. Having survived the Zeros, he had been shot at by a Wildcat as well. According to *Enterprise* legend, Smith stalked into Fighting Six's ready room, the flap on his holster unsnapped.

Gene Lindsey was gone, and with him eighteen others including Art Ely, Severin Rombach, and Pablo Riley. Only two missing men were eventually recovered.

Dauntless pilot Clarence Dickinson said of his friends in Torpedo Six, "The fact that they kept going in, I would expect it of them; I think everybody would have done that. Their thoughts were that whatever happened they were going in until the last man was gone. They were that kind of people."

MCCLUSKY

Nothing was going right for air group commander Wade McClusky. First, his regular gunner had been unable to fly, requiring a last-minute replacement. Then *Enterprise*'s launch had fallen behind schedule as McClusky circled overhead, burning precious fuel while waiting for the fighters and torpedo planes. After forty minutes he was ordered to proceed without the Wildcats and Devastators, though two Dauntlesses had aborted with mechanical problems.

Now, at the head of thirty scout-bombers, McClusky sought a moving target that defied discovery. Forty years old, the stocky New Yorker was a seasoned professional who had graduated from the U.S. Naval Academy eighteen years before, to the day. But now, pondering the time-distance equation, he pulled out his plotting board from beneath the instrument panel. He double-checked his navigation, confirming that the compass on his canopy frame read southwest. No error there. He was in the right place at the right time, but the Japanese had failed to show.

McClusky shoved the board back in place and faced a command decision. He had been airborne nearly three hours, and he knew the pilots of his two squadrons were watching their fuel gauges. Wingmen always used more gasoline than their leaders, needing to adjust throttle settings to keep formation. Worst off was Ensign Tony Schneider, whose engine was smoking, using far too much fuel. Nevertheless, he still plugged along in formation.

Fifteen minutes after passing the briefed contact point, McClusky exercised a combination of logic and intuition. Since the enemy fleet was not where expected, he reasoned that it had turned northerly, away from its previous course toward Midway. He eased into a gentle right turn. He would fly the reciprocal of the enemy's track for half an hour and, if nothing turned up, he could only return to the *Enterprise* with minimal fuel remaining.

Settled on their northwesterly heading, the Big E's dive-bombers droned along at 19,000 feet, pilots and gunners sucking bottled oxygen in the high, thin air, their Wright engines clattering along at minimum cruise power.

At the head of Bombing Six, Dick Best was increasingly frustrated. He trailed McClusky for another twenty anxious minutes—fifteen priceless gallons' worth—when the air group commander waggled his wings for attention. Almost four miles below, McClusky spotted the wake of a single ship, headed northeast. It had to be Japanese, and it was. A destroyer had been detached from the enemy armada to hunt a pesky American submarine, and now was making knots to rejoin the task force. McClusky turned starboard, taking up the ship's heading as its high-speed wake pointed like a white arrow on a deep blue canvas.

Five minutes later Wade McClusky was looking at Vice Admiral Chuichi Nagumo's Carrier Striking Force.

Flying behind McClusky, Scouting Six's Earl Gallaher gawked at the sight: "We knew that they had a lot but the ocean was covered with ships."

In Bombing Six, Lew Hopkins saw the carriers from fifteen miles, "and at that distance they looked like large water bugs scooting over the water."

In sight of a task force, Tony Schneider breathed a sigh of relief. He was flying on fumes and reckoned that Commander McClusky had taken the pilots home. At that point Schneider's Wright Cyclone hiccupped, gasped, and quit. He nosed down to maintain airspeed, intending to ditch beside a friendly vessel. Then he saw a huge ship with a pagoda mast. Only Japanese battleships had pagoda masts. Schneider turned away, knowing only that he wanted saltwater miles between himself and *Kido Butai*—the enemy carrier force.

Meanwhile, there were problems in the formation. Dick Best's left wingman, Lieutenant (jg) Ed Kroeger, had run out of oxygen and informed him by hand signals. The skipper began descending to 15,000 feet where the air was dense enough to permit unassisted breathing. But when Best again strapped on his oxygen mask, he inhaled what tasted like a mouthful of dust. Wracked by violent coughs, he finally cleared his head enough to concentrate on the war. Below his white-starred wings, wide open to attack, were four imperial carriers.

McClusky approached the target from the southwest, meeting Nagumo broadside to port. As the Big E's dive-bombers neared their pushover point, a former shipmate was dying far below. Lance Massey, the likable, ever smiling former Torpedo Six exec, led a dozen *Yorktown* TBDs inbound to the target. They were spotted by Nagumo's screening vessels, and in moments were beset by the Zero combat air patrol. None of his planes returned; only three of his fliers survived.

The dozen or more Japanese ships were maneuvering, producing concealing smoke and covering gunfire. *Enterprise*'s Dauntless crews did not know that their friends flying Devastators were attacking unsupported, sustaining appalling losses to fighters and flak. But in the precious minutes that followed, the upper air was free of Japanese interceptors. Wade McClusky, who had compiled an average record at Annapolis, was riding destiny's carousel with a once-in-a-lifetime chance to grasp history's golden ring. As

"Red Leader" he called "Red Base," providing the vital information of Nagumo's location, course, and speed, then deployed his squadrons for attack.

McClusky's immediate task was targeting. Facing four enemy flattops, he could only attack two. He led his Dauntlesses for the closer pair, radioing for Gallaher's scouts to take the port-hand carrier while assigning Best's bombers the beckoning rectangle to starboard. Since the air group commander normally flew with the scouts, McClusky kept his three planes with Gallaher's fourteen.

Farther back and somewhat lower, Dick Best squirmed in his seat, checked the deployment of his squadron, and prepared to make his dive on the closest carrier, as per doctrine.

Satisfied with his arrangement, McClusky retarded throttle, selected the diamond-shaped dive brake lever, and activated the hydraulic power pack on his right-hand console. He felt the perforated flaps opening at the trailing edge of his wing and beneath the belly, biting into the thin air, slowing his aircraft and providing the bomb-aiming stability that Douglas aircraft gave aviators of the U.S. Navy.

With that, he keyed his mike: "Earl, follow me down!"

At that moment, as Dick Best prepared to attack, he was startled beyond reckoning. A long vertical procession of blue-gray shapes plunged in front of him, narrowly missing himself and his wingmen. He realized what had happened: McClusky, instead of proceeding to the far target, had taken nearly the entire formation down on the nearest carrier, which according to doctrine should have been Best's. White waterspouts were already erupting alongside the long, yellowish rectangle.

With no option, Best pulled out of his dive and turned toward the other carrier to starboard. He had only his two wingmen, Lieutenant (jg) "Bud" Kroeger and Ensign Fred Weber. Best shot a glance to his right, as Weber had a tendency to drift out of formation, but this morning the youngster was sticking tight.

Whether the mix-up was McClusky's fault or Best's, the result was serious overkill: twenty-seven dive-bombers on one target. In any case, *Enterprise* aviators began pounding ordnance through the ancient pine flight deck of His Imperial Japanese Majesty's Ship *Kaga*.

KAGA

Kaga was coming port into the wind prior to launching Zeros. With most of two SBD squadrons streaming down from his port quarter, Captain

Jisaku Okada sought to confound them by reversing his turn. But the huge leviathan was ponderous in answering the helm. Okada may have done better to continue his initial turn, forcing the attackers to roll left to continue tracking.

Several Dauntless pilots reported their targets' decks crowded with armed aircraft awaiting launch. It wasn't true: at the time the bombers rolled in, all four flattops were fueling and arming dive-bombers and torpedo planes on their hangar decks. The only aircraft topside were a few fighters cycling through the schedule for the combat air patrol.

McClusky, who had never dropped a bomb from an SBD, missed the target. So did his two young wingmen. Earl Gallaher did not. He recalled, "It was just a perfect dive because the *Kaga* was heading into the wind so I was coming downwind onto a carrier that was on a steady course. My dive got really steep. I put my bombsight on that red rising sun on the bow of the carrier."

Gallaher considered the SBD "a wonderful dive-bombing plane," so he was confident enough to press his dive "as low as I dared and let the thing go."

In bombing practice, pilots frequently rolled into a steep bank to watch their hits or misses. Gallaher cautioned his men against the practice in combat, "But I couldn't resist the temptation myself and pulled up and watched it."

Gallaher's gunner, Chief Radioman Thomas E. Merritt, exclaimed, "God damn, that was a beaut, Captain!"

The bomb exploded aft—Gallaher thought it struck amid packed aircraft awaiting launch when there were no more than three. Ensign Reid Stone missed to port, then Ensign John Q. Roberts's plane was hit hard by flak. He managed to drop before plunging into the water.

Next down the chute was Dusty Kleiss, who saw flames gushing aft from the skipper's hit. The Texan shifted his aim point farther forward and punched his bomb into the deck alongside the number one elevator. Wingman Ensign James C. Dexter put a 500-pounder into the sweet spot, igniting a fuel cart ahead of the carrier's island. The result was devastating to the bridge crew and flight deck personnel. Most of the bridge was destroyed, and with it the captain, executive officer, gunnery officer, navigator, and communications officer. *Kaga* had been decapitated.

The second division dived with Dick Dickinson. He claimed a hit midships and his pilots probably got two more. Most were like Lew Hopkins, who said, "I do not know whether my bomb found its mark. I know my dive was good, my aim point was steady, and my plane was in balanced flight when I released."

Heavy casualties prevented a definite accounting of how some pilots fared. Dickinson thought he saw an explosion during the attack of Lieutenant Charles R. Ware's division. In any case, *Kaga* was sundered by at least five hits.

Pulling out of their dives, retracting their flaps, and bending their throttles, *Enterprise*'s scouts raced from the scene. The gunners had the best view of all. Riding backward, looking over their twin .30s, they took in the spectacle of a huge ship, still steaming at nearly thirty knots, spewing gasoline-fed fires and a small volcano cloud of dense, roiling black smoke.

At that moment it was the greatest show on Planet Earth.

The Japanese fighters had been chasing three torpedo squadrons (*Yorktown*'s had arrived), and inflicted ghastly losses: thirty-five Devastators had been shot down, leaving six to limp home to the two task forces. Now the Zero pilots expended their remaining ammo with a vengeance.

Kaga's losses were horrific: in her blasted, blazing hull more than 800 men were killed from her complement of 1,340.

AKAGI

Nagumo's flagship, *Akagi,* had spent an eventful morning dodging carrier- and land-based attacks. Like the other three carriers, she had burned the right incense—until *Kaga* began vomiting smoke and flame.

Recovering from his aborted dive on *Kaga,* Dick Best was appalled: only his two wingmen remained with him. What had moments before been a gorgeous setup had abruptly turned to hash. Well, so be it. He regrouped and headed for the next carrier about four miles away, willing to tackle one of the world's greatest warships with three planes.

Ordinarily Best liked to dive from the bow ("It forces you to get steep") but his target was broadside to him. No matter. Taking what he could get, Best waited until he was almost overhead, then once more extended the perforated flaps that kept his diving speed at 275 mph. With Fred Weber and Bud Kroeger on each wing, Best lined up Nagumo's flagship in his optical sight. He finessed stick and rudder, placing the aiming dot amidships, while in the backseat Jim Murray called out the numbers as the altimeter unwound at 400 feet per second.

The dive was good—very good. With the little ball pegged in the middle of the sight's housing—no lateral error—Best superimposed his aiming dot on the deck and pressed low. Murray said admiringly, "Nobody pushed his dive steeper or held it longer than Dick."

Weber and Kroeger dropped their half-ton bombs at about 1,500 feet. Best waited a few more seconds, pulled the double-knobbed handle, then hauled the stick into his stomach. Retracting their flaps, shoving up the throttles, the three Dauntlesses screeched out of their dives, hugging the waves.

Best's half-tonner was nearly a perfect center hit. It smashed through the planking of the flight deck, almost striking the number two elevator, penetrated to the hangar deck, and a hundredth of a second later exploded there. "I wanted to see the hit," he recalled, "so I laid my plane on its side and looked back over my shoulder. Murray called it amidships, abreast the island."

Weber got a near miss perhaps thirty feet to port, dousing the ship's island with saltwater. Kroeger's was an "edger," nicking the flight deck overhang and striking the waterline on the port quarter.

Best's hit was lethal. It probably destroyed the fire curtain separating the upper hangar from the middle elevator well, sending burning debris tumbling into the lower hangar deck, spreading the fire. It also might have cooked off some ammunition for the portside antiaircraft guns.

Far worse, the 1,000-pounder apparently exploded on an armed and fully fueled Nakajima bomber. *Akagi*'s entire torpedo squadron was parked on the upper hangar, ready to be raised to the flight deck. A string of convulsive explosions was ignited in the hellish confines of that enclosed steel space, spreading flames that set off more planes. The conflagration was unstoppable.

It wouldn't be known for years, but blast and fires killed 267 of *Akagi*'s complement—one man in six.

Racing from the scene, the *Enterprise* fliers were elated. They knew they had just knocked two enemy carriers out of the fight, and a third was spewing smoke and flames nearby, evidence of the near miraculous arrival of *Yorktown*'s Dauntlesses at the same time. In an unintended stroke of timing, Yorky's bombers punched three half-tonners into *Soryu*, sealing her fate.

Looking back over his shoulder, savoring the delicious taste of the moment, Dick Best remembered what Pearl Harbor had looked like on the evening of December 8.

So did Earl Gallaher, who exclaimed, "*Arizona*, I remember you!"

Dick Dickinson said, "We all could see the carriers burning; we knew that this was the whole heart of the war . . . to get those four Japanese carriers and with three of them burning I'm sure everybody was jubilant."

The aircrews who had swarmed *Kaga* had to shoot their way out. McClusky swooped out of his dive, flying as low as he dared to deny dozens of gunners a straight shot at him. Scooting along at perhaps twenty feet, he cleared the Japanese screen, reduced power, and turned northeast for home. About fifteen minutes later he was working at his plotting board when tracer bullets slashed around him and his gunner, Walter G. Chochalousek, opened fire. Two Zeros had caught the Dauntless low and alone.

McClusky the former fighter skipper knew what to do. When one Mitsubishi began a run on him, he turned into the attack, then quickly reversed to face the next pass. In a lopsided, five-minute dogfight, the Japanese pilots put fifty-five machine gun rounds and three 20mm shells into the SBD. They missed the engine and fuel tanks but some found flesh. McClusky recalled, "Suddenly a burst from the Jap seemed to envelop the whole plane. The left side of my cockpit was shattered and I felt my left shoulder had been hit with a sledge hammer . . . it seemed like the end. After an undeterminable period, probably only two or three seconds, I realized there was an unusual quietness except for the purring engine of the old Dauntless."

Finally one Zero made a mistake. Chochalousek drew a bead on the gray assailant, thumbed down both triggers, and put a stream of .30 caliber rounds into the fighter. It dropped away, possibly a kill, but more importantly its partner sought other sport.

Leading the third division of Scouting Six was Lieutenant Charles Ware, a Tennessee sharpshooter from the Annapolis class of '34. Previously a *Yorktown* pilot, he was shifted to *Enterprise* in time for the Wake Island strike in February.

Ensign John McCarthy—a Pearl Harbor survivor—glanced around and saw Ware's section, including Ensigns Frank W. O'Flaherty and James A. Shelton. McCarthy latched on to Ware, as did Ensigns Carl Pfeiffer and John C. Lough. Division integrity mattered far less than numbers: six SBDs with rear-firing guns meant better chances of survival.

Skimming the waves, Ware's pilots denied the fighters the advantage of a "submarine" attack from below. A succession of Zeros sped in from port, but none pressed their runs in the face of a dozen .30 caliber barrels. As McCarthy said, "The tracer display was very impressive."

The low-level shootout lasted a good twelve minutes as the Dauntlesses maneuvered together, their twin Brownings chattering in their staccato 2,400 rounds per minute. When the last Zero disengaged, the SBDs were low on ammo as well as fuel. The briefing had directed them to egress toward Midway to deceive the Japanese, but time was critical. It had taken extra minutes to circle around the three blazing carriers and set course for *Enterprise*.

But where was she?

Ware climbed to 1,200 feet and adjusted the throttle and fuel mixture for "max conserve." Departing the area, he and his radioman, Wiliam H. Stambaugh, saw a chilling sight. Overtaking them from astern were eighteen aircraft from the surviving enemy carrier *Hiryu,* outbound toward the American carriers. The dive-bombers were escorted by six Zeros, and their leader simply could not pass up a shot at some of the Americans who had just destroyed three fourths of Nagumo's flight decks. Lieutenant Yasuhiro Shigematsu pointed his fighter's black nose at the two-tone gray Douglases and took his pilots down to engage.

So began another gunfight.

During the combat Frank O'Flaherty's fuel gave out. His Wright Cyclone sputtered as it sucked more air than gasoline, and he was committed to a water landing. He got down nicely, and was last seen "in good shape" with Machinist Bruno Gaido of Marshalls fame.

The pursuit lasted an astonishing twenty minutes—one of the longest aerial engagements of the Pacific war. Ware and the remaining four pilots relied on smooth flying, turning as a unit into each attack, while their gunners tripped off short, accurate bursts as slashing Zeros crossed their sights. No attackers were splashed but two sustained heavy damage and limped away, out of the fight. The others hastened to catch up with their bombers.

Finally with time to consult one another, Ware and his pilots exchanged opinions as to the course home. They communicated by open and closed fists representing the dot-dash of Morse code. McCarthy believed that Ware was headed north of the course and nudged him to come starboard. Ware, confident of his navigation, blew the "kiss-off" signal, releasing McCarthy to find his own way home. John Lough went more southerly. The pilots slowly pulled away from each other, taking their fates in their hands, and finally each lost sight of the other.

John McCarthy found salvation. He ran out of fuel near the destroyer *Hammann,* which retrieved him and his gunner, Earl Howell. The other five crews were never seen again by friendly eyes.

More fortunate was Dick Dickinson. He made a smooth water landing five miles from *Enterprise,* just ahead of a destroyer. The "tin can" looked oddly familiar: then he realized she was *Phelps,* his first ship out of Annapolis.

More than four hours after launch, Dick Best landed aboard the Big E, snagging the first cable. ("I was a one-wire specialist.") He was exultant, realizing that, despite many missing Dauntlesses, the course of the Pacific war was shifting.

McClusky stretched his luck the last few miles. He squeaked aboard the Big E and immediately reported to the bridge with Gallaher and Best, showing the staff his plotting board. Everyone agreed: three carriers had been left burning, one by *Yorktown* planes. Finally *Enterprise*'s exec, Commander Walter Boone, noticed blood on McClusky's flight jacket. "My god, Mac, you've been shot!" McClusky was taken to sick bay where doctors began working on his arm and shoulder, pierced by multiple bullets and fragments.

In the ready rooms, silence reigned. The scouts and bombers had launched thirty-two SBDs and got fourteen back, some too damaged to fly again. Though two Bombing Six pilots had landed aboard *Yorktown,* they were out of the battle. But it was far worse in the torpedo ready room: Gene Lindsey was missing with nine of his crew.

Some of the Big E's Dauntless shortage was made up by *Yorktown* bombers, ordered to stand clear with enemy aircraft inbound. Bombing Three skipper Max Leslie and his wingman had ditched near a cruiser but Lieutenant Dewitt "Dave" Shumway led his remaining fifteen dive-bombers to *Enterprise.* He, Gallaher, and Best began forming a scratch team for the next launch. More Yorktowners also arrived as Lieutenant Wallace Short's morning search teams diverted to *Enterprise,* forming a small reserve.

The battle was far from over.

While *Akagi, Kaga,* and *Soryu* burned themselves out, *Hiryu* had escaped a similar fate. Despite the appalling reality visible on the horizon—three smoke pillars—Rear Admiral Tamon Yamaguchi was determined to continue the fight. His air group launched two strikes in two and a half hours: the dive-bombers followed by torpedo planes, both formations with fighter escort. Both strikes found *Yorktown.*

Old Yorky's peril was visible from *Enterprise.* To gunnery officer Benny Mott and others topside, distant enemy aircraft exploded "like firecrackers." But the Japanese were both persistent and skilled. The first attack scored three bomb hits, and "it looked bad" to Mott. The second mission punched two torpedoes into *Yorktown*'s hull; she went dead in the water.

After Jim Gray's high-altitude mission that morning, Fighting Six had been relatively unoccupied. But during the first *Hiryu* attack, Lieutenant (jg) Roger Mehle's pleadings for a vector produced results. Lieutenant Commander Leonard J. Dow, *Enterprise*'s fighter director, finally permitted the Wildcats to help Yorky. Mehle's guns malfunctioned but Ensigns Thomas C. Provost and James A. Halford double-teamed a dive-bomber.

During the afternoon attack on *Yorktown,* six *Enterprise* fighter pilots claimed three torpedo planes and two Zeros. Overall, in the war's biggest battle to date, Big E fighters claimed only nine kills and probably downed five.

HIRYU

Admiral Spruance knew that at least one Japanese flattop remained at large, and he intended to destroy it. He only needed her position, and that vital information came from a *Yorktown* scout about the time *Hiryu*'s squadrons crippled *Enterprise*'s older sister. Counting the displaced Bombing Three contingent, the Big E's air department prepared twenty-four SBDs, including Gallaher with six of his scouts and Best with four bombers.

Gallaher flew north of the morning's killing ground, noting the smoke pillars marking the demise of three imperial carriers. But the late-afternoon light slanting across the sea revealed *Hiryu* from Gallaher's aerie at 19,000 feet, and he led his two dozen Dauntlesses south of his prey in a wide, looping circuit to the west. Having found the "Flying Dragon," he began deciding how to slay her. He wanted the advantage of the lowering sun behind him, glaring into the eyes of alerted AA gunners when he dived.

Evaluating the enemy's disposition, Gallaher assigned targets. He would take his pilots down on the carrier while Dave Shumway's Yorktowners tackled the nearest battleship, northwest of the carrier. She was *Haruna,* the 37,000-ton World War I veteran reportedly sunk by a B-17 hero, Captain Colin Kelly, in the Philippines in 1941.

Whether due to the sun angle or inattention, the Japanese lookouts didn't notice the threat until Gallaher's bombers had nosed down for the run-in to the dive point. By then it was far too late. *Hiryu* was turning back to the southeast, perhaps to conduct flight operations, and remained unaware of her peril until two cruisers called out the threat. *Tone* and *Chikuma* were too far south to provide much protection.

Captain Tomeo Kaku was more decisive than his *Kaga* counterpart that morning. Caught in a port turn, he continued the maneuver, making full use of his smaller ship's agility. Aside from presenting a more difficult shot, his constant-radius turn forced the Americans continually to correct for the changing wind vector across the target.

Meanwhile, the Zero combat air patrol rolled in from its perch. The thirteen enemy fighter pilots were pros. Orphaned from *Akagi, Kaga,* and *Soryu,* they performed eye-watering aerobatics to avoid overshooting the SBDs in their four-mile plunge. The Mitsubishis could only slash at the rear of the Dauntless formation, but they were grimly determined. Knowing that *Hiryu* represented their last chance to keep their feet dry, they fought with focused ferocity.

Multiple factors conspired to foil Gallaher's attack. The carrier's hard turn, increasing flak, and the disconcerting Zeros disrupted some pilots' concentration. At that altitude and angle from the target, several Big E pilots lost sight of the carrier beneath their noses. Pushing harder, they got too steep, lacked time for proper tracking, and missed.

To the north, Dave Shumway made a command decision. He clearly saw the geysers erupting around the carrier and recognized that she might escape. That was "unsat": he had seen what came of allowing the enemy a shot at *Yorktown*. He shifted from the battlewagon and turned back to the carrier.

In the confusion, Shumway's Bombing Three nearly collided with Bombing Six. Joining from port, Shumway's formation veered ahead of Best's, resulting in a replay of the morning excitement. Best was forced to abort his dive, pull out, and try to re-form his quartet. In the process, Zeros riddled Ensign Fred Weber's plane; his tendency to lag proved fatal as he went down with Ordnanceman Ernest Hilbert. Fighters also claimed two VB-3 Dauntlesses: Lieutenant Obie Wiseman and Ensign John Butler, who both had made the Doolittle raid in *Enterprise*.

Dick Best had no time to count losses. He pulled his remaining pilots together and once again split his flaps, nosed over, and lined up his second carrier of the day. He recalled, "Everyone and his brother was firing at us." Trying to ignore the flickering muzzle flashes surrounding the flight deck, he set up his dive as he preferred: bow to stern. With his sight nailed well forward on the deck, he tugged the release and knew immediately that his bomb would hit.

Unlike the morning attack, Best did not try to observe the strike. He shoved the throttle to the stop, weaving continually to throw off the AA gunners, and recovered to the west. Shumway and company also scored as *Hiryu* took a tight cluster of four hits forward. She was opened like a tomato can: the forward flight deck was peeled back and the elevator blown out of its well, a large part lodging against the portside island. In the gaping chasm of the forward hangar bay, nineteen planes were immolated with scores of sailors and technicians.

Though mortally wounded, *Hiryu*'s engineering spaces remained intact. The ship continued plugging along at thirty knots or better, streaming smoke and flames. She was so obviously doomed that some bomber pilots near the end of the pack shifted back to *Haruna* and got two near misses.

Minutes later sixteen *Hornet* SBDs arrived, attacking the cruisers *Tone* and *Chikuma* without results or losses.

As the Dauntlesses turned for home, *Hiryu* and the Japanese empire were on their way to extinction.

That night Dick Best flopped into his bunk, musing on the greatest day of his aviation career: two missions, two bombs, two hits, two carriers. He was on top of the tailhook world.

Then that world collapsed.

Best coughed up clots of blood and kept coughing. It would not stop. Holding a stained handkerchief to his mouth, he reported to sick bay. More ill at heart than in body, he agonized over an uncertain future in the war he loved.

FRIDAY, JUNE 5

Little occurred during most of the second day, a development that irked the aggressive aviators whose blood was up. They chafed under the seeming lassitude on the flag bridge, as Spruance declined to pursue a beaten enemy. But the ready room strategists did not realize the admiral's priorities: defend Midway, which could still be vulnerable to surface bombardment or even an attempted landing.

From his Hawaiian headquarters Nimitz sent Task Force 16 an erroneous report of two damaged enemy carriers. By the time Spruance agreed to launch a strike, the distance was 275 miles—extreme range for a combat-loaded Dauntless. Nevertheless, the operations staff arranged for a massive blow of thirty-two *Enterprise-Yorktown* bombers and twenty-six from *Hornet*.

Spruance's chief of staff, Captain Miles Browning, insisted on a maximum effort with 1,000-pound bombs. The aviators were appalled: the drag imposed by the bulky half-tonners likely would increase fuel consumption beyond the margin of error. Mindful of the losses of the 4th, pilots envisioned even more ditchings.

Arrogantly confident, Browning insisted that if pilots paid attention to cruise settings they could get out and back. *Yorktown*'s senior bomber pilot, Dave Shumway, huddled with his scout skipper, popular, puckish Wally Short, and determined to talk to the wounded Wade McClusky in sick bay. Informed of the impending debacle, McClusky headed for flag country, meeting Scouting Six's Earl Gallaher en route. They also rounded up *Enterprise*'s Captain Murray, who at least could address Browning on even terms.

The result has been described as "a knock-down, drag-out scrap in a Bronx bar room." Amid rising voices and flaring tempers, Spruance was impressed with the junior officers' argument. Finally he said, "I'll do what you pilots want."

Miles Browning spun on his heels, stomped from the meeting, and indulged himself in a forty-five-year-old's temper tantrum by shutting himself in his cabin. Meanwhile, the air department proceeded arming Dauntlesses with 500-pounders.

The launch began that afternoon, Shumway leading the Big E contingent southwest. By the time a target was found the range had opened to 300 miles: one solitary Japanese ship.

She was *Tanikaze,* a 2,000-ton member of the new Kagero class, one of the finest destroyer designs of the war. As the sky rained Dauntlesses she dodged and weaved, evading more than forty bombs aimed at her. (*Hornet*'s scouts found no target.) Nine struck close enough to drench water on her, and bomb fragments killed six sailors. Her AA gunners expended most of their ammunition and knocked down Scouting Five's Lieutenant Sam Adams, who had found *Hiryu* the day before.

It was a long flight back in a darkening sky, and few of the pilots had ever made a night carrier landing, but almost everyone got down safely. One plane succumbed to fuel exhaustion, ditching near a destroyer.

That night the flight surgeons dispensed a blessed restorative to fatigued aircrews, who welcomed the shots of "medicinal" brandy.

SATURDAY, JUNE 6

From sea and shore, the searchers rose with the dawn, probing the western quadrant for sign of the retreating enemy. Scouts from *Enterprise* and *Hornet* scoured the area, and one of the latter flushed game. Four Japanese ships bore some 400 miles west of Midway, two limping along at an estimated ten knots.

They were large cruisers escorted by two destroyers. *Mogami* and *Mikuma* were 11,500-ton sisters, commissioned in 1935. They had collided during the night and both sustained serious damage, especially *Mikuma*. Their plight was compounded when the original American report erroneously read "one carrier and one cruiser." Though Spruance's staff had reason to believe all four enemy flattops were destroyed, nobody took anything for granted. *Hornet* launched a full deckload: twenty-five Dauntlesses with eight Wildcats. All her torpedo planes had been lost on the 4th.

The Big E had her own contribution: thirty-one Dauntlesses from four squadrons including Bombing Three and Scouting Five displaced from *Yorktown*. They were led by Wally Short, the VS-5 skipper, with Jim Gray's dozen fighters as unnecessary escort—Japanese aircraft were no longer present.

Bob Laub took *Enterprise*'s three remaining TBDs on the Devastators' last combat mission with Ensign Jamie Morris and Machinist Harry Mueller. One of the gunners was Ron Graetz, whose name providentially had missed the schedule on the 4th. He wrote, "Of course we enlisted men never got any amount of advance information but after we got airborne Mr. Mueller told me 'They wanted that cruiser destroyed at all cost.' However, Laub was to play it cautious since there were no more torpedo planes in the U.S. task force.

"Luckily for us, our TBDs were so slow that, when we came over the horizon so we could see the cruiser, the dive bombers were just beginning their dives and we just flew a big circle around that ship, swung in toward them occasionally, to draw some of their gun fire."

Arriving overhead to find one of the cruisers badly pummeled, Wally Short assigned targets, concentrating on the larger ship. With no interceptors and not much flak, the bomber pilots took their time, and they wrecked their targets. At least seven hits were claimed on the two cruisers, mainly *Mikuma*.

Graetz recalled, "We just watched the SBDs pound the living hell out of that baby. When we turned to return to the Big E, that ship looked like a big bath tub full of scrap iron."

Later that afternoon *Hornet*'s bombers returned, completing the execution. *Mikuma* absorbed at least five hits that tore her apart. She took 700 of her 888-man crew to the bottom.

The Battle of Midway was over—or so it seemed. But while Dauntlesses were demolishing *Mikuma*, the crippled *Yorktown* was stalked by a gutsy Japanese sub skipper who penetrated the escort screen, fatally speared her with two torpedoes, and slew the destroyer *Hammann* alongside. The survivors were transferred to other ships, and the Big E's big sister lingered until early the next morning, then capsized and sank.

A BATTLE WON

Though the battle had ended for the surviving ships, the fate of some human participants remained uncertain. Eventually six missing *Enterprise* pilots and five aircrewmen were rescued. They included Bombing Six's Tony Schneider with gunner Glenn Holden, who ditched within sight of the Japanese fleet. The last found was Torpedo Six's Machinist Albert Winchell and Radioman Douglas Cossett, who survived seventeen days in their raft.

For others, rescue did not mean salvation.

Ensign Frank O'Flaherty had ditched his Dauntless after the morning strike on June 4. His gunner was Bruno Gaido, who had manned the gun in a parked SBD during the Japanese bombing attack off the Marshalls in February. They were found by the Japanese destroyer *Makigumo*. She was a brand-new ship, three months in commission under Commander Isamu Fujita.

The fliers were interrogated by means that can only be imagined. But they provided no useful information; their description of Midway was speculative since they had never been there. Nevertheless, twenty-four-year-old Frank Woodrow O'Flaherty from Tonopah, Nevada, and twenty-two-year-old Bruno Peter Gaido of Beloit, Wisconsin, likely knew what to expect. Postwar investigation revealed that on the 15th they were tied with weights and thrown overboard.

Other casualties survived but were lost to the cause. The most notable was Dick Best. Back in Pearl he was examined by the senior medical officer (also named Best) who determined that the SBD's oxygen rebreather had become heated during the unusually long search on the 4th. The heat created gases that turned to caustic soda, activating latent tuberculosis. It meant permanent grounding.

Dick was aghast. "I'll lose *Enterprise*, I'll lose the squadron!" He locked his blue eyes on to Dr. Best. "You don't understand, Commander. I'm the best bomber in the Pacific—you'll set the war back five years!" Nevertheless, World War II continued without him, and Best was medically retired two years later.

RETROSPECTIVE

Enterprise Air Group took substantial losses at Midway: twenty-two pilots and twenty-two gunners plus six *Yorktown* fliers who launched from the Big E. Thirty-one planes were destroyed or written off among the seventy-eight on board at the start of the battle.

The victory belonged to the dive-bombers, but Bob Laub, the senior surviving "torpecker," wrote of his "sincere wish that some recognition be given to those who paid with their lives for a magnificent victory." In penning those words he wrote for all.

For decades the conventional wisdom portrayed Midway as the all-or-nothing roll of the Pacific dice. But with time and reflection, a more reasoned perspective arose. A Japanese victory at Midway would not have ended the war. American ships still would have dropped anchor in Tokyo Bay, if not in 1945, then certainly in 1946 or 1947. Public opinion, let alone global strategy, would have required nothing less. What Midway accomplished was ending Japan's early dominance in the Pacific, permitting America to take the offensive.

Well into the twenty-first century, Midway represents the pinnacle of achievement for the United States Navy. Nowhere else were the odds so long and the stakes so great, and in 1998 the Navy established "Midway Night" to commemorate the battle. Yet in 2009 the service had grown so politically correct that the chief of naval operations delivered a Midway speech without once mentioning Japan.

Nevertheless, *Enterprise*'s vital contribution remained a source of fierce pride for her men. In retirement, Dick Best probably spoke for most. He called Midway "Revenge, sweet revenge for Pearl Harbor. The Italians say it's a dish best served cold, and by June it was six months cold."

4

★ ★ ★

"We Didn't Know a Damned Thing"

Enterprise sustained heavy bomb damage in the August 24, 1942, Battle of the Eastern Solomons. Here repairmen shore up a damaged compartment on the ship's third deck. (USN via Tailhook Assn.)

After the shock and elation of Midway, *Enterprise* had a short period for grief, pride, and adjustment.

The time in Hawaii was not entirely restful. One evening at the Royal Hawaiian some Scouting Six fliers were toasting absent comrades within earshot of Army B-17 crewmen loudly claiming credit for sinking some Japanese carriers on June 4. Since the Navy pilots knew the enemy ships were untouched when the Dauntlesses rolled in, a vigorous dispute ensued. It took the shore patrol twenty minutes to restore order amid the overturned tables, broken plates, and prostrate bodies. Though grudges were nursed with black eyes and bruised knuckles, most Big E men seemed to feel better for the experience.

Then it was time to continue the war.

Before June was out, the ship and air group had a new organization with a new skipper and other key officers. Reshuffling personnel was inevitable, as men with combat experience were precious assets to be reallocated to new ships and units. Consequently, more prewar men left *Enterprise* in 1942 than any subsequent year.

At the end of June Captain George Murray turned over *Enterprise* to Arthur Cayley Davis, who had earned an exceptional scholastic reputation in the Annapolis class of 1915. He possessed Murray's self-confidence and ability but their contrasting personalities took some adjustment by subordinates. Whereas Murray had been approachable and pleasant, Davis was not given to small talk with the hired help.

Two other significant changes occurred after Midway. The departing executive officer, Commander Thomas P. Jeter, was one of the most popular men aboard—a rarity considering that XOs were responsible for discipline on warships. But "Jeets" was unusual. He had penned the doggerel added to the plan of the day for February 1 when Enterprise Air Group first launched for blood: "An eye for an eye and a tooth for a tooth; this Sunday it's our turn to shoot. Remember Pearl Harbor." By war's end Jeter would command his own carrier.

Also reporting aboard was the new air officer, responsible for flight operations. Commander John G. Crommelin, Jr., was a spare, plainspoken Alabaman; he would become Mr. Enterprise to every sailor and airman who served in the ship for the next fifteen months. He excelled at nearly everything: he had graduated near the top of the Naval Academy class of 1923, and his flying skill was legendary. Four younger brothers followed him at Annapolis, all but one becoming aviators. Two would die fighting Japan.

In unguarded moments Crommelin expressed himself irreverently; some would say he bordered on mutiny. Of one captain he said, "Oh, don't listen to that son of a bitch. He doesn't know what he's doing." On another occasion, learning of a new skipper, he exclaimed, "When is this ship ever going to get a break?"

Despite Crommelin's disrespectful statements, they were layered atop a more significant foundation—his undiluted devotion to United States Ship *Enterprise* and her crew. Small wonder that decades later he was still called "Uncle John."

Midway's staggering losses forced a reshuffling of the carrier decks. *Enterprise*'s fighters and bombers remained, but she absorbed the slain

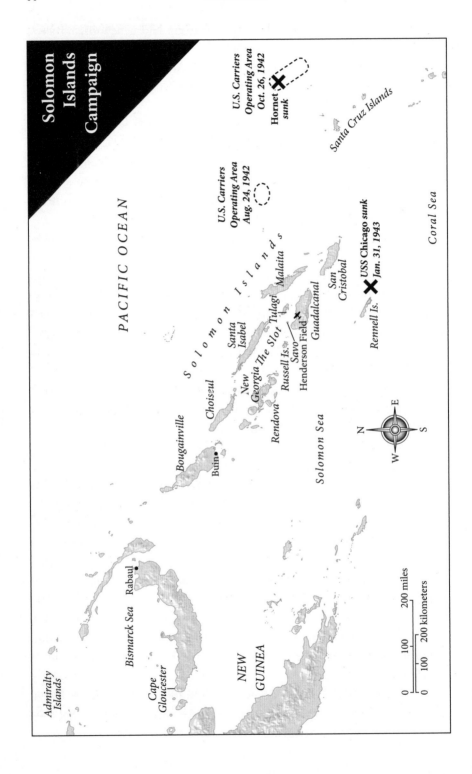

Solomon Islands Campaign

Yorktown's scouts and the reorganized Torpedo Three, formerly of *Saratoga*. Commanding the new air group was Lieutenant Commander Max Leslie, who relieved Wade McClusky in mid-June. Leslie was quiet, capable, and experienced, having led Bombing Three during the Doolittle raid and at Midway. There, despite the loss of his bomb en route to the target, he took his Dauntlesses down on *Soryu* and watched her destruction. His men thought the world of him.

New equipment arrived with Torpedo Three, which now flew Grumman's big-bellied TBF Avenger, a generational improvement over the late unlamented TBD Devastator. That summer *Enterprise* had the aircraft she would fly for the next twelve months.

Art Davis conned the ship out of the harbor on July 15, joining most of the screening vessels assigned for the next at-sea period. Very few men had any idea of their destination, but one look at the large assembly told them how much things had changed. For the first time the Big E had a battleship escort, the new *North Carolina,* 45,000 tons of sea power, and the even newer antiaircraft cruiser *Atlanta.* One of the familiar silhouettes was the cruiser *Portland,* veteran of Coral Sea and Midway. In Halsey's continued absence, commanding the *Enterprise* task force was a nonaviator, Rear Admiral Thomas C. Kinkaid, whose cruisers had provided antiaircraft escort in those battles.

COURSE SOUTHWEST

For ten days the force steamed southwesterly, and the scuttlebutt tended toward another series of smash-and-go strikes at Japanese-held islands. But upon reaching Tonga, two thirds of the way to New Zealand, *Enterprise* men gaped at something they had never seen: transports laden with the green-clad cargo of Marines: assault troops. That fact alone said much; this sortie would be no hit-and-run affair. America was about to launch its first offensive of the Second World War.

Wherever it was bound, the unprecedented assemblage bristled with power and authority. *Enterprise* was joined by the big, familiar *Saratoga* and a newcomer, the smaller *Wasp,* fresh from the Atlantic Fleet. After serving in the Mediterranean, she was needed to help fill the considerable shoes of *Lexington* and *Yorktown.* With more than seventy ships of all types, the assemblage at Tonga dwarfed any previous Allied armada—including the fourteen American, Australian, and Dutch ships that defended Java, and the two U.S. task forces at Midway.

The new mission was called Operation Watchtower. Its objective was an island called Guadalcanal, recently occupied by the Japanese.

After a 1907 Pacific voyage, novelist Jack London had written that if he wanted to inflict ultimate misery upon his enemies, he would banish them to the Solomon Islands. Ninety malarial miles long and ten sweltering degrees above the equator, "Guadal" was largest of the southern Solomons. Its otherwise obscure position commended it to the Naval General Staff in Tokyo because ships and bombers based there could interdict Allied sea lanes to Australia. As early as February 1942 the chief of naval operations, Admiral Ernest J. King, perceived Guadalcanal as "the tollgate" on the road to Tokyo, and after Midway that passage looked promising. Guadalcanal would remain the focus of the Pacific war for the next nine months.

Because Guadalcanal lay well beyond the radius of friendly land-based fighters, carriers were crucial to Watchtower. The American admirals were standing into uncharted waters, doctrinally if not literally. Carriers had never directly supported an amphibious operation, the most complex of all naval endeavors. It required close coordination not only between the Navy transports delivering the Marines, but between those two segments and the aviators protecting them from enemy aircraft while simultaneously supporting the infantry.

Common sense went against keeping irreplaceable flattops tied to a beachhead: they made too tempting a target for long-range Japanese bombers and submarines. Therefore, steaming south of Guadalcanal, Vice Admiral Frank Jack Fletcher committed his Task Force 61 to three days in the area, presumably long enough for the Marines to unload their cargo and get established ashore.

Operation Watchtower opened with concussive muzzle blasts early in the morning of August 7, eight months to the day after Pearl Harbor, and two months after Midway. Cruiser guns pounded the shorelines in a preparatory bombardment while eighteen transports and four converted destroyers began debarking the landing force of 16,000 Marines.

Enterprise's contribution to a powerful first launch of ninety-three aircraft was Fighting Six's patrol over the transports while nearly fifty *Saratoga* planes bombed and strafed Guadalcanal. Lieutenant Turner Caldwell took nine *Enterprise* Dauntlesses to Tulagi, across the sound from the main landing beach. There he joined *Wasp* pilots in working over the Japanese seaplane anchorage, wrecking nearly everything worth wrecking and some that was not. So far so good; the Americans had things their own way.

The Big E's Fighting Squadron Six now was led by Lieutenant Louis H. Bauer, a low-key, effective officer whose calm demeanor contrasted with Jim Gray's. Seven years out of Annapolis, Bauer had sea and sky in his blood: he had been a teenaged sailor and glider pilot. But the squadron was much changed. Of thirty-nine pilots, only eleven had joined before Midway. Nevertheless, with a heavy leavening of *Lexington* veterans, VF-6 became "Bauer's Flowers." Their trademark was the new skipper's mission-oriented attitude, as he valued ability above seniority. Consequently, experienced enlisted pilots frequently led two-plane sections and four-plane divisions with officers as wingmen. It was a stark contrast to the Imperial Navy, and fifty years later a Japanese ace quipped, "Now I know why you Americans won the war!"

Over 500 miles to the northwest, Imperial Japan possessed a powerful air arm: more than 100 long-range bombers and fighters at Rabaul, New Britain. The emperor's "sea eagles" quickly lofted twenty-seven Mitsubishi "Betty" bombers escorted by seventeen long-legged Zero fighters. The American carriers steamed south of Guadalcanal—about sixty miles from the transports off the north shore—and vectored fighters to intercept.

Fighting Six's Lou Bauer was not among them. Originally sent outbound from his patrol station, his division was recalled to circle the task force. Bauer was incredulous. He sensed the three-dimensional geometry of the developing situation and demanded a repetition of the order. When it came, the normally calm and composed skipper stewed in his cockpit. Later he learned that *Enterprise*'s fighter director wanted him in reserve in case the Bettys tried an end-around.

That left Lieutenant (jg) Ted Gay, a former enlisted pilot, to lead the interception. His wingman was Lieutenant Vince De Poix, an Annapolis man, who destroyed one bomber and stitched up another while old hand Gay claimed two probables. Unaccountably, the Zero escorts were out of position and responded belatedly before taking control of the fight. After shooting up Machinist Howell Sumrall's plane, they went after Machinist Julius Achten, who had downed a snooper at Midway. But Zeros were another matter: he ditched his battered Wildcat near a transport.

During the day, Fighting Six claimed ten shootdowns while losing three pilots and six aircraft. It was a cold-water shower for the Wildcat squadrons, which lost half the engaged fighters to the swirling, slashing Zeros, mostly flown by seasoned professionals. Some Japanese had been flying combat since 1937; many were aces, and they added to their scores over Tulagi.

One of the missing pilots was Lieutenant (jg) Gordon Firebaugh, a *Lexington* veteran. Leading his division against the bombers, he disappeared in the tussle. However, five Zero pilots knew exactly where he was. They ganged him repeatedly but found him no easy mark. With more than a thousand hours in fighters, Firebaugh timed his evasive maneuvers to near perfection. Time and again he spoiled the enemy's gunnery passes, keeping cool and shooting when he could. He destroyed one Zero that overshot him, then turned to meet each assailant. However, the next Japanese was sharp and hit the Wildcat with 20mm cannon shells.

Despite his crippled fighter, Firebaugh continued fighting back. When another Zero made a mistake, it paid the price. Having whittled the odds down to three against one, the determined aviator finally ran out of luck. Cannon shells ignited his fuel tank, sending searing flames into the cockpit. Firebaugh flipped his seat belt release, pulled his radio lead, and went over the side at 3,000 feet.

Though burned and plummeting through space, Firebaugh's brain was frosty cool. He waited to pull his ripcord until well clear of the fight, knowing that Japanese often gunned parachutes. When he popped his chute he swung a few times, then smacked into the sea. Once rid of his harness he shook saltwater from his eyes, heard a noise, and looked up. Two Zeros buzzed him but didn't shoot.

Badly burned, suffering a back injury, Gordon Firebaugh looked to the horizon. Santa Isabel beckoned northwest of Guadalcanal. He was alive and alone, and a long way from land. He started swimming.

The drubbing inflicted on American fighters was doubly shocking since Fighting Six had encountered few Zeros at Midway and lost no pilots there. Bauer's Flowers had been painfully plucked, and the skipper notified Pearl Harbor that he earnestly desired faster and better aircraft. "We didn't know a damned thing about Japanese aircraft," he recalled, lamenting that his knowledge of the Zero was gained firsthand. A *Saratoga* fighter pilot endorsed the sentiment, saying, "My Navy mentor was the Jap who shot me down."

The rose in Bauer's bouquet was a former enlisted pilot, Machinist Donald E. Runyon, widely considered one of the Navy's finest fighter pilots. He led his three wingmen into nine Aichi Val dive-bombers, operating separately from the Bettys. But while jockeying for position among some *Saratoga* Wildcats, the *Enterprise* division had to avoid flak bursts from friendly ships. Runyon led the first pass, missed, and watched enlisted pilot Howard Packard send a Val into the beach at Lunga Point.

Runyon then latched on to another dive-bomber which he gunned with Packard and his wingman. It went down inland, credited to Runyon. About two minutes later he claimed another Val, the best score of the day because Firebaugh's victories went unrecorded.

While Wildcats were fighting and dying, *Enterprise* dive-bombers also fought Zeros. Lieutenant Carl Horenburger's flight was holding north of Tulagi, awaiting a target from the controller. While circling at about 8,000 feet the eight Dauntlesses were stalked by two Zeros that ran in low and fast, planning a surprise attack from astern.

The Japanese leader was Flight Petty Officer Saburo Sakai, who was having a good day. He had just shot down a well-flown *Saratoga* Wildcat, then a *Wasp* Dauntless, running his tally to more than fifty Allied aircraft destroyed or damaged since 1938. With ammunition remaining, he expected to pick off an unwary American, then set course for Rabaul.

In Horenburger's rear cockpit was an alert young man, Machinist's Mate Herman H. Caruthers. Spotting the two assailants racing in, he waved to Ordnanceman Harold L. Jones in Ensign Robert C. Shaw's plane. Gesturing low and behind, Caruthers pointed out the threat. Both gunners deployed their twin .30 caliber mounts. Meanwhile, the pilots closed up the formation, concentrating their defensive firepower.

Sakai saw the movement and misinterpreted it. Normally fighters would not squeeze together: they would spread out to maneuver better. But Sakai thought he saw Wildcats rather than Dauntlesses and assumed the Americans were unaware of him. Only at the last moment did he realize his mistake: he was facing an alerted formation of dive-bombers, each with rear-firing guns.

Caruthers and Ensign Eldor Rodenburg's gunner, James W. Patterson, put their sights on the lead Zero and thumbed down their triggers. So did some others. At the same instant Sakai opened fire on Shaw's plane. Then Sakai's world exploded.

Machine gun bullets smashed into the Zero's windscreen; glass and fragments punched into Sakai's face, chest, left leg, and arm. His goggles were nearly shot off. In response, he jerked back on the stick and zoom-climbed high and right. Harold Jones quickly drew a bead, fired thirty rounds, and saw something fly out of the Zero's cockpit. Then the Mitsubishis were gone.

The entire episode had lasted seconds. In Shaw's rear cockpit, Jones took stock and found multiple hits. The radio between the cockpits was destroyed; two bullets had barely missed his legs; and his armor plate had stopped another. He estimated the Japanese had opened fire from barely 100 feet, close enough for vivid details to etch in his memory of the enemy: "I could see his face clearly, his body and head forced back against the headrest. The plane went almost vertically upwards and then fell smoking. That was the last I saw of him."

In the brief exchange of gunfire, Sakai's wingman also scored. A cannon round struck the vane of Ensign Robert D. Gibson's bomb, ricocheted into the plane's belly, and exploded beneath the pilot's seat. Gibson felt as though somebody had kicked him in the pants. He recalled, "My seat was armor plated and the blast was directed straight upward, tearing out my radio."

Bob Shaw fought for control of his own damaged Dauntless. The controls felt sloppy and he lost altitude. In the rear seat Jones assessed the visible damage and said that most of the starboard elevator was intact so Shaw decided they would not abandon ship. He turned for the task force sixty miles away and managed a safe landing.

Many years later the *Enterprise* fliers learned the rest of the story. In an epic of aviation survival, Saburo Sakai had navigated alone back to his base—a 500-mile flight while half blinded, bleeding, and battered by the wind streaming through his broken cockpit. He lost the use of his right eye but returned to flying and to combat.

Rear Admiral Kelly Turner's transport force weathered the Japanese storm as the Bettys and Vals only damaged a destroyer. In the air it was nearly even: sixteen American and seventeen Japanese planes lost to all causes. But in direct fighter combat, the Wildcats came off poorly, as nine of the eighteen engaged were shot down, versus two Zeros.

The day had been replete with lessons. The importance of teamwork was never better illustrated as the predatory Zeros had isolated some Wildcats and picked them apart. Additionally, fighter direction came in for scrutiny. Bauer remained bitter that the Big E's controller had kept the skipper's division as an airborne reserve rather than committing it to action. Though unusually capable—as an aviator he graduated from the U.S. and Royal Navy radar schools—Lieutenant Henry Rowe was an instructor without fleet experience. His *Enterprise* stint afforded an opportunity for practical work. Like many early fighter directors, Rowe was not enthusiastic about his job. As he said, "Pilots are supposed to fly." But he was determined to master his new job, and he stuck to it.

Despite their losses, Fletcher's fighters had prevented serious damage to American shipping. And *Enterprise*'s flight deck crew had set a blistering pace: 465 launches and recoveries, with seven fewer landings than takeoffs. The performance proved the value of larger air groups and experienced carrier crews.

The next day, August 8, Japanese squadrons again were overhead. Rabaul's air groups sent twenty-three Bettys with fifteen Zeros against the American ships still unloading in the sound. With advance warning from Australian coast watchers farther north, the Americans had about thirty minutes to respond.

Though *Wasp* and *Saratoga* contributed to the combat air patrol, Don Runyon led two other Fighting Six pilots into a formation of retreating Bettys. In the pursuit and shootout the *Enterprise* trio knocked down five bombers. Runyon downed a Betty and a Zero, matching his double the day before, while Ensign William Rouse won duels with enemy tail gunners to destroy two bombers. A pair of wayward wingmen—Ensigns Joe Shoemaker and Harry March—chased down a Betty near Savo Island but could not agree on who deserved most of the credit.

In all, the Wildcats and ship's gunners destroyed eighteen Bettys, three quarters of the attacking bombers. Japanese aircrews ruefully noted the bomber's combustible nature with unprotected fuel tanks and dubbed it "The Type One Lighter." But in two days Task Force 61 had lost one fifth of its fighters, reducing the three squadrons to seventy-eight Wildcats. That evening Fletcher noted that while strong enemy airpower remained in the area, no U.S. replacement fighters were available. The carriers had committed to three days tied to the beachhead, but Fletcher sought approval to withdraw beyond Japanese air range a day early. Vice Admiral Robert L. Ghormley, the area commander, approved. Apart from the need to preserve three irreplaceable carriers, many of the ships needed to refuel, and America possessed far too few fleet oilers at the time.

FLETCHER'S DECISION

Since 1942, three generations of baby Marines have absorbed the legacy of Guadalcanal with their boot camp mother's milk: Frank Jack Fletcher abandoned the First Division. In withdrawing the carriers twenty-four hours ahead of schedule, he forced Turner's transports to leave as well, most of the ships still bearing crucial supplies.

In truth, a major part of the problem was of the Marines' own making. They—and Turner—badly underestimated the time required to unload the transports, which had been improperly loaded in New Zealand. Because much of the food, ammunition, and heavy artillery were put aboard first, they were largely inaccessible until the last-loaded supplies were removed. Furthermore, Turner failed to keep Fletcher fully advised of the shipping situation off Tulagi. America learned a great deal about amphibious warfare at Guadalcanal, but most of the lessons should not have been necessary.

Whatever the Marines' concern, Fletcher's overriding priority was preservation of his carriers. It is impossible to fault him on that score: loss of one flight deck would have reduced the Pacific Fleet's available strength by 33 percent. Knowing that Japanese carriers were bound to react to his presence, Fletcher had to anticipate another Coral Sea or Midway. With new construction a year downstream, and only the *Hornet* in reserve, Fletcher's options were limited.

Among the flattops off Guadalcanal, the Big E was by far the most experienced. She alone had seven months of combat experience; she alone had fought enemy carriers; she alone had absorbed the hard lessons of Pacific Darwinism. Some *Enterprise* men were disappointed at Fletcher's decision to withdraw. One was gunnery officer Benny Mott, who thought the carriers should continue covering the transports while others felt "We had done our job." But few if any men aboard at the time realized the complexity of the situation: balancing force preservation with protection of the amphibious shipping off Tulagi; the poor communications; the concern about a Japanese carrier response. Nor, of course, wartime's unknowable factors.

Hours later, stark reality became vividly known.

On the night of the 8th off Guadalcanal's north coast, a Japanese cruiser-destroyer force inflicted one of the most lopsided naval defeats in American history. In a forty-minute slugfest four cruisers—one of them Australian—were sunk without significant damage to the enemy. It was the initial deposit in the repository that became known as Iron Bottom Sound.

Turner's transports lay completely vulnerable; he had no choice but to weigh anchor and pull out.

Yet as grim as the situation often appeared, occasionally some light glimmered through the gloom. A few days after Gordon Firebaugh disappeared on August 7, Fighting Six learned that he was safe with a coast watcher. The other missing Big E flier, Machinist William H. Warden, turned up in October.

Then, on August 20, two Marine squadrons touched down on Guadalcanal's newly prepared Henderson Field. Because Guadalcanal's code name was "Cactus" the twelve Dauntlesses and nineteen Wildcats were plankowners in what became known as the "Cactus Air Force." They were none too soon. Two days later, Catalina patrol planes spotted a small Japanese convoy headed for Guadalcanal, supported by fleet units. A battle was shaping up, requiring the carriers that Fletcher had to preserve.

Enterprise faced her second carrier engagement in less than three months.

SUBMARINES—AGAIN

Throughout August 1942 the Japanese navy posed multiple threats to Vice Admiral Frank Jack Fletcher's force near Guadalcanal. Much of the danger came from below.

The Big E had experienced little contact with enemy subs since December, but that summer off Guadalcanal brought numerous encounters. On the 12th some *Enterprise* bombers attacked the *I-175*, a sister of the boat that Clarence Dickinson had sunk near Hawaii on December 10. *I-175* had destroyed two Allied ships near Australia and damaged two more but had to turn for Rabaul and repairs.

Late that month fourteen Japanese submarines prowled the Solomons, mostly deployed in two patrol lines. About half of the enemy boats sighted American carriers in that period. On the 22nd, *I-121* crept into position off San Cristobal Island, southeast of Guadalcanal. She fired torpedoes at Rear Admiral Kinkaid's *Enterprise* formation, but the cruiser *Portland*'s lookouts saw the wakes in time to avoid them.

The pace accelerated the next day as the Big E's Scouting Squadron Five made three attacks. Lieutenant Turner Caldwell jumped *I-24* while *I-19* was surprised by Lieutenant Stockton Birney Strong and Ensign John F. "Jerry" Richey. The latter pair inflicted bomb damage, forcing the boat briefly to the surface, though it escaped. That afternoon Ensigns Elmer

Maul and Glen Estes straddled a large sub with their bombs, claiming a probable kill, but again the victim survived.

That was not the end of the submarine cat-and-mouse game. On the 25th two other subs stalked the Big E but were unable to coordinate their efforts. Meanwhile, on consecutive days *Wasp* Dauntlesses attacked other I-boats without success. Clearly the Imperial Navy knew where to look for Fletcher.

ANOTHER CARRIER BATTLE

Knowing that the Japanese needed to reinforce Guadalcanal, the Americans realized that a troop convoy was inevitable, and it would not come alone. With enemy carriers thought to be in the area, another flattop duel was shaping up, and the Big E made ready for battle. Meanwhile, on the 23rd much of *Saratoga*'s air group launched against the reported convoy but was thwarted by weather. Sara's planes diverted ashore to Henderson Field and returned to the ship the next morning. Because *Wasp* was detached for refueling, August 24 dawned with *Enterprise* and *Saratoga* facing three enemy flattops.

The Japanese deployed their forces in a typical dispersal: a main body with two heavy carriers and a detached force with a small one; a vanguard force of two battleships with seven escorts; a powerful advance force built around six cruisers with a seaplane carrier; and the troop convoy with escorts.

Task Force 61's main opponents were *Shokaku* and *Zuikaku*. Both commissioned in the summer of 1941, they displaced 25,000 tons or more and each embarked seventy-plus aircraft—a strong match for the Yorktown class. Both "Flying Crane" and "Auspicious Crane" had launched against Pearl Harbor and sank *Lexington* at Coral Sea. They would become the Big E's most frequent opponents. The third imperial carrier was *Ryujo*, displacing more than 10,000 tons and embarking thirty-three aircraft.

Frank Jack Fletcher's force steamed about 200 miles east of Guadalcanal that Monday, relying on PBY Catalina flying boats for distant reconnaissance. Monitoring the patrol plane network, Fletcher copied reports of a small enemy carrier: *Ryujo* about 280 miles northwest. As the distance closed to 200 miles, *Enterprise* launched twenty-three planes to track the known enemy flattop, aware that two more probably lurked nearby. Meanwhile, Japanese snoopers probed for the Americans, and *Saratoga* fighters splashed two uncomfortably close to the task force.

Before 3:00 on that afternoon of August 24, two *Enterprise* scouts sniffed out *Ryujo* and found "Prancing Dragon" capering southward with three escorts. Lieutenant Birney Strong and Ensign Jerry Richey—who had jumped a sub the day before—closed to near suicidal distance. Stalking the small carrier only five miles away, they remained on station for six long minutes to ensure their contact report went out. Then Strong led Richey for home, wondering whether they should have attacked. Two Dauntless scout-bombers against an alerted carrier force represented long odds, but Birney Strong's harshest critic was Birney Strong.

Meanwhile, Ensign Harold L. Bingaman's Avenger torpedo bomber and Ensign John H. Jorgenson's Dauntless also crept within five miles, working together despite their disparate aircraft. They stayed until two Avengers began dropping bombs from well above: Torpedo Three skipper Charles M. Jett with Ensign R. J. Bye. They scored no hits but the Japanese were put on notice: *Enterprise* aviators were persistent.

Saratoga copied the various reports and launched a deckload strike against *Ryujo* that put her on the bottom—the sixth imperial carrier sunk since early May. But Japan's heavy hitters remained to be heard from.

Japanese recon aircraft continued tracking Fletcher as Fighting Six splashed a twin-engine flying boat and a floatplane. Commanding the enemy's main body was Vice Admiral Chuichi Nagumo—victor at Pearl and loser at Midway. With a scout's report on Fletcher's position, he was determined to destroy an American carrier.

The Japanese excelled at multi-carrier operations. No other navy trained nearly as thoroughly, and it paid off. At 3:00 P.M. *Shokaku* and *Zuikaku* put up twenty-seven Aichi Val dive-bombers escorted by fifteen Zeros. Based on where the *Chikuma* floatplane disappeared, they knew where to hunt.

Meanwhile, *Enterprise* still had scouts aloft. Half an hour before the Japanese launched, a Bombing Six team found a target. The executive officer, Lieutenant John T. Lowe, and Ensign Bob Gibson found three cruisers and several destroyers. Waiting for his radioman to send a Morse code contact report, "Jiga" Lowe then led "Hoot" Gibson down on a big cruiser. She was *Maya,* ten years old and nearly 10,000 tons. Gibson recalled a textbook attack, "Keeping the sun behind me and facing a pullout in the direction of my carrier." But the big cruiser's turn presented a beam approach, giving the pilots a very narrow target instead of a long one. Both bombs missed slightly wide, and Gibson vowed, "From then on I knew that a hit resulted from putting a saddle on the enemy ship and riding that baby down to release."

At nearly the same minute, the Bombing Six skipper also had a target in sight. Probing a nearby search sector, Ray Davis passed up a cruiser-destroyer force preceding another group to the northwest. His judgment was rewarded as he skirted both enemy formations and—unknowingly—*Shokaku*'s radar coverage. The defenders' response was too late, as Davis and Ensign Robert C. Shaw climbed from search to attack altitude. They throttled back, split their dive flaps, and rolled in from 14,000 feet. Slanting downward in their seventy-degree dives, they kept their aiming points on the carrier's yellow deck, trying to keep a consistent hold as Captain Masafumi Arima slewed *Shokaku*'s 25,000 tons into a hard right turn.

Both bombs smacked the ocean thirty feet to starboard, inflicting slight damage.

Pulling in their flaps and shoving throttles to the stop, Davis and Shaw sped from the scene, harried by flak and fighters, not realizing that their attack had pulled away part of the strike group's fighter escort. Davis later declared, "The Japs followed us to hell and gone," but the *Enterprise* fliers escaped. The remaining twenty-seven Val dive-bombers and ten Zeros continued en route to Task Force 61.

In Task Force 61, radar director Hank Rowe managed his fighters like a stockbroker expending consumable assets: fuel and ammunition equaled time remaining on station. He told the Wildcats, "Many bogeys ahead. Get up high."

Between Wildcat scrambles to reinforce the combat air patrol, eleven *Enterprise* Dauntlesses and seven Avengers took off, seeking the *Ryujo*, which *Saratoga* planes had already sunk. The bombers got away just in time. With raiders barely twenty-five miles out, Big E went to general quarters.

Fletcher's fighters were fueled and ready on deck, ten miles separating the Big E and Sara. At 4:32 the radar watch reported "Many bogies range eighty-eight miles, bearing 320." The carriers came about southeasterly to launch into the wind. *Enterprise* worked up to twenty-seven knots, screened by *North Carolina, Portland,* and *Atlanta* plus six destroyers. The aerial picket was unprecedented: fifty-four Wildcats protecting the U.S. carriers.

The hostile "bandits" (no longer unidentified bogies) were tracked inbound just before 5:00 as Wildcats clawed for altitude. Two squadrons of American fighters were about to tangle with two squadrons of Vals in a twenty-minute gunfight.

As the raiders approached, the well-ordered CAP began falling apart. With so many contacts and too few radio frequencies, fighter directors began losing the picture. A junior officer described senior fighter director Lieutenant Commander Leonard "Ham" Dow as "sweating like a Turk" trying to interrupt the chatter of excited fighter pilots.

The first group of dive-bombers nosed down from 16,000 feet, making a high-speed descent over the top of the leading Wildcats. At that point the intercept turned into a tail chase. American fighters sparred with Zeros while the Vals pressed on toward *Enterprise*.

Don Runyon's four-plane division was one of those chasing the dive-bombers. As eighteen Vals approached from the north, nine swung wide to the east, and Runyon tapped the latter.

In the confusion, Americans reported fighting Messerschmitt 109s—not for the last time. Believing that the Japanese navy had imported some German aircraft, the impressionable aviators saw what they expected to see. But old hand Runyon knew what he was looking at. He cut the corner on the flanking arm of the aerial envelopment, closing to firing range on the easterly Vals. Diving in at high speed, he burned the first one, then pulled up into the sun. On his next pass he downed another bomber and drove two out of formation.

Repositioning to resume executing Vals, Runyon was jumped by a Zero. But the Japanese dived below and ahead of his intended victim. Runyon merely nosed down, put the gray fighter in his sight, and pressed the trigger. The Zero exploded.

Still determined, Runyon resumed his attack on the bombers, his six .50 calibers setting a third Val afire. As if that weren't enough, yet another Zero committed the same blunder as its partner. Runyon got hits, saw the Zero dive away trailing smoke—and then was alone. In minutes he had downed four enemies, chased two away, and damaged another. He had run his score from four to eight and remained the Navy's top-scoring F4F pilot of the war. With other Big E pilots he recovered aboard *Saratoga,* as *Enterprise* remained under attack.

Among the Fighting Six pilots cycling between both carriers was a twenty-one-year old enlisted flier, Lee Paul Mankin, who claimed two dive-bombers during the day. He especially appreciated the Big E's flight deck arrangement, recalling, "The *Enterprise*'s elevators were a lot faster than the Sara's, and that made a big difference in working the deck." The Big E's three fast elevators beat Sara's two slower ones (one inoperable) by a wide margin, especially when fighters had to be landed and launched in minimum time.

The two Wildcat squadrons claimed forty-four shootdowns (twenty-six by VF-6) and lost five. Two belonged to *Enterprise,* including Ensign Doyle Barnes, killed by friendly AA fire—often unavoidable in the maelstrom of flak and multiple aircraft. The Japanese actually lost twenty-five to American fighters and flak, still a crippling 43 percent attrition.

As the aerial gunfight played out, *Enterprise* committed eleven Dauntlesses and six Avengers against a reported surface force. Air operations officer John Crommelin had suggested the launch both as a means to strike the enemy and—more immediately—to clear the deck. With bombers inbound, the less fuel and ordnance on board the better. That decision may have saved the Big E.

Last off at 5:08 was air group commander Max Leslie in his Avenger; a glance backward showed enemy aircraft diving on the ship. But after escaping the raiders, Leslie had to contend with his friends. Passing over the escorting ships, he noted flak bursts from the battleship *North Carolina,* accompanied by holes in his port wing. He said, "I dived for the water and got out of there as fast as 175 knots would take me."

Radar blips faded as the surviving Vals entered the electronic dead zone directly overhead the force. That geometry forced the Big E to rely on human vision—no easy task, as gunnery officer Benny Mott reported, it was "late afternoon and the sky was considerably bluer than . . . earlier in the day."

Sharp-eyed Marine First Sergeant Joseph R. Schinka, boss of the Number Four gun battery, noticed something high above. As the Japanese leader nosed over from 16,000 feet, Schinka called, "Here come the bastards!" Though the bombers were far beyond the 20mms' effective range, he ordered his crews to commence firing: their tracers could coach the heavier guns on target.

A deafening cacophonic symphony erupted from *Enterprise* and her escorts: automatic 20mm, multi-barrel 1.1-inch, and bursting five-inch.

Spotters observed that the Vals dived at seven-second intervals with five or six down the chute at a time. There seemed no end to them: some sailors estimated forty though twenty-seven had launched.

As the attackers plummeted in from the port quarter, Captain Art Davis noted with professional detachment, "The dives were well executed and absolutely determined."

Lieutenant Commander Orlin Livdahl's gunners killed some Vals but the others came on, undeterred. Bombs, airplanes, and debris splashed into the water. Explosions erupted around the ship's 20,000-ton hull, cascading fountains of water.

Not all missed.

At 5:14 the *Enterprise* sustained her first wound as a 500-pound bomb splintered her deck near the aft elevator. It punched through five levels before its delayed action fuse went off. The explosion destroyed a pump room, ammo handlers, and a damage control station in the chiefs' quarters. Thirty-five men were instantly killed. The tremendous concussive effect in that confined space had to go somewhere—it sought its way upward, blasting a sixteen-foot hole in the overhead and warping the hangar deck upward nearly two feet. Throughout the ship, men felt the effect; some were knocked down or thrown from their seats.

Lieutenant William C. Williamson, Jr., of Gun Group Three, aft of the island, noticed a fire in an ammo locker. Juggling priorities, he pulled some gunners off one mount to fight the fire while ordering a pharmacist's mate forward, out of danger. Another bomb might hit, and Williamson wanted the corpsman available to treat additional wounded.

Amid the noise and fear and confusion, Photographer's Mate Robert F. Read, positioned near the starboard quarter, had the presence of mind to snap a quick shot of a Japanese plane floating within yards of the ship.

Then *Enterprise* took a second bomb within thirty seconds. Impact-fused, it hit only fifteen feet from the first, destroying the starboard aft five-inch gun gallery and the entire thirty-eight man crew, including Bill Williamson and Bob Read. Forty pounds of ready powder bags also erupted in secondary explosions, adding thick, black smoke to existing fires.

Like a boxer who has taken a one-two combination, *Enterprise* grunted from the blows, kept her guard up, and began counterpunching. Captain Davis continued maneuvering to spoil or at least compound the dive-bombers' tracking while the carrier's remaining gunners kept up a sustained barrage. So did the escorts as *North Carolina* claimed six and *Atlanta* one. Due to confusion and duplicate claims, the figure of two dozen AA kills (fifteen by *Enterprise*) was acknowledged on the high side. In any case, Big E gun crews fired nearly 14,000 rounds: everything from .50 caliber to five-inch.

★ ★ ★

While the Japanese attack continued, damage control crews went to work immediately. Previously some had bided their time playing chess—an impossibility when the ship began maneuvering at high speed. Sailors unspooled lengths of hose, doused fires, and began to control flooding. When time permitted, rescue parties looked for casualties, pulling wounded away from the carnage, knowing that some were beyond help.

Ensign James Wyrick felt the first hit and led his damage control crew to the impact area. He encountered heavy smoke and flames from the burning powder bags. The heat was so intense that some deck plates already glowed red. Wyrick recognized that more ammunition could cook off anytime and directed sailors to fling the powder overboard. Some men singed their hands but the job got done.

Meanwhile, the fight continued topside. Only two minutes after the first bomb, a third found the Big E. John Crommelin and others standing aft on the island saw it coming—in aviator's parlance it had them "boresighted." The exec was the last of several men through the hatch ("Only because they moved faster than I did"), narrowly escaping the blast on the flight deck.

The bomb impacted forward of the midships elevator, providentially a partial detonation. Even so, it left a ten-foot hole in the wood deck, knocked out the elevator control, and caused more casualties. The hit might have been catastrophic, as it exploded almost against the armor plate protecting the torpedo storage, but Newport News's workmanship met the test. Providentially, no fragments penetrated the inch-and-a-half armor.

Damage control is like politics—it's local. Each team positioned around the ship was responsible for its immediate area, though some crews could be directed elsewhere. The first bomb destroyed the ventilation trunk to the aft steering room occupied by seven men who almost immediately began breathing smoke. The ruined trunk also ingested waves of firefighting foam and boiling water from superheated decks. The only response, other than abandoning the space, was to seal it off. Eager, sweaty hands spun the overhead valves and turned off the vents.

Lacking outside air, the compartment quickly morphed from heated to hot to searing. Sometimes the normal ambient temperature was 120 degrees Fahrenheit, though men who worked there could tolerate it for the duration of a general quarters drill. But now a chief electrician, Alexander P. Trymofiew, looked at the thermometer. He had been aboard since 1938 and had never seen anything like it: 140 and rising. He was probably the only man who knew the temperature but thought better of mentioning it.

The physiological effects were terrible: skin wrinkled as men watched, growing taut over muscles. At 160 degrees dehydration was nearly complete; breathing was painful. Drinking bottled water did little good, as men threw up.

Finally Chief Machinist William A. Smith called the steering room on a sound-powered phone. He was from A Division, responsible for auxiliary power, and instructed the men how to remove access panels for some unpolluted air. Trymofiew tried following instructions but he and the others were too weak. The men didn't even try to talk—it required too much effort. One sailor dropped his pipe but lacked the strength to pick it up.

On the bridge, skipper Art Davis had his hands full. *Enterprise* plunged ahead at twenty knots, streaming smoke tinged red with flame from hits aft. Though the Japanese were gone, the ship swerved into an abrupt starboard turn, unbidden by the captain or anyone else. The helmsman, Chief Quartermaster Cal Black, spun the wheel to no avail. He had experienced nothing comparable in his two and a half years aboard.

The cause of the problem was invisible to the bridge crew. Far below and astern, the steering engine in Trymofiew's compartment had locked up, jamming the rudder twenty-two degrees right. The Big E was a runaway, stampeding through her own nautical herd. She blared a warning siren to other ships: "Steering control is away from the bridge." Davis ordered "all stop," then "full back" to avoid hitting a destroyer. Reducing speed to ten knots, he tried steering by the ship's propellers, to no effect.

Machinist's Mate William N. Marcoux was the only man remaining conscious in the steering room. Realizing that no one else was likely to correct the measure, he thought of his ship: "I kept telling myself that the Big E depended on me." Somehow he stretched his strength to reach the control panel to start the backup unit. Then he fainted and fell to the catwalk, immobile.

Lieutenant Commander Carl Yost, the assistant engineer, tried to coordinate efforts to reach the steering room. But each crew that tried penetrating to the dark, smoke-choked, Dantesque nether region was forced back. Those with emergency oxygen packs succumbed to the pervasive, bake oven heat. As each man fainted he was dragged to safety by shipmates tugging on safety lines.

Finally Art Davis looked to Chief Smith, who had provided phone advice to the steering room crew. He was another of the seemingly inexhaustible stash of plankowners: men who had been aboard since the beginning; who knew their jobs and their equipment inside out. Smith merely said, "I'll go."

Like the others, Smith collapsed in the searing heat. He was pulled to safety by sailors who applied artificial respiration. Seeking another way through the wreckage, Smith was making progress when he fainted again. Once more he was retrieved and revived. The third time he took another plankowner, Cecil S. Robinson. Together they pushed their way into the steering compartment, momentarily puzzled at finding it empty. The seven men previously there had seemingly vaporized. But Smith and Robinson focused on the immediate job: restoring control to the rudder. They cranked up the auxiliary unit, permitting the rudder to return to center. *Enterprise* straightened out of her wild right-hand circuit.

Smith and Robinson cleared away some of the debris and allowed minimal air to flow, helping relieve the appalling heat. But they felt their strength ebbing, then draining: it was difficult to stand. A man's life force was sucked out of him as the temperature topped 170 degrees.

Smith barely reached safety before collapsing again. Once restored, he made his way to the bridge where, grimy, sweat-soaked, and barely upright, he estimated that steering control probably could remain with the captain. On the way back he fell to his hands and knees on the hangar deck, gagging and choking with dry heaves. Then he returned to the hellish place he had just vacated, intending to oversee the process.

On his third descent into the compartment, Smith saw the temperature gauge pegged at 180 degrees. He greased the rudder shafts to prevent them from binding in the severe heat. With the temperature gradually abating, Chief Smith stayed for most of the next twenty-four hours. Finally Commander Yost gave up trying to order him out. Eventually Smith received a well-deserved Navy Cross and commission as lieutenant (junior grade).

Only later was the mysterious disappearance of seven sailors explained. One died of heat stroke but the other six only recalled having been revived on the hangar deck. Under questioning by Commander Yost, Electrician's Mate Ernest R. Visto finally admitted that he had left his battle station to look for his trapped shipmates. Because of his corn-fed Midwestern heft, Visto was unable to use an oxygen apparatus but made his gas mask work long enough to retrieve all seven unconscious men. He said, "Well, I did have to lug and shove them around, more or less."

While Fletcher fought off Nagumo's squadrons, *Enterprise*'s bombers probed the gathering dusk without success. Owing to the late hour, Turner Caldwell's eleven dive-bombers diverted to Guadalcanal, almost doubling the number of Marine Dauntlesses there. Thus *Enterprise* Flight 300 was enrolled in the Cactus Air Force, remaining ashore the next four weeks. The Navy fliers experienced a grueling ordeal: upon departure from the island Caldwell told correspondent Richard Tregaskis, "There's a point where you just get to be no good; you're shot to the devil and there's nothing you can do about it."

Meanwhile, Max Leslie, the Big E's air group commander, proceeded his lonely way in his Avenger, trying to catch his bombers and torpedo planes. Unable to raise anyone by radio, he did not realize that Caldwell's Dauntlesses had diverted ashore.

Leslie found nothing but waves breaking over a reef, which apparently had been reported as wakes of enemy ships. With fuel running low, he navigated back to the task force in the gathering evening gloom. Finally he heard the blessedly familiar voice of a friend: "Max, keep coming and gain some altitude." It was Commander "Ham" Dow, Admiral Fletcher's communications officer. Dow had concluded that the lone radar blip likely was his Annapolis classmate, and to Leslie the message was "the best news I ever received."

Leslie was directed to land aboard *Saratoga,* which briefly lit up to guide him in. Still new to the big Grumman, he had logged fewer than five arrested landings in the Avenger, none at night, "but I was more than willing to try." He turned up the groove, slow and steady in the big Grumman, and snagged a wire. He had been airborne nearly five hours. After reporting to Fletcher, Leslie retired to the admiral's big brass bed.

Meanwhile, Admiral Kinkaid had accepted the risk of running landing lights, and *Enterprise* began recovering aircraft at 10:00 P.M. The pilots were careful to land port of centerline owing to an eighteen-inch bulge in the flight deck aft. An Avenger crashed on deck, the pilot's forward view obscured by an oil-streaked windscreen, forcing the other bombers to divert to *Saratoga.*

While the searchers and strikers were away, damage control continued unabated. *Enterprise* had taken on 240 tons of water, and some of the lower compartments flooded to four feet or more. One of the bombs had torn a six-by-two-foot hole in the hull, just above the waterline. The damage control officer, Lieutenant Commander A. Herschel Smith, devised a plan to plug the breach, requiring a dam built around the gash from the inside. Supervised by Chief Carpenter William L. Reames, damage control men and shipfitters coped with darkness and water nearly to their armpits. With battle lanterns providing minimal light, the men built a barrier of two-by-sixes, wrapped it with wire mesh, then crammed the space between the boards and the hull with mattresses, pillows, and anything else that fit. Then, shoring up the barrier, the crew wedged the structure against the hole to prevent more intake. That chore accomplished, they started pumping water from the compartment.

Then it was time to count the dead.

Enterprise sustained seventy-eight killed and ninety wounded—a shocking figure, as the ship and air group had ninety-three fatalities in the previous nine months. En route to Tonga for temporary repairs, the Big E's dead were buried at sea, each body weighted with a fifty-five-pound shell. Ten had been burned or blasted beyond recognition.

Among the dead was Bosun Max Lee. On December 7 he had prophesized his death, intoning, "I'll never get out of the Navy alive."

Enterprise proceeded to Pearl but she was not finished with Guadalcanal, and "that damned island" was not finished with her.

5

★　★　★

"A Fighting Chance"

Rushed back to Pearl Harbor from Guadalcanal, the Big E had priority for repairs before returning to the Solomon Islands in October 1942. (USN via Tailhook Assn.)

The healing season ran from late August to mid-October as *Enterprise* recovered from her Eastern Solomons damage, mostly recuperating in Hawaii. Those two months brought her back into fighting trim as she received a new captain and a new air group. Meanwhile, *Saratoga, Wasp,* and *Hornet* continued operating in the Solomons.

But not for long. Japanese submarines remained plentifully aggressive, and on August 31 Sara took her second torpedo of the war. She was out of action indefinitely. Two weeks later Commander Takakazu Kinashi's *I-19* fired perhaps the most destructive salvo in submarine history. *Enterprise* aircraft had driven him down just before the Eastern Solomons battle, but on September 15 Kinashi had a gorgeous target in his crosshairs. He fired six fish; three destroyed *Wasp* and others ran on to hit the battleship *North Carolina* and a destroyer that eventually sank. Kinashi got away clean.

Enterprise was needed more than ever.

The new skipper was Captain Osborne Bennett Hardison, a brilliant scholar and excellent administrator. Hardison had been a prodigy: he entered the University of North Carolina at fourteen and graduated when his contemporaries were finishing high school. From there he matriculated to Annapolis, excelling in gymnastics and ranking ninth in the class of 1916. Like most 1942 carrier captains, he had little experience commanding ships, but he was blessed with a fine bridge crew.

Previously Hardison had been chief of staff to Artemus L. Gates, undersecretary of the navy for air. Between juggling political footballs in Washington's potentially toxic environment, Hardison proved himself invaluable to the secretary by helping streamline the naval aviator training program. Gates then "firewalled" Hardison's fitness report, giving him stratospheric endorsements and a preferred next assignment: a West Coast carrier.

Departing Washington on October 6, Hardison reached Pearl two days later and immediately reported aboard *Enterprise* for a brief period as Art Davis's understudy. In a turnover ceremony Hardison assumed command at noon on the 20th, the peak of his twenty-six-year career.

Hardison stood six-foot-two, lanky and lean with close-cropped graying hair. He often gave the impression of being distracted—Yeoman Bill Norberg said he appeared "in a daze"—but beneath the surface was the scholastic mind that grasped details and retained them. Norberg added, "He was a country boy at heart and not above a casual conversation."

The Big E's new unit was Air Group 10, composed of Bombing 10, Scouting 10, Torpedo 10, and Fighting Squadron 10. The group commander was tall, gangly Commander Richard K. Gaines, an athlete from the bottom of the class of 1925, whose sporting activities included shooting craps. He was among many officers caught in a career time warp: more an administrator than an operator; his seniority was urgently needed but he possessed minimal background for the new position.

Fortunately Gaines had help, and was not above using it. The fighter skipper was four years junior but Gaines would lean heavily upon him. Lieutenant Commander James H. Flatley crammed a heavy reputation in a small package. Short and slightly built, he had been flying since 1931, mostly in fighters, and enhanced his name aboard *Yorktown* at Coral Sea. With Jimmy Thach and Butch O'Hare, he became one of the most influential fighter leaders of the war.

Flatley also was a keen judge of talent. He recruited some former Dauntless pilots into Fighting 10, including Lieutenants John Leppla and

Stanley Vejtasa, both Coral Sea veterans. The Grim Reaper squadron blossomed under their tutelage, evidenced by the emblematic flying skeleton, dubbed "Old Moe" for "Mow 'em down." Vejtasa deemed the Reapers "A fine bunch of kids, very, very good and progressive and they learned very quick."

The new pilots also were suitably impressed. One was twenty-two-year-old Donald Gordon, who never forgot his initial meeting with the skipper. "He asked me if I had a nickname and because I had thick hair in those days I said, 'I'm called Curly.'"

Flatley replied, "Curly's no name for a fighter pilot. From now on you're Flash." Don Gordon remained Flash the rest of his life.

Heading the bombers was Lieutenant Commander James A. "Tommy" Thomas, known as "Shorty" at Annapolis where he was an enthusiastic boxer and runner.

Like Captain Hardison, James R. "Bucky" Lee of the scouts was an exceptional scholar from Carolina, standing third in the Annapolis class of 1928. He adjudged his aircrews, like the rest of the air group, as "raring to go."

Leading Torpedo 10 was John Austin Collett. He could not resist zinging Flatley by adopting his own version of Old Moe: a buzzard brandishing a swab with the motto "Mop 'em up!" Collett believed in the potential of night carrier operations and swiped the first radar-equipped Avenger in Hawaii.

The ship and air group were urgently needed back in the Solomons, so training in Hawaii was brief. Rear Admiral Thomas Kinkaid remained aboard as overall commander of Task Force 61 comprising *Enterprise*'s Task Force 16 and *Hornet*'s Task Force 17, the latter under former Big E skipper George Murray. Kinkaid wanted a night flying capability, so some of Gaines's pilots were rushed through carrier qualifications. One was Don Gordon, who said, "I did night qual in the Wildcat in October before we deployed—one night landing after four day traps. I was one of twelve pilots to get the one qualification landing, and only made one during the deployment."

Enterprise departed Pearl on October 16, escorted by the cruisers *Portland, Atlanta,* and five destroyers. Including spares, the Big E embarked ninety-five aircraft—more than she had ever crammed onto her flight and hangar decks. There was no doubt where they were headed.

With the Japanese expected to launch their strongest effort yet to nail down Guadalcanal, Admiral Nimitz wanted a proven fighter. Two days after *Enterprise* sailed, a new South Pacific theater commander took over in New Caledonia, issuing a blunt directive: "Kill Japs, Kill Japs, Kill more Japs!"

Wild Bill Halsey was back.

News of Halsey's promotion was well received in *Enterprise*, where hundreds of men fondly recalled him. He had been absent from the Pacific since June but now, back in fighting trim, he fielded "the hottest potato they ever handed me." With the Big E and *Hornet* task forces operating under Kinkaid, Wild Bill took heart. He reckoned, "Carrier power varies as the square—two carriers are four times as powerful as one. Until the *Enterprise* arrived, our plight had been almost hopeless. Now we had a fighting chance."

Nevertheless, Halsey faced a touchy Solomons situation. Although Army troops were reinforcing the Marines, American airpower at Guadalcanal had dwindled alarmingly: at mid-month the Cactus Air Force counted just seventy-four aircraft—less than one carrier air group—with few replacements available.

Apart from ground combat, Guadalcanal was under near continuous attack by Japanese aircraft and surface bombardment. Now the enemy launched powerful fleet units in a rare effort of army-navy cooperation. The Imperial Navy was to ensure control of the waters surrounding Guadalcanal long enough to put a decisive force ashore.

At sea, the Imperial Navy fielded four carriers: *Shokaku* and *Zuikaku* from Eastern Solomons two months before, with *Zuiho,* plus *Junyo* in the advanced force. (Had *Hiyo* not been sidelined with engine trouble, she could have determined the outcome of the battle.) The surface combatant ratio wasn't even close: thirty-five Japanese to twenty-one American. Rear Admiral Willis Lee's Task Force 64 included a battleship with nine cruisers and destroyers but his unit would take no part in the coming air battle.

The emerging arena was north of the malarial Santa Cruz Islands, nearly 400 miles east of Guadalcanal.

At midday on the 25th, Catalina patrol planes alerted Kinkaid to the Japanese carriers some 350 miles north of Task Force 61. Simultaneously, other patrol planes reported a Japanese carrier plus six escorts. That was enough for Halsey. Chafing at his New Caledonia headquarters, he signaled, STRIKE REPEAT STRIKE!

That order prompted a twelve-plane search. Bucky Lee led his scouts off *Enterprise* at 1:35 P.M., ahead of a long-range strike optimistically planned for thirty-five aircraft. The operations plan called for the scouts to find the enemy and radio his position to Dick Gaines's formation, which would save time by already being airborne.

None of it worked.

Only twenty-three strike aircraft got off the deck, and Gaines searched too far south. Probing through the darkening sky for an enemy still beyond range, the aviators ran out of daylight, visibility, and fuel. Beneath a waning moon they turned for home, Tommy Thomas's Dauntlesses jettisoning their bombs to lighten the load for the gas-shy return. Some pilots barely got in. "Swede" Vejtasa wore out one glove, hand-pumping fuel from his Wildcat's inoperative drop tank, and narrowly missed being killed on deck when the next fighter snagged the arresting cable immediately behind him.

Between ditchings and crashes, the fruitless mission cost *Enterprise* seven planes and three fliers. Many of the pilots complained about Kinkaid's staff work, claiming a fifty-mile difference in the briefed ship's position upon return. But there was no point in grousing. Kinkaid had closed the distance on the Japanese force during the 24th, making clear what would happen in a day or so.

UNCLE JOHN

On the eve of battle men spoke low, quickly, earnestly. Many wrote letters—not necessarily last letters, but you just never knew. All coped with the mounting pressure in their own way. For instance, Lieutenant John Hicks of the air department discussed literature with Associated Press correspondent Eugene Burns, who had covered the Pacific since Pearl Harbor. On December 7 his dispatch was the first to the mainland but authorities had shortstopped it, and his scoop died aborning. Now he was positioned for an exclusive. On the night of the 25th, after the recovery of the failed dusk strike, Burns followed his instinct to the seat of power.

Air officer John Crommelin—Uncle John to aviator and whitehat alike—was on top of the situation. That night he convened a pilots meeting in the wardroom. The fliers sat by squadrons, arrayed around the felt-topped tables, clanlike in that rare company of warriors. Some off-duty ship's officers stood along the bulkheads, absorbing the atmosphere.

"This may be the beginning of a great battle," Crommelin began. He let that sentiment sink in, then put things in perspective. He said that four Catalinas had tracked the Japanese carriers en route but only one got back.

Actually, in recent days four were shot down with one surviving crewman. The crucial information—the enemy's location—had been purchased in blood.

"You men will have the privilege tomorrow of proving the worth of your training, your schooling, our way of life as against the Japs." Crommelin spoke of what lay at stake after dawn: the lives of thousands of marines and soldiers on mud-soaked, blood-spattered Guadalcanal. "The Japs are determined to drive us out of the South Pacific. If they get through to Guadalcanal with their carriers tomorrow, the Japs will take it. If Guadalcanal falls, our lifeline to Australia will be menaced." His gray eyes tracked around the room. "To stop them, you must knock out their carriers." He added a spur to the impetus of his message by stating that all the aviators' training was pointed to this time and place. "If you're going to miss with your bomb, you might as well stay home and let a *good* pilot take your place."

In his soft Alabama accent, Crommelin added a final heartfelt sentiment, direct from his Southern roots. "We are on the right side of this war. God is with us. Let's knock those Jap bastards off the face of the earth. God bless you."

Correspondent Gene Burns jotted a note to himself: Uncle John's mixing piety and profanity did not seem incongruous.

As they filed out, the last thing any man in that room wanted to do was disappoint Uncle John Crommelin.

DAY OF BATTLE: SANTA CRUZ

On October 26, *Enterprise* found herself short of aircraft. An accident and the previous evening's abortive mission had reduced Commander Gaines's inventory to seventy-eight planes, only sixty-four operational. *Hornet* was in better shape with seventy-three "up" birds, but Task Force 61 faced long odds.

Breakfast for officers was served at 4:00 A.M. For those with an appetite, the galley offered hotcakes with ham and eggs, and those tired of coffee could drink pineapple juice. The fare prompted the usual dark humor about condemned men and hearty meals.

The ship went to general quarters at 5:50 A.M. Half an hour later the sunrise revealed scattered cumulus and rain showers, which could make things hard for searchers and good for ships under attack.

After Midway and Eastern Solomons, *Enterprise* understood the choreography of carrier combat: preliminary probing by long-range patrol planes followed by ship-based scouts updating the contacts, tracking the various enemy task forces as long as fuel and fate allowed. The nautical ballet began just before dawn as sixteen Dauntlesses lifted off, hunting southwest through north to 230 miles, seeking a fresh scent of the Catalina reports. The scouts sniffed out the enemy at 6:17.

Bombing 10's Lieutenant Vivien Welch and Lieutenant (jg) Bruce Mc-Graw passed up a Japanese scout plane, suspecting that something bigger lay ahead. They were right. Using the 50 percent cloud cover, they probed the edge of a surface force and sent a reasonably accurate position report, noting two battleships with many escorts. It was McGraw's first taste of combat: his parents had been divided whether he should study medicine or the ministry so he compromised and became a dive-bomber pilot.

Meanwhile, nearly two hours outbound, Bucky Lee scouted with Ensign William E. Johnson. Two search sectors north of Welch, they spied large ships some thirty miles to the west and closed the distance. At fifteen miles the pilots were certain: enemy carriers, the first they had ever seen. Lee began a full-throttle climb to give his radioman altitude for a report. In the rear cockpit Chief Irby Sanders's educated fist tapped out the vital information on his Morse code key: two flattops and escorts. The position report was excellent: about ten miles from Nagumo's three carriers. *Shokaku* and *Zuikaku* stood out while the smaller *Zuiho* was obscured by clouds.

Lee watched with professional detachment while his prey began maneuvering and escorts emitted a smoke screen. Climbing through 3,000 feet, he and Johnson were intercepted by seven Zeros that raced in head-on. From there it was a gunfight.

As Lee recalled, "Things happened fast. About the time my plane was hit in the windscreen with small caliber, I got off a burst of forward .50 caliber at the leading Jap." Lee had the fleeting impression that the Zero exploded.

Bill Johnson optimistically claimed downing two fighters while the Dauntlesses found cover in the clouds. The aggressive Lee tried to gain position for a bombing attack but was foiled each time he stuck his nose in the open. Eventually the two scouts got separated and wisely turned for home.

Minutes later another search team tried to gain attack position. Lieutenants (jg) Leslie Ward and Martin Doan Carmody swapped gunfire with the same Zeros as Lee and Johnson, and both sides claimed kills. The Big

E fliers returned to base after nearly four and a half hours, and though no planes were shot down, *Enterprise* was keeping the pressure on Nagumo.

Four sectors to the northwest, Radioman Clarence Garlow in scout S-13 had copied Welch's report. He jotted the position and notified his pilot, who immediately went to work on his plotting board.

Stockton Birney Strong was short, slight, intense. Colleagues quickly learned that there was no point asking about his credentials because he would gladly tell you: he was the best there was. The maddening thing was, he could prove it.

Strong grew up in Washington, D.C., raised by his mother, the widow of a naval officer. "Stock" or "Birney" graduated in the middle of the Annapolis class of '37, where the annual concluded, "His good common sense has carried him past many reefs; he will succeed in any career where good judgment and cool nerves are prime requisites." *The Lucky Bag* got that right: it also noted appropriately that his favorite sport was "shooting holes in bullseyes."

Earning his wings in 1940, Strong became a *Yorktown* scout pilot and made most of her stops: Marshalls and Gilberts, New Guinea, Coral Sea. That August he reported aboard *Enterprise* with an impressive 800 hours of carrier flying and a Navy Cross.

In contrast to Strong's family background, his wingman was an orphan. Ensign Charles Irvine affected a close-cropped haircut that earned him the nickname "Skinhead." He was delighted to fly with Stockton Birney Strong.

Welch's report of battleships placed Admiral Nobutake Kondo's heavyweights about 150 miles from Strong's sector. Running the time-distance equation, it looked as if the Dauntlesses might make the diversion with enough gasoline to return home. Strong began a cruise-climb, seeking optimal use of his fuel to gain attack altitude.

Partway along the new course, Strong's radioman, Clarence Garlow, monitored Lee's report of carriers. Strong's memory defaulted to the situation at Eastern Solomons two months before. He had passed up a shot at a Japanese carrier in favor of taking his information directly home. Few people said anything, though John Crommelin had expressed keen disappointment.

Strong eased into a thirty-degree turn to starboard.

Navigation was tricky, as the scouts' altitude and low clouds complicated estimation of wind direction and velocity. Nevertheless, Strong stuck to his course, west-southwest.

He nailed it.

Twenty minutes after hearing Lee's report, the searchers found Nagumo's carriers as two of the three flattops emerged from clouds into sunlight. Skinhead Irvine tucked up close to his leader as both gunners shoved their canopies forward and deployed their twin Brownings. They were ready for a shootout.

But the timing was providential, as the Zeros were then harrying Ward and Carmody. No time to waste. Strong signaled to Irvine: they would take the nearest carrier. From that point on it was Dauntless 101: basic dive-bombing. Strong activated his dive flaps as Irvine slid away, allowing proper interval. Then they nosed over from 14,000 feet.

In a thirty-second plunge, the SBDs were in and out of the clouds. No matter: Strong's excellent sense of spatial geometry told him where the target should appear. Making 275 mph, he broke clear at 1,500 feet, greeted by the gorgeous sight of a Japanese flight deck.

The ship looked like a big one: the pilots reckoned Shokaku class. In fact, she was the much smaller *Zuiho*. "Fortunate Phoenix" was a priority target and the *Enterprise* fliers had her boresighted. With no flak or fighters, they had time to remember Crommelin's words the night before: "If you're going to miss with your bomb, you might as well stay home and let a *good* pilot take your place."

Both were good pilots.

The two 500-pounders punched into the flight deck, aft. With near instantaneous fuses, the bombs exploded on the wood planking, rendering the ship incapable of operating aircraft. That was the good news. The bad news: *Zuiho*'s air group was already en route to Task Force 61.

The explosions drew vengeful attention from Zero pilots. Spotting the two Americans wave-hopping through the destroyer screen, three *Zuikaku* fighters pounced in a forty-mile tail chase. During the prolonged shootout Garlow and Elgie Williams, Irvine's gunner, both thought they scored. They actually got one fighter between them, but it capped a tremendous performance, one of the finest missions ever flown from aircraft carriers. Everything came together: precise navigation, excellent communications, astute tactics, perfect bombing, superb fuel management—and undiluted courage.

By the time the scouts were headed home, the battle had become a brawl. Both sides launched large formations against one another in a confusing series of overlapping actions. Japanese scouts had found two American carriers, and Nagumo—mindful of the severe penalty for waiting at Midway—threw a heavy punch just before Strong and Irvine attacked. *Shokaku, Zuikaku,* and *Zuiho* had launched sixty-two planes. Nagumo had forty-four more ready, and Rear Admiral Kakuji Kakuta was spooling up twenty-nine on *Junyo,* operating independently.

Kinkaid's carriers also were lofting strike groups. *Hornet* put up nearly thirty planes at 7:30, and half an hour later *Enterprise* sent off Dick Gaines leading eight Avengers and three Dauntlesses with eight fighters. That effort was followed at 8:15 with *Hornet's* second launch: twenty-five planes for a total of seventy-five Americans en route to various targets.

Each formation operated in its own bubble as the players crossed their three-dimensional arena, climbing at perhaps 130 miles per hour. Inevitably, the opposing teams began to clash.

Trailing *Hornet's* first strike by a few minutes were Air Group 10's twenty planes. About sixty miles outbound, Gaines's formation was climbing through 9,000 feet when the roof fell in. With a 5,000-foot altitude advantage, the nine *Zuiho* Zeros escorting *Shokaku's* torpedo planes could not resist a juicy setup. They circled the slow-climbing Americans, then dived out of the sun from six o'clock high.

Torpedo 10 skipper Jack Collett went down in the first pass. He jumped from his flaming Avenger but was never seen again; neither was his gunner. Radioman Tom Nelson kicked his way free, plunged overboard, pulled his ripcord, and swung beneath his canopy as a Zero hosed a vengeful burst at him. Nelson splashed into a safe landing.

Belatedly alerted, the Avenger turret gunners started shooting. Their concentrated fire torched one Zero, which exploded.

The Japanese kept coming. They shot down Ensign John Reed, and only the radioman got out before the Avenger blew up. The engine and propeller narrowly missed Lieutenant Macdonald Thompson's plane. His radioman, Chuck Shinneman, gaped at the spectacle, watching the prop still spinning.

Other Zeros shot Dick Batten's Avenger out of formation. Fighting serious damage and a fire, he dropped away, heading home. Batten's gunner was Rex Holmgrin, who at least "had the satisfying privilege of seeing four Jap planes come out and hit the water. They don't bounce."

On the port side of the formation, Wildcats tried to intervene. Ensign Willis Reding released his drop tank, lost fuel suction, and his engine quit. His wingman, Raleigh Rhodes, had his own problems since his external tank refused to drop. Rhodes followed the descending Wildcat until Reding's engine returned to life.

On the opposite side of the bombers, Jim Flatley's four Wildcats played catch-up. Responding to the ambush, his quartet exchanged gunfire with the fast, slashing Zeros and destroyed one. Meanwhile, another Japanese pressed an attack and his luck against the remaining Avengers. Charging in close from low astern, he offered a no-deflection target to Chuck Shinneman in the belly of Thompson's plane. The Zero absorbed about fifty fatal rounds of .30 caliber.

The five surviving Avengers regrouped, forming up with the three unmolested Dauntlesses, and continued on course. Flatley stuck with them—militarily the right choice, but his stomach churned in the knowledge that behind him four of his men still fought for their lives.

In the prolonged, hard-fought battle, both sides took losses. John Leppla of Coral Sea fame probably was wounded, as his Wildcat descended straight ahead. Trying to cover him, Al Mead claimed three Zeros, and certainly got one. Moments later, too low to jump, Mead ditched his battered plane.

"Chip" Reding and "Dusty" Rhodes rejoined to put up a terrific fight, using the defensive weave that Flatley had taught them. Despite shot-up aircraft, they kept flying for five minutes before the disparity of odds and performance rang down the curtain. Rhodes went over the side at perhaps 500 feet—fearfully low. He popped his chute immediately, swung once, and hit the water. Reding nursed his perforated Wildcat homeward.

It had been a rough initiation for Air Group 10. *Zuiho's* fighters downed three Avengers, three Wildcats, and inflicted serious damage on two more planes. Twelve Americans went down; four would survive a three-year ordeal as captives. Despite their initial advantage, the Japanese lost four Zeros.

Gaines's surviving pilots pressed ahead, still seeking targets. But with the remaining Wildcats short on fuel, the bombers had to settle for their first opportunity: the enemy's thirteen-ship vanguard force. Consequently, four Avengers went for the cruiser *Suzuya* but only two torpedoes released on the first try. Both missed, as did the third on the next run.

Meanwhile, Lieutenant (jg) Glen Estes's three Dauntlesses dived on a big ship resembling a Kongo class battlewagon. The aviators might have been excused the error since they were unfamiliar with Japanese ships; they actually holed the 11,000-ton cruiser *Chikuma.*

With that action, *Enterprise's* offensive role in the battle was over.

PLAYING DEFENSE

The nature of carrier combat was never better illustrated than that morning off Santa Cruz. Two forces operating more than 120 miles apart exchanged near simultaneous blows in about twenty minutes. *Hornet* dive-bombers fought their way into the Japanese carrier force and pounded the veteran *Shokaku*. Between Strong's and Irvine's attack on *Zuiho* and the *Hornet* contribution, two of the four enemy flattops were out of the battle.

However, at 8:40 the Big E's announcing circuit blared throughout the ship: "Put on flashproof clothing." Five minutes later *Enterprise* gained the safety of a rain squall, where she awaited word of her sister's fate to the southwest. The largest air strike yet launched against American carriers was headed for Task Force 61.

Thirty-eight Wildcats were airborne but poorly positioned. Rather than specific compass headings, the inexperienced fighter director radioed bearings relative to the ship, which most of the pilots could not see.

The first Japanese formations got through Task Force 17's fighters and flak, and around 9:20 Big E men learned that *Hornet* was hit. Five minutes later American radar scopes were clear but the damage had been done. In two strikes the attackers inflicted horrific damage upon *Hornet*: four bombs, two torpedoes, and two die-hard aviators who crashed her in their doomed planes. The fact that she remained afloat spoke volumes of her design and construction.

Twenty miles farther east, Kinkaid's *Enterprise* force prepared to repel a major air attack.

Meanwhile, Lieutenant Richard K. Batten's Avenger aborted a landing aboard *Enterprise,* prompting what historian Norman Polmar termed "one of the most bizarre incidents of the war."

Batten's plane had been shot up in the outbound ambush, and he was unable to jettison his torpedo. His crew insisted that "Red" Batten could fly a washtub and, despite damaged controls, he made a safe water landing near the destroyer *Porter.* As the ship backed off the knots enough to deploy a boat, lookouts shouted a warning—torpedo on the port bow. Incredibly, the Avenger's fish had activated itself and swam away from the sinking Grumman.

Overhead, Wildcat pilots Albert "Dave" Pollock and Jim Dowden spotted the threat and dived in, trying to detonate the warhead with gunfire. Their well-intended action was misinterpreted by shipboard gunners, who shot back.

Moments later the Mark 13 speared *Porter* midships and—in contrast to many American torpedoes—detonated on impact. The explosion rendered *Porter* irretrievably damaged, and she was sunk by another destroyer two hours later.

As if that weren't enough, the second Japanese strike group arrived: most of the forty-four planes from *Shokaku* and *Zuikaku*. Shortly before 9:30 they strobed on the cruiser *Northampton*'s radar some eighty miles northwest of the task force, giving the defenders time to prepare. However, Tommy Thomas's Dauntlesses, readied on deck for a follow-up strike, were ordered to shut down. There was no time for the Big E to launch.

The radar information arrived just as cooks and stewards were passing out battle rations: sandwiches and beverages. Sailors—especially those topside—paid little attention to food at that moment.

Five minutes later the Big E reported her peril: two dozen raiders (nineteen *Shokaku* dive-bombers and five fighters). Captain Hardison changed course, circling to port as the Vals got in above the prowling Wildcats. The bridge rang up twenty-seven knots, and the engineering division complied, firing up the boilers to produce 247 turns per minute on the big propellers.

Amid the tension and churning fear, Kinkaid turned to the correspondent sharing the bridge. "Burns, you're the most favored civilian alive. You're seeing the greatest carrier duel of history. Perhaps it will never happen again."

Only two Fighting 10 ensigns intercepted before the bombers rolled in. Maurice "Wick" Wickendoll experienced maddening gun problems, leaving twenty-two-year-old Ensign Edward L. Feightner to do most of the shooting. "Whitey" was considered a natural pilot: as a Michigan teenager he had ferried a Ford Trimotor before his official solo. Swede Vejtasa considered him "a solid citizen," and Whitey proved it by torching one plane that splashed near the cruiser *Portland*.

Vejtasa jumped the Vals a few minutes later. "I was able to get behind them and shot two of them apart. Really blasted them quick like. I pulled away and one of my wingmen said, 'Torpedo planes below, eleven o'clock!' It was Flash Gordon. He had eyes like an eagle, that guy."

At that moment on the flight deck, plane captain Edmond G. Johnston was riding his Dauntless as it was towed aft for the next launch. He was passing the forward elevator when nearby sailors called, "Enemy planes overhead!"

Johnston recalled, "Looking up, I saw a small speck of a plane as it turned over into a dive. At this time the plane was almost over the port bow." He started to get out of the cockpit, then realized the plane had not been chocked. He tried setting the parking brake, but it wouldn't hold as the carrier heeled into an evasive turn. Johnston continued tapping the toe brakes on the rudder pedals, trying to compensate for the ship's movement.

One division of Vals was led by Lieutenant Keiichi Arima. With his pilot, Petty Officer Furuta Kiyoto, they had hit *Enterprise* at Eastern Solomons. Now for the second time in eight weeks they dived on the Big E, making use of the precious gifts of time and opportunity.

At 10:17 the enlisted pilot put his 550-pounder on the centerline near the bow. The armor-piercing bomb punched through the flight deck and detonated outside the hull. The concussion knocked a parked Dauntless overboard, taking Machinist's Mate Sam D. Presley with it; like Bruno Gaido off Kwajalein, he had been firing the rear-seat guns. Fires burned in the forecastle for nearly half an hour.

Seconds later the next bomb struck aft of the forward elevator and fractured into two deadly components.

Still sitting in his Dauntless, E. G. Johnston watched the developing attack. As the next Val dived closer, he could see the bomb under its belly. "I felt the Jap had me in his sights so I let the SBD roll a little. . . . The Val let his bomb go, and he seemed to be following it down." The weapon appeared to grow from the size of a baseball to medicine ball proportions. As the Japanese pulled out of his dive, seemingly below 1,000 feet, Johnston was convinced that the bomb was going to hit him. He began reciting the Act of Contrition but only started, "O my God, I am . . ." when he felt "the most terrific explosion I have ever heard."

Part of the bomb exploded on the hangar deck, flinging shards upward through the flight deck. Later Johnston counted twenty-two holes in his airplane, from the size of a penny to that of a large man's fist.

The hangar deck explosion wrecked seven aircraft. The other part penetrated lower, exploding in officers' berthing where it killed forty damage control men and medical personnel, and started sporadic fires.

Four sailors also were killed when an antiaircraft shell "cooked off" in an adjacent ammunition handling room. William Pinckney, a Carolina sailor, was knocked unconscious but regained his senses and struggled upright. He was an officers' cook—a common rating for black sailors at the time. But he was an old hand, having been aboard nearly three years. Other mess men knew that he enjoyed Duke Ellington and rooted for the Dodgers.

Bill Pinckney groped through the blackened, burning, reeking compartment, feeling for the ladder leading to the hangar deck. He bumped into Gunner's Mate James R. Bagwell, who was too weak to climb the ladder. Despite the weight disparity, Pinckney picked up the larger man and hefted him toward the hatch. Near the top, he touched a severed electrical line that delivered a stunning shock. Both men tumbled to the deck, insensate. When they came around again, Pinckney again hoisted Bagwell and shoved him through the opening.

At that point the twenty-seven-year-old cook might have called it a day. As he related, "When the first guy seemed to be surviving pretty good, I went below to see if I could help someone else." Finding only burned, blasted bodies, he climbed out again—and collapsed. He had suffered puncture wounds and third-degree burns to his hands, back, and one leg.

Ten months later Pinckney received the Navy Cross. He died in 1976 and a destroyer bearing his name was commissioned in 2004.

Barely two minutes later, hit number three exploded in the water to starboard, sprung several hull plates, opened two empty fuel bunkers, and scoured an engine turbine bearing. On the flight deck a second Dauntless went overboard while another bounced into the catwalk.

The ship's gunnery department remained in the very capable hands of two lieutenant commanders: North Dakotan Orlin Livdahl and Rhode Islander Benny Mott. Though four years senior, Livdahl had agreed to Mott's suggestion to use selected observers and the flight deck loudspeaker system. The spotters were sailors with exceptional vision, Yeoman Jack Rountree and Seaman Roger McCabe. Mott reckoned they could see the spots on a fly at 10,000 feet.

During the dive-bombing attack, Mott, atop the ship's mast, strove to keep track of the Vals emerging from the 6,000-foot overcast. He recalled, "I had some well trained spotters with me in Sky Control, and they would tap my shoulder the moment a plane appeared out of the cloud and I would roar out over the bull horns the direction of the planes, and tell the gunners what planes to get on."

Enterprise ceased fire at 10:20. The entire episode had lasted three minutes. Sailors thought that the raiders dropped twenty-three bombs (it was fewer), scoring two hits and a rattling near miss.

In the brief interim, reports reached the bridge of periscopes in the area—later identified as porpoises. But few men aboard warships ever see the action, real or imagined. Most were like radar technician Ray Blood, locked in his compartment, who could only offer his shipmates a can of black olives.

Then at 10:35 more attackers swept in.

Zuikaku's fifteen Nakajima "Kate" torpedo planes burst out of the storm cloud to the north, splitting for a two-pronged attack. As the task force steamed southwesterly, eight Japanese aimed for the bow and eight more with four escorting Zeros swung around the stern.

South Dakota's 45,000-ton bulk matched the Big E's every turn, maintaining a constant thousand-yard position off the starboard quarter. Making twenty-seven knots, both ships kept up a wall of flak, augmented by the new twin- and quad-mount 40mm Bofors. The Swedish-designed weapons threw a 1.57-inch explosive projectile that could take an airplane down with one well-placed hit. Two cruisers and eight destroyers added to the aerial wall of steel.

Swede Vejtasa already had gunned two dive-bombers in the previous attack but he was out of position to intercept the easterly torpedo planes. Climbing as fast as his Wildcat permitted, the blond Montanan lined up a string of Nakajimas only ten miles out. Chasing them into thick cloud, he was cool and professional, switching off his two outboard guns to maximize his ammunition. He figured that four .50 calibers would suffice. Decades later an interviewer asked if he had been scared. The blue eyes twinkled: "Gosh no. It was *fun*." Swede was credited with downing five torpedo planes for an American record of seven kills in one mission. However many he splashed, he undoubtedly helped save *Enterprise* while Lieutenant Leroy "Tex" Harris also helped break up part of the attack.

One crippled raider flew on, set afire by Vejtasa. Nearly out of ammo, Swede flew into the streaming flames, pondering the chances of severing the enemy's tail with his propeller. But the Kate's slipstream bounced him away, allowing the courageous Japanese to fly into the destroyer *Smith*. Afire across the bow, the little ship swerved into *South Dakota*'s wake, largely extinguishing the flames. But other planes lined up on the carrier and battleship.

Unperturbed, Kinkaid paced the flag bridge, bareheaded, puffing cigarettes, and occasionally offering unsolicited advice. At one point he scolded *South Dakota* for shooting at American aircraft. Meanwhile, on the lower bridge Yeoman Bill Norberg also was bareheaded, though not by choice. The earphones of his sound-powered headset afforded precious little protection.

Meanwhile, gun crews demonically loaded and fired. Some five-inch crews claimed kills at 2,000 yards—a nautical mile—but other planes kept coming. The surviving Kates bore in low and fast, splitting for an attack on both bows and aiming for the Big E's damaged hull. Those to starboard were the first to launch their torpedoes, which boiled through the water at more than thirty knots. On the bridge, Osborne Hardison—who had never commanded a ship—judged the developing time-space problem.

Fortunately, the new captain received valuable help from his navigator. Commander Richard W. Ruble was a sharpshooting poker player from Denver. Admired by his Annapolis classmates ("3.0 in academics and 4.0 in females"), he admitted that he seldom allowed studies to interfere with his education. In his sixteen months aboard, he had become a skilled ship handler.

Hardison alternated between the port and starboard wings of the bridge, better to gauge the evolving geometry in trying to avoid an intersection of two wakes: *Enterprise*'s and a torpedo's. He ordered hard a-starboard, swung the bow into the oncoming spread of torpedoes, and in naval parlance "combed the wakes" by turning parallel to their track. His timing was exquisite: the nearest fish boiled past perhaps thirty feet away.

Moments later the port-hand Kates reached their release point. The Big E's adroit maneuvering temporarily placed them out of position, gaining precious time to meet the threat. Antiaircraft gunners kept up a barrage of fire: five-inch, 40mm, and 20mm. Like wing-shot ducks, three planes tumbled into the flak-spumed sea but two more kept coming. One apparently stalled in an abrupt turn and lurched into the water. The survivor made a good drop but one fish was not enough. Hardison countered with another evasive turn, the torpedoes streaked past, and the attack was over.

Enterprise had dodged nine torpedoes. Probably no other American carrier had ever done as much.

The torpedo attack ended at 10:53 with nine of sixteen Kates downed. Somewhere in the maelstrom of noise, gunnery officer Benny Mott could not contain his enthusiasm. "That's good shooting, lads" blared from the flight deck loudspeaker.

At noon the Big E's signalmen ran the diamond-design "Fox" flag up the halyard as the ship turned into the wind, indicating flight operations. Orbiting aircraft descended into the landing pattern, which quickly became crowded with *Enterprise* planes and *Hornet* orphans. The operation was interrupted when jittery gunners opened fire on approaching planes—six Dauntlesses.

Enterprise ran in and out of rain squalls—a double-edged factor that cut both ways. It shielded the carrier from the enemy but delayed gas-hungry planes from roosting.

Following the torpedo attack, the ship's air-search radar antenna stopped rotating. Only one man stood a chance of repairing the vital gear. Lieutenant Dwight M. B. Williams was called "Brad." He was also perhaps the first radar officer so designated in the Navy. He had reported aboard in November '41 and nursed the Big E's set through the inevitable temper tantrums that characterized early electronics. Despite dive-bombers above and pounding, concussive antiaircraft fire below, he scaled the tripod mast, lugging his tools with him.

Williams found poor purchase on the mast: peeling paint, rusted bolts, and a sooty coating of exhaust stains. Realizing that he needed three hands, he secured himself to the mast so he could work with two.

Then more dive-bombers arrived.

Despite the clutching fear, Williams experienced an eerie recollection. He remembered the words of his Quaker teacher, "If thee follows thy father's footsteps by entering the military service, thee shall probably die a violent death!"

Simultaneously, landing signal officer Robin Lindsey had "cut" only a handful of planes onto the deck when the AA guns erupted again. This time it was for real: the third Japanese raid had arrived. Lindsey dropped the paddles he used to guide landing pilots and raced for a nearby dive-bomber. Manning the guns of a parked Dauntless had become something of a Big E tradition.

The newcomers were from *Junyo*: eighteen Vals with a dozen escorts. The dive-bombers rolled in at 11:20. Big E gunners splashed four, and appeared to dissuade some others. The best bombing was a "paint scraper" to starboard, springing more plates and letting seawater into some compartments.

The same explosion also deafened Brad Williams for weeks. However, by then he had cured the problem, and radar operators resumed scanning. But as the antenna rotated through its arc, Williams was still secured to the mast. He shouted loud, eloquent profanities until Benny Mott's gunnery crew heard the commotion from atop Sky Control in the ship's mast. Finally the devoted radar officer edged his way down into the ship's island. After the war, Uncle John Crommelin was outraged to learn that Williams had received no recognition for his exceptional courage, and tried to get Williams a Navy Cross, to no avail.

In Damage Control Central, Lieutenant Commander Herschel Smith received reports via sound-powered phone, and directed the necessary assets to each site. He and his assistant, Lieutenant George Over, were well experienced: they had done the same thing at Eastern Solomons. Besides sending firefighting and structural crews to damaged areas, they coordinated placement of large fans to suck thick, cloying smoke from cramped compartments.

Perhaps cautious after witnessing their friends' fate against the Big E, the surviving Vals went elsewhere. Battleship *South Dakota* and the cruiser *San Juan* both were hit without serious damage.

After the third attack, *Enterprise* sailors allowed themselves to believe the ordeal was over. The chaplain, Lieutenant Merle Young, decided there was no further point in kneeling on the deck to pray because his left knee got sore. According to legend, the padre switched to his right knee thereafter.

At 12:35 *Enterprise* resumed landing operations. With the forward elevator jammed in the up position and the mid-elevator jammed down, the deck quickly became crowded. Plane handlers maneuvered aircraft nose to tail in a dense pack to accommodate the overflow. With each "cut the throttle" signal, Robin Lindsey used up more precious deck space for another airplane. At one point his talker relayed word from the bridge: cease landing operations. The risk of a terrific smash-up was only increasing.

Lindsey briefly chewed on the situation. Most of the planes still airborne were Dauntlesses—the most effective aircraft in the fleet. He told his assistant to pull the plug on the sound-powered phone. "I don't want to hear anything from anybody." Nothing more was heard.

As the available parking area diminished, Lindsey began artfully landing each pilot closer and closer to the stern. At length he was catching aircraft on the third arresting wire; then the number two wire.

Then the last arresting cable was all that remained. Assistant LSO Jim Daniels bet Lindsey a dime for every plane trapped on the number one wire. Unfazed, Lindsey put the next eight aircraft on the remaining cable, "like it was a Sunday picnic," Swede Vejtasa said.

The last pilot around the pattern was Vejtasa, who had given precedence to his inexperienced wingmen. Driving up the wake, hanging on his

Wildcat's prop with tailhook dangling, Vejtasa kept his eyes on the LSO platform. He had enormous confidence in Lindsey, who returned the sentiment. Flatley regarded Swede as perhaps the finest aviator afloat, and in seconds that opinion would be confirmed or denied. An error by the LSO or the pilot could destroy most of America's remaining naval airpower in the Southwest Pacific.

With the Wildcat farther from the ramp than he had ever done, Lindsey gave Swede a "high dip"—descend a few feet—then slashed his paddles downward and across his body. Swede chopped the throttle, dipped the nose, brought the stick back—"I was looking at the ramp"—and snagged the cable.

Robin Lindsey had put Swede Vejtasa onto the number one wire with the deck locked. It remains *the* virtuoso performance in the LSO's esoteric trade. Every pilot or sailor who saw it recognized the significance. Vejtasa climbed out of his Wildcat to shake hands with Lindsey as scores of men cheered, waved, and applauded.

Enterprise had shoehorned fifty-seven more planes onto the deck; others had to ditch but the fliers were rescued.

During the afternoon Nagumo's last punch landed while *Hornet* was under tow. She took another torpedo, leading the crew to abandon her. She drifted that evening, horribly battered but still afloat, until the Japanese finished her off. *Enterprise* remained the only survivor of her class.

Nagumo had flung 138 sorties at Kinkaid, more than at Midway and Eastern Solomons combined. He lost ninety-nine planes, and his personnel losses were catastrophic for Japanese naval aviation. In sinking an American carrier, the Imperial Navy lost more aircrew at Santa Cruz than at Midway. The deficit proved irreparable.

POSTMORTEM

After the battle, the wounded were treated and the dead tended to. In addition to sixteen missing aircrew, forty-four ship's company had been killed. Chaplain Young moved among the severely wounded, offering solace while other men did what they could. Dauntless pilot Bruce McGraw decided to help the medics. He knelt beside a critically burned sailor who asked for morphine. The doctor said the man wouldn't last more than ten minutes; McGraw sat with him until he died.

Other casualties experienced even worse. Assistant LSO Jim Daniels saw a horribly wounded, legless man use his remaining arm to pull himself to the deck edge. A corpsman advised against helping him. Aghast, Daniels watched the sailor achieve his goal by rolling overboard.

That evening some curious sailors wandered aft where the bodies were prepared for burial; an eerie-ghastly sight. There were pale, nude corpses with visible wounds—some catastrophic—and others with sutures visible where medics had rendered a final cosmetic courtesy. Each body was wedged into a mattress cover with a five-inch shell to ensure that the body would sink. Then the cover was stitched closed and the package hefted onto a flag-covered board, ready to be tilted overboard into oblivion.

Enterprise had taken some hard knocks but she had thrown an amazing amount of lead: more than 50,000 rounds from .50 caliber up to five-inch, including 4,000 rounds of the new 40mm. Livdahl and Mott thought that their gunners splashed thirty of eighty-four attackers while escorting ships downed ten more. The postmortem was predictably optimistic. The Navy credited *South Dakota* with twenty-six (she claimed six more), an action resented by Livdahl's men. Years later, Mott met "SoDak's" captain, Thomas L. Gatch, who said, "I know the *Enterprise* shot down most of those planes. When I went to Washington, the new battleship program was in trouble with Congress and the press. They wanted to cancel some of them. I went along with the story about the *South Dakota* even though I didn't want to."

In his after-action report, Captain Hardison was lavish in his praise, recommending more than seventy medals plus commendations. He was most impressed with the standout performance of Birney Strong, whom he recommended for the Medal of Honor for the flawless long-range attack on *Zuiho*. Strong received another Navy Cross, as did Swede Vejtasa. Flatley thought that Swede deserved the Medal of Honor since no American had ever been credited with seven kills in one mission, and Butch O'Hare had received "the Congressional" for five victories. But by the time the paper mill finished grinding, the Cross had been elevated from its previous position below the Distinguished Service Medal.

After Santa Cruz, squadron commanders wrote the necessary letters. Jim Flatley especially took the responsibility to heart: eight Grim Reapers were missing. He knew his pilots more as family than subordinates, and every letter to next of kin was personalized. Bespeaking the quiet intensity of his Catholic faith, he wrote one family, "God in His divine wisdom calls us when He wants us. I confidently hope that when our call comes, we will find your son waiting for us in Heaven. When we do meet him, again he will be the same smiling, gentle but strong man that remains now in our memory." Later he ordered miniature wings of gold sent to the wives and mothers of missing pilots.

Despite the loss of *Hornet,* Santa Cruz could be called an American victory. The strategic status quo remained unaltered, and both sides recognized that the battle for Guadalcanal, now nearly three months old, could only continue.

On October 30 *Enterprise* dropped anchor in Nouméa's mountain-rimmed harbor, Halsey's SoPac haunt at New Caledonia. The squadrons moved ashore to Tontouta, living under canvas and bathing in a stream.

Halsey assigned battleships *South Dakota* and *Washington* to anchor at the harbor entrance, preventing any further harm from befalling his remaining carrier.

The Big E laid up alongside the repair ship *Vestal,* which spared no effort in getting the *Enterprise* back in the lineup. *Vestal* had a story of her own: commissioned in 1909, she survived the Great War and Pearl Harbor (moored alongside *Arizona*), then fetched up at Tongatabu that summer. Her crew was incredibly adept: in two months the men logged repairs on nearly sixty ships, including *Saratoga* and two battlewagons.

Enterprise repairs began immediately. A sixty-foot section of the hangar deck was bulged over a foot upward, and the aft elevator machinery room had flooded. Elsewhere, frames, floors, and bulkheads were blown out or badly warped, and forward berthing spaces were destroyed. After assessing the situation, *Enterprise* damage control officer Herschel Smith consulted with *Vestal*'s crew, which estimated three weeks to effect repairs. That did not suit Halsey's schedule: he allowed eleven days. Priority was given to the hangar deck and elevator areas, sparking a nonstop cacophony as cutters, welders, structural and system crews all clanged and clattered in a round-the-clock frenzy. The patch job wasn't pretty—some hull damage remained—but the Big E was put right with all three elevators operable, though nobody wanted to test the forward lift, which remained up. Work was still under way with dozens of *Vestal* sailors and Seabees aboard when the carrier departed.

On November 11—Armistice Day—*Enterprise* raised steam and hoisted anchor to depart Nouméa with Air Group 10 restocked. Two weeks after Santa Cruz the Big E again stood guard off Guadalcanal, the last carrier available to face the impending crisis.

6

★ ★ ★

"The Most Exciting Part of Your Day"

A Bombing 10 radioman-gunner exchanges information with his pilot, while the aircraft's plane captain looks on, early 1944. The pilot's life preserver bears the emblem of Scouting 10, absorbed into the bombing squadron in early 1943. (National World War II Museum)

The *Enterprise* task force arrived south of Guadalcanal on Friday, November 13, and that ominous date represented the impending climax of the campaign. In less than forty-eight hours spanning three days there occurred two nocturnal surface battles, a naval bombardment of the American perimeter ashore, a prolonged bloodletting among Japanese transports, and numerous aerial combats. The combined three-day toll was appalling: twenty-six ships sunk, 100 aircraft destroyed, and 3,600 lives lost. Though

Enterprise was well removed to the south, her contribution was vital, as Air Group 10 made a huge difference.

Thanks to the repair ship *Vestal*'s tireless crew and the Seabees, the Big E was able to operate aircraft and steam unimpeded for the coming showdown. But the carrier showed her scars: part of the hull was still bulged from Santa Cruz bomb damage, and she hemorrhaged a trace of oil from her battered fuel bunkers.

Commander Dick Gaines led a reduced air group of seventy-seven planes including thirty-one Dauntlesses, thirty-seven Wildcats, and nine Avengers. Since Jack Collett's death at Santa Cruz, Torpedo 10's "Buzzard Brigade" was headed by Lieutenant Albert "Scoofer" Coffin. His 1934 Annapolis classmates considered the extroverted Hoosier ever cheerful, especially in a tight spot: "When aroused, Albert moves with the passion and fire of a Latin in the body of a Nordic giant." Furthermore, he was admired for his drinking stamina "when many another had sunk behind the bar."

NOVEMBER CRISIS

Both sides funneled troops and supplies to Guadalcanal, usually by night to avoid air attack. In early November the "Tokyo Express" offloaded six or more ships a day on the island's western shore while American transports anchored in the northern sound. Neither side could gain a decisive advantage in troop strength, turning the campaign into an attrition battle entering its fourth month.

Now Halsey had valuable radio intelligence: the Japanese were coming, and coming hard with troop transports and powerful surface units. Their landing, labeled "Z Day," was expected on the 13th.

At dawn that day Task Force 16 bore about 400 miles southeast of the island, but Rear Admiral Tom Kinkaid was taking nothing for granted. With reports of two Japanese carriers approaching from the north, he ordered scouting flights to 230 miles. (Of the two reported flattops, *Hiyo* was being repaired at Truk and *Junyo* remained out of range.)

Nevertheless, *Enterprise* and the Cactus Air Force still faced serious opposition. From Rabaul, New Britain, and environs nearly 200 Japanese naval aircraft lay within range of Guadalcanal. But no matter: Kinkaid had orders from Halsey. Despite the odds, Air Group 10 was to break up the enemy convoy bound for Guadal, and Kinkaid cranked on twenty-five knots to close the distance to the reported enemy ships during the night. Against the chance that some Japanese ships would get through, Halsey hedged his bets. He ordered Rear Admiral Willis Lee to detach from Kinkaid, taking the battleships *South Dakota, Washington,* and their escorts to shortstop the Japanese.

It proved an astute decision but Task Force 16 was not where Halsey expected it to be. Kinkaid was out of position for the battlewagons to reach Ironbottom Sound in time.

The Big E faced her own continuing battle that Friday. Captain Hardison had his ship's construction and repair division work with *Vestal's* men, some still embarked to put right the damage not corrected at Nouméa. On the second and third decks—below the hangar deck—artisans with cutting torches debrided torn or twisted steel frames while welders followed up, filling and patching where needed. As after Eastern Solomons, new doors were fitted and tested for watertight integrity. *Enterprise* was again battleworthy.

But at Guadalcanal, the battle had already begun.

In the wee hours of the morning, thirteen American and fourteen Japanese warships clashed near Savo Island, scene of the U.S. Navy's debacle the night after the Guadalcanal landings in August. Though the numbers were similar, the tonnage vastly favored Japan with two battleships intent upon wrecking Henderson Field with a nocturnal bombardment.

At sunup the nautical detritus of the battle was evident to anyone airborne near Savo's conical edifice. During the night's slugfest one Japanese and two American destroyers had sunk; three U.S. destroyers were dead in the water, while two cruisers crept toward Lunga Point's anchorage. The survivors were cruisers *Helena, San Francisco,* and *Juneau* with three destroyers—insufficient to repel another attack.

Most notable of all was the Japanese battleship *Hiei,* her 36,000-ton bulk battered by close-range gunfire. Marine pilots reported her soon after dawn, circling aimlessly northeast of Savo's brooding monolith, barely under way while tended by a destroyer. The American cruisers finished off another Japanese "tin can," but aerial scouts reported two groups of enemy warships inbound: battlewagon *Kirishima* and seven destroyers. It became a race as to who would arrive first: the Japanese or Lee's two battleships.

More than 300 miles southeast of Guadalcanal, Task Force 16 went to general quarters as Kinkaid's squadrons launched ten scouts and a combat air patrol. With the forward elevator still questionable, it made sense to send the big torpedo planes ashore. Scoofer Coffin led nine Avengers for

Guadal that morning, relying on John Crommelin's hand-drawn maps. Lieutenant John Sutherland, a *Hornet* veteran, led six escorting fighters.

Approaching the search area from the east, the carrier aviators gaped at the tonnage dotting the waters between Savo and Guadal. Scoofer Coffin led the formation into cloud cover at 5,000 feet, closing the distance until near enough to pounce on *Hiei*.

Coffin set up an anvil attack, taking his four Avengers to the battlewagon's port side while sending Lieutenant Macdonald Thompson's quartet wide to starboard. Lieutenant (jg) John Boudreaux's ninth plane, bearing bombs, made an overhead attack.

Hiei had been pounded by naval gunfire during the night and swarmed by land-based aircraft that morning. But she still had plenty of fight; some aviators were astonished at the amount of flak she put up. Fighting 10's Lieutenant (jg) Henry Carey, an urbane Ivy Leaguer, had strafed men-o'-war at Midway but he had seen little to compare to *Hiei*: "My God, what a wall of fire they put up as we made our attack over the top of those torpedo planes."

The fighter pilots went low to strafe, trying to suppress AA fire against the Avengers, but the Wildcats did little more than chip the paint. Eight Mark 13 torpedoes entered the water, and the Buzzard Brigade optimistically reported three explosions against the target. No bomb hits were observed from Boudreaux's lone Avenger.

Coffin led his small strike group into Henderson Field, drawing a heartfelt welcoming committee headed by the Marine air commander, Brigadier General Louis Woods. He had no idea the *Enterprise* fliers were inbound but warmly shook hands and slapped backs, exclaiming that Torpedo 10 resembled angels descending from heaven.

The Guadalcanal of November remained ruggedly expeditionary, but much improved over what Turner Caldwell's *Enterprise* Flight 300 had found in August. Marines still insisted that Cactus was the only place on earth where you could stand up to your knees in mud and get dust in your eyes. However, Henderson Field was almost fully covered by pierced steel planking, with improved maintenance and servicing facilities. Communications were better; there was early-warning radar; and a separate fighter strip was operational east of Henderson.

Meanwhile, the frenetic pace of operations continued. Less than three hours after landing, six of Coffin's crews participated in the seventh and last mission against battered, bleeding *Hiei*, less than a fifteen-minute flight from Henderson. In all, she absorbed nearly 100 sorties of Marine, Navy, and Army aircraft. Beneath lowering clouds northwest of Savo, the Avengers shrugged off still formidable flak to claim three more hits, one by the skipper. Lieutenant (jg) George Welles's hit on the stern probably mattered most. *Hiei* was further immobilized while at least two other torpedoes were seen to hit the hull—and sink. On the way out, gunner Robert Gruebel glimpsed the leviathan in extremis, "afire and the stern was awash."

Coffin's crews were lucky. They missed the sequence of Zero patrols cycling southward from Rabaul and Buin, harassing Henderson's squadrons. However, American aircraft losses were surprisingly small: two Dauntlesses with their crews and a Wildcat whose pilot survived.

Hiei was abandoned during the night and sank unwitnessed.

Torpedo 10 had helped sink the first Japanese battleship of the war, and the first destroyed by the U.S. Navy since 1898. In observance of the occasion, Coffin and company enjoyed unusually good fare courtesy of the ever capable Seabees: bully beef and hotcakes, washed down with grapefruit juice mixed with torpedo alcohol. When Lieutenant James "Irish" McConnaughhay expressed concern about use of the valuable fluid, he was told that Seabees knew the Mark 13 carried enough alcohol for a 2,000-yard run but pilots preferred to drop at half that distance. Without realizing it, the Buzzard Brigade had fuel to burn.

With hundreds of orphaned sailors ashore, the word got around: Rear Admirals Daniel Callaghan and Norman Scott had been killed while losing the cruiser *Atlanta* and four destroyers, plus four cruisers and a destroyer severely damaged. The battle cost Japan *Hiei* and two destroyers; and saved Henderson Field one night's pasting.

But only one night. Before dawn on November 14 Halsey received word from the Marines, "Being heavily shelled." The unrelenting barrage from two cruisers lasted nearly ninety minutes, but was poorly directed. Henderson Field escaped damage—a gift from the war gods—and at sunrise the Cactus Air Force counted more than fifty operational aircraft.

They were badly needed. Aerial reconnaissance tracked eleven Japanese transports and eleven destroyers trailing a vanguard built around four cruisers. The transport group embarked some 7,000 imperial soldiers (the Americans estimated nearly twice as many), possibly enough to decide the campaign.

Normally *Enterprise* would have launched an early search on the 14th, sniffing the surrounding sea for hostile ships. But the tropic weather brought heavy rain, delaying the mission until after daylight. Ten scouts set out on their wedge-shaped search sectors while three bombers patrolled the task force perimeter looking for submarines—always a concern in Solomons waters.

Shortly before 9:00 the scout team of Lieutenants (jg) Martin Doan Carmody and William E. Johnson spotted the threat. About 150 miles northwest of Guadalcanal they assessed the situation and sent a contact report. Their count was close to actual, though they reckoned some of the eleven destroyers were cruisers. Though two Dauntlesses against twenty-two enemy ships represented an immense risk, they attacked anyway. Both bombs missed but tall, square-jawed "Red" Carmody shot up a destroyer on the way out. His gunner, John Liska, glimpsed a plane hitting the water. It was Johnson who fell prey to six Zeros belatedly arriving on station, though he and Radioman Hugh Hughes took a Japanese with them. Carmody shaped course southerly for the Big E.

About ninety minutes after launching the scouts, *Enterprise* again turned into the wind and lofted seventeen Dauntlesses under Bucky Lee with Flatley leading ten Reapers, two of whom strayed from the fold and lost their aerial shepherd. The Japanese cruiser-destroyer force that attracted Lee had been spotted by Lieutenant (jg) Bob Gibson, formerly of Bombing Six. With Ensign Richard Buchanan, "Gibby" snooped the enemy task force for an hour, patiently awaiting confirmation of his contact report. Once it arrived, he was free to pursue his ambition: bombing Japanese ships. From 18,000 feet he selected an obvious cripple: the big cruiser *Kinugasa*, limping along from damage inflicted by Cactus bombers that morning.

Diving from astern, the Dauntless pair put both 500-pounders close aboard, opening seams to port and destroying the ship's steering. It was fatal damage. Incredibly, Buchanan's plane took a main-battery round through the tail, leaving an eight-inch hole where the shell failed to detonate. During the egress, Gibson laid the stick over and kicked the rudder pedals, offering the most difficult target possible. He said, "When you're jinking out of an enemy fleet it's the most exciting part of your day."

In Gibson's slipstream was another search team, Ensigns Robert Hoogerwerf and Paul Halloran. Seeing *Kinugasa* in her throes, they passed her up for fresher meat. Since the Japanese ships had divided, each pilot went for a separate group. Hoogerwerf near-missed *Suzuya*, the force flagship, without inflicting damage, and set course for the Big E. Halloran never turned up.

He pressed his attack so low that one wing snagged *Maya*'s mast, and his ruptured fuel tanks sprayed burning gasoline across the superstructure. The Japanese jettisoned their torpedoes to prevent the warheads from cooking off.

Next on the scene were Bucky Lee's sixteen dive-bombers. His team was loaded with talent, including standouts Tommy Thomas, Birney Strong, and Howard "Red Bird" Burnett, but they scored no direct hits. They made for Henderson Field where they could refuel and rearm. At the same time two of Flatley's Wildcats landed ashore as he led the others back to the ship.

Meanwhile, the Japanese transport force came doggedly on at ten knots, shrugging off attacks from Marine, Navy, and Army aircraft. The ships could not be permitted to put their human cargo ashore: that much was clear. Therefore, Captain Osborne Hardison and air officer John Crommelin—not always mutual admirers—went to work. They fashioned a plan to hit the transports as heavily as possible. There was no doubt who would lead the attack.

That afternoon Jimmy Flatley launched at the head of a dozen Wildcats and eight Dauntlesses, bound for the reinforcement convoy. The twenty-plane strike had orders to sink some ships and recover ashore, joining two dozen *Enterprise* planes already there. The plan left seventeen Wildcats aboard: a minimal number for air defense, but a worthwhile gamble.

Arriving over the convoy, Flatley took charge. Some bomber pilots were worried about Zeros overhead, but with cool deliberation Flatley broadcast, "Okay everybody, quiet down. The Zeros haven't seen us, and I don't want any wing rocking or canopies flashing. We're going to concentrate on defending the bombers and hitting the transports."

As strike coordinator, Flatley assigned targets to the dive-bombers, preventing too many from attacking one ship. He radioed Red Carmody, who had found the transports twice that day, assigning him "the number one transport on the right side," and so on. Years later Red reflected, "In combat, Jimmy was unflappable."

The bombers hit two transports, slowing them for further attention. Leaving a top cover, Flatley led his division below 2,000 feet, strafing the decks packed with brown-clad soldiers. The effect of six .50 calibers on such dense targets was visible to the pilots; the carnage was horrific.

The other Wildcats did their job, running interference for the bombers. The aggressive Carmody pressed his dive to minimum range, watching his bomb burst on a transport. Outbound he was jumped by two Zeros. Alerted by his gunner, Carmody shoved the stick forward, descending to 100 feet off the water, maneuvering according to Radioman John Liska's directions. Liska was an old hand: he'd been John Leppla's radioman-gunner at Coral Sea over six months previously. While the Dauntless dodged the fighters, one of the Reapers dashed in and shot the closest Zero into the water. Liska used the opportunity to put dual streams of .30 caliber into the other, claiming a flamer.

So it went. Throughout the afternoon the Cactus Air Force threw strike after strike at the determined Japanese force. Some pilots logged a numbing nine hours in combat, and sometimes attacks averaged one plane per minute. Inevitably planes, crews, and equipment got switched, traded, and hijacked. Marine crews flew Navy aircraft and vice versa. Somebody made off with Bucky Lee's parachute, and he never saw it again. He continued flying anyway, trusting whoever had packed the chute in the next bomber. As it developed, he didn't need one.

Zeros intercepted several flights but generally the Wildcats handled the bandits. In one dogfight Ensign Ed Coalson ("a prince of a young fellow" in Vejtasa's estimation) found himself the meat in a four-cornered Zero sandwich. Defying doctrine, he looped up, over, and behind one assailant, finishing close enough to flame the Japanese, who made a water landing.

Still, there were losses. A late afternoon strike departed Henderson under Tommy Thomas leading six other Dauntlesses. Despite a lack of escorts, he proceeded up "The Slot," the long stretch of water approaching Guadalcanal between New Georgia and Santa Isabel. The evidence of previous attacks was obvious: two ships burning in the background; three or four stationary; another limping off westerly. But others continued doggedly southeast. Thomas faced a decision: attack immediately from only 12,000 feet and likely avoid interception, or climb for altitude to execute an optimal attack. He chose the latter.

The defenders made good use of the time. Six Zeros slammed into the bombers, sparking a violent set-to with losses on both sides. Thomas's pilots and gunners were impressively accurate, splashing three Japanese, but the enemy was skilled and persistent. Zeros expended hundreds of 20mm and 7.7mm rounds, downing two Dauntlesses. Vivien Welch and Don Wakeham disappeared with their gunners. Ensign Jeff "Tiny" Carroum kept airborne long enough to drop his bomb, then caught a load of flak. He splashed into a safe landing and exited the sinking plane with Radioman

Robert Hynson. Their raft was lost with the plane, leaving them on their own, sustained only by their Mae Wests.

Another bomber pilot was jumped by a Mitsubishi leech that sank its teeth into the Dauntless's skin. Diving away, Ensign Len Robinson kept his bomb to increase his vertical velocity, and hauled back on the stick, to no avail. Down to 300 feet, he dodged and weaved while the determined Zero pilot kept up a steady fusillade. After a thirty-mile tail chase to the Russell Islands, the Japanese aviator gamely rocked his wings in a parting salute, out of ammunition.

The remaining Dauntlesses attacked undamaged ships, but without result. Thomas, Ed Stevens, and the ever present Bob Gibson headed for Henderson.

That week Guadalcanal represented the crossroads of America's war, where naval aviators often met old friends. They included Jimmy Flatley, who recognized a marine sitting in a Wildcat. The leatherneck was Lieutenant Colonel Joe Bauer, a year behind him at Annapolis, now running Cactus fighter operations. Already a double ace, he had assigned himself to a mission to gain more trigger time. Flatley scrambled up on the high wing, traded good-natured Navy-Marine insults, and looked forward to renewing their acquaintance that evening. "Indian Joe" agreed, then taxied out for takeoff. He never returned.

Nevertheless, wave upon wave of American planes pummeled the convoy, ships were struck, stopped, then sunk. At sunset four transports remained headed for Guadal's northwest coast, shepherded by five destroyers. Four other escorts busily pulled surviving sailors and soldiers from the sea, then resumed the southeasterly course. It was apparent that some enemy troops would get ashore.

But another act in the naval drama remained in the wings. That night of the 14th–15th, the Second Naval Battle of Guadalcanal involved the biggest battleship fight to date: *Hiei*'s sister *Kirishima* and twelve other Japanese ships against Rear Admiral Willis Lee's *South Dakota* and *Washington* with four destroyers. Hundreds of Americans ashore—marines, soldiers, and sailors—sought a vantage point to watch the pyrotechnic drama playing out in the waters to the north. It was a grim show: three American tin cans were crushed and one dented, but *Kirishima* and a Japanese destroyer were sunk. Guadalcanal's status quo remained unchanged—it seemed the situation could go either way.

In the early morning of the 15th, Rear Admiral Raizo Tanaka's last four transports ran themselves aground, disgorging their troops. A destroyer also landed its soldiers, for a total of 2,000 Japanese with four days of supplies put ashore. It was pitifully little to show for the immense effort, and could not shift the balance of power on Guadalcanal. Throughout the day *Enterprise* aircrews joined their Marine and Army associates in destroying the beached transports or sinking the drifting remnants out in the sound and the Slot.

FAREWELL, CACTUS PATCH

Though the crisis apparently had passed, Kinkaid decided to keep most of Air Group 10 on Guadalcanal. It was not a popular decision with Halsey. While jauntily confident ("after the beating he had taken, the monkey would withdraw"), he was concerned about his only carrier-qualified squadrons in the region. The Japanese navy had a nasty habit of pulling off the seemingly impossible, and however unlikely, another bombardment of Henderson Field might deprive Halsey of an invaluable asset. But Willis Lee's battleship force remained on hand for the moment, so *Enterprise* headed for Nouméa.

The air group began trickling out of Cactus over the next two days. Most of Bucky Lee's and Scoofer Coffin's outfits flew 650 miles south to Espiritu Santo in the New Hebrides, losing two Dauntlesses and an Avenger to weather, but the fliers were rescued. The other personnel boarded transport planes for the southerly trek, leaving three dozen carrier aircraft at Henderson and the fighter strip. The Marines were grateful.

Air Group 10 was astonished when a dead man turned up living. Jeff Carroum had disappeared on November 14, but he spent seventy-three hours alternately swimming and floating to reach land twelve miles distant. His gunner, Bob Hynson, had died of exhaustion on the second day. Carroum, small and slight, somehow survived three days without drinking water while exposed to the unrelenting tropic sun.

After crawling ashore in the Russells on the 17th, Carroum found helpful natives who hid him from the Japanese. There he joined Marine Sergeant Thomas Hurst, who had been shot down two days before Carroum. A Catalina flying boat fetched them to Tulagi on the 26th. Thus, Jeff Carroum was added to the growing list of surviving *Enterprise* fliers including the crews of Harold Nixon off Samoa and Albert Winchell after

USS *Enterprise* at sea in 1938, embarking upon a seven-year career unlike any ship before or since. (USN)

Enterprise's "royal" court during the equator crossing rite with the Royal Baby second from right. (Joel Shepherd, Enterprise Assn.)

A Northrop BT-1 of Bombing Six enters the landing pattern c. 1940. (Commander Pete Clayton, USN Ret.)

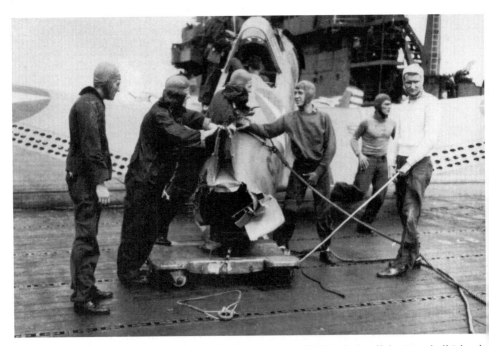

A determined Japanese bomber pilot tried diving into the Big E's deck off the Marshall Islands in February 1942. One wing severed this Dauntless's tail, barely missing Machinist's Mate Bruno Gaido manning the machine gun. (USN via Tailhook Assn.)

Lieutenant Commander C. Wade McClusky, Enterprise Air Group commander who made the crucial decision to continue hunting the Japanese carriers at Midway. (USN via Tailhook Assn.)

Douglas Devastators of Torpedo Six prepare to launch into the Battle of Midway, June 4, 1942. Of fourteen Devastators launched, only four returned to the ship, and one was jettisoned. (USN)

Taking the offensive: *Enterprise, Saratoga,* and *Wasp* bound for Guadalcanal, August 1942. It marked the beginning of a six-month struggle that left the Big E the only American carrier still in action. (USN via Tailhook Assn.)

LEFT: *Enterprise*'s most devoted enemy, Lieutenant Keiichi Arima of the Japanese carrier *Shokaku.* Flying with pilot Furuta Kiyoto, Arima's bomber scored damaging hits on the Big E at Eastern Solomons in August and Santa Cruz in October. Arima survived the war. (Ron Werneth.)

RIGHT: Scout-bomber pilot Stockton Birney Strong was one of *Enterprise*'s prominent personalities. After Eastern Solomons he vowed never to pass up another shot at a Japanese carrier and succeeded brilliantly at Santa Cruz. Nominated for the Medal of Honor, he received a second Navy Cross. (National World War II Museum)

Lieutenant Commander Jim Flatley and the "Grim Reapers" of Fighting 10, first blooded at Santa Cruz. (USN via Tailhook Assn.)

When enemy bombers got past the Big E's fighters, her defense lay in the hands of shipboard gunners such as these 20mm crews practice firing in 1942. (Joel Shepherd, Enterprise Assn.)

Lieutenant Stanley "Swede" Vejtasa, fighter pilot extraordinaire, credited with downing seven Japanese attackers on October 26, 1942. Jim Flatley considered him "the finest aviator afloat." (National World War II Museum)

With Japanese aircraft inbound, flight deck crewmen scramble to move fighters and dive-bombers out of the way as the ship heels in a starboard turn. (USN via Tailhook Assn.)

Landing Signal Officer Robin Lindsey gave a virtuoso performance at Santa Cruz, directing aircraft to land on the last available arresting wire. (USN via Steve Ewing)

Bomb splinter holes in the port bow, seen during repairs after Santa Cruz. (USN via Tailhook Assn.)

In early May 1943, after the Guadalcanal campaign, *Enterprise* is escorted on part of her homeward journey by the battleship *Washington*. (USN via Tailhook Assn.)

A typical ready room briefing with navigational and tactical data noted on the chalkboard. (USN via Tailhook Assn.)

Among the Big E's most forceful personalities was air group commander William R. "Killer" Kane: inspiring leader, enthusiastic aviator, and devoted enemy of the Japanese Empire. (USN via Tailhook Assn.)

During 1944 operations, Jig Dog Ramage exits the cockpit of his Dauntless while radioman-gunner David Cawley stands by. Sailors are immediately on hand to refuel and rearm the bomber for its next mission. (USN via Tailhook Assn.)

Bombing 10 aircrew keep occupied in their ready room. Acey-deucey was a popular pastime: players bet on whether the next card would fall between the two dealt faceup. (National WW II Museum)

An *Enterprise* damage control party during a drill. When oxygen bottles were unavailable, some sailors wore handkerchiefs over the mouth and nose to reduce smoke inhalation. (National World War II Museum)

William I. Martin (center), commander of Torpedo 10, with his aircrewmen, Jerry T. Williams (left) and Wesley R. Hargrove (right). Both were lost when Martin's Avenger bomber was shot down off Saipan in June 1944. (National Museum of Naval Aviation)

Back aboard the Big E after their respective dunkings off Saipan, Lieutenant Commanders Bill Martin (Torpedo 10) and Killer Kane (Air Group 10) exchange experiences. (USN via Tailhook Assn.)

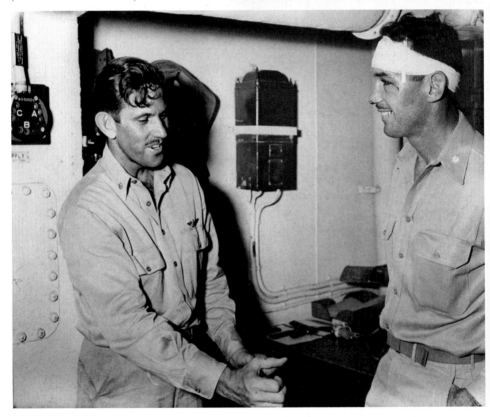

Enterprise Avengers caught a Japanese convoy off Guam on June 12, 1944, and sank the 1,900-ton freighter *Nitcho Maru*, which lost most of its cargo overboard. This photo became one of the most-published images of the period. (National Museum of Naval Aviation)

During the Battle of Leyte Gulf, *Enterprise* squadrons helped sink the veteran Japanese carrier *Zuiho* on October 25, 1944. (USN via Tailhook Assn.)

Among the unheralded contributions to carrier aviation are aircraft mechanics and weapons-specialists. Above, *Enterprise* technicians prepare an F4F Wildcat for flight on the hangar deck in early 1942, and below, ordnancemen load incendiary clusters into an Avenger's bomb bay, summer 1944. (Both USN via Tailhook Assn.)

Emergency crews douse a fire caused by a Hellcat night fighter's belly tank. (National Museum of Naval Aviation)

A typical working day for flight deck crewmen was fourteen hours or more. These Big E "airdales" flop as the opportunity arises. (USN via Tailhook Assn.)

A wounded aircrewman is removed from a battle-damaged Helldiver, fall 1944. (USN via Tailhook Assn.)

Avengers secured on the flight deck, facing the setting sun—beginning another "workday" for Night Air Group 90. (USN via Tailhook Assn.)

In a beautiful piece of flying mated to an exceptional photographer, the Big E's last kamikaze perhaps two seconds from impact, May 14, 1945. (USN via Tailhook Assn.)

Seen from the battleship *Washington*, *Enterprise*'s forward elevator is blasted almost 400 feet in the air from the kamikaze hit on May 14, 1945. (USN via Tailhook Assn.)

Enterprise docks at Staten Island, New York, after her last Magic Carpet voyage on January 14, 1946. Aboard were 3,557 GIs and WACs. (Joel Shepherd, Enterprise Assn.)

The *Enterprise* stern plate at the River Vale, New Jersey, Veteran's Memorial Park during the December 2000 dedication. (Robert Secor via Joel Shepherd, Enterprise Assn.)

Midway—men who shared an essential quality: when faced with appalling odds, a primal refusal to quit.

But the Japanese were not ready to quit, either. On November 30, in the campaign's fourth clash near Savo Island, the Imperial Navy inflicted another drubbing upon the Americans. At the cost of one ship, eight Japanese destroyers—most encumbered with supplies—sank a U.S. cruiser and left three others hors de combat.

HOLIDAY REINFORCEMENTS

Meanwhile, on November 16 *Enterprise* returned to Nouméa, where she received additional repairs. The air group established itself ashore, settling into living areas both assigned and opportune. As befitted the skipper of Scouting 10, Bucky Lee took himself on a snooping expedition in a "borrowed" jeep under the sound military premise that time spent on reconnaissance is seldom wasted. He made friends with the CO of a repair facility featuring cots, sheets, showers, and edible food served on tablecloths. The aviators settled in, determined to enjoy themselves as long as conditions and hospitality lasted.

It wasn't nearly long enough. On December 4 the ship got under way and the squadrons flew out, exercising the deck crew—and the much studied forward elevator. Captain Hardison finally reckoned that the time had come for a test, and authorized the V-1 Division to push the down button. The elevator worked in both directions. The Big E was 100 percent back in business.

Three days later the crew marked the first anniversary of Pearl Harbor. There were still hundreds of men aboard who remembered that Sunday: the disbelief that morphed into shock and roiled into burning anger. Twelve months of near constant combat and the loss of 250 shipmates had shaped and honed the Big E as an institution. The post-Pearl rage had settled into a grim resolve: kill enough Japs, sink enough ships, down enough planes, then dare to dream of home.

As correspondent Gene Burns had noted, after Santa Cruz "then there was one." But in early December *Saratoga* returned to the South Pacific, easing some of the pressure off *Enterprise*, which mainly operated out of Nouméa. Meanwhile, taking up some of the slack was a new breed of flattops, oilers hastily converted to escort carriers (CVEs). Though small and slow, they still provided valuable service with as many as thirty aircraft.

Two "baby flattops," *Chenango* and *Suwannee*, were available in the Solomons but admirals were still learning how to use them.

After a week at sea *Enterprise* began another lay-up period at Espiritu Santo. Over the next three weeks the ship sortied occasionally, allowing the air group to refresh its carrier qualifications and escape the South Pacific fauna ashore, including rodents, reptiles, and insects. At Guadal, Nouméa, and Espiritu, some men acquired lasting maladies beyond the routine misery of dysentery, dengue fever, and malaria. Some, for instance, caught a foot infection generically termed "the crud" that could last twenty years.

Despite the religiosity of the name, Espiritu Santo did little to enhance the holiday season. Many *Enterprise* men observed their second Christmas at war, with the inevitable homesickness partly alleviated by an avalanche of gift packages and delayed mail.

Some sailors expected little from home and bluntly said so. Twenty-two-year-old Ordnanceman Jim Shepherd of the V-5 Division had reported aboard in October and wrote his parents in Ohio, "Pass the word around to the folks to forget the Xmas presents this year as I'm definitely not going to send any myself. Not even so much as an Xmas card so far as I know."

A NEW YEAR DAWNING

In late January *Enterprise* patrolled the now familiar waters south of Guadalcanal, mostly as a precaution. But some Japanese units remained active. Screening a convoy unloading the evening of January 29, the cruiser *Chicago* had been attacked by astutely flown Bettys from Rabaul. They attacked near Rennell Island 120 miles south of Guadalcanal, and put two torpedoes into her.

Enemy interest resumed at dawn on the 30th. That morning Fighting 10 chased a snooper, which observed *Chicago* towed by a tug, escorted by six destroyers.

Shortly past 4:00 P.M. Wildcats prowling near *Chicago* learned of a new threat. Flatley's exec was big, strapping Lieutenant William R. Kane, a fearsome collegiate wrestler who had been "Killer" since Annapolis. Orbiting the cruiser with a Betty in sight, he kept Ensign Ed Coalson and sent a passel of others to deal with the snooper southwest of Rennell. The youngsters were eager: Navy fighters had claimed no kills since the slaughter of Tanaka's transports in mid-November. So, romping with the Mitsubishi like a Wildcat's chew toy, Bill Leder and Wick Wickendoll did the deed.

However, the harm had been done. If not before, surely now the Japanese knew where to find a juicy target.

At 4:45 a dozen Bettys made straight for *Enterprise*, fifty miles southeast of the limping *Chicago*. The Big E had ten Grim Reapers airborne: Lieutenant Macgregor Kilpatrick's six, plus four under Flatley, covering another U.S. cruiser force to the northeast. Kilpatrick met the raiders head-on, and they recognized a no-win setup. They came hard about to the north, heading for *Chicago* northeast of Rennell.

"Mac" Kilpatrick and his wingman, Ensign Robert Porter, tied into the bombers. Making overhead and high-side runs, denying the enemy gunners a decent shot at them, they splashed three in minutes, the smoke pyres visible from *Enterprise*. The remainder lowered their noses and began a slanting approach toward *Chicago*. The big Mitsubishis steadily pulled away, exceeding 300 mph in their descent.

From his position near the cruisers, Jimmy Flatley sized up the situation and headed west, hoping to intercept the bombers. Neither time nor geometry worked for him. Nor did mechanics. Only one of the Reapers was able to release his drop tank; the others remained stubbornly stuck, incurring drag, reducing speed.

The Bettys had no such problem. They dropped out of the cloud deck, finding just one destroyer between them and their prize. Antiaircraft fire erupted from every ship that could bear, but to little avail. Several torpedoes entered the water, and four of them boiled into *Chicago*'s hull. Unlike those made in the USA, Japanese torpedoes typically ran as advertised, and when they struck, they exploded. *Chicago*'s guts were ripped out; she sank in twenty minutes. Another torpedo smacked the new destroyer *La Vallette*, killing twenty-two men, but she survived.

Flatley gave chase with Russell Reiserer, Roland Witte, and Peter Shonk. Like most fighter pilots, while chasing attackers, Flatley accepted friendly AA fire as part of the trade, but nobody tolerated getting hosed while heading outbound. As at Pearl Harbor, Navy gunners still tended to shoot at anything, no matter that single-engine gray-painted Wildcats bore no resemblance to twin-engine green Bettys.

Belle of the brawl was young Whitey Feightner, who reeled in three bombers during a low-level tail chase. Closing on one Betty fast from astern, he held his trigger down. If the bomber hadn't exploded he would have collided. Back aboard ship, Flatley learned of the youngster's triple victory and paid him high praise, "You're a fighting fool, aren't you?"

The Japanese paid a price for their victory. Fighting 10 expended 11,000 rounds of .50 caliber to claim eleven kills, though apparently two bombers fell to AA gunners. In fact, the Japanese lost eight Bettys in the attack, and another crashed on landing.

The Guadalcanal campaign continued into early February when the last emaciated Japanese were withdrawn from the island. The news was released to the American public on the 11th, ending the six-month bloodletting. If Midway had ensured that Japan could not win the Pacific war, Guadalcanal meant that America could not lose.

Some veteran campaigners were headed home, including Jimmy Flatley. Yet for all the fiery motivation in that slender frame, he could not bring himself to say farewell to his squadron. Instead, he wrote a heartfelt letter, handed it to Killer Kane, and departed USS *Enterprise*.

The skipper left the Reapers in good hands, saying he could choose no finer relief than the Killer. His parting sentiment was, "Take care of yourselves. Stick together and don't forget to respect that airplane. Every time you see a Jap, remember Leppla, Mead, Rhodes, Caldwell, Davis, Fulton, Barnes, Miller, Edwards, and Von Lehe."

Finally, he wrote, "Rip 'em up and down, but do it smartly. . . . Meanwhile, keep your chins up and don't forget that little guy who called himself Reaper Leader."

THE MEANING OF GUADALCANAL

Both sides recognized the crucial importance of the Guadalcanal campaign, where prolonged, large-scale attrition was inflicted upon both sides. There had never been so intense a period of naval and air combat: those six months cost twenty-nine American ships and thirty-eight Japanese, while total aircraft losses topped 1,300. Naval historian John Lundstrom reckoned that *Enterprise*'s contribution to victory was exceeded only by the surface forces that prevented two potentially disastrous bombardments.

Richard Frank, author of the campaign's preeminent study, concludes, "The whole campaign teetered so close to failure for so long that any number of things could have sent it to an American disaster. Probably the single most perilous moment where *Enterprise* could have been the tipping point was at Santa Cruz, where we were very lucky not to lose her and her air group as well as *Hornet*. Practically speaking, when you get to November, this has all sorts of implications against the convoy and the Japanese naval forces."

Enterprise fully matured at Guadalcanal: her aircrews supported the initial landings; met the Japanese thrusts in August and October; contributed Flight 300 to the island's defense; shared in the destruction of *Hiei*, got the greater portion of the cruiser *Kinugasa*, and destroyed four or more transports. *Enterprise* squadrons operated cheek by jowl with the Marines ashore, integrating effectively into the cobbled-together Cactus Air Force.

At Midway the Big E had earned every dollar invested in her. At Guadalcanal she returned that investment with compounded interest.

7

★ ★ ★

"A Long and Teedjus Journey"

The "gedunk," the ship's soda fountain where sailors bought ice cream, soft drinks, and doughnuts to dunk in coffee. (USN via Tailhook Assn.)

If 1941 was *Enterprise*'s year of preparation and 1942 was the year of combat, then 1943 came closest to a year of rest.

Enterprise began regenerating herself that spring: absorbing new men who would benefit from the skills, knowledge, and wisdom of the old hands. Enthusiastic, fresh-caught aviators unpacked their bags at Espiritu Santo and began absorbing the *Enterprise* ambience. Everybody was impressed with Fighting 10's new skipper, Killer Kane, the Annapolis wrestling star. Then-Ensign Dick May recalled, "He was built like a strong Abe Lincoln, tall and lanky. Some of us young bucks thought we could gang up on him and take him to the ground, and eventually we did, but it took six of us!"

At Espiritu, Fighting 10's organization was reshuffled. Previous wingmen and section leaders were promoted to lead their own two-plane sections or four-plane divisions, and Swede Vejtasa began auditioning new talent. Most new pilots emerged from Training Command with excellent technical skills, as pound for pound the U.S. Navy arguably produced the finest fliers on earth. But beyond that, the new aviators craved what young men have always sought—acceptance, respect, and a fervent desire to avoid failing their fellows.

In assessing potential wingmen, Vejtasa sought an arcane mixture of head, heart, and hands coupled with an avid willingness to learn. A good wingman was not only skilled but reliable—a teammate one literally could trust with one's life. Swede went through most of the replacement pilots before he got to Dick May, a slender Oregonian. "Stay on my wing," was all Vejtasa said, and they took off in a pair of Wildcats.

Concentrating as if his life depended on it—which it might have—May did whatever was necessary to keep Vejtasa's starboard wingtip in view. Somewhere in the evolution, May risked a glance through the top of the canopy and saw palm fronds close aboard. With growing confidence in the youngster's ability, Vejtasa had led him through a low-level aerobatic routine, skimming the treetops. Upon landing, the finest fighter pilot afloat pronounced the rookie his new number two.

Six decades later May asserted, "The fact that I was Swede Vejtasa's wingman means more to me than the fact that I later made ace in another squadron."

Although Uncle John Crommelin remained the ship's executive officer—second only to the captain—he still loved to fly, and grasped any opportunity. In those days a "three-striper," a full commander, was a very senior officer who often could make his own rules. Crommelin did just that. One morning he appropriated a torpedo plane and took off to indulge his passion. A group of junior birdmen watched the proceedings, having no idea of what they were about to see.

The Avenger leveled off at 1,500 feet and abruptly rolled on its back. Hanging in his straps in the spacious cockpit, Crommelin pushed forward on the stick, stalling the big Grumman, then booted the left rudder, forcing the plane into an inverted spin. He kept it in that condition through two or three turns before a seemingly effortless recovery, and made a three-point landing.

The youngsters gaped at the spectacle. A few snorted, "Hell, if that old man can do it, so can I!"

Cooler, wiser heads dissuaded them. That old man of forty had gifted hands—and experience.

THE BUZZARD BRIGADE

Torpedo 10 called itself the "Buzzard Brigade," and logged numerous "proficiency flights" to Efate in the New Hebrides, returning with Avengers laden with liquid cargo. The 400-mile round-trip benefited an entrepreneur named Tom Harris, whom the squadron deemed "our genial south seas trader who has some interesting connections in various islands."

The booze runs afforded an opportunity for aircrews to qualify for their monthly flight pay. Some aviators outside the Buzzard Brigade took advantage of Scoofer Coffin's generosity, including landing signal officer Robin Lindsey and Scouting 10 exec Bill Martin. On one occasion Martin fetched back a fifty-five-gallon oil drum filled with rum. Such hauls met with heartfelt approval in the air group, since official emporiums such as the officers' club at the fleet landing were a considerable walk from the bomber strip. Besides, the bar opened at 1:00 P.M., only serving gin until 2:00, and progressing through beer, rum, and finally bourbon at 4:00.

On another occasion Coffin, ever mindful of his men's welfare, arranged a trade to the squadron's benefit. Approaching the captain of a civilian cargo vessel, he offered a straight-across swap: a ride in a Navy airplane for a quantity of milk. Coffin reckoned it a no-brainer: his overhead cost was exactly zero (the U.S. government provided the airplane and the fuel) and he obtained enough "moo juice" for the entire squadron for one meal. One flier recalled, "For a group who hadn't had a glass of fresh milk for nine months, it was liquid gold."

Conventional wisdom held that alcohol fueled all wars—generally true throughout the twentieth century—but ordinary pleasures such as milk and dairy products also boosted morale. Aboard ship, ice cream was especially valued but in limited supply at the soda fountain, which sailors called the "gedunk," from a place where snacks could be dunked in coffee or other beverages. Experienced gedunkers knew that the early sailor got the goodies, so lines formed before the canteen opened. Machinist's Mate Freddie Chafin had learned a few things in his three years onboard, and conceived a way to accelerate the ice cream output by two or even three times. Unfortunately, he left the ship that summer before implementing his "supercharged" gedunk.

BROTHERS AND OTHERS

For most men, the variety of life ashore had its limits. On a weekly basis or so, some of the beached air group returned to the ship for some good food, a real shower, and a clean, soft berth. In late April Avenger gunner Chuck Shinneman was told he had a visitor on board. The officer of the deck asked, "Do you have a brother in the Navy?"

Shinneman allowed as he did, and was told his sibling had just headed for the flight deck. There Chuck found Ensign John R. Shinneman—his brother, Jay. The Grim Reapers of Fighting 10 had just received a batch of replacement pilots, and Jay would remain for the next combat deployment.

Other brothers came and went during that period, including two of the four Hoover boys from Denver. All were prewar Big E sailors, able to stay aboard despite the Navy's normal policy after the five Sullivans were lost on the cruiser *Juneau* at Guadalcanal. Bill Hoover, a bugler, and Paul, a bosun's mate, were reassigned after three and two years, respectively. Medical Corpsman Victor had left just before Midway but Machinist Howard remained from 1941 until early 1946. In all, at least six sets of brothers—fourteen men—served in *Enterprise,* of whom A. J. Davis was killed at Eastern Solomons and Lewis Flack at Santa Cruz. Additionally, Chief Machinist's Mate Allen Patten reported to the Big E in 1942 after serving with his six brothers aboard *Nevada,* the only battleship to get under way at Pearl Harbor. Their father later entered the Navy during the war.

The bombers also experienced change in the slender, intense form of Stockton Birney Strong, whom Captain Osborne Hardison had recommended for the Medal of Honor after Santa Cruz. In February—after more than a year in the Pacific and six months aboard *Enterprise*—Strong assumed command of Bombing 10.

Among the replacement pilots was Lieutenant (jg) James D. Ramage, the same Jig Dog who had joined *Enterprise* directly from Annapolis in 1939. Back then he was part of the ship's company but now, a newly minted aviator, he was exactly where he wanted to be, flying from the Big E. When Jig reported to the squadron, Strong looked up at him—most people were taller—and said in a level, gunfighter's tone, "Ramage, I am going to make you the second-best dive-bomber in the Pacific Fleet."

With only fifteen hours in Dauntlesses, Jig Dog received two sessions of field carrier landing practice under the expert tutelage of Robin Lindsey and Jim Daniels. Lindsey exuded confidence: "I'll get you aboard." And he did.

Ramage was unusual in that he served aboard *Enterprise* both as a blackshoe surface officer and a brownshoe aviator. He typified the growing talent pool available in early 1943. When Birney Strong greeted new pilots he was not merely accepting another batch from Pensacola or Corpus Christi. He was grooming his men for greater responsibilities—leaders as well as warriors; thinkers who could sink enemy ships with minimum loss. A dive-bomber pilot had to possess the same fiery desire to hit the target that Strong and Chuck Irvine had demonstrated at Santa Cruz—diverting far off their assigned sector to grasp the rare opportunity to bomb a Japanese carrier, outfox the Zeros, and dodge the flak, then manage their fuel to within a few gallons to make it home. Strong was a hard taskmaster—some said harsh—but he was also a keen judge of talent. He looked at James D. Ramage and liked what he saw. With a confidence just short of cockiness, the youngster held promise. Strong departed the Big E later that year, but in his wake he left a crop of dedicated warriors including a few, like Ramage, who would command squadrons and air groups.

Other old hands also rolled out. In early April Captain Hardison left after nearly six months in command, relieved by Samuel Paul Ginder, a forty-eight-year-old Pennsylvanian who would remain almost until year's end.

EASTBOUND—BUT NOT FAR ENOUGH

Three weeks later music rent the tropic air while *Enterprise* steamed away from Espiritu, the crew in a jaunty mood. The ship's band lustily played "California Here I Come" as the Big E set course for Pearl Harbor and points east.

Nearing Oahu, the air group launched on May 8 and landed ashore. Hours later, approaching the channel entrance, *Enterprise* received a Morse code light message from shore. The form went from the signal officer to the bridge, where Captain Ginder read it. He passed the sheet to John Crommelin, whose intimate relationship with the crew was far beyond anything the skipper could achieve.

Uncle John read what he read, then he said what he felt. He spoke into the main circuit that was heard throughout the ship. The gist of the message: *Enterprise* would remain at Pearl Harbor training a new air group for about six weeks.

Enterprise seemed to lower three feet in the water as morale plummeted to the keel and sulked there. But PacFleet had no option: carriers were still rare, and none could be spared specifically for training. The first new-generation flattops, Essex and Independence class, would not begin arriving for two to three months. They would spearhead the upcoming Central Pacific offensive, but before then the Big E was badly needed to keep new air groups current in carrier operations. As usual, she was invaluable.

There was some small compensation. On May 27 Admiral Nimitz came aboard in Pearl to present *Enterprise* with the Presidential Unit Citation—the first ever to an aircraft carrier. The citation lauded the ship and her squadrons "For consistently outstanding performance and distinguished achievement during repeated action against enemy Japanese forces. Her aggressive spirit and superb combat efficiency are fitting tribute to the officers and men who so gallantly established her as an ahead bulwark in defense of the American nation."

The battle honors listed eight actions from February through November 1942, excepting the Doolittle raid, lest the Japanese infer too much even if they suspected that the U.S. Army bombers came from a carrier.

Meanwhile, some of the Big E's aggressive spirit was demonstrated ashore. One evening at Pearl's enlisted men's club some *Enterprise* marines and some leathernecks of the newly arrived *Essex* "got into a little discussion about which one was the Big E." Before the dispute ended—it was not really settled—blood was drawn on both sides. *Essex*'s air group commander was Charles D. Griffin, who admitted to divided loyalties since he had flown from *Enterprise* for three years before the war. He recalled, "It took half the officers on both ships to get 'em separated. We suggested it might be a good idea to save some of this for the Japs."

Then the Big E got back to work. From late May to mid-July she exercised Air Group 12, which eventually deployed in *Saratoga*. Lieutenant Commander "Jumpin' Joe" Clifton's fighter squadron was the first in Hawaii with the new F4U Corsair—a fast, versatile, bent-wing Vought design. The temporary assignment proved prophetic, for in the coming year *Enterprise* would receive her own bent-wing Corsairs—as night fighters.

By mid-July the promised six weeks had stretched to ten, but finally the training period was over. Captain Ginder ordered the crew to set the sea-keeping detail, single-up lines fore and aft, and finally to cast off. With her turbines thrumming, her four bronze screws churning the familiar waters, *Enterprise* exited the channel, came around to port, and navigator Oscar Pederson set course for "Uncle Sugar." Pederson was an old Pacific hand—he had commanded *Yorktown*'s air group at Coral Sea and Midway—and he knew the way home.

That course was approximately 045, northeast. Next stop: Bremerton, Washington.

Inevitably, the trip home involved gambling, however illicit. During the slow voyage to the West Coast, some Dauntless pilots had an extraordinary game under way with Ensign Leonard Robinson dealing. One night from home the game was draw poker, nothing wild, pot limit. As Robinson recalled it, he dealt the cards in the shortest poker game of World War II.

The player to Robinson's left held three kings; Dan Frissell and "Red" Hoogerwerf had six- and seven-high straights, Frank West held four nines, while "Bird Dog" Ramsey had two pair. Red Bird Burnett—a fearsome competitor in all things—was dealt the three, four, five, and seven of spades with a red six.

The bidding quickly got out of hand. The player to Robinson's left wound up with a full house, kings over eights. West, with four of a kind, stayed pat.

Came the crunch. At the end, with eight grand on the table, only West and Burnett remained in the pot. West still declined to draw, so it came down to Red Bird's next card. Time stopped in that tight steel space. Pulses pounded and perspiration dripped; lips were licked. Eight thousand dollars in 1943 was two years' income for many Americans. But in the Pacific it was different. Said Radioman Ron Graetz, "Money meant nothing to us out on the waters. What could we do with it? It was easy come, easy go."

Len Robinson flipped Burnett the last card. Red Bird turned it over . . .

Six of spades. A seven-high straight flush!

Robinson recalled West's reaction. "He tore up the cards, upset the table, scattered the chips, threw chairs, mouthed a number of special words. Needless to say, no more poker tonight. Maybe never for Frank."

Games were where you found them, including under the captain's nose.

For much of the war the chief master at arms was big, burly Chief B. H. Beams, essentially the ship's police chief. He was so large that it was said his initials stood for "Bulkhead," and that's how he was known. But he preferred persuasion to force, and rarely had to exercise his considerable brawn. He had been aboard since before Pearl Harbor and was well known to officers and men.

One day in 1944 Chief Beams entered the captain's office to find a blanket spread on the deck with a small poker game in progress, the skipper being absent. At that point Bulkhead faced an ethical dilemma: he could bust the miscreants for violating gambling regs, or he could pretend he hadn't seen what he saw.

But there was a third option. BH glanced around, made sure that no one else was within earshot, and asked, "What's the ante?"

A sailor replied, "Four bits, Chief."

BH lowered his bulk to the deck, reached into a pocket, anted up 50 cents, and bought into the game. According to a witness, "In almost no time he built up his earnings to $17,000!" (At 2010 rates, Beams's take amounted to more than $200,000.)

"And then, just as quickly, he lost every cent of it and out he went as happy as a lark." Widely respected and admired by the crew, Beams remained aboard until VJ Day.

BREMERTON AT LAST

Enterprise dropped anchor at Bremerton on July 20—the first time she had been stateside since September 1939. Changes immediately occurred.

John Crommelin, newly promoted to captain, transferred to the staff of an escort carrier division. More than any of her skippers, he left an indelible mark on *Enterprise* and her men. From that day on, no *Enterprise* sailor or aviator was beyond Uncle John's aid. Whatever his duty or location, time and again he reached down to help a former shipmate, whether he knew the man or not.

Air officer Tom Hamilton spoke for many in describing Crommelin as "a truly great officer." Hamilton said, "He had his own way of doing things which was sometimes hard to follow, because it might not be exactly standard with other carriers' operations. So we had to adjust them some, to operate the same way other carriers did. But we always felt that his legacies permitted us to do carrier operations a little better."

Crommelin was succeeded—nobody could replace him—by Commander Cecil Gill as exec. He proved competent if not lovable.

The air group also changed hands as Tommy Thomas rolled out, relieved by Commander Roscoe Newman, who took charge at Sand Point Naval Air Station, across the sound from Seattle. An easygoing Southerner, Newman would take the squadrons back to the Pacific for their second combat deployment.

While the crew and air group enjoyed leave, the ship remained at Puget Sound Navy Yard for much-needed repair and update. Over the next several weeks *Enterprise* teemed with sailors, yard workers, construction and repair crews, all working toward a top-to-bottom, stem-to-stem transformation.

When the air group returned aboard that fall, the Big E had been made over. Through 1942 she had been modified as limited time and resources permitted. But in 1943 her original configuration, though only five years old, needed more extensive upgrades. Those came from the Bureau of Ships and Bureau of Aeronautics, which had studied the sanguinary lessons of Midway and Guadalcanal. At Bremerton, with months in a stateside navy yard instead of several days or a few weeks at various war zone facilities, *Enterprise* received the long-delayed attention she needed to fight and survive against the growing Japanese air threat.

The most visible change was topside, where more antiaircraft guns were installed, along with more electronic antennae. New SK and SM height-finder radars sprouted from the island while the older SC-2 model provided backup air search.

Long gone were the troublesome 1.1-inch "Chicago piano" antiaircraft guns, replaced by the hard-hitting 40mms after Guadalcanal. Additional 20mm Oerlikons also sprouted around the flight deck. The ship now boasted six quad 40mm mounts and eight twin mounts, forty barrels in all. Bitter experience had shown that attacking aircraft needed to be engaged as far out as possible. Therefore, the 40s and five-inchers could be coupled to fire control radar for greater long-range accuracy.

The deck itself was expanded, emerging from the yard eighteen feet longer and five feet wider, affording more space for aircraft and handling gear. Other equipment included new fire pumps and more powerful aircraft catapults to accommodate new-generation aircraft.

The extra weight of the larger flight deck and three dozen more AA guns affected the ship's center of gravity, making her more susceptible to rolling motion, whether from high seas or abrupt maneuvers. Consequently, the Bureau of Ships recommended adding antitorpedo blisters along three quarters of the hull's length on both sides. The advantages were twofold: offsetting the extra topside weight, and providing underwater defense against the weapons that slew *Yorktown* and *Wasp* and contributed to the deaths of *Lexington* and *Hornet*.

When she floated out of dry dock, *Enterprise*'s full-load weight had grown from the original 25,484 tons to 32,060—a gain of more than 25 percent. But most of it was armor and muscle. If she was bigger and bulkier, she was also a tougher target—and more lethal.

She was also harder to see. The ship emerged from Bremerton with a new paint job called Measure 21, two shades of dark blue to reduce visibility from above. At sea level it tended to confuse observers as to her direction.

As the Big E evolved, so did the air group. Her squadrons would operate thirty-six new Hellcat fighters, thirty-seven Dauntlesses, and eighteen Avengers. The F6F Hellcat was successor to the F4F Wildcat: bigger, faster, and longer-ranged. Bearing a family resemblance to other kittens in the Grumman litter, the new cat's claws and fangs would make a strategic difference in the Pacific. Over the next two years, F6Fs were largely responsible for destroying enemy airpower, accounting for nearly as many Japanese planes downed as all Army fighters in the Pacific and China combined.

The greatest change in the air group occurred almost invisibly. Bill Martin, previously the scouts' skipper, took over the torpedo squadron when dedicated scout units were absorbed by the dive-bomber squadron. Quietly, efficiently, and almost evangelically, Martin began reshaping Torpedo 10 and eventually naval aviation.

Fond of singing about "Booger County" Missouri (where "it was a long and teedjus journey" to just about anywhere), William I. Martin was a big, capable officer out of the Annapolis class of '34. His middle name was Inman but colleagues said that "I" stood for "Instrument," reflecting his passion for nocturnal flight "on the gauges." As a junior officer he had written the first instrument flying manual for carrier aviators. That was an innovation, as at the time night flying was seldom done from carriers other than predawn launches because there was no doctrine for nocturnal missions, either offensive or defensive. But Martin saw the enormous potential in airborne radar, and resolved to exploit it.

Martin took the squadron from Seattle to Pasco, 250 miles inland, where better weather permitted more intensive training. He became the high priest of Navy night flying, having written his own scripture and imbuing his aircrews with the conviction of true believers.

Other personnel changes also would be felt, including the position of air officer. Stepping into the slot was Commander Tom Hamilton, who was equal to the challenge. Husky and jug-eared, Hamilton stood six-foot-one, a trim 185 pounds, mostly muscle. From the Annapolis class of '27, he had starred on the 1926 football team that was acclaimed national champion with a 9-0-1 record. The tie was against Army, 21–21, but time ran out when the crowd ran onto the field, preventing the final play with Navy on

Army's two-yard line. Subsequently Hamilton was best known as Navy's football coach, compiling a 19-8 record in the 1934 to 1936 seasons.

Hamilton had drawn the attention of Rear Admiral Arthur Radford, chief of naval aviation training in 1941. Radford charged the coach with developing a program for training physical conditioning instructors in preflight schools. But besides athletics, they kept their warrior eyes on the martial ball, recognizing that the Axis powers possessed "a cold-blooded will which pushes aside all rules to win."

Despite the effects of the Great Depression, Hamilton saw too many cadets as products of "a soft, luxurious, loose-thinking, lazy, peace-time life in our homes and schools, and must be prepared physically and mentally to meet and defeat pilots and personnel of our enemies who have been thoroughly trained in a purposeful and wartime physical and mental system for years; in fact, from childhood." While *Enterprise* aircrews of 1942 had proven themselves efficient warriors, the next crop of carrier fliers would largely be wartime-trained, drawn from a different manpower pool than those who flew at Midway and Guadalcanal. Radford's support of Hamilton's approach would pay long-term dividends.

On September 25, 1943, *Enterprise*'s keel again felt saltwater. An extraordinary amount of work had been accomplished in two months: she was practically a new ship. Sam Ginder eased her out of the navy yard into Puget Sound, where she tested her new equipment and began melding hundreds of new sailors into the institution called the Big E.

About 40 percent of the crew had turned over during the refit, but the *Enterprise* culture remained intact. As Hamilton recalled, "It was one of the most remarkable things that the old crew—and personnel was changing all the time—would pass on their know-how and their pride to the new crew members, and they would carry on in that same fashion." Thus passed October 1943, four weeks well spent integrating the veteran ship with its new sailors via the bonding cement of old hands still aboard.

On November 1 *Enterprise* recovered her airmen, the veteran Air Group 10. That morning Roscoe Newman's squadrons flew out from Sand Point, dropping into the racetrack pattern overhead the ship as the LSOs waved each pilot aboard. The time between landings frequently was more than the air department liked, but Hamilton's crew knew that intervals would tighten up as the old hands regained their finesse and new pilots gained experience. The salient point was that the U.S. Navy's most experienced carrier was reunited with its most experienced air group.

HAWAII AGAIN

Enterprise eased into her old berth at Pearl Harbor on November 6 while the air group settled into Puunene Naval Air Station on Maui. The next day the Big E got her seventh full-time captain as Sam Ginder turned over to Matthias Bennett Gardner. A scholar of Osborne Hardison's stripe, Gardner hailed from the Annapolis class of 1919. Chief Yeoman Bill Norberg described him as "a stern disciplinarian who had very little interchange with enlisted personnel other than in the line of duty. Like Captain Davis at Guadalcanal, he was very sure of himself and made good decisions."

Gardner was an accomplished aviator and a mission-oriented leader with extensive staff experience during the Guadalcanal campaign. The task force commander was Rear Admiral Arthur Radford, the administrative water walker who, with Tom Hamilton, had supervised the huge expansion of naval aviation training in 1941. He was destined to wear four stars.

While Roscoe Newman's Air Group 10 squadrons continued training ashore, they were relieved by Air Group Six with a new leader—the most famous aviator in the U.S. Navy.

Lieutenant Commander Edward H. O'Hare was a stocky twenty-nine-year-old Annapolis product who, in a blazing six minutes in February 1942, had become the Navy's first ace by defending the old *Lexington* off New Britain. Credited with five kills, he received the Medal of Honor but his demeanor changed not at all. Unfazed by his celebrity, he remained "Butch" to contemporaries and "Mr. O'Hare" to subordinates. Few leaders in naval aviation were so widely respected as O'Hare for his personal qualities and professionalism.

O'Hare was among friends: air officer Tom Hamilton had been an Annapolis football coach when O'Hare was a midshipman. A former Fighting Three squadron mate was Lieutenant Commander Robert W. Jackson in air plot; he would fit into O'Hare's plans for radar-controlled intercepts.

Shortly after taking over Air Group Six, O'Hare borrowed one of Lieutenant Commander John L. Phillips's Avengers. Phillips was no stranger to the Big E—he had been among the original Torpedo Six complement with brand-new Devastators when the air group formed in 1938. Some observers may have thought that the new commander was merely acquainting himself with the air group's equipment, but O'Hare had plans for the big, versatile Grummans. He intended to deny Japanese bombers the cover of darkness.

While *Enterprise* was inbound from Bremerton, O'Hare began building an interim team to implement his ambitious night flying program. Knowing that Air Group 10 would be ashore for a while, Butch arranged for Commander William A. Dean's Fighting Two to augment Air Group Six during the upcoming invasion of the Gilbert Islands.

In the few days available, O'Hare consulted with ship and task group planners, learning the Big E's role in the upcoming occupation of the Gilberts. Operation Galvanic marked the kickoff of the long awaited Central Pacific offensive, Admiral Nimitz's northern thrust through Japan's outer defensive perimeter in concert with General Douglas MacArthur's southern approach through New Guinea to the Philippines. *Enterprise*'s role in the Guadalcanal campaign had helped secure MacArthur's flank; now she was poised at the tip of Nimitz's spear with growing strength.

The Gilberts operation was an ambitious plan: simultaneous landings at Makin and Tarawa, two atolls some 100 miles apart and requiring separate carrier groups to support the amphibious forces. Gone were the days of single- and two-carrier task forces; now American industry, organization, and determination had forged naval-air forces of growing size and power. In all, eleven fast carriers were deployed in four task groups throughout the region, either bombing Japanese bases before the invasions or positioned to intercept enemy fleet units that might contest the landings. At long last, the Big E was no longer alone.

In the brief period available, *Enterprise*'s crew became accustomed to rubbing elbows with a living legend. In passageways, wardrooms, and mess facilities, officers and whitehats learned that Butch O'Hare was the real deal. He could draw a crowd just by walking past a group of sailors, but inevitably he greeted everyone, regardless of rank. He trailed morale in his wake like phosphorescence on a nocturnal sea.

On November 10, less than a month after assuming command, O'Hare watched Air Group Six (including Fighting Squadron 2) rendezvous with *Enterprise*. Seventy-one fighters, bombers, and torpedo planes wheeled overhead, arrayed by sections, divisions, and squadrons. With ample sea room offshore, Matt Gardner pointed the Big E into the wind as the landing signal officer picked up each homing pilot in turn.

Perched in "vulture's row" on the port side of the island, O'Hare noted his pet Hellcat enter the pattern. Bearing the group commander's traditional 00 side number, it was flown by a self-conscious youngster, Lieutenant (jg) John F. McCloskey. He was so self-conscious that his first two passes at the deck resulted in wave-offs.

In carrier aviation, at least half of a pilot's reputation is composed of his landing grades. The ready room atmosphere is an unrelenting pressure cooker where any lapse or perceived weakness is seized upon and mercilessly examined until the next unfortunate draws the pack's attention. The LSO gave McCloskey the "cut" on his third attempt, and with earnest gratitude the pilot felt the sudden stop of an arrested landing as he was tossed forward against his shoulder harness. Turning over "Zero Zero" to the flight deck crew, he descended to the fighter ready room, knowing exactly what awaited him.

Minutes later another Hellcat banged down hard and bounced into the port catwalk. The drop tank was crushed, spewing high-octane fuel onto the flight deck, where the gas ignited from the engine exhaust. In seconds the F6F was afire. As Ensign Byron Johnson struggled to escape the cockpit, men watched incredulously as a lone khaki figure sprinted to the burning fighter and climbed on the wing. While the "hot poppas" in their asbestos suits sprayed foam on the blazing engine area, Lieutenant Walter L. Chewning ignored the searing heat to help Johnson out of the cockpit. Chewning's first day as catapult officer with the new air group aboard provided an unforgettable introduction to the Big E.

While the squadrons exercised that afternoon, further planning for Galvanic proceeded. The task force commander was well known to *Enterprise,* as Rear Admiral Charles Pownall had overall command of the four task groups with eleven carriers. He was the same Baldy of prewar days, finally shed of Genial John Hoover.

Under Radford, *Enterprise* was teamed with two new Independence class light carriers, *Belleau Wood* and *Monterey.* All groups would coordinate their movements, aimed at Dog Day, November 20, when the Second Marine Division would assault Tarawa Atoll.

Seizure of Makin Atoll preceded the larger event at Tarawa. As one of a handful of combat-experienced aviators aboard—let alone a Medal of Honor ace—O'Hare exhorted his junior officers with some ready room pep talks. But he also offered one-on-one advice to new "nuggets" understandably concerned about impending combat. He told a Fighting Two pilot, "There isn't a Jap plane made that I can't shoot down. This F6F you're flying is better than anything they've got. So you can't lose! Go in there and knock 'em out of the sky."

Certainly the tonnage assembled off the Gilberts inspired confidence. Six fast carriers and three new battleships represented an enormous amount of sea power in 1943, and that's what bore down upon the islands on November 18, two days before the landings. But however much the Japanese were impressed, they stood up to the Americans. That night a dozen land-based Betty bombers lifted into the darkness, seeking the intruders, and five never returned. The Americans got away clean.

AT WAR ONCE MORE

Reveille on the 19th—D minus one—announced the first battle dawn for the new air group. With blue flames flashing from engine exhausts, four Dauntlesses were catapulted off, making room for conventional takeoffs by other aircraft, turning up with propellers churning the darkened air, awaiting an unwary sailor. Next the first Hellcats launched as O'Hare led his wingman, Ensign Andrew Skon, into the air. In twenty-eight minutes Walt Chewning's practiced flight deck crew had thirty-four planes airborne.

The Big E was back.

Beneath a crescent moon, O'Hare led his two squadrons westward to the target. Thirty-three tricolored airplanes prepared to pounce on Makin Atoll as sunlight peaked the eastern horizon.

During the run-in, automatic gunfire sparked upward, rising through the dawn toward the Big E's airmen. Butch O'Hare, the astute old pro, timed his fighters' runs to beat down the inevitable antiaircraft fire for the bombers. He led his division low, recovering from a screeching dive at only 300 feet, ensuring that most of his .50 caliber ammunition went where it belonged. Bill Dean's fourteen planes followed, raining expended cartridge cases on the radio station, King's Wharf, and the surrounding gun pits. Pilots in action for the first time realized with a rush: "I'm in combat!" Later, with the studied casualness that comes with experience, they would claim membership in a global brotherhood: the Loyal and Fraternal Order of Them What Have Been Shot At.

Lieutenant Ike Hampton's Dauntlesses were close behind O'Hare's Hellcats. The dive-bomber crews saw no ground fire coming their way as they dropped their ordnance from 2,000 feet. But there were glitches in the play: three bombers were unable to release their half-tonners, an unsatisfactory development for *Enterprise*'s experienced ordnancemen.

Throughout the day the Big E launched successive strikes, the second deckload featuring Lieutenant Commander Phillips's Avenger torpedo bombers. During the approach one of the escort fighters noticed a float biplane that could only be made in Japan. The plucky enemy aviator turned to close on the bombers, matching his ungainly "Dave" against the Torpedo Six formation. It was an execution more than a combat: Hellcat pilot Lieutenant Leroy Harris—the same Tex formerly of Flatley's Grim Reapers—notched his third kill of the war.

O'Hare led the fourth mission of the day, and afterward he settled down with a cup of coffee to assess results. Though three planes had been written off, there were no combat losses in five missions.

D-Day at Makin came dreadfully early: 2:30 A.M. on November 20. It bespoke a long day of operations conducted extremely close to shore, as the task force drew within fifty statute miles. Barely two hours later—well before sunup—*Enterprise* sent off her first launch of thirty-five strike aircraft plus the usual fighter patrol.

O'Hare was bedeviled by man and nature, as the ship's actual launch position was sixty miles in error, and darkness compounded the problem. He arrived over Makin with just Andy Skon clinging to his wing to escort seventeen bombers. Eventually three more planes—one each Hellcat, Dauntless, and Avenger—rendezvoused with O'Hare, who descended to strafe ahead of the bombers. In the growing light the pilots saw the amphibious force offshore, then focused on their targets.

The bombers deposited their ordnance around the main wharf. A Dauntless went down with the crew recovered, as the other pilots earned their flight pay that morning. When Rear Admiral Richmond Kelly Turner's troops secured the island, they reported about forty Japanese killed in the defending trenches as well as the garrison commander.

Entirely unlike the bloody battle at Tarawa, Makin was almost convivial. Later that day, Torpedo Six skipper John Phillips checked in with the air coordinator allocating targets to each squadron. Probably thinking of topless island women from *National Geographic,* the coordinator radioed, "If you see any nice females down there, save me one."

Phillips took up the spirit of the occasion. In his Virginia drawl he commented, "It looks like all the girls have skivvy shirts on." The coordinator commiserated, "That's too bad." Eventually somebody with command authority in his voice cut in, requiring an end to nonregulation chatter.

The U.S. Army's 27th Division secured Makin on the 24th, suffering sixty-six dead whereas only five of the 400-man Japanese garrison surrendered. But it was a different situation at sea. Supporting the Tarawa landing, the light carrier *Independence* was torpedoed in a dusk air attack on the 20th, forcing her out of the lineup for eight months. Four nights later the escort carrier *Liscome Bay* was sunk by a Japanese submarine nearly fifty miles southwest of Makin, killing nearly two thirds of the crew.

Among the survivors was John Crommelin, who had left the Big E in September. His boss, Rear Admiral Henry Mullinix, was lost with 643 other men. Crommelin barely survived—he swam away from the shattered carrier and was pulled from the water, burned but able to return to duty. Meanwhile, his brother Charles continued the family's war against Japan, leading the new carrier *Yorktown*'s air group.

SHOTS IN THE DARK

The successful Japanese torpedo attack on the *Independence* and other nocturnal missions only reinforced O'Hare's support for carrier-based night fighters. It was painfully clear that not even radar-controlled antiaircraft guns could repel a determined night attack. The defenders had to engage the raiders farther out, and that meant fighters.

Supported by Rear Admiral Radford and Captain Gardner, O'Hare had consulted with air officer Tom Hamilton to produce the "bat team" concept. Lacking radar in his fighters—a concept racing toward fruition on the U.S. East Coast—O'Hare mated Hellcats to Avengers equipped with air search radar. The Avenger would locate Japanese bombers and, if necessary, guide the Hellcats to the intercept. It was a rudimentary procedure but it held promise.

Coordinating the bat team operation would be the Big E's fighter director, Lieutenant (jg) George P. Givens. Highly experienced, he learned his trade at Midway and the Guadalcanal battles, and had earned the signal accolade of the confidence of Fighting 10's first skipper, Jimmy Flatley.

Fitted with bomb bay fuel tanks, Phillips's Avengers could remain aloft more than eight hours, avoiding the time and trouble of landing aboard at night. His radar operator was a twenty-five-year-old electronics wizard, Lieutenant (jg) Hazen B. Rand. Five years younger was the turret gunner, Ordnanceman Alvin B. Kernan, who had served aboard *Enterprise* from late 1941 and awaited his turn at pilot training.

A second Avenger joined O'Hare's lineup, flown by Lieutenant John McInerny, teamed with Fighting Two skipper Bill Dean and wingman Lieutenant Roy "Butch" Voris in their Hellcats.

O'Hare recognized that he needn't wait for an air attack to develop. If one or both Avengers could intercept the snoopers that preceded each Japanese strike group, an attack might be averted. Therefore, the night-blind

Helicats were reserved for repelling bombers approaching the task group—a worst-case scenario.

O'Hare's bat team went to work the night of the 20th, standing watch in case their esoteric services were needed. No enemy aircraft approached close enough to justify catapulting the Avengers off the Big E until early morning of the 24th, and even that proved unnecessary. The airborne flight crews saw a garish gout of yellow-red in the distance, unaware that the *Liscome Bay* had blown up. The closest call was John McInerny's, sweating out the mission with erratic engine performance. He wheezed into the traffic pattern and got the LSO's "cut" signal with perhaps five gallons of fuel remaining. The rest of the bat team followed an hour later when the ship recovered the dawn fighter patrol. It had been a tantalizing, frustrating six-hour mission.

So it went: a nightly cat-and-mouse game played in three dimensions as Bettys probed the task force defenses. On the 24th one snooper over-flew the *Belleau Wood* at perhaps 500 feet; sailors on deck clearly saw the bomber's exhausts and heard the rumbling twin engines. Though the Japanese dropped flares, they never spotted their prey. The perfect discipline of American naval gunners that night stood in steely contrast to the spastic chaos when *Enterprise* pilots flew into Pearl on December 7.

"Tojo the lamplighter" was active again the next night, dropping flares. Two groups tried to bracket the task force but Radford kept turning away, showing his stern to the interlopers, who lost a bomber to a terrific AA barrage from the battleship *North Carolina*. The Bettys came and went too fast for *Enterprise* to launch a bat team, and the Japanese motored back to Maloelap Atoll in the Marshalls, gleefully claiming three American carriers sunk. The enemy must have marveled at the Yankees' inexhaustible supply of capital ships, for there were always more carriers, battleships, and cruisers to replace those reported sent to the bottom.

The next chance came the following evening, the 26th. *Belleau Wood* Hellcats dealt with some pesky snoopers late that afternoon: a sign that a night attack was likely. *Enterprise*'s night fliers were trying to eat when the call came to man aircraft. O'Hare dashed topside still grasping a sandwich. An old salt, he knew the conventional wisdom about never passing up a chance to eat or sleep.

With her bow into the wind, *Enterprise* launched Bat Team One: Phillips's Avenger with O'Hare and Skon. They lifted off at 6:00 P.M. and flew into legend.

Almost immediately the fighter director gave the team a vector for another snooper, a move that Arthur Radford rescinded, concerned that the Hellcats could not find the Avenger when full dark settled.

Beneath a 1,500-foot cloud base on a moonless night, the three airborne pilots had their hands full. Just flying straight and level under those conditions challenged many airmen, but O'Hare, Skon, and Phillips had to keep track of each other and watch for the enemy as well. Strapped into their cockpits, instrument lights dimmed or switched off, they droned through the oceanic vastness, relying on radio and radar for salvation.

Chasing radar vectors, O'Hare and Skon remained within sight of Phillips for a while but his Avenger couldn't keep up with the Hellcats. Ironically, it didn't matter. In the back of the TBF, Hazen Rand expertly deciphered the esoteric data rendered in green phosphors, coaching his pilot onto a heading for some of the fifteen Bettys hunting the task force.

After an hour aloft, Phillips noted burning patches on the water—float lights providing a datum line that the Japanese mission commander could use to guide his pilots onto the American ships. When any Bettys closed the range, a torrent of AA fire erupted from the task force. Sailors gawked at the light show as large- and small-caliber flak leapt into the dark void, sparking red, orange, and white. Some of it connected; one Betty splashed. Meanwhile, *Enterprise* and her teammates kept maneuvering to confound the enemy's tracking and prevent a broadside aspect that would invite a torpedo attack.

But the Japanese were persistent. Aided by the Big E's radar crew, Rand got the contacts he needed and brought Phillips in behind some Bettys. The distance closed: from three miles to two to one. At that point the torpedo skipper called, "I have them in sight." He announced he was attacking.

A flaming aircraft strobed in the darkness, then another five minutes later, and some men assumed O'Hare had just added to his tally. In truth both kills belonged to Avenger pilot John Phillips, though the Bettys went down fighting. Rand took a grazing hit to one foot, and the incendiary round started a small fire in the radioman's compartment, which he smothered with a blanket.

Meanwhile, radar plot tried to put O'Hare back on the Avenger's wing. Phillips flashed his running lights to help with a rendezvous. Looking aft from his turret, Kernan counted one, two . . . *three* aircraft approaching. His adrenaline spiked. With Phillips and the fighter director both screaming for the gunner to open fire, Kernan placed his illuminated sight reticle above the nearest Hellcat and tripped the trigger. At that moment the enemy nose gunner began shooting from about 200 yards. Then it was over. Kernan's target swung away from the formation, disappearing to starboard.

Standing in the Big E's radar room, Tom Hamilton listened to the terse, arcane chatter. He thought he heard O'Hare say, "Oh, I'm hit." Almost immediately word flashed out: O'Hare was in the water, nearly thirty miles southwest of *Enterprise.*

"I called to Butch to keep talking so we could get bearings on him, but he didn't answer," Hamilton recalled. "We searched for a couple of days and never did find him. That's a sad, sad story."

The beloved Butch was gone. For decades speculation ran toward the theory that Alvin Kernan's burst at a ghosting target had downed the ace, but that remained speculation. Far more likely, O'Hare had passed below and ahead of a Betty, and the nose gunner loosed an optimistic fusillade that connected.

Butch O'Hare's death affected *Enterprise* as few losses ever did. The crew felt that it had lost more than a leader—it had lost a friend and mentor, someone who understood the men, and appreciated sailors as much as pilots and aircrew.

Then, having absorbed the loss and measured its depth, the Big E shrugged if off and got back to work. It was the best way to honor the legacy that Butch had bequeathed—and it was war.

While the *Enterprise* with Air Group Six supported the Gilberts-Marshalls operations, Air Group 10 relished the training time in Hawaii. Recalled Jig Dog Ramage, "The fighters were over at Kahului, and the bombers and torpedo planes were at Puunene. It was just ideal. You could take off with a load of anything you wanted; you could bomb, strafe, you could fly at night, you could do anything. There was all the sea room in the world. There was just nothing you couldn't do."

Bill Martin worked his torpedo crews hard, especially by flying a lot of hours after dark. He explained, "We took off many times in the rain and into squalls . . . but no flights were canceled while we were at Maui. A 4.0 movie wouldn't cancel it!"

The squadrons flew "group gropes" duplicating a deckload strike with a dozen Dauntlesses, six Avengers, and twelve to sixteen Hellcats. Jig Ramage explained, "The low escort fighters would start in to the target just before the bombers went in. The bombers would then go in, and the torpedo planes simultaneously would pull out to either side and do a spiral and come on in low for their torpedo attack or from about 5,000 feet if they were going to drop bombs. We could get the full strike group on and off the target in less than two minutes. It was quite a devastating shot."

Unlike most units, Air Group 10 performed "night bounce drill" over the holidays, most pilots logging two nocturnal carrier landings. It wasn't much, but it was far more than most aviators received at the time. The long-term dividend on that investment would be paid in the Central Pacific six months later.

Any carrier existed to support its air group, but some individuals kept the ship afloat by the emotional buoyancy called morale. In the *Enterprise,* nobody contributed more than Ensign Gerald J. Flynn, who arrived in May 1943.

An elfin reservist, Jerry Flynn was 130 pounds of Irish spirit. In the Lookout Division he was responsible for lookouts, but that was merely for starters. In almost no time he became "the most visible person on the ship." He was a natural morale officer: he'd been head cheerleader at Notre Dame. Talk about the Fighting Irish: Flynn's father had fled the auld sod after a colorful affiliation with the IRA. Despite Jerry's five-foot-seven stature, he coached the ship's basketball team and found time to run the radio station, with an evening "gossip column" laced with his own brand of irreverent Hibernian humor.

Thus modified structurally, modified organizationally, and fortified spiritually, the *Enterprise* faced a new year at war.

8

★　★　★

"If Any of Them Lived, It Wasn't Our Fault"

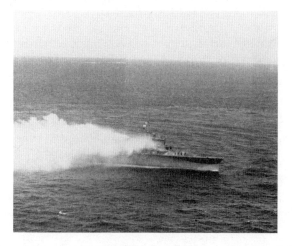

A Japanese destroyer, probably the 1,100-ton *Wakatake,* under attack by *Enterprise* aircraft off Palau on March 30, 1944. (National Museum of Naval Aviation)

January 1944 began *Enterprise*'s third year at war, and that month she was reunited with old friends.

Commander Roscoe Newman had shaped up Air Group 10 during the time in Hawaii, and his three squadrons were primed for whatever awaited the ship. But before deploying, the air group also absorbed a remarkable cadre of aviators and support personnel: a specially trained night fighter unit.

Night fighters were well established in Britain and Germany, as Europe's nocturnal skies thrummed and blazed with bombers and fighters playing a lethal three-dimensional game of blind man's bluff. But the huge majority of RAF and Luftwaffe night stalkers were twin-engine fighters with two- or three-man crews to split the duties of flying and operating radar. Carrier-based night fighters did not have that luxury; they were modified single-engine, single-seat naval aircraft.

U.S. Navy night fighters had made immense progress since the efforts that cost Butch O'Hare two months before. Each large carrier now had a detachment of dedicated night fliers—radar-equipped Grumman Hellcats or Vought Corsairs with the performance of single-seat fighters rather than the bulky Avengers that Commander John Phillips had teamed with O'Hare's Hellcats.

Enterprise's night owls belonged to Lieutenant Commander Richard E. Harmer's Night Fighting Squadron 101, with five pilots flying four F4U-2 Corsairs maintained by a few electronics experts. Operating Corsairs off carriers was remarkable enough in daytime, given the Corsair's man-killer reputation. Notoriously difficult to land aboard ship, the F4U-2 had been beached by the Navy and mostly given to land-based Marine squadrons.

Harmer's aircraft were modified with a bulbous radar housing on the starboard wing, and one gun was removed to make room for the electronics. Nobody had routinely flown night fighters from carriers, and some doubted that it could be done. "Chick" Harmer thought otherwise.

A FAST CARRIER FORCE

In January the Pacific Fleet established the Fast Carrier Task Force with flattops capable of more than thirty knots. It was the most powerful, mobile, and longest-ranged striking arm yet assembled. When assigned to Admiral Raymond Spruance's Fifth Fleet the fast carriers operated as Vice Admiral Marc Mitscher's Task Force 58. The Big E knew both admirals from the days of two-carrier task groups. Spruance had ridden her to victory at Midway when Mitscher commanded *Hornet*.

Enterprise became the flagship of Rear Admiral John W. Reeves's Task Group 58.1, teamed with the Essex class carrier *Yorktown*, named for *Enterprise*'s late sister, plus the light carrier *Belleau Wood*. The other three groups were similarly composed, with the entire force comprising six big-deck carriers and six light carriers escorted by two battleships, seven cruisers, and thirty-five destroyers. Nothing remotely comparable existed anywhere else. (That month the British Royal Navy had four fast carriers; Japan had three, plus six light carriers capable of less than thirty knots.)

The Big E got to know Admiral Reeves in all his moods. His nickname, "Black Jack," was not due to any acumen at cards. Tough, demanding, and often abrasive, he was nevertheless experienced and capable. Combined with the often distant, sometimes edgy Captain Matt Gardner, Reeves's tenure in the ship was not regarded as a high point by many aviators and sailors. Gardner had little contact with enlisted men beyond what was required in the line of duty.

Fortunately, the *Enterprise* corporate mystique always came through. One of the linchpins in early 1944 was air officer Tom Hamilton. Bombing 10's Jig Dog Ramage said of him, "Tom Hamilton was very close to the pilots like John Crommelin was. Captain Gardner wasn't at all. . . . He really didn't do anything. On the other hand, Tom Hamilton was always around."

The Big E was not about to concede anything to the new-generation ships. As Hamilton explained, "If the Essex class carriers which were bigger, could carry more planes, the *Enterprise* was determined to carry the same number of planes. This necessitated . . . developing the catapulting of planes for the initial launch. The Big E did not have the side deck elevators nor did we have the space that the Essex class carriers had."

Hamilton also acknowledged the ship's depth of talent. "We had a great group of officers," he recalled. "Walt Chewning was in charge of our catapults and arresting gear, and I think he was mostly responsible for developing the technique that we had in catapulting the early planes of our launches. Since then, catapulting has become standard in all the carriers, but *Enterprise* made the first widespread use of it."

Task Force 58 departed Pearl on January 22, supporting Operation Flintlock, the seizure of the Marshall Islands. The primary objectives were Kwajalein and Eniwetok atolls, ideal bases to support further American offensives through the Central Pacific. Kwajalein was especially valuable—with the world's largest lagoon it would be a magnificent fleet anchorage.

The first mission was almost old-home week for the Big E, revisiting Taroa in Maloelap Atoll where the lone *Enterprise* had logged her first offensive operation of the war that long-ago February of 1942. After the November 1943 conquests in the nearby Gilberts, the Marshalls represented the next coral stepping-stone toward Japan itself, 2,500 miles to the northwest.

Barely a dozen of the pilots on board had been shot at; Bill Martin was the only one in Torpedo 10. But as the ships ran in toward the target, the Japanese were only a remote concern. Amid darkness and worsening weather, air group commander Roscoe Newman was first off the catapult in his radar-equipped Avenger, available to help the new pilots form up beneath low, leaden clouds. On deck, plane handlers coped with the blackout and a pelting rain, seeking traction in leather-soled shoes on drenched wood spotted with hydraulic fluid and engine oil. Nevertheless, they cycled each aircraft into the prescribed launch sequence.

Of eighteen Hellcat fighters launched against Taroa that morning, two disappeared. The fate of Lieutenant (jg) Ed Tolin and Ensign Billy Steward remained unknown, but probably they succumbed to vertigo and flew into the water. When the weather clamped down behind the fighters, with almost zero ceiling and visibility, there was no choice but to suspend launch operations. The Hellcats proceeded, often singly or in pairs, while the bombers and torpedo planes awaited better conditions.

In the dark and gloom, few of fighter skipper Killer Kane's Grim Reapers could identify Taroa Island, let alone their briefed targets. But two pilots had the priceless asset of luck. Lieutenant Rod Devine, a lanky flier from Walla Walla, Washington, broke out of the clouds at 8,000 feet with his wingman, Ensign Jim Kay. They gawked at the spectacle presented to them: four Zeke fighters (previously called Zeros) on a reciprocal heading 1,000 feet below. Everybody saw everyone else at the same time, and the fight was on.

In the next several seconds Devine dived onto the tail of the nearest Zeke, triggered three bursts, and saw the Japanese gush flames and swerve into the water. Before the other Japanese could reach the clouds, Kay drew a bead on one and fired. Hits sparkled around the cockpit and engine before he lost sight of it, claiming a probable kill.

A new pilot, Louisianan Lieutenant (jg) Edwin Reulet, tangled with two opponents. He met the first one head-on, swapping gunfire nose to nose, and flamed it at close range. Next he pounced on a Zeke crossing his gun sight, applied the proper deflection, and fired. Armor-piercing and incendiary rounds lit up the fuselage, sending the fighter down almost immediately.

Nearby, second-tour aviator Don Gordon also found aerial targets. Intending to strafe the big airfield, he came across several Zekes below him. With his wingman watching his tail, Flash Gordon dived on a vulnerable Japanese and held down his trigger for an extra-long five-second burst. He fired at least 400 .50 caliber rounds—one sixth of his ammunition—and was gratified with the result. The Zeke rolled inverted and crashed into the water offshore, Gordon's third victory of the war.

With Japanese fighters downed or dispersed, the Big E's Hellcats proceeded to beat up the defenses. Antiaircraft positions were identified in the growing light, and subjected to low-level strafing that killed or dissuaded the gun crews. By the time the bombers rolled in, there was little flak, none effective.

Air Group 10's Avengers and Dauntlesses arrived with squadrons from *Yorktown* and *Belleau Wood*. At the head of fourteen Torpedo 10 planes, Bill Martin opened his bomb bay doors and slanted into a dive. His aim was excellent as his eleven bombs slammed across a valuable target—Taroa's fuel and ammunition storage. His ordnance erupted in vivid orange-yellow gouts, touching off a memorable string of secondary explosions that engulfed the area. The other bomber pilots went for parked aircraft, runway intersections, hangars, and workshops—anything that looked worth wrecking.

So it went throughout the day: a long cycle of launches and recoveries. But early that evening, with only the combat air patrol still airborne, radar operators reported unknown aircraft inbound. Sailors topside looked in the direction of the increasing flak as nine planes came out of the lowering sun. The Hellcats pounced as Lieutenant Bud Schumann's pilots identified the strangers as twin-engine, twin-tail Nell bombers—the same type that nearly hit the Big E in those same waters in 1942.

One bomber gushed flame and crashed into the waves about ten miles out. Some shipboard gunners yelped in glee at the sight. Then the loudspeakers blared, "Cease fire!" It made no sense—the other intruders were still flying.

Gradually the awful reality became known: the bombers were U.S. Army B-25s, arriving unannounced. One man was lost from the downed plane, based on Tarawa some 600 miles away. Investigation revealed that the Army fliers were keeping low to evade enemy radar while attacking shipping. Admiral Mitscher expressed the Navy's regret but noted—properly—that without information of the B-25s' presence, his pilots and gunners could only assume they were hostile.

Two days later, American assault troops splashed ashore on Kwajalein Atoll and Roi-Namur, seizing both in less than a week. Meanwhile, the fast carriers continued flying strikes and patrols, keeping the pressure on the Japanese. In all, the Big E lost four Hellcats and three pilots, but Air Group 10's new pilots and aircrewmen had justified the confidence Roscoe Newman showed in them.

For the next operation, confidence would come at a premium.

MIGHTY TRUK

Before the war, hardly anyone had heard of Truk Atoll in the Caroline Islands, 1,000 miles west of Kwajalein. Even the name was widely mispronounced: "Truck" rather than "Trook." But the Japanese touted Truk as "the Gibraltar of the Pacific," and some Americans regarded it as the emperor's Pearl Harbor. In any case, Truk was the Imperial Navy's most important base beyond the home islands, and eventually the fast carriers would have to tackle it.

Previously a German possession, the Carolines had been ceded to Japan after the Great War. Over the previous two decades precious little light had escaped the Japanese security blanket, but in 1943 the Americans got occasional peeks beneath the shroud. Long-range PB4Y Liberator bombers had snooped Truk on occasion. Based on their partial photo coverage and considerable electronic eavesdropping, Vice Admiral Mitscher's fast carriers pointed for Truk in mid-February.

As usual, intelligence was incomplete. During briefings en route to the launch point, *Enterprise* aviators were told that Truk's airfields hosted about 185 planes. The actual number was twice that figure, including reinforcements bound for the Solomons.

Enterprise's lineup was the same team under new management. Air group commander Roscoe Newman was elevated to Admiral Reeves's staff, with the intent that fighter skipper Killer Kane would relieve Tom Hamilton as air officer. But the Killer steadfastly refused—not what was expected of well-behaved Annapolis graduates. Kane was determined to keep flying and shooting—some said because he had been the duty officer at Pearl Harbor Naval Air Station on December 7. Whatever the reason, he got his way. He became air group commander just before the Truk operation, though Fighting 10 hardly knew the difference. Bud Schumann officially became the squadron skipper but to the pilots Killer Kane remained "Reaper One."

The other change involved Torpedo 10. More than two weeks earlier, Bill Martin had broken his left elbow in a freak accident, and though he tried to prove he could function in the cockpit, the staff remained skeptical, including the flight surgeon. But nobody wanted to be the one to say Bill Martin couldn't lead his squadron on its most important mission yet. The decision was kicked upstairs—literally—where Captain Gardner sat on the bridge. He absorbed the information, noted the pleading in Martin's brown eyes, and thought for a few seconds. Then he said, "No." Torpedo 10 would hit Truk without the skipper.

Two hours before dawn on February 16 the first fighter sweep departed five flight decks—seventy Hellcats including a dozen from *Enterprise*'s

Fighting 10. Hungry and eager, Killer Kane led his Reapers into one of the most spectacular dogfights of the Pacific war.

The low sun on morning clouds produced an unforgettable panorama as aircraft turned, dived, fired, and flamed. Parachutes blossomed in the lightening sky—nearly all of them made in Japan. One squadron commander called it "a Hollywood war." In the opening minutes of the dawn combat, Kane downed three Zekes and his wingman, Lieutenant (jg) Vern Ude, got two more, then dropped down to strafe parked aircraft.

Other Reapers were just as busy. Lieutenant (jg) Walter Harman claimed two Zekes and a "Rufe" floatplane fighter. "Frenchy" Reulet, who had downed two planes at Kwajalein, claimed three Zekes to become the squadron's first ace of the second cruise.

But it wasn't entirely one-sided. Though the nearly fifty Japanese fighters were outnumbered, some were flown by experts. The section of Lieutenant Jack Farley and Ensign Linton Cox sparred indecisively with some Zekes, then Farley sighted a Rufe. He shot it down but lost contact with Cox, who apparently fell victim to one of the Zekes. Then Farley was hit by an unseen assailant, taking a 20mm shell in his cockpit. Despite wounds to his left arm and leg, he decided to use his remaining ammunition in strafing. He caught another Zeke taking off, dropped it into the lagoon, and set course for the Big E.

Besides Cox, three other Hellcats failed to return to the task force, but air superiority now belonged to the Americans. The Reapers claimed thirty kills during the day, topping the claims under Jimmy Flatley at Santa Cruz fifteen months before. With air superiority assured, successive strikes were launched, producing perhaps the biggest haul of Japanese shipping of the war. It far exceeded the scourging of the enemy transports at Guadalcanal.

That afternoon Jig Dog Ramage led a bombing attack on Japanese ships. Looking down from his Dauntless, seeing thousands of tons of vessels either sinking or sunk, he reflected, "It was a good day to remember Pearl Harbor, because it was the first time that we'd really gotten an opportunity to get at their ships."

One of the vessels in the lagoon drew attention by its size. She was *Tenno Maru,* a 6,000-tonner seized from the Dutch for use as a hospital ship. She was marked as a noncombatant but her two escorts—the size of patrol craft—were fair game. With bombs expended, the outbound Dauntlesses attacked with the pilots' forward-firing .50 calibers. The effect on the escorts' thin hulls was devastating, and both began sinking.

Jig Dog Ramage was raised a Christian in Iowa but he had no problem with slaying Japanese who could swim to shore. Years later he said, "They had a lot of people in the water, life boats, rafts, people in life jackets. But most of our .50s were out of ammo by that time, so I put my SBDs into a circle at about 100 feet and let the rear gunners kill the rest of them. I don't know how many there were in the water, but if any of them lived, it wasn't our fault."

SEIZING THE NIGHT

That night *Enterprise* hit Truk again, expanding the realm of carrier aviation beyond anything previously attempted.

Based on marginal torpedo performance at Guadalcanal, Torpedo 10 favored bombing. The Buzzard Brigade found that very few Mark 13s would run "hot, straight, and normal." Of the squadron's first six torpedoes dropped in combat during 1944, two ran wild in circles, one "with its head above water like a wild hippopotamus." Two others hooked at least 300 yards and missed, and two apparently were dud hits. "We definitely saw one bounce," Bill Martin insisted.

The squadron experimented with various combinations of speed and altitude for bombing, settling on 180 knots (205 mph) at 250 feet. As Martin explained, "When the target disappeared under your nose, you counted 'one alligator two' before releasing, and you'd hit the hull almost every time."

Frustrated and proud, Martin watched twelve of his Avengers flung off *Enterprise* that night. They formed up behind his exec, Lieutenant Van V. Eason, and headed into the quarter-moon darkness at 500 feet, 100 miles out. Each plane carried four 500-pound bombs.

Riding with Eason, radar officer Lieutenant William B. Chace occupied "the cheap seats" in the bomber's belly. As he described the position, "The tunnel did not provide much comfort. It was a noisy, enclosed capsule with very limited visibility. After days of intensive combat, it became encrusted with and smelled of engine oil and transmission fluids. There was no physical access to the cockpit, therefore it could produce a discouraging claustrophobia for the uninitiated."

Nevertheless, Chace saw the atoll on his scope from twenty-two miles. The formation broke into two divisions, Eason taking his five planes to the northeast while Lieutenant Russell "Kip" Kippen led seven to the northwest. As the range closed, the best radar operators could detect ships anchored close to shore.

However, small islets dotting the two anchorages posed problems, as ships could blend with the ground return. But aided by the partial moon, aircrews identified vessels alongside the islets, selected their targets, and turned in to attack. The bombers were briefed to depart from their two starting points at one-minute intervals, avoiding congestion over the target.

For more than twenty minutes Torpedo 10 hunted carefully, patiently through the tropic darkness. Several Japanese gun crews hosed off optimistic bursts at engine noise or dim shapes ghosting through the night sky, but seldom came close until a plane had overflown its target. Usually dropping two bombs per pass, the pilots remembered their skipper's "one alligator two" mantra, thumbed the release button, and began hitting ships with astonishing regularity.

Torpedo 10's unrivaled character was Lieutenant (jg) Charles English Henderson III, who had joined the squadron after Guadalcanal. Fun-loving, irreverent, and lethal, the Marylander made four runs, dropping one bomb each time. His two crewmen observed two hits and a near miss.

The twelve Avengers made twenty-five passes, claiming thirteen hits and seven near misses, with five misses or results unobserved.

Eleven planes came home, including Eason's and another shot up by flak. The missing crew was that of Lieutenant (jg) Lloyd Nicholas, probably shot down pressing an attack.

The next day aerial reconnaissance brought proof of Martin's concept. Eight ships (including two precious tankers) were assessed sunk or destroyed and five were damaged by bomb blast. Twelve bombers had scored thirteen hits, at night, with one loss. Martin noted that typically a daylight bombing attack would yield fewer hits with equal or greater losses.

Admiral Raymond Spruance allowed his surface ships to sink or finish off a few of the Japanese vessels, but overall the operation was a triumph for carrier airpower. The two-day operation sank thirty-one merchantmen, two light cruisers, four destroyers, and four auxiliaries.

For its role in smashing Truk, Air Group 10 lost six fliers and four planes—light casualties by some reckonings, but each empty chair in the ready room bespoke an emptiness that some men would suppress for decades, and some would never replace.

NIGHT STALKERS

While Torpedo 10 demonstrated what night bombing could achieve, Chick Harmer's night fighter pilots fretted at the few chances to prove themselves.

A carrier's daily air plan often involved fifteen hours of flight operations, typically from 4:30 A.M. to 7:30 P.M. By sundown, flight deck crews were exhausted from pushing airplanes, launching and recovering aircraft, and manhandling ordnance.

If night fighters were launched, the deck crew had to push perhaps thirty aircraft forward to clear the landing area. After the night fliers returned, those same planes had to be moved aft again for the morning launch. Few captains or admirals considered the extra effort worthwhile for one or two night fighters, especially when radar-controlled antiaircraft guns might defend the ships. That was a factor the night of February 16 when a night Hellcat chased a Japanese bomber toward the task force. The radar controller ordered all guns to cease fire, lest the friendly get hit. But the enemy exploited the opportunity and put a torpedo into *Intrepid*. She limped away for repairs in Hawaii, taking Harmer's second night fighter detachment out of the war.

With few night sorties, the Corsair pilots soon grew rusty. Consequently, Harmer conceived a compromise. He and his most experienced aviator, Lieutenant (jg) Robert F. Holden, would take most of the night work while the other three pilots flew as opportunity arose.

But Harmer was a nocturnal evangelist. He was so convinced of his unit's capability that "We even took the duty when other carriers refused to launch their night fighters." His relationship with Tom Hamilton, the normally genial air officer, became strained. Harmer joked, "He almost became physically ill every time he saw me."

Harmer himself had the chance to prove what a radar-equipped fighter could do. Three nights later, off the Carolines on February 19, *Enterprise*'s fighter director coached him onto a twin-engine bomber and got his teeth into it. In two passes Harmer shot up the intruder, glimpsing a brief fire in one engine, then lost sight at 800 feet where his radar mixed with ground returns.

Though his prey escaped, Chick Harmer had logged the first radar interception by a carrier-based night fighter.

THE PALAUS AND BEYOND

After Truk the fast carriers continued their transpacific tour, visiting violence upon distant corners of the Japanese empire. On March 11 old hands found themselves again looking at Espiritu Santo in the New Hebrides. *Enterprise* even tied up at her old berth from late 1942. But the visit was short lived: four days later the forecastle crew hoisted anchor and the Big E was en route to Emirau in the Bismarck Archipelago, northeast of New Guinea. It was almost a live-fire exercise for the invading Marines, who encountered little opposition.

The next step was a long one, 2,700 miles westward. The Palau Islands provided Japan a major base protecting the eastern flank of the Philippines. When *Enterprise* aviators got a look at the island group, they were at once impressed and disappointed. Mostly, however, fliers commented on the immensely rugged terrain and unlikely place names such as Arakabesan and Babelthuap. Hellcats caught few airborne targets but the bombers found significant shipping.

On March 30 the Big E's bombers went to work. Lieutenant Commander Ira Hardman's dozen Dauntlesses coordinated with Bill Martin's six Avengers, the latter armed with torpedoes for a change. The *Enterprise* fliers were among a strike group that jumped a small convoy off Babelthuap, concentrating on *Wakatake,* a second-class destroyer misidentified as a light cruiser in the dim dawn light. Otherwise the scaly old vessel, rated at 1,100 tons, would not have warranted 24,000 pounds of ordnance.

The Mark 13 torpedoes performed about as well as the Buzzard Brigade expected, which is to say, miserably. The two that ran more or less straight were either set too deep or failed to detonate.

The Dauntlesses did better as a heavy bomb hit staggered *Wakatake,* which immediately slowed. But her gunners, fighting for survival, remained active and accurate. They hit one plane in its dive, probably killing the pilot, as the bomber dived straight into the sea with no apparent effort to pull out. Hardman limped his battered plane homeward but heavy oil loss ruined his engine and he splashed into a controlled landing. He was rescued with his gunner.

The dead pilot was Lieutenant (jg) Charles B. Pearson, a young officer beloved throughout *Enterprise.* A stellar Dartmouth athlete, he had it all: brains, ability, and personality. Like nearly 400,000 other Americans of their generation, neither Stubby Pearson nor his back-seater, Thomas W. Waterson, had the chance to grow to maturity.

It was precious small consolation, but *Yorktown* Avengers finished off the stubborn *Wakatake,* lost with her captain and most of the crew. Overall, carrier aviators sank nearly twenty ships and numerous small craft, serving notice that Tokyo could no longer assume the Palaus were immune to attack.

HOLLANDIA

The next stop, April 1, was Woleai in the Carolines, left to wither on the Pacific vine. That month Jig Dog Ramage succeeded Lieutenant Commander Richard Poor at the head of Bombing 10. The promotion formalized Ramage's de facto status. "Before that I was exec and strike leader, so I was just as happy as I could be." Since squadron COs worked through the air group commander rather than reporting to the captain, the arrangement suited them. Said Ramage of Gardner, "He didn't even know who I was."

Jig Ramage was nothing if not focused. He said, "Our world was the ready room, the cockpit, and the target. Nothing else really mattered until we won the war."

The new skipper's attitude was appreciated by the troops. Aircrewman Jack Glass said, "He certainly was a great leader and one we never questioned."

The bomber squadrons were thrilled with Killer Kane as air group commander. "Killer was just great," Ramage exclaimed. "He ran things very low-key but competently, and we never worried much about Jap fighters. The other great thing about Killer was radio discipline. We could get an entire deckload strike on and off the target without any radio calls."

Kane's only foible was his vision. Notoriously nearsighted, he managed to remain flying by applying his forceful personality with flight surgeons and landing signal officers. Nor was he alone. One of his junior aviators, Ensign Lester Gray, could not clearly see the LSO's paddles until nearly over the flight deck. Much later he confided, "A fifth of booze went a long way in the middle of the Pacific."

The last week in April took the Big E 800 miles south as Task Force 58 supported General Douglas MacArthur's landing at Hollandia on New Guinea's north coast. It was the first time the fast carriers supported a major Army operation, and inevitably the two forces crossed paths. MacArthur's Fifth Air Force was heavily engaged in New Guinea, a fact soon evident to *Enterprise*.

The Big E's aircraft recognition officer was the irrepressible Ensign Jerry Flynn, in charge of the lookouts on the flag bridge. One day during the Hollandia landings, Black Jack Reeves asked, "Mr. Flynn, what kind of plane is that out on the horizon?" Flynn glassed the aircraft and replied, "Admiral, it looks like a B-25 to me." Reeves responded, "It looks more like a B-26 to me."

Ever irreverent, Flynn said, "Well, Admiral, I'll bet a week of my salary against a week of yours!"

To Black Jack Reeves, the ensign's response sounded something akin to mutiny. As Tom Hamilton recalled, "The admiral didn't like that very much, so he wrote a letter to Captain Gardner and asked that Mr. Flynn be put in his room for a couple of days to think things over. But he was soon back on duty doing a good job . . . running the ship's radio station with a gossip column every night and kept the ship's company in good humor."

Another man in good spirits was Chick Harmer, who conclusively proved his night fighter capability the night of April 24. In barely an hour he made three radar contacts. Once the fighter director coached him within two miles of the enemy, the Corsair's centimetric radar glommed on to the target, allowing the pilot to complete the intercept. The ensuing shootouts were conducted within 300 yards range as Japanese tail gunners finally spotted the Corsair. Nevertheless, Harmer shot down one bomber and damaged another, while the third escaped due to his faulty ammunition.

On offense and defense, the Big E had written night flying history, and would continue to do so.

TRUK REVISITED

Task Force 58 revisited Truk on April 29. The naval-air complex, though much depleted, retained operable facilities that Pacific Fleet commander Admiral Nimitz wanted further reduced. There were few ships, but among the remaining targets were the navy yard, aircraft maintenance facilities, and miscellaneous installations.

Aerial opposition over Truk was tiny compared to the first raid. The Reapers claimed only seven kills including two Zekes by the consistent Rod Devine.

That afternoon a Reaper met his match during a photo escort mission. Lieutenant (jg) Robert Kanze found himself nose to beak with a lone, aggressive Zeke, and neither pilot flinched. Streams of .50 caliber and 20mm converged as the fighters exchanged fire, and both scored. They passed close by one another, both streaming flames.

Kanze opened his canopy, unhooked from his restraints, and went over the side. Two parachutes descended toward the lagoon, where Kanze splashed into a safe landing. He inflated his rubber raft and awaited events. With daylight running out, there was no chance to rescue him before nightfall.

The next morning Torpedo 10 spotted a yellow dot afloat near the reef, and reported Kanze's position for a pickup. But before long, the fighter pilot had company. Two Avengers fell afoul of Truk's practiced gunners, putting Lieutenant Robert S. Nelson's and Lieutenant (jg) Carroll Farrell's crews in the water.

Air-sea rescue was conducted by Kingfisher floatplanes, and two of the ungainly angels arrived from the battleship *North Carolina*. After landing on the water and trying to retrieve Kanze, one plane capsized. The other Kingfisher, flown by Lieutenant (jg) John Burns, landed successfully. Burns picked up Kanze and his would-be saviors plus both Avenger crews, then motored several miles through choppy waves to meet a lifeguard submarine. The crew of USS *Tang* could hardly believe the spectacle: a battered Kingfisher bearing seven men on its wings plus Burns and his back-seater. Burns's plane had to be scuttled but at least there was no Japanese intervention. It was a blessed event, as U.S. intelligence learned that most of the aviators captured in February had been murdered.

Since January the fast carriers had roamed the Central Pacific at will, supporting amphibious landings and striking far-flung enemy bases in a convincing demonstration of growing power and competence. *Enterprise* aviators and their fellows had engaged in spectacular dogfights and sunk record numbers of Japanese ships, extending the limits of American naval hegemony ever westward. But one factor remained absent: the Imperial Navy. No major Japanese combatants had been brought to battle since 1942, and not even Air Group 10's remaining first-cruise pilots had seen an enemy flight deck. Jig Dog Ramage spoke for all when he said, "We really wanted a shot at the Jap carriers." That opportunity was about to appear on the horizon.

9

★ ★ ★

"Vector Two-Seven-Zero"

Plane directors guide just-landed Hellcats to the parking area forward on the flight deck, February 1944. Note the third fighter just touching down, indicative of the minimum landing intervals common to the Big E. (USN via Tailhook Assn.)

Task Force 58 spent most of May 1944 at newly won Majuro Atoll's huge anchorage in the southern Marshalls, absorbing recent lessons, integrating new faces, and preparing for the next sortie. Meanwhile, sailors and fliers mused about the upcoming operation. It was fairly easy to guess, even for boiler-room strategists.

Japan had seized the Mariana Islands from America in December 1941, their importance apparent with one glance: they lay 1,500 miles due south of Tokyo. The Army Air Force had already begun staging long-range Boeing B-29s from India through China to hit a few targets in southern Japan, but the Asian logistics required huge effort for minimal return. If the Marianas were again in American hands, the huge bombers could strike directly at the enemy home islands.

Operation Forager's immediate objective was Saipan, northernmost of the main Marianas, with Tinian nearby. Nearly 100 miles south-southwest lay Guam, the largest island and the ultimate goal. Imperial General Headquarters in Tokyo could read a map as well as the U.S. Joint Chiefs of Staff: both sides prepared for a major battle in mid-Pacific.

Task Force 58 now comprised fifteen fast carriers supporting Admiral Kelly Turner's amphibious force of 535 ships with 127,000 assault troops. Black Jack Reeves still rode *Enterprise,* now as commander of Task Group 58.3 with *Lexington* plus light carriers *Princeton* and *San Jacinto*. Vice Admiral Mitscher flew his three-star flag as commander of all Task Force 58 in *Lexington,* so Reeves's group steamed with the entire fleet's command element.

Guam was 1,800 miles and five days sailing from Majuro. Upon departure on June 6 the men of the Fifth Fleet learned of events on the other side of the globe as Allied forces landed in northern France. Response in the Pacific was varied. Some sailors cheered, while those with brothers or schoolmates in Europe may have been subdued. But most remained focused on the immediate task—the near certainty of a naval battle. Task Force 58 staffers with inside information began laying bets: a fleet engagement before June 20.

The Imperial Navy had not deployed since *Enterprise* sustained damage and lost her sister *Hornet* at Santa Cruz in October 1942. Few aviators had ever seen an enemy carrier, even in Air Group 10. Commander Richard "Killer" Kane intended that his three squadrons would put Japanese flattops on the bottom.

But first air superiority had to be won over the Marianas. D-Day for the invasion of Saipan was the 15th, with operations beginning on D minus four. The Big E's catapults slammed Hellcats off the deck on June 11 as the first fighter sweeps lifted into the moist tropic air east of the islands. Eleven Japanese naval air groups in the Marianas possessed hundreds of aircraft— there could have been 500—with perhaps 150 more within range from the Carolines and Palaus. Forager, as the operation was code-named, shaped up as a slugfest.

Fighting 10's part of the afternoon chore was Saipan and Tinian, where Zekes were encountered. Typically leading from the front, Kane gunned two bandits, claiming a kill and a probable, while other Reapers claimed six more.

A standout was twenty-one-year-old Ensign Lester Gray, who found all the business he could handle between Saipan and Tinian. He misidentified a

Zeke as an Army "Oscar" fighter but shot it down nonetheless. Then, outbound, he came across Lieutenant (jg) Tommy Harman, who had splashed a Zeke before his Hellcat was hit by AA fire. Gray took Harman's gimpy Grumman under his wing just as three Zekes appeared overhead, two chasing a *Bunker Hill* Hellcat. Gray added power, pulled up, rolled out behind one of the Zekes, and shot it into the water. Subscribing to the maxim about the best defense, Les Gray ignored the odds and pressed his offensive tactics. He latched on to a well-flown Zeke that attempted to evade in a series of aerobatic gyrations but fell to Gray's marksmanship. Only later did Gray learn that the grateful *Bunker Hill* pilot was Whitey Feightner, one of the original Grim Reapers.

Two lieutenants (junior grade) got wet that day. Merle P. Long's Hellcat caught a load of flak, forcing him to ditch well off Saipan, and Richard W. Mason bagged a Zeke, then became a victim himself. But as at Truk, dedicated floatplane pilots were on hand to fetch downed aviators.

On June 12 the task force got down to business with six strikes against Saipan's airfields and other installations. Torpedo 10 Avengers found a nautical target in form of a 1,900-ton cargo ship northwest of Saipan, and Lieutenant (jg) Shannon McCrary clobbered it with his 500-pounders. *Nitcho Maru* rolled onto one side and capsized, strewing the ocean with floating oil drums. Much of the crew was fished out of the water by American ships.

Meanwhile, Lieutenants (jg) Cliff Largess and CB Collins sank ships in Saipan's Tanapag Harbor. Like some others of his generation, Collins had no first or middle names—he was simply "CB," which his squadron mates changed to the more combative "Crossbow."

The bombers were less fortunate. During the first strike Lieutenant James G. Leonard's Dauntless was slashed by antiaircraft fire; he went down with back-seater Robert D. Wynn. On the next launch Lieutenant (jg) Cecil R. Mester crashed just ahead of the ship but was picked up with his gunner. They and the two downed fighter pilots were returned to the Big E in exchange for the going rate of five gallons of ice cream per flier—a twenty-gallon haul for the rescue destroyer.

THE SAGA OF BILL MARTIN

As a strike leader, Bill Martin was flying every day, often twice. At dawn on D minus two, June 13, he led seven Avengers and nine Dauntlesses escorted by ten Hellcats against Japanese gun emplacements on Saipan's southwest coast. Joining a similar *Lexington* formation, Martin radioed the strike co-ordinator, Commander Robert Isley, and both Avenger squadrons attacked together, splitting the defenses.

It was a good, solid plan that did not work. The Japanese were ready and immediately bracketed the American formation at 8,000 feet. Lieutenant (jg) Murphy D. Powell was one of the flak suppressors supporting the bombers. He was seen entering his dive but never rejoined. Then Isely's Avenger was hit hard and went down with the crew.

Martin, ever aggressive, pressed through the barrage while Radioman Jerry Williams monitored the altitude. He had just called 4,000 feet when Martin dropped his bombs and the plane was viciously rocked by a direct hit.

Tossed against his shoulder harness, Martin felt flames in the cockpit as the Avenger rolled inverted. He tried yelling for Williams and gunner Wesley Hargrove to get out. Then an eerie calm settled over him.

"On the count of one, I released the safety belt. On the count of two, I pulled the rip cord. On the count of three, I felt the parachute take up the slack in my harness, and on three and a half, I hit the water." Almost without realizing it, he had been pitched from his cockpit at nearly 350 mph.

Martin was stunned but not so dazed that he forgot his Missouri childhood. He recited the Twenty-third Psalm, then thought of his two crewmen who went down with the plane, burning nearby. Both were old hands from 1942. He wiped moistness from his eyes that had nothing to do with saltwater.

Then Martin began thinking. He was within easy view of the beach, where Japanese began shooting at him. Inhaling deeply, he began swimming underwater toward the reef, only surfacing to inhale again amid the snap-crack of rifle bullets striking around him. Then, about 500 yards offshore, he noted two boats setting out from Garapan. Martin resolved to use his .38 revolver and die fighting—he knew too much about the invasion plans to be captured.

At that moment two blessed Avengers rumbled overhead, forcing the boats back to shore. With that respite, Martin picked up his waterlogged gear, including his parachute, and stumble-ran across the reef. He had the presence of mind to count nineteen steps for the intelligence officers. Then, on the seaward side, he deployed his rubber raft. From that vantage he watched approvingly as his exec, Van Eason, arrived with the next strike, pounding more positions ashore.

Though sick from ingesting seawater, Martin had strength enough to rig his parachute overboard to reduce his drift. He knew that America owned the Pacific Ocean outside the reef, and felt confident of rescue.

Shortly two more Big E planes turned up—Martin's own Lieutenant (jg) Gilbert Blake escorted by a Reaper Hellcat. The Avenger dropped a large rescue pack with enough supplies to sustain a man for a week or more. With that, "Gibby" Blake rocked his wings in a comforting gesture: "See you, Skipper."

Later that day salvation arrived as a Curtiss Seagull floatplane alit near the yellow raft. With Martin safely aboard, the little biplane returned to its roost, cruiser *Indianapolis,* the fleet flagship. There, with dry clothes and "a drink of something that tasted so terrible that I had two," Martin related his observations to Admiral Raymond Spruance. The next day Martin was transferred back to the *Enterprise* for a heartfelt reunion with the Buzzard Brigade. He was flying again two days later.

By the time Martin was back aboard, even more pressing news was buzzing around the ship. For the first time in twenty months, Japanese carriers were drawing near.

SAIPAN

D-Day at Saipan dawned bright and relatively clear, the object of so much concentrated sea power that even experienced aviators gaped at the spectacle. Nonetheless, the Japanese continued resisting and the Reapers lost Lieutenant (jg) Karl Kirchwey, possibly killed by "friendly" antiaircraft gunners.

The Japanese carrier fleet was still distant, tracked by American submarines, but enemy land-based aircrews swarmed to the task force. Shipboard radar operators glommed on to seven fast twin-engine bombers, inbound at some 280 mph. Radar-controlled antiaircraft guns opened up, dropping one plane right away. But the others came straight in, penetrating the task group's destroyer screen as gunners leveled their barrels, firing horizontally into the twilit sky. In succession five more bombers tumbled into white-fountained splashes, fuel and oil blazing on the surface.

One plane dropped a torpedo fairly close to *Enterprise,* forcing Captain Gardner to veer to port. The wake bubbled past the hull where some sailors watched, stunned. It was the first time since Santa Cruz that the Big E had to dodge torpedoes.

The low-angle AA fire took its toll. A 20mm shell fractured on one of the forward gun tubs, knocking two men down, though they rebounded.

But an errant 40mm round struck one of the five-inch mounts, killing Seaman John Shandley. Friendly fire was the price of doing business, and it didn't relent the next morning.

On the 16th Killer Kane was the day's first strike coordinator when, inevitably, somebody didn't get the word. Passing over the amphibious craft some twenty miles offshore, Kane ran afoul of nervous gunners who fired on aircraft heard better than seen in the predawn gloom. If their judgment was miserable, their aim was good: the Hellcat took a major-caliber hit in the port wing.

Kane choked down the instinct to abandon ship and dived away from the threat, radioing his identity in unmistakable Anglo-Saxon imperatives—to no avail. Firing contagion took over as more flak burst and rippled through the dark. Killer shot a glance at his instruments, noted oil pressure falling toward zero, and set up for a water landing. He touched down all right—no mean feat in low visibility—but the jarring halt tossed him face-first into his gun sight. Bleeding from a cut forehead, he climbed out and inflated his life raft. His Hellcat sank as the sun rose, leaving Killer Kane afloat with his headache and a fuming anger. He was quickly rescued and made his way to the *Enterprise,* where he was galled to learn he was off flight status—with the biggest battle of the war just over the horizon.

JUNE 19

On the morning of June 19, fourteen of Mitscher's fifteen carriers had never fought enemy flattops. *Enterprise,* however, had sunk or crippled Japanese carriers at Midway, Eastern Solomons, and Santa Cruz. Entering her fourth carrier battle, she faced nine imperial flight decks including her old foes *Shokaku* and *Zuikaku.*

The Big E began the day long before dawn when fifteen Avengers launched on a radar search at 2:30 A.M. They scouted to 375 miles, seeking Vice Admiral Jisaburo Ozawa's carriers, which remained beyond range. Martin's crews returned more than four hours later.

Possessing longer-ranged aircraft, the Japanese could search and strike beyond reach of the Americans, who were further hampered by having to turn into the easterly wind to conduct flight operations. Each turn upwind took Task Force 58 farther from the enemy fleet. Consequently, throughout the day Ozawa threw four attacks at Mitscher, some 325 sorties, which, though significant, were fewer than Vice Admiral Nagumo's six decks had launched against Pearl Harbor.

During the morning, Mitscher's fighters capped the Marianas airfields, catching Japanese planes arriving from distant bases or trying to take off. Remaining in reserve, the Grim Reapers could only sulk in their ready room, hearing snippets of information as sister squadrons claimed thirty-five kills over land. On a day of battle like no other, Killer Kane sulked most of all, his head still bandaged from his ditching. Meanwhile, the squadron kept three or four divisions of four pilots each fully briefed and ready to man aircraft.

Also that morning Avenger-Hellcat search teams crossed paths with Japanese scouts, downing a dozen or more. Clearly the enemy was at hand, as long-legged Mariner flying boats informed Mitscher of Ozawa's force well to the west. For the time being, Task Force 58 had its hands full preparing for fleet defense.

At 10:00 the Americans sniffed their first electronic scent of inbound trouble. Vice Admiral Willis Lee's battleships were deployed west of the carriers, providing early warning. Twenty minutes later *Enterprise*'s task group was 100 miles west of Guam and nearly 350 from Ozawa. Mitscher began clearing his flight decks, reinforcing the combat air patrol and sending the bombers to restrike Guam's Orote Field and other facilities. Bill Martin's and Jig Ramage's two squadrons orbited to the east while the Hellcat fighters prepared to engage.

Seventy-five miles out, the raiders circled to regroup before their attack. It was a gift to the defenders. Blunt noses well up, climbing under full power from their Pratt & Whitney engines, Hellcats clawed for altitude to pounce on the intruders. A dozen Reapers and elements of seven other squadrons got their fangs into the sixty-nine-plane raid.

Leading the *Enterprise* contingent was skipper Bud Schumann, who suffered radio problems at the worst possible moment. But old hand Don Gordon heard the controller order "Vector two-seven-zero" and immediately acknowledged, turning due west, leading the Hellcats well over the six American battleships, which were already putting up an impressive flak display. Shortly Flash Gordon spotted a flight of dive- and torpedo bombers. Ignoring the Zero escort ("I didn't think they could damage anyone but me"), he piled into the formation. From there it was a downhill chase; Gordon destroyed one while Lieutenant (jg) Richard Mason and Ensign Charles Farmer also chased torpedo planes toward the incredible rippling, bursting wall of flak. Flying as low as fifty feet, the Reapers could hardly see the battleships through the AA gunfire but returned reporting three kills. For Gordon, it was nearly a replay of Santa Cruz in '42, where he pursued Japanese bombers almost into the task force's gunnery.

But the scale of the Marianas battle dwarfed Santa Cruz. The scene that morning was unprecedented: scores of enemy planes thrusting through the twin pickets of Hellcats and flak in a sky laced with flashing steel and erupting shell fire. Though the battleships could not hurt the enemy fleet, they proved an attractively lethal target. One Japanese pilot used the priceless opportunity to plant his bomb on *South Dakota,* inflicting minor damage. Overhead *Indiana,* Gordon took in the sight of a lifetime: a flak curtain rising to 20,000 feet above two dozen American ships spouting yellow-orange muzzle flashes; enemy planes spurting gouts of flame or vaporizing from direct hits; varicolored parachutes descending through the three-dimensional violence and spreading blossomlike on the surface of the sea.

And there was more to come.

That afternoon Rod Devine got the squadron's best steer of the day from the fighter director. Taking two divisions to Orote Point, he flew into a low-level dogfight and did not mind being outnumbered.

Devine was a highly proficient fighter pilot: he entered the fight with four previous victories, and in a sizzling shootout he doubled that tally. He chopped up two Zekes and flamed a Val and a Judy dive-bomber. Lieutenants (jg) Phil Kirkwood and Vern Ude logged triples, while James F. Kay, Merle Long, and Bob Kanze recorded doubles. It was especially rewarding for Kanze after his dunking by a Zeke at Truk. In all, the eight Reapers claimed sixteen kills in ten minutes.

Throughout much of the day Chick Harmer's night fighters provided top cover for rescue operations, freeing a few more Hellcats for defensive patrols. That afternoon Harmer's Corsair teamed with Fighting 10 exec Lieutenant Henry C. Clem's Hellcat to cover a cruiser floatplane picking up downed aviators.

Inbound to the position off Guam, the *Enterprise* pilots heard a frantic call for help from a Curtiss Seagull, call sign "Ace." Under attack by a lone Zeke, the floatplane was defenseless on the water. While Harmer covered Ace, Clem bent his throttle to catch the Japanese, who climbed sharply. The Hellcat pulled almost straight up, and Harmer feared for Clem's eagerness. Moments later the American stalled and dropped nose-down, closely pursued by the Japanese, who clearly knew his trade. The enemy pilot fired one lethal burst that sent the Hellcat into the sea. Ace hollered, "They got one of our guys!"

Chick Harmer shoved everything forward with his left hand: throttle, mixture, and propeller control. He barely got within range and fired a long burst at the fleeing Zeke, which emitted smoke but kept going.

Returning to the floatplane, Harmer knew what he would find. Sick at heart, he saw oil and debris on the water where Clem had gone straight in. Decades later, Japanese historians revealed that the Zeke pilot, Lieutenant Shinya Ozaki, belly-landed on Guam but died of his injuries after his twelfth aerial victory.

The Hellcats had done their work extremely well. *Enterprise* gunners only shot at four attackers that day, downing one and claiming shares in three others.

Shortly the returns began trickling in. It looked as if Task Force 58 fighter pilots had downed about 400 enemy aircraft, and American submarines sank two of Ozawa's carriers. The latter was a galling situation for aviators who still craved a shot at rival flattops.

On the biggest day of aerial combat in American history, Killer Kane could stand it no more. Exercising his command prerogative, he pronounced himself ungrounded and put his name on the schedule for a search mission. Escorting Avengers that evening, he came across two extremely unfortunate floatplanes and destroyed both, one only fifty miles from the task force. Thus the Killer made ace with one to spare, but he still rued missing the day's unprecedented hunting.

Actually about 260 enemy planes were downed, plus more destroyed ashore or sunk with the carriers *Shokaku* and *Taiho*. Sho, the Big E's old rival from Eastern Solomons and Santa Cruz, had fallen prey to an American submarine but her sister *Zuikaku* remained afloat and potentially a threat. In exchange, twenty-nine American planes were lost.

Destroying Japanese aircraft in squadron-sized lots was satisfying, but Marc Mitscher and every aviator afloat wanted carriers. With Ozawa's beaten force steaming northwesterly, Mitscher faced a stern chase. Task Force 58's primary obligation was to support the amphibious force, but Raymond Spruance's Fifth Fleet was authorized to engage Japanese carriers if the opportunity arose. The pursuit was on.

JUNE 20

Throughout the 20th the fast carriers gulped bunker fuel by the ton, trying to close the distance. *Enterprise* launched a special search mission at 1:40 that afternoon: four teams each with two Avengers and a Hellcat sweeping pie-shaped sectors far to the west. "Hotshot Charlie" Henderson spotted a Japanese plane and gave chase. He shoved his throttle to the firewall and slowly reeled in the speedy "Jill" reconnaissance plane, finally firing from directly astern. Henderson conceded his success was "more credit to the manufacturer of my plane than to me as the pilot."

Lieutenant Robert S. Nelson also saw a Japanese scout but ignored it. Then, about four hours into the mission, he noticed a slight disturbance on the horizon. It was hard to tell, peering between rain squalls, but it looked like ships.

In the adjacent sector another Torpedo 10 crew also found something. Lieutenant (jg) Edward Laster, wingman to Robert R. Jones, had a better perspective than Nelson. The Avenger crewmen had found something not seen in twenty months—Japanese aircraft carriers.

The pilots immediately checked their navigation, plotting the position and opening up with contact reports. Nelson radioed in the clear: "Enemy fleet sighted." He gave the latitude and longitude with an estimated speed of twenty knots. Meanwhile, Jones's radioman, Robert Grenier, tapped out a Morse code message that began, "Many ships." Both reported positions were within a few miles of each other. However, Nelson's wingman, Lieutenant (jg) James S. Moore, was doing his own navigation and found a one-degree longitude error, equal to sixty miles. A correction was immediately sent to the task force.

"Railroad" Jones made tracks for *Enterprise* to report in person while Nelson stuck around. He was fascinated to see a Japanese carrier only a few miles away, "leaving a circular wake as it turned after we had been in view for four or five minutes." On the return leg, escort pilot Lieutenant (jg) Ed Colgan dived on a green-colored Japanese aircraft. His Hellcat snacked on the Kate torpedo plane, then continued homeward.

Tom Hamilton and Killer Kane had a strike group ready to launch: twelve Dauntlesses, five Avengers, and a dozen Hellcats. They were just part of a massive 240-plane mission from three of the four task groups.

Standing at the head of Bombing 10's ready room, Jig Ramage announced, "We're going to be gas misers." It was a fairly long way outbound—at least 250 miles—and the return flight would be made in darkness. Ramage suggested that his pilots manually manage their fuel flow rather than trust the "auto lean" setting.

The carriers swung their bows into the wind and began flinging airplanes off their decks at 4:25 P.M. Fourteen aircraft aborted, leaving a long aerial trail of 226 planes cruise-climbing into the afternoon sky.

About twenty minutes en route, the squadrons began receiving priority radio traffic. Jim Moore's report of the one-degree easterly error finally caught up with the airborne pilots, who began recomputing the time-distance equation. Leaning over his chart board, Ramage saw that the actual range to target was a little over 300 miles. He accepted the likelihood that he would have some boating experience that night.

Well along at the end of the aerial procession—Dauntlesses were the slowest carrier aircraft—Bombing 10 glimpsed strange ships to port, south of the outbound track. *Wasp*'s air group jumped on the Japanese oilers but everyone else continued west, seeking "the fighting navy."

They found it beneath an immense anvil-shaped cumulus cloud, backlit by the slanting rays of the westering sun.

Enterprise's formation arrived overhead the Japanese Second Carrier Division with *Lexington*'s Air Group 16, the only other unit still flying Dauntlesses. Strike leaders began assigning targets among the three carriers escorted by a battleship, a cruiser, and eight destroyers.

Ramage coordinated with Lieutenant Van Eason's Avengers to attack two flattops carving high-speed wakes on the cloud-shadowed sea. Trusting Killer Kane's Hellcats to handle the defending fighters, Jig Dog was satisfied with his pilots' positions, then reduced power and opened his dive flaps. Suddenly he heard Chief Dave Cawley's voice on the intercom, warning of bandits overhead. Ramage glanced around, astonished to see a Zeke close aboard. The Japanese turned away, leaving Ramage to nose into his seventy-degree dive. At that moment he inherited the legacy of previous Bombing 10 CO Stockton Birney Strong, who had said, "I am going to make you the second-best dive-bomber in the Pacific Fleet."

Ramage's target likely was *Junyo* as he assigned Lieutenant Lou Bangs's second division to *Ryujo*. Flak erupted from the enemy ships, but at long, long last, with a Japanese flight deck in his sight. He recalled, "The carrier below looked big, tremendous, almost make-believe. I had a moment of real joy. I had often dreamed of something like this. Then I was horrified with myself. What a spot to be in!"

Ramage pressed his dive to the limit, only 1,500 feet. He punched the bomb release, felt the half-ton weight leave the airplane—and pulled on his stick.

Even under the stress of a high-G recovery, Ramage felt his bomb explode in the ship's wake. Then Cawley was firing his twin Brownings, and a Zeke overshot the Dauntless. Ramage and the Japanese exchanged glances, then the Zeke was zoom-climbing for altitude.

Looking down, Ramage saw waterspouts erupt around his target. One pilot was unable to drop his bomb but one of the other four seemed to hit the flight deck overhang.

Nearby, Lou Bangs's Dauntless division got split up during the approach and went for separate targets. In all the confusion, smoke, spray, and gathering dusk, it was difficult to tell who did what. But later Lieutenant (jg) Harold F. Grubiss was credited with a hit on *Hiyo*, which took a bomb to the bridge, and Bangs saw his explosion knock some planes off *Junyo*'s deck.

Eason's Avengers opened their bomb bays and slanted down on the light carrier *Ryujo*, drawing heavy gunfire from the escorting battleship. Though the Grim Reapers fought to keep interceptors off the bombers, perhaps twelve Zekes harried the Buzzard Brigade crews. Van Eason's gunner, L. W. Hughes, likely scored, as a Zeke dropped away trailing smoke.

Dropping in line astern to cover a wider area, Eason's pilots claimed a 50 percent hit rate from their sixteen bombs. Japanese records only mention near misses on *Ryujo*, though some damage was inflicted.

During the approach, attack, and withdrawal, *Enterprise* Hellcats fought a series of brief engagements with Ozawa's CAP. The Reapers claimed seven kills, two by Ensign Jerome L. Wolfe, Jr., who got separated from Killer Kane.

Tommy Harman's Hellcat quartet was bounced by an estimated fifteen Zekes. Turning in to the threat, shoving up the power, Harman and Ensign William T. Howard each gunned an enemy. The second section, Lieutenant (jg) John Shinneman and Ensign Jack Turner, fought a separate battle, scoring hits and disengaging. Somewhere in the hassle Turner's plane took damage and he had to ditch, awaiting rescue the next day.

Outbound from the Japanese fleet, pilots looked for friends or at least friendly strangers. Nobody wanted to be alone for the nearly 300-mile return trip, especially with nightfall pending. Behind them, minus twenty planes lost in combat, the departing Americans reckoned they had justified Marc Mitscher's risky long-range strike. In truth, only *Belleau Wood*'s Avengers achieved significant success by sinking the carrier *Hiyo*. Four other carriers were struck, most notably *Junyo*, which took two hits and six rattling near misses. Bombing 10 undoubtedly contributed to her damage.

Flying east through the darkening sky, pilots leaned out their fuel mixtures, striving for the most efficient power settings. When tanks began running dry, the calls were overheard with ambivalence: to some pilots they were plaintive, to others aggravating. Some fliers turned off their radios and proceeded east through a moonless sky.

Nearing the task force, aviators were astonished at what they saw. Almost every ship was lit up, running truck lights and shining high-powered signal lamps like vertical yellowish beacons. Marc Mitscher's staff had decided to ignore the danger of Japanese submarines in favor of dozens or scores of young lives. The word went out: "Turn on the lights."

Enterprise's first Avenger home was piloted by Lieutenant (jg) Joe Doyle, who safely snagged an arresting wire—and his wheels collapsed. There was no time to study the problem, as Avenger T-49 was quickly jettisoned to clear the deck.

Behind Doyle, others were trying to stretch their fuel and their luck. Ralph Cummings came close—his engine ran dry in the traffic pattern so he ditched near the ship. He unlimbered his flashlight and visually hailed the cruiser Baltimore, which rescued his crew.

Like many pilots that night, Crossbow Collins mistook an escort's lights for a flattop. By the time he realized he was lined up on a destroyer, he had enough fuel for one pass at Enterprise's fouled deck. Collins made a good water landing and engaged in a brief tug-of-war with gunner Bill Langworthy, as they pulled opposite ends of the fuselage-mounted life raft.

Van Eason also came close to landing. But he was cut out of Lexington's pattern by panicked or unobservant pilots who forced him to go around. Out of fuel, Torpedo 10's exec set his Avenger down in the water. Radioman Joe McMullin had experienced a dunking at Santa Cruz and said Eason's ditching was no rougher than a normal carrier landing.

Enterprise's landing signal officer was Lieutenant Horace Prolux, previously a Bombing Six aviator who had an extremely busy evening. Among those he had to wave off was Jig Ramage, who finally squeezed into Yorktown in Task Group 58.1. There he had an unexpected reunion with "my old hero," Captain John Crommelin on Rear Admiral Jocko Clark's staff.

Meanwhile, "Hod" Prolux brought aboard seventeen planes from five other carriers. That night it was any available flight deck. The only Bombing 10 pilot who didn't get aboard was Lou Bangs. He ran out of fuel, and with his gunner wound up on the destroyer Cogswell with Van Eason's crew. Remarkably, the relatively short-ranged Dauntlesses sustained the fewest losses to fuel exhaustion of all bombers on "the mission beyond darkness."

Chick Harmer was airborne that night, not hunting Japanese but seeking lost friends. Employing his Corsair's air-search radar, in a two-hour sortie he tacked on to three groups of wayward aircraft and shepherded them back to the task force. He considered it one of the most satisfying missions he ever flew.

One other Big E pilot failed to return that night. When noses were counted, Killer Kane was missing.

FRUITLESS PURSUIT

In the wee hours of the 21st the tireless crews of Bob Nelson and Jim Moore sought to repeat their find of the previous afternoon—and they did. Incredibly, they loitered for an hour over Ozawa's four task groups, sending updates on enemy position, course, and speed. Torpedo 10's sterling work over those two days raised the bar for carrier-based reconnaissance, confirming the importance of night flying mated to radar.

Based on the contact report, sixteen *Enterprise* bombers with a dozen Hellcats tried to restrike the enemy fleet later that morning, but the gap had widened to some 350 miles. With the Japanese well out of range, the Battle of the Philippine Sea was over, and the Great Marianas Turkey Shoot entered legend.

But work remained to be done. Task Force 58 searched for missing aircrews and reshuffled the very mixed decks throughout the force. Fifteen *Enterprise* planes returned to the Big E, so a tentative accounting could begin. Six Air Group 10 planes had been lost on the 20th but only Jack Turner's was due to enemy action, and he was rescued.

Through June 29, follow-up strikes were launched against Guam and Pagan to keep the pressure on Japanese bases and intercept enemy aircraft funneling into the area. But after the excitement of the 19th and 20th it was pretty tame. One day only fifteen planes were launched and recovered.

On the 22nd a destroyer approached *Enterprise*, blinking the Morse code numeral 6, alerting the Big E that the message was for her. On the signal bridge the sailor on the light acknowledged the message, which began How . . . Oboe . . . William . . . break . . . Mike . . . Uncle . . . Charlie . . . How . . . and so on.

Once received, the message read, "How much ice cream is Killer Kane worth?" Whoops of delight erupted from the signal bridge, immediately relayed to exec Tom Hamilton. In minutes he was on the microphone, letting the Big E know that her air group skipper was coming home.

That afternoon Kane was transferred on lines suspended between the two ships, exchanged for twenty gallons of ice cream—four times the going rate. He looked even worse than before, with his head rebandaged and his face bruised from another impact with a gun sight.

According to Hamilton, "You never saw such elation on a ship and when Killer came over on the high line from the destroyer back to the *Enterprise,* I have never seen such an expression of love of a whole ship of men for one individual."

Kane related his story from two nights previously: waved off for a fouled deck, he quipped that while other pilots were running out of fuel, he ran out of altitude and flew into the sea. If so, it was understandable: he had logged ten hours that day.

Behind the scenes, some fliers wondered if the Killer hadn't outdone himself. His nearsightedness was a poorly kept secret, and by rights he should not have been flying from carriers. However, nobody—but nobody—was going to tell Killer Kane that he should stop flying.

AFTER THE BATTLE

Overriding the thrill of getting at enemy carriers and welcoming shipmates back from peril was something else: a sense that somehow the battle had not gone quite right. The aviators—wearing their sporty brown shoes in contrast to the regulation surface officer's black shoes—muttered among themselves. For all his intellect, they held, Spruance had muffed a golden opportunity. The ready room majority held that Ozawa should have been pursued to destruction so Japan's carriers would pose no future threat. But the cockpit perspective was strategically myopic, as some dedicated aviators later acknowledged. Fifth Fleet's primary responsibility was supporting the amphibious force, protecting its vulnerable shipping from an enemy end run. However unlikely that prospect, it was recognized by Nimitz, who had given Spruance as much latitude as possible. As he had done at Midway, Spruance accomplished both his missions: he protected the troops ashore while inflicting as much damage as possible on the enemy. Only six of Ozawa's nine carriers steamed home, their decks nearly devoid of aircraft. The Hellcats had shattered Japan's carefully nurtured tailhook squadrons, shot to rags and tatters and beyond rebuilding.

Much of *Enterprise*'s limited combat the next week was logged by the night fighters. On June 27 Corsair pilot Bob Holden splashed a Betty ten miles south of the force. The next night Harmer's squadron closed its victory log as Holden downed two more and Harmer another. Night Fighting Squadron 101 finished the cruise with five kills and no losses, despite flying the Navy's most challenging aircraft—at night.

On June 29, Air Group 10 ended its deployment with a thirty-plane strike against Orote Airfield. Upon return to the task force some of the youngsters allowed their exuberance to show: they broke Kane's ironclad discipline, indulging in aerobatics and unprofessional banter on the radio. After several minutes Black Jack Reeves personally intervened, putting an end to the performance. But the survivors felt justified: they had lost a dozen pilots and seven aircrew during five months of almost constant operations, and now they were going home.

Enterprise was staying.

10

★ ★ ★

"Only Human"

Enterprise sailors enjoy some time ashore at Majuro Atoll, 1944. Note two battle-ships anchored just offshore. (National Museum of Naval Aviation)

Midsummer 1944 brought change to *Enterprise* resting at Majuro Atoll in the Marshall Islands. Rear Admiral Black Jack Reeves departed, as did Captain Matt Gardner, stars in his near future as a task group commander. He was not widely missed in the Big E, though some men had glimpsed his softer side. Despite their occasionally testy relationship, Gardner gave Chief Yeoman Bill Norberg a parting gift: an autographed pencil portrait of Gardner.

With no new captain available at Majuro, exec Tom Hamilton assumed temporary command. Though only a commander, he was skipper for most of July, returning the ship to Pearl for a new propeller and a new air group. Docking on the 16th, *Enterprise* remained for a month, and it was a crowded four weeks.

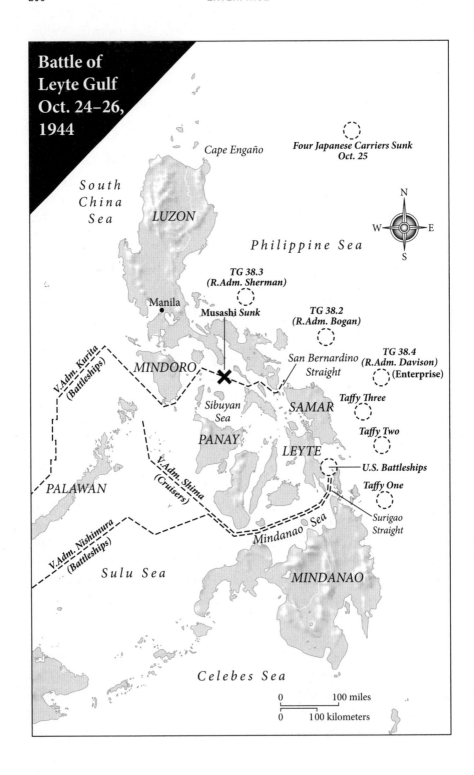

Battle of Leyte Gulf Oct. 24–26, 1944

South China Sea

LUZON

Cape Engaño

Four Japanese Carriers Sunk Oct. 25

N
W — E
S

Philippine Sea

Manila

TG 38.3 (R.Adm. Sherman)

Musashi *Sunk*

TG 38.2 (R.Adm. Bogan)

San Bernardino Straight

TG 38.4 (R.Adm. Davison) **(Enterprise)**

V.Adm. Kurita (Battleships)

MINDORO

Sibuyan Sea

SAMAR

Taffy Three

PANAY

LEYTE

Taffy Two

V.Adm. Shima (Cruisers)

U.S. Battleships

PALAWAN

Taffy One

Surigao Straight

V.Adm. Nishimura (Battleships)

Mindanao Sea

Sulu Sea

MINDANAO

Celebes Sea

0 ——— 100 miles
0 ——— 100 kilometers

The new captain, Cato Douglas Glover, Jr., had been one of Admiral Nimitz's senior planners. As such, Glover possessed a broader grasp of Pacific strategy than any previous skipper. He also represented the trend to rotate staffers to sea commands, a policy that kept information flowing up and down stream while giving senior officers important career benchmarks. Subordinates remembered the Alabaman as a gentle, soft-spoken leader who treated everyone as an equal. He was probably the most approachable of *Enterprise* captains, taking an interest in the welfare of his sailors. He conversed casually on the wing of the bridge, and encouraged youngsters to attend college on the newly enacted GI Bill.

Assigned a new air group, *Enterprise* spent five days exercising her squadrons. Air Group 20 operated under drawling Commander Daniel F. Smith, Jr., widely known as "Dog." The 1934 Annapolis yearbook described him as "The embodiment of the fabled Texan, six-foot-two, lean and rangy, possessing that sun-cured color and out-thrust chin."

The fighter skipper was Frederick E. Bakutis, a Bay Stater who lettered in track at Annapolis. He had been flying since 1939, previously serving in two carrier squadrons. A natural musician, he often unlimbered his guitar to accompany whatever was playing on the radio or Jerry Flynn's *Enterprise* broadcast.

The bombers belonged to darkly handsome Robert Emmett Riera from Pensacola. Called by his middle name and known for his appetite, he brought a new aircraft to the Big E. The Curtiss SB2C Helldiver had experienced a painful gestation, often shedding its tail and demonstrating poor carrier suitability. Few bomber pilots liked it as much as the beloved Dauntless, which though slower was a more accurate bomber and more reliable aircraft. The Helldiver belatedly entered combat in November 1943, but only after the Marianas did it fully replace the Dauntless aboard ship. Riera and company were determined to tame "The Beast" and exchanged their "dash one" Helldivers for much-improved SB2C-3s shortly before joining *Enterprise*.

Torpedo 20's first skipper was Lieutenant Commander David Dressendorfer, who rotated out before the squadron deployed. His parting prediction: the air group could be one of the best ever, but one man in three would perish. He proved perilously close to right. Dressendorfer was succeeded by Samuel Lee Prickett, Jr., from Alabama. Unlike the air group commander and other squadron COs, Prickett was not an Annapolis product.

The night fighter skipper was well known in the Big E. Lieutenant

Commander Jim Gray was back aboard more than two years after Midway. As the squadron commander, Gray led Night Fighting Squadron 78's Detachment One while subordinates took four other "dets" to other carriers.

The new outfit was proud to find itself aboard *Enterprise*. Recorded the torpedo squadron, "We went aboard the Big E, the Navy's finest carrier. The ship was loaded with officers and men of whom the Navy should be proud. For the most part, they had long sea duty behind them, and by usual standards, should have been relieved. They met us newcomers with open arms, made us feel part of them. We all respected the Big E's gallant war record, and looked up to the men aboard, especially the deck crew, the Navy's best."

Smith and Bakutis had drilled their fighter pilots extensively at gunnery and rocket firing, sometimes three ninety-minute flights per day. In California and Hawaii the squadrons had evolved from "group gropes" into a smoothly choreographed, three-dimensional routine, not only by day but with predawn launches and join-ups. Air Group 20 arrived in the Big E as a smoothly functioning team.

Tom Hamilton, now reverted to executive officer, liked what he saw in the new arrivals. He considered Smith's crew "a very aggressive, an excellent air group." The pilots were obviously competent, and proud of their factory-new aircraft sporting an overall gloss blue in place of the previous blue shades over white.

With the new aircraft color scheme, *Enterprise* herself received new paint. While at Pearl the ship was decorated in Measure 33, the "dazzle pattern" of haze gray, pale gray, and ocean gray. Because she was the only survivor of her class, Variant 4AB was unique to the Big E: a combination of scallops and angles designed to confuse enemy submarine skippers as to the ship's size and direction of travel.

Departing Pearl Harbor on August 16, *Enterprise* steamed into Eniwetok, the fleet anchorage in the Marshalls, 2,700 miles nearer Japan. A few hundred *Enterprise* veterans recalled the early days of 1942 when the most that the Pacific Fleet could manage was a one-day raid on the Marshalls. Now it was an American lake.

After four days at Eniwetok the task force set course 1,600 miles west, to attack the barren, obscure Bonin Islands. En route the planned Fifth Fleet to Third Fleet transition was accomplished at sea. Halsey in *New Jersey* took over, but the change was hardly noticeable to ships' crews. Now part of the Third Fleet, the fast carriers became Task Force 38 but still operated under Mitscher. *Enterprise* with *Franklin, Belleau Wood,* and *San Jacinto* became Rear Admiral Ralph Davison's Task Group 38.4. Davison rode the newer *Franklin,* as "Big Ben" had more staff space and the latest communications gear. It was a startling change for the Big E, accustomed to having a flag officer aboard almost continuously since 1941.

Air Group 20 went to work in earnest on August 31, beginning three days of pounding the Bonins 750 miles south of Tokyo. To a former fleet planner like *Enterprise*'s Captain Glover, the islands represented one portion of the immense Pacific chessboard, with squares defined by degrees of latitude and longitude. Carriers were naval queens, with supreme mobility and reach, able to strike almost any square on the board. While Davison's group interdicted the Bonins, other task groups struck other squares—the Palaus east of the Philippines and Wake Island, keeping the Japanese off balance and uncertain. One island in the nearby Volcano group would emerge from obscurity six months later—Iwo Jima.

From the Bonins south-southeast to the Palaus and east to Wake covered much of the western Pacific, an oceanic triangle 2,000 to about 4,500 miles on a side, with one point resting on Wake. It was a huge expanse of 4.4 million square miles, and the United States Navy owned nearly all of it. Nimitz wanted more.

On the first day of the Bonins operation, Dog Smith's squadrons put up an unusually large strike—forty aircraft. They got a two-for-one opportunity, hitting Chichi Jima's harbor and airfield while inbound, and Haha Jima to the south on the return leg. With no enemy aircraft on either small island, and no significant shipping, to some men the operation had the feel of a training exercise. *Franklin*'s Hellcats claimed a dozen kills over Iwo Jima 150 miles south while *Enterprise*'s pilots had no opportunity. But Chichi's flak was lethal: a variety of automatic fire and bursting rounds slicing up from the island's craggy greenness. In three days Air Group 20 lost three Helldiver bombers, with Ensign Stuart Ferguson and Radioman James A. Bain the first fatalities, plus two Hellcat fighters and an Avenger torpedo plane. Though cruiser-based floatplanes provided the now accustomed air-sea rescue service, six missing planes made Chichi a rough initiation.

After a brief stop at Saipan—now an advanced fleet base that Killer Kane's crews would not have recognized two months previously—the fast carriers headed south. Task Group 38.4 struck Yap in the Carolines on September 6, looking like another in-and-out affair. Dog Smith was up front for the afternoon strike with fighter skipper Fred Bakutis and his exec, Joseph T. Lawler, leading three divisions. But Yap's gunners were among the most practiced in the western Pacific, and they shot down Bakutis's number four man, Lieutenant (jg) Harry Brown. Seconds later Lawler's two wingmen disappeared. Ensigns Joseph E. Cox and H. A. Holding either collided in the dive or succumbed to flak. It all happened so fast: nobody saw what happened to the latter pair. Air Group 20 was learning the ropes as everyone did—the hard way.

While some fliers felt that Yap yielded little for the effort expended, one innovation emerged from the Carolines raids as Fighting 20 initiated napalm to carrier combat. The gelatinous substance, the consistency of applesauce, was poured into Hellcat drop tanks with an impact fuse. When dropped it burned with hellish intensity to destroy foliage and camouflage covering Japanese facilities. *Enterprise* pilots found that perhaps half of the tanks failed to drop or explode, and a return pass to ignite them with machine gun fire often was not worth the risk.

BLOODY PELELIU

The next operation was no smash-and-go affair; it was the prelude to a major amphibious landing at Peleliu 600 miles east of Mindanao. While the other three task groups probed the Philippines, Davison took *Enterprise, Franklin*, and their consorts to the Palaus where Air Group 10 had pummeled shipping in March, six long months before.

The Japanese had thirty years to construct defenses, and made use of the time. Joe Lawler, the low-key yet effective fighter exec, later said, "Koror Island was the capital of the Palau group, and the Japanese had the first team on their guns, which were supplied with ample ammunition."

Among the targets were ships that in fact were floating flak sites. On September 10 torpedo exec Ross Manown's Avenger crew was lost with the bombers' Lieutenant George Gibson and his gunner, plus another aircrewman killed. It was a rough way to learn the rules of the new league, but thereafter Air Group 20 restricted attacks on Koror to 4,000 feet, above the worst of the light flak. Even so, on the 13th the torpedo squadron lost a crew over Peleliu.

D-Day was the 15th, providing *Enterprise* aircrews with an inspiring spectacle. None had seen anything comparable: streams of amphibious tractors and landing craft churning the ocean toward Peleliu's beaches, dominated by high, craggy hills providing some of the war's best defensive terrain. It was frustrating for Dog Smith's aviators, who bombed, rocketed, and strafed inland of the beaches. Yet despite repeated runs and expenditure of all ordnance, the enemy gunfire seemed unabated. When the carriers disengaged on the 17th, the First Marine Division proceeded to climb, fight, and bleed its way in the questionable need to conquer the island.

In vivid contrast, the carrier sailors were able to indulge in some nautical foolery. On the 19th the task force crossed the equator southbound, affording the Trusty Shellbacks a rare opportunity to inflict traditional degradation upon the new crop of Pollywogs. The initiation ceremony was not always observed in wartime, but with no urgency at the moment, the Big E repeated the ritual she had first sponsored on that long-ago shakedown cruise in 1938. Some *Enterprise* men still aboard remembered the occasion, but the principals were mostly departed. The role of Neptunus Rex was played by Chief D. C. Gensel, who brought experience and enthusiasm to the part.

There followed three days at Manus in the Admiralties, north of New Guinea, devoted to rearming, refueling, and what passed for recreating. Ship's crews crowded ashore to indulge in horseplay fueled by warm beer— six per customer at least age twenty-one. But the equatorial climate tended to melt much of the enthusiasm, and some sailors returned to the relative luxury of their ships and bunks.

To some, the interlude bordered on surreal. On the far side of the planet the World Series was played that month—the famous crosstown rivalry between the National League Cardinals and American League Browns. *Enterprise* radiomen passed the word: the Cards took it 4–2, retaining MVP Stan Musial (hitting .304 in the Series), who was not due to report for induction until next year.

OKINAWA BOUND

When Task Force 38 deployed again in early October, Halsey took everything he had: seventeen fast carriers, six battleships, fourteen cruisers, and nearly sixty destroyers. The target was Okinawa, barely 350 miles south of Japan. The big island was on the list for conquest in the coming spring, but first it had to be softened up.

For a change, aerial opposition was anticipated, and Fighting 20 contributed three divisions, each of four planes. But the Japanese were caught by surprise, so on the morning of October 10 Bakutis's Hellcats went down low and close to the runways and parking ramps, strafing dozens of parked planes to destruction.

The following strike arrived over the briefed target on Nakagusuku Bay, but better hunting was reported off Naha Town. Of five Japanese transport or cargo ships sunk there, *Enterprise* bombers found four transports and an escort that was initially thought to be a destroyer, and divvied them up by two-plane sections. Diving out of the west from 12,000 feet, ignoring generally inaccurate flak, the Helldivers were deadly: the strike coordinator reported hits on every ship with very few misses. One transport blew up and others were set afire. The escort went under while the bombers shared a transport with the torpedo planes. On the way out Emmett Riera's Helldiver pilots got a rare opportunity to strafe with their 20mm cannon, chewing up a coastal vessel that appeared sinking.

Nearly a year after being established and following almost two months in combat, Air Group 20 had achieved high competence. Smith's aircrews could put thirty-plus planes on and off a target in a few minutes, leaving it burning, sinking, or wrecked. But the fighters had lacked any opportunity to engage airborne targets. That was about to change.

On the evening of October 11 Jim Gray stalked a Betty bomber fifty miles west of the task force. It was a perfect intercept: he closed to 100 yards, unseen by the Japanese until he opened fire. When he pulled off the kill he was so close that he could see flames burning inside. Officially it was Fighting 20's first victory, as the night detachment had been absorbed into Bakutis's outfit. The nocturnal Hellcats already had paid a price, however, losing three planes and a pilot in accidents.

The next morning the fast carriers tackled Formosa (now Taiwan), seventy-five miles off the China coast and loaded with Japanese naval and military facilities. Third Fleet devoted three days to pounding the huge island—13,000 square miles, fourteenth largest in the Pacific—beating down enemy airpower as a prelude to the upcoming Philippine landings 500 miles to the south. Smothering Formosa was a daunting task: it had been a Japanese possession since 1895, with nearly fifty years to develop bases and defenses. The island was crammed with bombers, fighters, and hundreds of antiaircraft guns, from 25mm up. But its importance could not be ignored, as Japanese naval aircraft from Formosa had overwhelmed Americans on Luzon in 1941. The remarkable range of Japanese planes had enabled Tokyo's conquest of the Philippines.

Enterprise contributed a dozen Hellcats to the early fighter sweep, and Fred Bakutis's crew eagerly hunted near major airdromes: Tainan, Ein

Ansho, and Takao. Air group commander Dog Smith opened the action, splitting a Zeke with Lieutenant (jg) Thomas J. Woodruff.

Over the next twenty minutes other Fighting 20 pilots tied into Japanese army fighters—stub-nosed "Tojos"—and Zekes. Bakutis gunned a pair of Tojos while lanky Ensign Alex Phillips claimed a quartet of Zekes. Equally lethal was Ensign Douglas Baker. He dived onto a string of Tojos and flamed the last one in line. Seconds later another crossed his nose, affording him a smooth tracking shot. The target gushed flames and the pilot went over the side. Seeking his wingman, Baker glanced down and saw another opportunity. He rolled into the Navy's patented overhead gunnery pass, allowed full deflection, and fired. His aim was perfect and the Tojo blew up. Next Baker joined another lone ensign, Robert Nelson, and killed a Zeke. A twenty-three-year-old Oklahoman, Baker was on his way to top shot in the squadron.

After its long apprenticeship in aerial combat, Fighting 20 counted twenty-one kills.

Though the morning sweeps eradicated one third of Formosa's aircraft, and the second launch obliterated most of the others, there were still losses. An Avenger crew and two Helldivers fell to Takao Harbor's thick flak, plus a Hellcat, but the survivors were scooped up by submarine.

The next day, the 13th, involved far less combat as the Japanese ceded control of Formosa airspace. Big E fighters splashed eight planes, nearly all snooping the task group, but Joe Lawler found an opportunity offshore. Returning from a strike on Taipei, he spotted a life raft with "a lonely aviator who was waving frantically." Lawler decided to cover the shootdown until a submarine arrived.

In his low orbit, Lawler looked around and saw a sleek Japanese aircraft outbound from shore. The Japanese apparently saw the Americans at the same time, as he abruptly reversed course. The "Paul" was fast for a floatplane—good for 270 mph—and Lawler shoved his throttle through the "gate," the wire preventing accidental use of water injection that temporarily cooled the engine. With the big Pratt & Whitney surging at maximum power, the Hellcat overhauled the ungainly floatplane. Lawler centered the Paul in his gun sight and held the trigger down until the victim exploded.

About five minutes later, regrouping his division, Lawler was surprised to see another floatplane. Knowing that Japanese tended to strafe life rafts, he repeated the process again, executing an Aichi "Jake" from below.

Eventually Lawler heard from the duty submarine, inbound to the raft, and took his flight back to *Enterprise.*

That same day Lieutenant (jg) William F. Ross's Avenger was shot down with Radioman Harry H. Aldro and Ordnanceman Charles E. McVay. As his plane dropped out of control, Ross heard his friends calling, "Bail out, Shorty!" He went over the side, pulled the ripcord, and landed in the surf. The Japanese opened fire, striking him in one shoulder. Then they decided to let him live. Ross was taken to a hospital where he received a visitor a few days later—a Japanese pilot who claimed shooting him down. Ross's two crewmen were murdered eight months later.

On the evening of the second day, four Bettys penetrated Task Group 38.4 to launch torpedoes at *Franklin. Enterprise* sailors standing topside saw a gout of flame erupt from a bomber that skidded across Big Ben's deck, but no serious damage was done.

Day three of "the air battle of Formosa" sent Davison's group about 250 miles south to harass airfields on northern Luzon. Bakutis's pilots found some grounded planes to strafe but little else. The operation was judged a success, however, not only in reducing enemy airpower but in sinking more than twenty Japanese merchant or cargo ships and tankers.

TO THE PHILIPPINES

Tokyo could not let the Philippines go uncontested. The archipelago not only dominated the western Pacific but stood astride Japan's essential petroleum route from the East Indies. That was the reason for seizing the islands immediately after Pearl Harbor. Consequently, the American offensive to regain the islands would likely result in fierce resistance ashore and a great naval battle.

The campaign to liberate the Philippines began in earnest on October 15. That morning each of the Big E's squadron skippers led their respective commands shoreward—thirty-three blue aircraft bearing the air group's white triangle on the tails. The target was Manila.

East of the capital it became apparent that the Hellcats would have to shoot their way in, clearing a path for the bombers. Japanese army fighters easily outnumbered the sixteen Hellcats and tried luring them away from the Helldivers and Avengers. Fred Bakutis was having none of it. Consequently, the mission turned into the biggest dogfight yet: eleven Oscars downed against no American losses. Doug Baker claimed two and became the squadron's first ace.

Unpestered by enemy fighters, Riera's and Prickett's bombers had a clear shot at Manila's airfields. Low clouds prevented the customary steep dives from altitude, so the Helldivers and Avengers flattened their approaches and ran in through some of the thickest flak yet seen. All released ordnance from minimum altitude, destroying parked planes and cratering runways.

One of the pilots heading outbound was Lieutenant Edward B. Holley, who had flown from *Enterprise* at Guadalcanal. Amazed when a Zeke appeared ahead of his Avenger, he barely had to change his flight path to hose it with his wing guns. It was the first time an enemy aircraft got within shooting range of an Air Group 20 bomber, and nearly the last.

Action shifted seaward at mid-afternoon as Japanese formations pressed hard against the carriers. In a running battle from sixty down to twenty miles from the force, Bakutis's fighter pilots claimed another seventeen victories, running the day's total to a record thirty-five. Moreover, the skipper and his wingman splashed a twin-engine "Dinah," apparently serving as strike coordinator, orbiting at 23,000 feet.

But there were losses. Ensign Norman Snow's Hellcat was shot up in a dogfight, forcing him to ditch near a destroyer. He got out but drowned despite efforts of the ship's crew to save him. Another ensign, Bruce Hanna, collided with a bomber, losing a wing and barely escaping his doomed Hellcat by parachute. This time some rescuers were successful.

The Americans kept pressure on Philippine airfields over the subsequent days. On the 17th Dog Smith led a sweep to Mabalacat East, fifty miles north of Manila. The Hellcats dived in, strafing and rocketing, when Zekes belatedly took off. Smith recognized a rare opportunity and jumped on it: in less than a full turn he shot down two, then found another on his nose. The Zeke turned away, offering Smith a belly shot, and he triggered a lethal burst. Three kills in perhaps sixty seconds with fewer than 850 rounds of .50 caliber. Other Hellcats claimed four more.

The next day *Enterprise* launched five fighter sweeps and bombing strikes, with the fighters claiming twenty-seven shootdowns around Clark Field, the big facility the Americans built between the wars. Alex Phillips downed an Oscar to make ace on his twenty-third birthday. Doug Baker was over Manila twice that day, killing two fighters and sharing a third in the morning, then adding another that afternoon. The day's record for VF-20 was twenty-seven against five losses to all causes—further proof of the growing disparity between U.S. Navy pilots and their opponents. Long gone was Japan's qualitative edge that the Big E knew from 1942.

However, the 18th was the worst day of the war for Air Group 20. Fifteen planes were lost to all causes, evenly divided among the three squadrons with six fliers missing. Of three downed Hellcat pilots, only Lieutenant William N. Foye got out of his sinking plane in Subic Bay. Unknown to his friends, the injured pilot was plucked up by friendly Filipinos.

EMERGENCY RECALL

After a month at sea and frequent losses, *Enterprise* and her consorts were ready for some downtime. But en route to Ulithi in the Carolines on October 21, prospects for rest and relaxation were dashed. Third Fleet ordered an immediate reversal, and Davison's task group came hard about. It took a while for word to filter down, but sailors' suspicions soon were confirmed. The Japanese fleet was out for the first time since the Marianas operation in June.

The enemy plan was ambitious and complex: three powerful units operating across a 600-mile north–south axis from well off Luzon's northern tip down to the central Philippines. Two battleship groups would penetrate the islands from the west, surprising American amphibious forces in Leyte Gulf, while Tokyo's four remaining carriers would draw off Halsey far to the north. It shaped up as the last great naval battle in history.

Davison laid on the knots as Task Group 38.4 pounded west at high speed. At dawn on the 24th, *Enterprise* and *Franklin* were to launch search teams from maximum range east of Luzon: 375 miles instead of the typical 250. Four wedge-shaped sectors were assigned, two for each carrier, extending west of the island chain. Dog Smith's crews drew the two southern sectors.

Major elements of the Japanese fleet were reported eastbound in the Sulu Sea, west of the Philippines. The *Enterprise* contribution was two sector searches launched at 6:00 A.M., each with six bombers and eight fighters instead of the usual three or four planes per sector. To make the distance, the Helldivers carried underwing fuel tanks and two 500-pound bombs. They wasted no time, departing the force in fifteen minutes. Their search leg—southwest through west—took them over the width of the myriad Philippine islands, which in bright sunlight assumed an almost fluorescent greenness.

Just before 8:00 one team found three destroyers "apparently going no place in particular" and left them for possible attack on the return leg.

Around 8:30 Lieutenant Raymond E. Moore's search team struck gold about 100 miles northwest of the fabled isle of Zamboanga, in the northern part of *Enterprise*'s sector. The aircrews correctly identified two Fuso class battleships (39,000 tons with fourteen-inch main batteries) plus a Mogami cruiser and four destroyers, northbound at fifteen knots. *Fuso* was a favorite in the imperial household: Emperor Hirohito's brother had served aboard her twice. Her sister *Yamashiro* trailed with her own escorts, presenting two distinct targets.

Moore radioed his skipper in the adjacent sector, and Emmett Riera turned northerly to link up. Between them they had a decent strike group: a dozen bombers and sixteen fighters. Helldiver pilot Ensign Robert J. Barnes called the sight of the majestic Japanese southern force, cutting broad white wakes below him, "something you dream about as a dive bomber pilot. The anti-aircraft was terrific."

From ten miles the battlewagons' main batteries fired fused rounds, bursting at 12,000 feet. Spectacular explosions detonated within 500 feet of the Big E's aircraft, erupting in red, blue, yellow, and white flashes. The long-range antiaircraft fire was surprisingly accurate, causing some fliers to flinch in their cockpits. The phosphorus rounds impressed everybody over the ships that morning: brilliant white bursts in the sky, flicking greedy tendrils outward from the explosion, seeking a daring or unfortunate pilot.

With everyone now present, Riera led the bombers to 15,000 feet while assigning targets. The Helldivers' 500-pounders could not inflict serious damage on battleships, but it was unthinkable to pass up the opportunity. Riera took the lead battlewagon, *Yamashiro,* sending Moore's team after *Fuso*, farther astern. As Fred Bakutis led his Hellcats down to suppress flak with rockets and gunfire, the Helldivers timed their dives to near perfection, plunging on both leviathans simultaneously, out of the morning sun. The setup prevented enemy gunners from concentrating their firepower on one group of planes, yielding better survival prospects for the aviators.

It was a sight for the fliers to remember all their lives: high-velocity rockets snaking out, bursting on gray steel hulls and superstructures, while bombs left Helldiver bellies at about 2,000 feet. All the while Japanese gunners put up a wall of five-inch flak, often accurate in altitude but wide in deflection. However, it was thick—so thick that some pilots could not easily discern hits or misses on the ships.

Bombing 20 claimed hits on both battleships. *Fuso* took a quarter-ton bomb alongside the number two turret, exploding inside the hull and killing the crew of a secondary battery. Some old seams failed, allowing seawater to intrude, but pumps handled the inflow. *Fuso* also had a large fire amidships to aft, still burning when the attackers pulled off half an hour later. She heeled out of column to port, slowing visibly.

Meanwhile, *Yamashiro* sprung some plates from near misses. Then a Helldiver pilot put one of his bombs on her stern, igniting a depth charge, rupturing an aviation fuel tank, and incinerating two floatplanes. She developed a serious list approaching fifteen degrees that was corrected by counterflooding to port. From overhead—and from some attending vessels—the old battlewagon appeared in trouble with thick, roiling smoke. But eventually the persistent flames were doused and she continued on course.

Cruiser *Mogami* also was attacked—no stranger to *Enterprise* aviators, who had mauled her at Midway and seen her west of Saipan. Three bombs splashed close aboard but the veteran warship escaped damage. In fact, she coolly launched a floatplane during the bombing attack, as Vice Admiral Shoji Nishimura badly needed reconnaissance information.

Strafing Hellcats made a stinging impression: as a Japanese officer recalled, "enemy bullets showered like rain near the bridge, and pierced here and there." About twenty men were killed aboard *Yamashiro,* and a petty officer on the bridge was wounded within a few feet of Admiral Nishimura, who appeared impassive. He remained focused on his ultimate mission— sailing out of Surigao Strait that night to fall upon American shipping in Leyte Gulf.

Bombing 20 was impressed with Fred Bakutis's fighters, describing their performance as "outstanding." The Helldiver crews appreciatively noted that the escort maintained position, then dived ahead of the bombers, strafing and rocketing, suppressing AA fire "with complete disregard of personal safety." It was no more than fighter pilots were supposed to do, but the bombers' sentiments were no less heartfelt.

Somewhere amid the flak, Bakutis took hits to his engine, forcing him to ditch east of the Japanese force. Surprisingly detached, he was intrigued with the clarity of the water, able to watch his Hellcat descend beneath him, spinning idly into the depths. While his friends circled low overhead, Japanese main batteries continued firing from as much as ten miles off. A Helldiver ignored the gunfire to drop the fighter skipper a two-man raft, which he inflated and boarded. With nothing else to be done, the dark blue planes set course for *Enterprise,* arriving after nearly six hours in the air.

★   ★   ★

Of the three Japanese armadas committed to the Philippines, Vice Admiral Takeo Kurita's center force had been reported by American submarines passing Palawan Island early on the 23rd. The subs did well, sinking two cruisers and crippling another. Aboard *Atago,* Kurita had his flagship shot out from beneath him. Still, he retained an extraordinarily powerful armada with five battleships, nine cruisers, and thirteen destroyers. He continued eastward into the Sibuyan Sea, bounded by Mindoro and Leyte islands.

An *Intrepid* search team from Task Group 38.2 found Kurita about noon on the 24th, more than 300 miles north-northeast of Nishimura as *Enterprise* was readying a deckload strike of nine bombers, eight torpedo planes, and sixteen fighters. The Big E, with her strike cocked and ready, launched at 1:15. After one turn near the ship, the thirty-three planes headed out, rendezvousing en route to conserve fuel for the 300-mile trip. With Fred Bakutis adrift somewhere off Zamboanga, Jim Gray assumed command of the fighters.

By the time Air Group 20 arrived over Kurita's force, other task groups already had weighed in over the previous four hours. In beautiful weather with thirty-mile visibility, the Big E's squadrons arrived at 3:00.

The Japanese were deployed in two units, one astern of the other. Dog Smith took his squadrons to the western formation, selecting the obvious target, the huge battleship *Musashi,* named for Tokyo's province. Commissioned in August 1942 at the time of the Guadalcanal landings, her AA armament was vastly upgraded, notably from twenty-four to 130 25mm guns. Intelligence estimated the Yamato class battleships at 50,000 tons but they easily topped 60,000. Whatever their bulk, they were the largest things afloat.

Pilots and aircrewmen who were not even in training two years before gawked at *Musashi.* From about fifteen miles away she began throwing huge explosive shells that erupted in a colored kaleidoscope: purple, red, blue, yellow, and white. None came close to the Big E formation, but it was still unnerving.

Smith continued west of the target, then came about northerly to place the afternoon sun behind him. The Helldivers and Avengers were directed onto the battlewagon while the fighters were to suppress AA fire from the escorts.

Like a thoroughly trained football team, Smith's squadrons proceeded with their well-rehearsed choreography: the Hellcat blockers providing interference for the running backs in Helldivers and Avengers.

The three-dimensional offensive pattern had been crafted to present the two-dimensional defense with an insoluble problem: in very limited time, recognize the developing play and try to counter it before the ball carriers crossed the goal line.

From there on it was almost routine, as Smith had imprinted the process on his aircrews through months of drills. Lieutenant Commander Sam Prickett took his torpedo planes forty-five degrees to port while the Hellcats dived the opposite way. The Helldivers pressed ahead to the pushover point, presenting Kurita's gunners with a three-axis threat. Settled into their runs, the bombers dived from overhead, the fighters from the southeast, and the torpedo planes turning in from the southwest. The Japanese gunners—hundreds of them on a dozen ships—were presented with a bewildering arabesque of assailants from high above, from medium altitude and almost from sea level; from port and starboard.

Leading a fighter division was Joe Lawler. "From about 17,000 feet we pushed over rapidly and settled in about a 60 degree dive. As soon as I could get the sight on the cruiser I opened fire with six guns, firing short bursts all the way down. . . . At about 3,500 feet the ship looked big in the gunsight and . . . I salvoed six rockets. I could see some people manning exposed antiaircraft guns, all shooting like crazy."

From directly above *Musashi* looked immense, and she was—nearly as long as *Enterprise* and much wider. Tracking her in their steep dives, speed brakes deployed, Jim Cooper's nine Helldivers probably scored four hits with half-tonners, smothering the port bow, killing all the forward damage control team and wrecking the chief steward's office.

Meanwhile, Prickett's eight Avengers split for a coordinated attack from both sides. The Mark 13 torpedoes entered the water, plunged to perhaps 150 feet, then powered up to their selected depth. Boiling through the waves at thirty-three knots, they armed their warheads after a 200-yard run and streaked ahead. Gone were the "wild hippo" characteristics that bedeviled Scoofer Coffin's and Bill Martin's pilots. At least three of Torpedo 20's fish struck the hull—two forward and one amidships—detonating with tremendous concussive force from the 600-pound warheads, smashing through steel and springing adjacent plates from the hydrodynamic shock.

From their cockpits, pilots and aircrews could not easily discern between torpedo hits and bomb near misses, nor could they tell how hard they had struck the target. Vertical white spouts leapt from the dark blue sea beside the great gray vessel, cascading onto its decks. Youthful optimism usually perceived what young eyes wished to see, but that day one thing was obvious: the huge battlewagon was taking a hellacious beating. The torpedo hits flooded a cooling room and a hydraulic machinery compartment, further impeding the ship's steering. Far below deck, repair crews slaved unceasingly, shoring up leaks in the central damage control spaces.

In about five minutes Dog Smith's thirty-three planes delivered their ordnance, scored hits, and got away clean. The Hellcats fired some five dozen rockets at three of *Musashi*'s escorts, with a destroyer battered by a terrific explosion that further suppressed AA fire.

Pulling away, *Enterprise* fliers reported the battleship smoking heavily, down by bow, apparently immobile. Actually she was still doing fifteen knots or better, but not for long. Within minutes nearly three dozen more planes from *Franklin, Intrepid,* and *Cabot* rolled in.

Predictably, accounts vary of the terrible carnage inflicted by successive attacks. The Americans thought that *Musashi* absorbed nineteen torpedoes plus seventeen bombs and as many near misses. Japanese records conceded eleven torpedoes and ten bombs. Whatever the numbers, the damage was real enough: the battle flag was lowered and, in ultimate extremis, the emperor's portrait was passed to another ship. At 7:30 that evening, with a thirty-degree list, *Musashi* began turning turtle. Six minutes later she rolled over to port, sinking bow-first on the way to the bottom 4,000 feet down, taking more than a thousand of the 2,400 men on board.

Meanwhile, cruiser *Myoko* turned back with torpedo damage, leaving Kurita with twenty-three vessels including four battleships. Nevertheless, he reversed course and was last seen steaming westward, apparently beaten.

During the day's multiple attacks, Japanese gunners downed eighteen of the 259 carrier planes that swarmed over the armada, but none from *Enterprise*. It was a momentous day for carrier aviation, avidly shared by Big E aircrews and sailors who were eager for more. Late that afternoon Davison's Task Group 38.4, about 120 miles east of San Bernardino Strait between Luzon and Samar, joined 38.3 with *Essex, Lexington,* and light carrier *Langley*. But that morning in Leyte Gulf, Rear Admiral Frederick C. Sherman's group had lost *Princeton* to conventional air attack—the first fast American carrier sunk since 1942.

Shortly after 8:00 P.M. Big E men felt the ship turning as she came starboard, engines sending vibrations through deck plates upward through the soles of sailors' shoes. Soon the word got around: Rear Admiral Jerry

Bogan's 38.2 also had linked up while 38.1 was being recalled from refueling to the east. Joined by Vice Admiral Willis Lee's battleships, the task force headed north at high speed in response to electrifying news: Japanese carriers off the northeastern tip of Luzon.

Tom Hamilton recalled, "The last report was about 9:30 at night that the Jap force at San Bernardino Strait had turned back. We had no flag aboard . . . but we had the flag circuits, so Captain Glover shared that information with me. We applauded Admiral Halsey's decision to attack the northern force."

Hamilton had known Halsey at Annapolis when the future admiral was commander of the Academy station ship and boxing coach. Hamilton knew Halsey as a battler, and expected more battle to come.

ANOTHER DAY, ANOTHER BATTLE

Jim Gray retained his dual capacity as interim skipper of Fighting 20 and running the night fighters. At 2:15 A.M. on the 25th he splashed a Mavis seaplane snooping the task group. It was the start of another long day.

Beginning at 5:40 *Enterprise* catapulted seven two-plane search teams covering the western quadrant. They found nothing, but close in their slipstream were other scouts and powerful airborne strikes to minimize response times if something turned up. Before long, word arrived of the enemy northern force, 120 miles north-northwest. Vice Admiral Jisaburo Ozawa had four carriers, two battleships, and escorts—an irresistible target. Which was exactly what the Japanese intended.

Big E sailors weren't the only ones who knew Halsey's combative nature—so did the enemy. The genial, occasionally boozy Bill of 1942 had evolved—some said mutated—into the ferocious, headline-hunting Bull. Ozawa, who had commanded during the Marianas battle, assessed that America's most aggressive admiral could not pass up a shot at Japan's remaining carriers. By drawing most of Third Fleet north, the amphibious forces of Seventh Fleet could be attacked in Leyte Gulf with relative impunity by the two battleship units pummeled the day before.

Enterprise's air plan provided four strikes: two in the morning, one at midday, and the last in late afternoon. Dog Smith led the first off at 6:00 A.M., taking eight bombers, seven Avengers, and eight Hellcats. The group received real-time information as Riera's bomber pilots heard a report that the enemy flattops were turning in to the wind to launch planes.

Within sight of Ozawa's force, *Enterprise* aviators gaped at the scene.

To many fliers the four carriers escorted by battleships "looked like the whole Japanese Navy." After the previous day, that assessment was not far wrong: the flattops were *Zuikaku* with the smaller *Zuiho*, *Chitose*, and *Chiyoda*, the only flattops able to put to sea.

The *Enterprise* formation passed up the first two carriers encountered, which were assailed by other air groups. The largest was *Zuikaku*, last of the six Pearl Harbor attackers. But one of the smaller carriers was making full speed. She was *Zuiho*, which Birney Strong and Skinhead Irvine had clobbered at Santa Cruz two years before. She had survived the Marianas debacle, though she had not been attacked by *Enterprise*'s Air Group 10.

Diving out of the southwest from 12,000 feet, sun behind them, Emmett Riera led his seven pilots down nearly vertically, each peeling off and following one another in a lethal waterfall of stooping Helldivers. They received very little antiaircraft fire during their thirty-second dives. As each bomber dropped a pair of 1,000-pounders, *Zuiho* appeared smothered by near misses. Then one bomb hit the stern, bulging the flight deck, and the ship temporarily lost steering. *Zuiho* began burning from the hit and damaging near misses as the bombers pulled off amid increasing gunfire from a battleship, two cruisers, and about five destroyers.

Meanwhile, the Avengers descended to within a couple hundred feet of the waves to launch torpedoes, though it's uncertain whether any connected. But *Enterprise* pilots also hit two cruisers and three destroyers with rockets.

Ozawa had launched his remaining aircraft on combat air patrol, and the Japanese pilots fought with desperation, knowing their remaining flight decks were at stake. Some unusually competent Zekes shot down Joe Lawler's wingman, Ensign George Denby. Another Hellcat fell to flak but both pilots survived.

On the egress, pilots picked their way through the gray forest of Japanese superstructures. Bob Barnes declared the flak "the most intense I have ever seen, with all ships firing everything they had . . . every ship you flew by was shooting at you."

Departing *Enterprise* at 6:45 A.M., the second strike was the day's smallest—just fifteen aircraft with one of the two Avengers tacking on to *Franklin*'s group. Opting for the battleships, the Big E's fliers probably tagged the *Ise*, distinctive with her stern-mounted flight deck.

Dog Smith had a day like no other, leading three of the four strikes—once with merely forty-five minutes between sorties. In all, he logged more than ten hours in the air. Meanwhile, the flight deck crew also toiled throughout the day, inspecting, arming, and fueling the planes as they landed and were prepared to fly again. *Enterprise*'s "airdales" demonstrated why they had long been the fleet standard. Four strikes went off without a hitch, each with bombers, torpedo planes, and fighters arranged on deck, properly armed, fully fueled, and inspected.

The noon launch dispatched twenty-one planes, targeting what appeared to be an "Otaka class" escort carrier. In truth she may have been the 11,200-ton *Zuiho* again, as the tough flattop continued absorbing American ordnance. By then *Chitose* had already died, leaving her sister *Chiyoda* the only other small-deck carrier. Whatever the target, *Enterprise*'s fliers claimed two fish and four or more bomb hits. Whoever did the deed, about 3:30 that afternoon *Zuiho* slid under stern-first, rolling to starboard, taking 214 imperial sailors with her.

An hour before, the Big E bade a respectful if not fond farewell to *Zuikaku,* the Auspicious Crane that had spread her destructive wings across the Pacific from Pearl Harbor onward. Her squadrons had helped sink the first *Lexington* at Coral Sea, attacked *Enterprise* at Eastern Solomons, and contributed to *Hornet*'s death at Santa Cruz. Mainly victim of the new *Lexington*'s Air Group 19, she sank with more than 800 men.

Dog Smith's last flight was to his liking: at 4:20 he headed up sixteen Hellcats packing 1,000-pounders, with no bombers to escort. Fighting 20 reported numerous hits on a light cruiser and a possible hit on a battlewagon. One Hellcat went down but again efficient rescue work retrieved the fliers from all five aircraft, including an Avenger and Helldiver.

In four strikes totaling seventy-seven aircraft, the Big E expended a dozen torpedoes, seventy bombs, 107 rockets, and 27,000 rounds of machine gun and cannon ammunition—vastly more than the thirty-one bombs that twenty-eight Air Group 10 planes had dropped that long-ago June evening over Ozawa's Mobile Fleet. But such was the changed nature of naval air combat in just four months—a day-long pounding versus a one-shot fling into the dark. Air Group 20 claimed shares in two carriers (which may both have been *Zuiho*) plus damage to a battleship, three cruisers, and four destroyers.

Despite the exultation of sinking so many capital ships—some old enemies of two or three years standing—*Enterprise* men marveled at events to the south while Ozawa was suffering. The decoy had worked: with Halsey drawn northward, the presumably beaten enemy center and southern forces (both hit by *Enterprise* the day before) had nearly succeeded. Nishimura's southern force, with *Fuso* and *Yamashiro,* died trying to penetrate Rear Admiral Jesse Oldendorf's gray rampart of old battleships and new destroyers defending Surigao Strait. But Kurita with mighty *Yamato* and her consorts had emerged from San Bernardino Strait to be confronted and repelled by an undersized escort carrier group off Samar. It was a scandalous multilevel command failure that went unpunished. The theater commander, General Douglas MacArthur, had failed to coordinate Army-Navy communications, leaving Halsey of Third Fleet and Thomas Kinkaid's amphibious Seventh Fleet (he of *Enterprise*'s flag bridge at Santa Cruz) pursuing their own goals. Consequently, neither admiral bothered to guard the vital San Bernardino Strait. To discipline, let alone remove, three senior commanders was politically unthinkable in Washington.

Thus ended the three-day slugfest generically called the Battle of Leyte Gulf, fought on the sea and in the air. The Imperial Navy lost four carriers, three battleships, eight cruisers, and a dozen destroyers. Air Group 20 had attacked three major fleet units in two days—a pace of operations never to be repeated.

Other than the light carrier *Princeton,* American losses were limited to the morning surprise on the 25th when Kurita's battleships and cruisers jumped the escort carrier force called Taffy Three. Two baby flattops and three escorts were sunk in repulsing the Japanese center force.

In the assessment of historian Evan Thomas, "For the Imperial Japanese Navy, the battle was a death knell. Never again would the Japanese be able to put to sea to engage the Americans in a fleet action. Without a fleet, the Japanese home islands were cut off, starved, and exposed to American attack."

LEYTE DENOUEMENT

There was no respite after the largest naval battle of the war. The fast carriers turned their attention northward, striking the Visayans in the central Philippines, and the upper portion of Luzon. The attacks kept the pressure on the Japanese now that American troops were ashore.

During a sweep on October 27, *Enterprise* pilots found the 2,500-ton destroyer *Shiranui.* Steaming to the aid of another destroyer run aground, she was caught north of the island of Panay. Big E bombers scored at least three hits, sending her down bow-first. The six-year-old ship was lost with all hands.

The next two days passed in active routine, but on October 30 the task group faced Japan's newest, eeriest weapon—suicide planes. Off Samar, the large island southeast of Luzon, the raiders were tracked by radar within eighteen miles when *Franklin*'s search radar failed. Admiral Davison got word to *Enterprise*, which had to pass the information back to the flagship.

In the intervening few minutes, radar plots got confused. *Enterprise* sent Hellcats out on the correct bearing but the pilots missed the bandits a couple of miles away. A second vector put *San Jacinto* fighters onto the enemy, downing four Zekes, but the suiciders were then in their high-speed dives toward the ships. Minutes later three Zekes and three Judy dive-bombers were sighted overhead. Three went for *Enterprise* and *San Jacinto*; two near-missed "San Jac." The last one slanted into a shallow run aimed at the Big E's starboard side. The gun boss withheld his five-inchers for fear of hitting friendly ships, but the 20mm and 40mm mounts opened up a thick, accurate fire. All the while Tom Hamilton stood exposed on the island, re-laying what was occurring for the hundreds of sailors belowdecks.

Set afire by repeated hits, the Zeke came straight in, unwavering. Per-haps by then the pilot was dead, as he needed only a slight course correc-tion. But the burning fighter flashed just over the flight deck astern of the island and went into the water to port. It exploded so close that aluminum pieces dropped into the catwalk.

Meanwhile, three suiciders were drawn to *Franklin*, two miles off the Big E's port beam. The first was shot down close aboard but the second dived into the flight deck, igniting a huge fireball that killed or wounded eighty-six men. The other plane, burning but under control, plunged into *Belleau Wood*'s stern, inflicting some ninety casualties.

Franklin fought fires for more than an hour before smothering the flames. At day's end it was apparent that she and *Belleau Wood* would be headed for a West Coast shipyard. Big Ben had been tagged twice in two weeks; some Big E men began thinking CV-13 truly was unlucky to draw such attention.

The kamikaze experience was unnerving, even for *Enterprise* veter-ans. They had just seen the new enemy up close: the lethal determination of Japanese pilots who dived into American ships without flinching. It wasn't like Lieutenant Nakai in his doomed bomber off Kwajalein twenty months before. That had been a desperate, valiant last act that fighting men understood. But now, off Samar, the lesson was obvious to everyone from seaman to admiral: the only way to defeat the dedicated kamikaze was to kill him.

The next afternoon *Enterprise* regained her flagship status as Rear Admiral Davison brought his staff over from *Franklin* en route to Ulithi. Extremely bright and well read, Davison had a friendly, even fun-loving nature that contrasted with *Enterprise*'s previous admiral, Black Jack Reeves. Davison had spent all but four years of his career in aviation, winning his wings in 1920 at age twenty-four—about as young as an Annapolis graduate could manage at the time.

Late on the 30th, in the Sibuyan Sea, a sharp-eyed lookout on the submarine *Hardhead* spotted something three quarters of a mile off. Investigation turned up Fred Bakutis—dehydrated, hungry, blistered by sea and sun, but alive. "His physical condition was excellent considering that he had been in a small life raft seven days," *Hardhead* reported. He recovered enough to resume flying and shot down two more enemy aircraft when the air group transferred to *Lexington* in November.

Enterprise got one leader back but lost another. On November 10 Emmett Riera was tapped to take over *Hornet*'s air group in Task Group 38.1. The previous air group commander, Fred Schrader, had been killed at Formosa, and with no immediate replacement available, Riera moved to Air Group 11. He was succeeded by Lieutenant Commander Raymond E. Moore on November 10, the anniversary of the squadron's establishment.

The next morning—ironically, Armistice Day—*Enterprise* squadrons attacked ships in Ormoc Bay on Leyte's north coast. Planes from three task groups sank four destroyers and four cargo vessels but Dog Smith's men stood out. During their attack one destroyer capsized while another, weaving erratically, exploded. So did a cargo ship. A smaller escort lost its bow and went dead in the water.

But losses continued. Over the next ten days the torpedo squadron lost a crew while the fighters were especially hard hit, with five pilots killed around Manila and another on the farewell look at Yap.

In the win column, Bakutis's fliers added a dozen victories on the 13th, and the next day Doug Baker ran his string to twelve. After two years, Don Runyon's *Enterprise* record of nine had finally been broken.

On the evening of the 19th two fighter divisions under Lieutenant (jg) Lafe Shannon splashed three Bettys west of the task group. They brought

Fighting 20's tally to 135 in barely five weeks—top score for all Big E squadrons throughout the war. Moreover, Bakutis's pilots had done a superb job on escort—as good as the Grim Reapers. While aboard *Enterprise* only two of the bombers even got a shot at a Japanese aircraft. The torpedo squadron lost twenty-one men and the bombers eight, but none to enemy fighters.

During its three-month *Enterprise* deployment Air Group 20 lost forty-two men and forty-seven planes. It was a heavy toll, more than Air Group 10 had lost on either deployment from late 1942 to mid-1944. But the fall campaigns were the most intensive yet conducted in the Pacific.

At Ulithi on November 23, Air Group 20 "cross-decked" to *Lexington* where Dog Smith's squadrons would complete their tour in late January. Marking the departure, *Enterprise* gave Smith's outfit a whimsical "letter of introduction" to "the Lex." Therein CV-6 cautioned against excessive trust by CV-16, *Enterprise*'s air department noting that any carrier could only do so much with an air group and, after all, "The Big E is only human."

Enterprise ferried *Lexington*'s Air Group 19 to Pearl Harbor, arriving December 6. Veterans of 1941 reflected on what a difference three years made. The Pacific war had completely reversed course in that time, but the press of operations remained insistent. Any hopes for Christmas in Hawaii were quickly dashed, as the Big E was urgently needed in an entirely new mission.

11

* * *

"Live with Great Enthusiasm"

Lieutenant (jg) Shunsuke Tomiyasu, the twenty-two-year-old suicide pilot who knocked *Enterprise* out of the war on May 14, 1945. (Kan Sugahara via *Naval History* magazine)

Bill Martin was back.

If any aviator was Mr. Enterprise, it could only be Commander William I. Martin, veteran of both Air Group 10 deployments in the Big E. After flying with Scouting 10 at Guadalcanal and leading Torpedo 10 to Truk and the Marianas, he was ready for a record-setting third cruise in *Enterprise.* Now in December 1944 he had an unusual command.

Night Air Group 90 was only the second such unit in the Navy. Its fighter squadron had been cobbled together on the East Coast that spring, the amalgam of four Hellcat outfits under Lieutenant Commander Robert J. McCullough. The attached Avengers were expanded into Night Torpedo

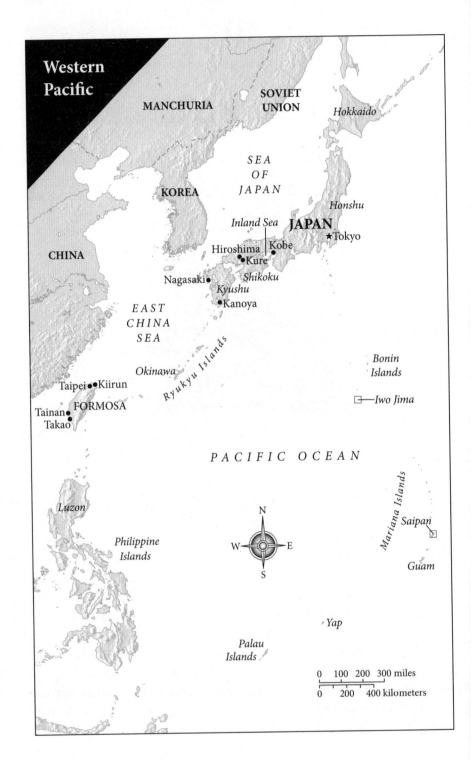

Western
Pacific

MANCHURIA

SOVIET
UNION

Hokkaido

SEA
OF
JAPAN

KOREA

Honshu

Inland Sea

JAPAN

CHINA

Hiroshima
Kure
Kobe

★Tokyo

Nagasaki
Shikoku

Kyushu
Kanoya

EAST
CHINA
SEA

Bonin
Islands

Okinawa

Ryukyu Islands

Iwo Jima

Taipei Kiirun

Tainan FORMOSA
Takao

PACIFIC OCEAN

Luzon

Mariana Islands

Saipan

Philippine
Islands

W   E

N

S

Guam

Yap

Palau
Islands

0 100 200 300 miles

0   200   400 kilometers

Squadron 90, led by another *Enterprise* veteran, Lieutenant Russell Kippen.

Martin assumed command in late September, shortly after the air group arrived in Hawaii. Almost immediately he called an all-hands meeting in the Barbers Point hangar. Addressing some 230 men of both squadrons and air group staff, he spoke earnestly, directly. "We're going to get in trouble. Anybody who doesn't want to go along, one step forward."

Heads turned as fliers and sailors looked around, half expecting some to accept the offer. None did. With that, Martin said. "Dismissed," and the men returned to work. Among them, radar technician Arnold Olson was impressed. He recalled, "That was the first time I saw Commander Martin and it might have been the last time, but I sure didn't want to be left behind!"

Air Group 90 contained 103 officers but only a dozen ensigns—far fewer than daytime air groups owing to the requisite experience. Martin wanted his aviators to have fifty daytime carrier landings and twenty-five or more night traps before entering combat. He had assembled a passel of devoted night owls—true believers like himself. Toward that end, he brought along some of his Torpedo 10 talent, including Bill Balden, Crossbow Collins, Hotshot Charlie Henderson, Cliff Largess, and radar wizard Bill Chace.

It was no surprise that *Enterprise* became the first big-deck night carrier. She had pioneered almost every advancement in nocturnal flattop aviation, from Butch O'Hare's bat teams to Bill Martin's attack missions and Chick Harmer's Corsair night fighters. Martin's former shipmate Turner Caldwell (of *Enterprise* Flight 300 at Guadalcanal) already led the first full-time night air group from the light carrier *Independence*.

For her new role, *Enterprise*'s typical loadout was thirty Hellcat night fighters and two photo planes plus twenty-seven radar-equipped Avenger bombers, all sporting a horizontal arrow on the tail. Fifty-nine aircraft were far fewer than the ninety-three authorized for the recently departed Air Group 20, but Martin's were optimized for night flying. They provided more bang for the buck, around the clock.

The ship itself reflected the new mission. White "victory lights" on stiff rubber posts were placed to port and starboard on the deck, forming a reference from the first crash barrier back to the ramp. The standard red deck-edge lights were aligned alternately to port and starboard—aft and outboard thirty degrees—to allow pilots to see them early in the carrier approach. Providing greater depth perception, the two light arrays notably

improved pilots' ability to line up properly with few corrections from landing signal officers. Consequently, night flying pilots seldom received wave-
offs.

Night operations were further enhanced by control of the "Snapper"
air traffic director in the Air Defense Forward position. Once cleared by
the bridge to permit homing aircraft to enter the landing pattern, Snapper
advised each pilot of his position abeam by radar, ideally 1,600 yards out.
A secure VHF radio circuit permitted a running commentary when needed.
Finally, nocturnal LSOs wore illuminated suits with lighted wands instead
of the usual paddles.

Two months after the sprawling Leyte Gulf battle, the war continued apace.
On Christmas Eve the new skipper, Captain Grover B. H. Hall, took *Enterprise* out of Pearl, and Air Group 90 flew aboard, paying tribute to its
legendary carrier. Martin led his Avengers in a letter E while McCullough's
Hellcats formed V for victory. All aircraft got safely aboard, and the crew
began settling in for the ship's third wartime Christmas. Said Yeoman John
MacGlashing, "Everyone tried to stay busy and not talk or think about it,
but it was tough."

Some levity emerged among the serious business at hand. Reporting
aboard with the new ship's band was Wilton Syckes, previously Maryland's
sixteen-year-old finalist in the national violin championships. The Navy had
turned him into an even more versatile musician, and Syckes drew some
attention when he struggled up the gangway with his trombone case in addition to his violin and seabag.

The crew immediately recognized the new captain as an enthusiastic
ship handler. Unlike other Big E skippers, Hall had a previous ship command, the escort carrier *Charger*. He impressed all *Enterprise* men—and
worried some—because "he drove that ship like a Model A Ford." Despite
his often nonregulation demeanor, "Dynamite" Hall clearly knew his business.

As a dedicated night carrier, *Enterprise* relied even more heavily upon
radio and radar than other flattops. The electronics shop got a gross of
condoms, not for use as prophylactics at exotic ports, but to protect the
radar antenna waveguides on Avengers. The gadgetry required skilled attention by men such Arnold Olson, another teenaged violin prodigy who
became an electronics technician. He was surprised to be accepted at radio
school, insisting that his previous experience was tuning in *Fibber McGee*

and Molly or *Amos 'n' Andy.* From there it was a logical step to aviation, with one chilling aspect: radar techs were not to allow themselves to be captured, lest they reveal valuable information.

All manner of equipment had to be checked and tested. For instance, the transponder in the identification friend or foe (IFF) set had six vacuum tubes requiring frequent inspection. But the electronics were state-of-the-art: the aircraft radar altimeter was unusually good for the era, accurate within five feet, and the Avenger's search radar could pick up a large ship at forty miles or more.

Off duty, the new air group's enlisted men learned the Big E's nooks and crannies as had their predecessors. Nickel-dime blackjack and craps games were safely held in recessed spaces on the hangar deck. Shipboard imbibers had their own schemes as a symbiotic relationship grew among various divisions. The entire Navy knew about the recreational use of high-grade torpedo alcohol, and the ship's ordnance department also had extra bombsight alcohol, since the Nordens were almost never used. Meanwhile, the air group and M Division (main engines) collaborated on a still in the engineering spaces, safely out of view. The resultant white lightning was barely palatable, but potent, which was generally the priority.

The Big E quickly adjusted to her backward schedule. The day crew worked from 6:00 A.M. to 6:00 P.M., when the night shift took over to conduct most operations. The night crew normally was roused at 3:00 P.M., receiving a hot meal from 11:30 P.M. to 1:30 A.M.

Because aircraft carriers are perhaps the noisiest work environment of all, and because general quarters could sound anytime, crews were given unusual latitude for rest. Officers generally allowed fliers and sailors to "caulk off" whenever and wherever they could catch a nap.

The attrition began two days out. Two fighters and a bomber were lost, the first two on launch and the other in a hard landing. Another Avenger went in the water while landing on the 29th. A pilot and aircrewman died in those incidents—further reminder that there was no such thing as "routine" carrier operations.

New Year's passed with little observance at sea, but the Big E perked up on January 5 when she rendezvoused with Task Group 38.5. The group commander was known to *Enterprise.* Promoted to rear admiral, former skipper Matt Gardner had left the ship in July after the Marianas operation and now commanded the world's first night carrier task group. *Enterprise* was teamed with the light carrier *Independence,* whose Night Air Group 41 remained in the capable hands of Big E alumnus Turner Caldwell.

Caldwell's unit was experienced, having joined the task force in August. His pilots had tracked Vice Admiral Kurita's force eastbound through San Bernardino Strait the night of October 24–25, but the information was discounted by Third Fleet staff. Air Group 20 had seen the results of that lapse when Kurita broke into Leyte Gulf the next morning.

RETURN TO THE PHILIPPINES

Task Force 38 was headed for the Philippines again, contributing her nocturnal capability to supporting the Army landings at Lingayen Gulf on Luzon's west coast. The first launch on January 7 sent McCullough's Hellcats to an area known to *Enterprise* pilots: Clark Field, Manila. Fifteen night fighters were catapulted into the predawn darkness 235 miles offshore, but three rebounded with radar problems. McCullough led his dozen remaining planes into heavy flak, strafing visible targets, but the Japanese gunners were experienced. Three Hellcats were holed, the skipper's being the hardest hit. McCullough faced a serious challenge—getting aboard with damaged controls, sticky throttle, and no hydraulics. His plane skimmed over the arresting wires, smashed through the barriers, careened off parked aircraft, and tumbled overboard to port. Sailors standing on deck looked down at the sinking, bashed-up Hellcat and reckoned that Mr. McCullough was gone.

Incredibly, the skipper got out of his cockpit and was picked up by the plane guard destroyer. His injuries were pronounced "repairable" and he returned to duty.

Meanwhile, the flight schedule proceeded as planned. Lieutenant Carl Nielsen led four Hellcats to northern Luzon where he found airborne targets. In ten minutes he claimed a Dinah, Zeke, and an Oscar—a triple kill, extremely rare for night fighters.

Two more fighter divisions pounced on Lingayen Gulf and Clark Field, strafing and rocketing beneath moisture-laden clouds. But visibility worsened, and on the way back Ensign Charles Gibson and John Sowell collided. Sowell was seen parachuting into the sea but neither pilot was ever found.

The torpedo planes also kept busy. Charlie Henderson led Lieutenant (jg) Gilbert "Gibby" Blake to bomb Aparri and Laoag airfields, where fires were reported. Lieutenant (jg) Joe Doyle and Lieutenant (jg) Cliff Largess also struck Aparri and another field but claimed no damage in the full dark. Lack of observable results would become a continuing irritant to aggressive aviators.

INDOCHINA INTERLUDE

Third Fleet commander Bull Halsey was in a collecting mood that January. Not content with sinking four carriers and one of the world's two biggest battleships at Leyte, he wanted two more battlewagons on Third Fleet's scoreboard. Intelligence hinted that the sisters *Ise* and *Hyuga* might be holed up at Cam Ranh Bay, French Indochina, and that's where Task Force 38 headed. It was a historic moment—the first time an Allied naval force had turned a wake in the South China Sea since 1942. And what a force it was: 101 ships including thirteen fast carriers and six battleships.

Rear Admiral Matt Gardner's two night stalker carriers began flinging dark blue airplanes into the dark black sky at 3:00 A.M. on the 12th. They represented the tip of Halsey's spear, the first of some 1,500 sorties that trolled Tonkin Gulf waters and owned Vietnamese skies. But Indochina proved vacant of capital ships. First by radar, then by God's light in the misty gray dawn, it became obvious that *Ise* and *Hyuga* were absent— actually anchored at Singapore, 800 miles southwest.

Bill Martin and company were nearly as disappointed as Bill Halsey. Torpedo 90 had an antiship strike prepped with Avengers on deck, armed with torpedoes—this time, torpedoes that worked. But with no ship targets, *Enterprise* ordnancemen downloaded the fish and uploaded bombs, each Avenger receiving the now standard loadout of four 500-pounders.

Despite a lowering ceiling and reduced visibility, Russ Kippen's eleven bombers sniffed out a large coastal convoy: fifteen ships whose escort included a light cruiser. Kippen took her for himself—she was the 6,000-ton *Kashii*—and straddled her with two bombs. Other Avenger pilots also scored as Lieutenant (jg) Joseph F. Jennings claimed two hits on an escort that caught fire, and Ensign James D. Landon put a quarter-tonner on a merchantman's stern. All the while, Hellcats suppressed anti-aircraft fire with shallow strafing runs—more time to shoot than steep approaches—and lit up ships with rocket hits. In all, the *Enterprise* fliers sank one merchantman and left two in fiery distress. *Kashii*, apparently wounded, turned for the beach and later was finished by bombers from Task Group 38.3.

Aerial opposition was negligible as carrier pilots only logged a dozen shootdowns through the day. Bob McCullough's Hellcats flew two missions to Saigon's airport—the fabled Tan Son Nhut of a later war—but had to be content with strafing.

The next day, January 13, the Big E crested pitching waves and driven, horizontal rain on the periphery of a typhoon. In aviator parlance, the weather was "dogshit" with low ceilings, shrieking winds, and impossible operating conditions. Many sailors climbed into their racks and stayed there, enduring the ship's bucking, pitching motion while those ambitious enough to eat—let alone hold a cup of coffee—sometimes needed two hands. Like all Pacific seamen before them and after, the Big E had long since learned the ultimate reality of the world's greatest ocean.

On January 16–17 the fast carriers struck the China coast, sustaining heavy losses to Hong Kong's appalling flak, which aviators described as "intense to incredible." Task Force 38 lost twelve planes the first day and forty-nine the next, to all causes. Bob McCullough's eight night owls found relatively little action during a twilight fighter patrol. A Hellcat chased down a Tojo over Canton but it was not worth the losses: one fighter simply disappeared in the wind-driven darkness; another flew into the water; and three more crashed or flopped on deck. Two pilots were dead.

FORMIDABLE FORMOSA

A week later the fast carriers returned to Formosa, keeping the pressure on enemy naval and air bases. Once the Americans' presence was known, the Japanese broadcasters collectively known as Tokyo Rose asserted that few ships would survive the China Sea venture. *Enterprise* men ignored the propaganda while appreciating Rose's music.

Based on intelligence reports, Bill Martin planned an eight-plane attack on shipping in Kiirun Harbor at the island's north tip. The January 22 mission started poorly: two Avengers aborted on deck, requiring two spares to launch, then another returned with engine trouble. Nevertheless, before dawn Martin and Russ Kippen proceeded with three planes each. Armed with bombs and rockets, the attackers expected to strike hard and fast, hit any ships possible, and get the hell out.

It didn't work.

Japanese radar plotted the Americans inbound, affording time to prepare flak and searchlights. With blinding lights shining into their cockpits, and possibly engaged by radar-controlled antiaircraft guns, Kippen's pilots were overwhelmed. He radioed that he had trouble seeing and was dodging heavy flak, but attacking nonetheless.

Sizing up the situation, Martin began circling at 6,000 feet, an obvious target drawing frequent gunfire. But his gutsy act permitted some of the others to penetrate the defenses down low, bombing and rocketing targets that briefly appeared in the garishly lit darkness.

Martin's flight pressed hard, claiming a small cargo vessel and igniting fires along the wharf. Then they turned seaward, beginning to realize that half their number was missing. Whatever happened that night, Russ Kippen disappeared with his wingmen, Lieutenant (jg) Lester Koop and Ensign John Wood, and their crews. Nine well-trained fliers were gone, but more importantly, valued shipmates.

The task force swiped at Okinawa on the way to Ulithi, losing another *Enterprise* man en route. A memorial service at sea honored the eighteen pilots and aircrewmen known or suspected dead since departing Hawaii, but Kippen's loss was especially felt. The torpedo skipper had survived what had seemed the worst: Truk and the Marianas. The VT(N)-90 (Night Torpedo Squadron 90) diarist recorded, "Many of us have flown and lived with him so long in this squadron and VT-10 that his loss seems impossible. To all of us he was an intrepid pilot, a true friend and shipmate."

The two weeks in Ulithi were largely devoted to nautical housekeeping—"A clean sweepdown fore and aft!"—and recreation. Many sailors found the brief time ashore unsatisfying and opted for shipboard diversions, including reading backlogged Christmas mail. Basketball and volleyball were popular pastimes—a physical outlet for nervous tension, and an advantage that carriers enjoyed over ships with less space. But beneath the relative ease and surface levity, some men noted a restrained pensiveness absent four weeks before, when missing friends still lived.

Then it was back to sea, and back to war.

DESTINATION TOKYO

With Admiral Spruance and Vice Admiral Mitscher once more in command, the fast carriers deployed as Task Force 58. Destination: Japan. Of more than 100 ships present, only *Enterprise* and perhaps three others had plied enemy waters—nearly three years before, on the Doolittle raid.

With *Independence* returned to daytime operations, her foreshortened silhouette was replaced in Task Group 58.3 with *Saratoga*'s looming bulk—a startling contrast, but she brought extra strength to Rear Admiral

Gardner's unit. Sara embarked a unique air group with a day and night fighter squadron plus the night torpedo outfit. The object: round-the-clock air operations in the teeth of the enemy's homeland. Two days of strikes against Honshu were planned for mid-February, keeping Tokyo's attention away from the actual target, the sulfurous porkchop-shaped island called Iwo Jima.

The North Pacific weather remained seasonal: cold, cloudy, drizzly, and gray with choppy seas. Upon launching in Japanese waters early on February 16, pilots found that their wings accumulated ice above 3,000 feet, but formations usually got in beneath the ceiling. *Enterprise* fighters took off late that afternoon, and immediately lost one of their number. Ensign Francis "Tex" Luscombe—who possessed an enviable reputation as a ladies' man—splashed down near the ship. He got out of his Hellcat and was seen clinging to the belly tank but drowned just as help arrived.

The other eleven pilots proceeded to assigned targets, strafing and rocketing Honshu airfields. The Hellcats tangled with a couple of Japanese navy fighters without result, and though one pilot ditched with battle damage, he was saved.

Subsequently the new torpedo exec, Charlie Henderson, took his Avenger offshore with an important new mission. "Radio countermeasures" was the phrase of the era, jamming enemy radar with an airborne transmitter. Riding with Henderson were Lieutenants (jg) Ted Halbach and Henry Loomis, working their electronic esoterica in the bowels of the big Grumman. Naval aviation was maturing, and *Enterprise*'s sophisticated air group pointed the way to the future.

Nocturnal attack missions occupied the 17th with loss of an Avenger crew, evidently victim of vertigo—the night flier's occupational hazard. Despite minimal observed results, *Enterprise* had just inscribed another page in naval aviation history. She and her consorts had done what some military authorities considered impossible: gone head to head with a major land-based air power, won local air superiority, and got away clean. It boded ill for Tokyo's immediate future.

Meanwhile, the task force heeled through rough seas, southbound some 600 miles to Iwo Jima.

IWO JIMA AROUND THE CLOCK

Arriving off the island on the 19th, *Enterprise* and *Saratoga* began flying combat air patrols to protect the amphibious forces sending two divisions of Marines ashore with one remaining afloat. But Tokyo could not afford to cede Iwo, which could support long-range fighters to escort B-29s from the Marianas. Bombers and kamikazes flocked southward from Japan, seeking the priority targets—carriers. Night Fighting 90 splashed a bomber the first night, but the American aerial picket was not perfect. On the 21st *Saratoga* got clobbered.

In barely three minutes the Pacific veteran took five bomb hits that turned her flight deck into an inferno of burning aircraft. Her fires attracted more raiders, and two hours later she sustained another hit. With her air group largely destroyed and 123 men dead, the huge carrier was knocked out of the war. *Enterprise,* now almost wholly responsible for the amphibious ships' nocturnal air defense, transferred to the Seventh Fleet.

As usual, the enemy was not the only threat. On the night of the 22nd Crossbow Collins's flight descended out of the overcast during a "red alert." Jittery American gunners who had been subjected to kamikazes began shooting, and other ships joined in. The lead Avenger gushed smoke, started down, and was lost from sight. Ensign Henry Hinrich's plane also took fatal hits, but he managed a successful ditching. His crew attracted a patrol craft whose sailors remained skeptical of the fliers' identity until unmistakable American profanity removed all doubt.

The highly regarded Crossbow Collins, another Buzzard Brigade veteran, was lost with both crewmen. Charlie Henderson became VT(N)-90's third skipper in thirty days.

At 4:30 P.M. on February 23 Bob McCullough's night fighters launched on a combat air patrol—nothing remarkable at the time. But it began an incredible string: seven days of continuous flying. Partly the record was possible owing to the arrival of five *Saratoga* pilots whose talents would have gone wanting otherwise. The Big E lofted an average of two fighters per hour, day and night, flying sweeps to Chichi Jima and patrols over Iwo. Meanwhile, Henderson's Avengers jumped on targets of opportunity elsewhere in the Volcanos and Bonins, dropping fragmentation clusters on facilities and grounded aircraft. Three planes were lost during the week but all fliers were saved, and an enemy bomber fell to a nocturnal Hellcat.

All the while air operations continued unabated. The hangar deck was never idle, and the flight deck thrummed with activity. Landing signal officers exchanged their daytime paddles for illuminated wands while mechanics and ordnancemen kept aircraft flyable, serviced, and armed.

At 11:30 on the night of March 2, *Enterprise* landed the last airborne night owl, completing 175 hours of continuous flight operations. Nothing remotely similar had ever occurred—nor could it.

In those seven days more than fifty American vessels were damaged in collisions or heavy seas, or hit by enemy gunfire; one was sunk. But Japanese aircraft hit only one destroyer on February 28 and struck another with dud ordnance March 2. Night Air Group 90's air defense record was just about perfect.

KAMIKAZE HATCHERIES

Following a much needed rest at Ulithi, *Enterprise* and her escorts hoisted anchor and sortied on March 14, again bound for the home islands. With the Okinawa invasion slated in two weeks, Admiral Spruance wanted to beat down the kamikaze hatcheries with a series of strikes on Kyushu airfields, within range of Okinawa's landing beaches. Beginning the night of the 18th, Martin's aircrews harried enemy bases during hours of darkness, also targeting known radar sites.

For a change, there were airborne targets aplenty. That night Lieutenant (jg) Robert Wattenberger's controller put him onto an extremely elusive target that he pursued "all over the Western Pacific through clouds, around the fleet, into rain squalls one after another," before shooting it down. No less persistent was Lieutenant (jg) Wesley Williams, who stalked his intended victim through weather for three hours. Two other pilots also dispatched enemy aircraft, though yet another Hellcat was downed by American sailors. The pilot was rescued, but perennially trigger-happy gunners remained a threat to friendly fliers.

The aerial hunting continued into the 19th when the fighters claimed a destroyed and a probable—and the Avengers got a kill. The torpedo pilot was the ever-aggressive Charlie Henderson, who latched on to a huge "Emily" flying boat and sent it diving into the water at 5:00 that morning. Twenty-four hours later another Torpedo 10 alumnus, Cliff Largess, downed one, possibly two, bogies. Thus the big, ungainly Avengers continued justifying the confidence showed by Butch O'Hare and John Phillips in late 1943.

Operating in a confined area off Japan, the carriers were not hard to find. Japanese aircraft streamed out from shore on four consecutive days, and they learned how to do it right. Some broke through the fighters and flak, and on the morning of the 18th a skillful enemy dive-bomber pilot—mistaken as a friendly by radar operators—got a shot at the Big E.

Among those on deck was nineteen-year-old radar technician Arnold Olson, working on a Hellcat on the starboard catapult. "The Jap roared right over the flight deck, bow to stern," Olson recalled, and the bomb struck the forward elevator. "The fuses broke off the bomb and it rested in the middle of the deck by the island. A couple of heroes rolled it to the stern and dumped it overboard." It was an unexpectedly up-close look at the war for a violinist whose promising Disney orchestra debut had been sidelined by Pearl Harbor. One man was mortally wounded but the ship got off lightly—some night shift sailors were not even rousted from their bunks.

Yet more was to come. The next day, March 19, the day crew was wakened at 3:45 A.M., stowed bedding and combustibles in flash-proof covers, and went to breakfast. Men assumed general quarters stations at 5:13, sixty minutes before sunrise. Faced with capable, zealous enemy airpower as little as fifty miles off Japan, Grover Hall kept *Enterprise* at GQ from before dawn to after dusk—all battle stations manned and the ship buttoned up.

That morning *Wasp* in Task Group 58.1 took hits that killed 100 men but her damage control team was expert at its task, and the carrier steamed away under her own power. Minutes later *Enterprise*'s former teammate *Franklin* was hammered by enemy dive-bombers when the ship was not at general quarters. Big E men standing on deck or peering from the island watched the sickening plume of greasy black smoke on the horizon where *Franklin* spewed flames with flashes of igniting ordnance. Eight hundred men were killed—the worst toll for any American carrier—and Big Ben was towed out of the area, en route home and forever out of the war.

Predictably, the Japanese kept coming, and on the 20th another determined Judy pilot staked his claim to *Enterprise*. Eluding the Hellcats long enough to draw a bead, he dropped out of the low overcast full on the bow and put his 550-pounder within fifty feet of the hull, inflicting minor damage. The assailant sped for home, flak bursting in his slipstream. Some of the gunfire was ill directed, with five-inch rounds from escorting ships erupting close aboard the Big E. In two shells the proximity fuses sensed a solid object and, as intended, detonated. The fifty-five-pound projectiles burst above antiaircraft crews forward, scything down men in the exposed mounts. Six Hellcats fueled and armed for launch burst into flames, and the gasoline-fed fire quickly spread across the deck. Nonetheless, the institution that was *Enterprise* immediately responded, faced with the worst damage sustained since Santa Cruz. Lieutenant Commander John Munro's thoroughly drilled damage control teams began fighting the fires, but the heat ignited thousands of rounds of antiaircraft and machine gun ammunition, forcing most of the crews away from the danger.

The flames blazed and the smoke thickened, choking crucial spaces in the island. The Combat Information Center was abandoned, as were the main radio and flight control stations. CIC and radio crews moved to backup positions but the ship relied on her escorts for primary air defense and reports on new threats. More Japanese planes attacked the task group, targeting *Hancock* and *San Jacinto,* but the attackers died trying.

Meanwhile, the Big E continued her fight. Some fire hoses burned through, and in one place the flight deck wood was charred away, exposing the hangar deck to the conflagration topside. Had the fully serviced aircraft and ammunition magazines there caught fire, it could have proved catastrophic. From his position in Damage Control Central, Munro isolated the threat by dousing part of the hangar bay with overhead sprinklers.

Captain Hall turned the ship crosswind, sending the worst of the smoke away from the hull, while sailors in respirators moved in on the blazing forward part of the flight deck. Heads bent against the searing heat, wielding fog nozzles and directing white streams of thick, aqueous foam, gradually they beat down the blaze, starving it of fuel and oxygen.

In less than an hour *Enterprise*'s fires were doused and she maintained station in the task group. Ten men had died, including an officer who panicked and jumped overboard.

REPAIRS, BEER, AND MORALE

Back in Ulithi on March 24, the Big E focused on healing. The R Division—repair—maintained a nearly nonstop work schedule, augmented by crews from the heavy repair ship *Jason,* the first vessel of her kind.

Some *Enterprise* men were able to unwind a bit from the constant strain of almost nonstop operations, and the searing memory of March 20. A beer party ashore permitted most sailors to imbibe more than two or three bottles for a change, and undoubtedly some minors snagged a few as well.

In ten days the chore was done, and the Big E returned to work. As the lone remaining night carrier, she was once more under familiar management with Rear Admiral Arthur Radford's Task Group 58.4, including *Yorktown, Intrepid,* and light carrier *Langley.* Big E veterans recalled Radford as commander of their task group for the Gilberts-Marshalls operation of late 1943. Additionally, *Intrepid* now flew Air Group 10 under prewar

Enterprise pilot John Hyland, making the group's third combat cruise. Radford's formation arrived off Okinawa on April 7, one week after the invasion began.

Carrier units supporting Operation Iceberg were deprived of the advantage of mobility. Confined to a box of ocean within reach of Okinawa, the flattops were relatively easy to find, and Japanese aircraft from Kyushu flew thousands of sorties on both conventional and kamikaze missions. Thus, April and May became the zenith of the war for Tokyo's "special attack" squadrons and the nadir of U.S. Navy fortunes against the suicide threat.

Despite top-notch leadership, morale began to slip, and Bill Martin took time to poll his aviators. Considering that many were volunteers, the results were disappointing. Of the eighty pilots in Air Group 90, only ten remained enthusiastic about night flying whereas twenty-three said they did not want to continue the mission. The others—more than 40 percent—did not object to their current assignment but would not join another night air group.

Few pilots would admit it, but night flying lacked the glamour and attention of daylight operations. With far fewer discernible results to show for their losses, decorations were rare. Though few aviators were medal hunters, nearly all craved basic recognition for performing a difficult, dangerous mission supremely well. Thus far McCullough's Hellcats had little opportunity for aerial combat: since January they had logged only thirteen kills by nine pilots, while the Avengers had bagged three.

Bomber pilots needed a confirmed hit on a major enemy warship for a Navy Cross—almost impossible in night flying. The magnificent intelligence work that Torpedo 90 performed in the February missions against Tokyo went unheralded because of the secrecy enshrouding the electronic "ferret" mission. One crew alone had catalogued two dozen Japanese radar sites—invaluable information that remained classified.

For whatever reason—largely unjustified optimism—some aircrews began dreaming of rotating home after the next sortie. However, for the present there was no option but to continue the work. And there was work aplenty off Okinawa, as the Japanese aircraft resisted heavily, frequently, and persistently.

The kamikazes came out in strength on April 11 with *Enterprise* targeted time after time. Her gunners blew up a suicider that morning, exploding so close that a man was blown overboard but rescued.

That afternoon a bomb-packing Zeke—misidentified as a Judy—dived in steep and fast. It absorbed an incredible amount of flak before smashing into the water mere feet from the starboard bow, where the bomb exploded. Subsequently another kamikaze dived on *Enterprise* but her forward gun crews were alert, vigorous, and accurate. Their barrage deflected the attacker into circling for a better opportunity, affording other ships a decent shot, and they killed the attacker. Other Japanese penetrated the task group's screen, but were destroyed before inflicting damage.

Enterprise was badly shaken. The two very near misses had destroyed a radar mount, dented hull plates, dislodged some generator mounts, and punctured some fuel bunkers. But the ship remained in position, carrying her share of the load.

Radar screens showed more "bloodsuckers" orbiting in the gathering dusk, and Air Group 90 went on the offensive. Hellcats and Avengers carpeted the intermediate kamikaze bases between Okinawa and Honshu, bombing and strafing airfields on Amami Shima and elsewhere. Yet another Torpedo 10 veteran followed Charlie Henderson and Cliff Largess's example when Lieutenant Ralph Waldo Cummings glommed on to a Japanese transport plane, overtook it, and opened fire. His twin .50 calibers were adequate to the job, and the "Tabby" dropped into the sea.

On April 14 *Enterprise* learned of the death of President Roosevelt. For Big E men, it was farewell to the individual most responsible for their ship, dating from that otherwordly period twelve years previously when reconstruction funds were allocated for two new carriers. Navy Secretary James Forrestal ordered flags flown at half-mast for thirty days. He added, "Wearing of mourning badges and firing of salutes will be dispensed with in view of war conditions." Little was known of FDR's vice president, a Great War artilleryman from Missouri.

Once more in Ulithi, the all too familiar repair routine returned, again with the skilled artisans from repair ship *Jason*. In order to access the underwater damage, *Enterprise*'s port tanks were partly flooded to induce an eight-degree list, making walking the interior spaces a dizzying experience. More than two weeks were required to put right the kamikazes' vengeance, and the crew could not help notice that "the fightingest ship" in the U.S. Navy was spending an inordinate amount of time in harbor. At that time Rear Admiral Matt Gardner departed, no longer having a nocturnal task group to command.

During the farewell dinner for the admiral—a rare banquet with turkey, dressing, and even cigars—Captain Hall poured cold water on the warm embers of an early return stateside. In fact, he stated that the ship was needed in northern climes in about ten days, and would meet that commitment. Gardner's parting comments left a glimmer of hope, hinting that Air Group 90's relief should arrive "soon," though he pointedly omitted any specifics.

Enterprise calendar watchers knew that Air Group 10's second cruise had lasted six months from January to July 1944, and Air Group 20 had left after nearly four months before transferring to *Lexington* for two more. At the four-month mark, the night fliers reckoned they could expect at least sixty more days. Recorded Torpedo 90's log, "A blue funk settled about the ship."

Unknown in *Enterprise*, Air Group 91 was inbound aboard the new carrier *Bon Homme Richard* but would not reach Ulithi until the end of May. Until then, the Big E was the only night owl in Admiral Spruance's barn.

A MEMORABLE MAY

On May 3 *Enterprise* rejoined the fleet, something of an orphan. As the lone night carrier she fetched up in Rear Admiral Frederick Sherman's 58.3, which included the task force flagship. *Bunker Hill* embarked Vice Admiral Marc Mitscher with his operations officer well known to *Enterprise*: Commander Jim Flatley. Now commanding fifteen fast carriers, Mitscher reckoned he had enough power to go against mainland Japan again, as no flattops had been tagged since *Intrepid* on April 16. Additionally, the staff planned offensive day and night sorties over the Amami Shoto islands to wear down Japan's airfields between Kyushu and Okinawa.

At 3:45 A.M. on May 9, four *Enterprise* fighters launched on a dawn combat air patrol over Amami but one plane nosed into the water off the port beam. Lieutenant (jg) James T. Tucker was never found, and the cause of the accident—vertigo, engine failure, faulty instruments—remained unknowable. He was the squadron's eleventh fatality, and would prove the last.

Meanwhile, the kamikazes were relentless. Hundreds of Japanese fliers expended themselves fruitlessly against the U.S. Navy's defenses, shot out of the sky by radar-directed Hellcats and Corsairs, or blown apart by massive shipboard gunfire. But always more attackers came, and some were skillful, lucky, or both. On May 11 two of them combined both factors and damn near destroyed USS *Bunker Hill*.

The combination of Japanese bombs and aircraft smashing into her deck and structure ignited horrific fires that killed more than 350 men. Some *Bunker Hill* fighters had just returned from CAP and, seeing the volcanic flames erupting from their ship, the pilots dropped into *Enterprise*'s landing pattern. It was the first time Corsairs operated from her deck since Chick Harmer's night fighters almost a year before.

Marc Mitscher's staff, forced off his flagship, moved aboard *Enterprise*. There Captain Hall and the exec, Commander William Kabler, showed the displaced officers to their new quarters, making room in the limited staff spaces. However, not much space was required since thirteen of Mitscher's staff had been killed. As *Bunker Hill* was escorted from the area, Mitscher and company turned their attention to continuing offensive operations, which suited Bill Martin just fine.

Martin proposed a series of attacks on Japanese airfields in the home islands, extending nocturnal coverage even farther afield. For that kind of aggressive action, he looked no further than Charlie Henderson, who favored any kind of airborne mayhem. On the first night Martin and Henderson led their Avengers to Kyushu targets and generally enjoyed themselves, attacking unwary airfields and military facilities. At one field Henderson even found a mock carrier deck outlined by lights, which he promptly bombed.

The second night, May 12—seventh anniversary of *Enterprise*'s commissioning—was different. The Japanese anticipated a return engagement, and dozens of powerful searchlights split the darkness, many radar-controlled. Some pilots' night vision was ruined, and others reported their aim was spoiled in the garish light. However, others like Martin actually relished the opportunity to duel with searchlight crews, foiling their radars by dropping metal strips cut to match known radar wavelengths, and shooting, bombing, and rocketing any movement on the ground.

That same night, Big E fighters staked out Kanoya and Kagoshima Bay where they claimed eight kills in the predawn. Lieutenant Owen Young came close to instant ace status with three Jake floatplanes and a "Tony," plus a "Pete" floatplane shared with Lieutenant (jg) Charles Latrobe, who downed another by himself. Lieutenants K. D. Smith and John Kenyon also splashed singles for the squadron's best day's—or night's—work.

The next morning, the 13th, Charlie Henderson spent an active quarter hour, probably downing a rugged "George" fighter and dropping a Rufe floatplane. It ran his official wartime tally to three destroyed and a probable—flying Avengers. Significantly, no *Enterprise* planes were lost on either night.

THE LAST KAMIKAZE

When the sun appeared over the Philippine Sea at 5:30 A.M. on May 14, the ship had been at general quarters for ninety-three minutes. Hatches were dogged; guns were manned; and battle rations available. Two kinds of sentries stood watch: sailors with keen eyesight watched topside while the Argus-eyed sentinel called radar swept the sky with electronic vision beyond the horizon. The dawn revealed good flying weather: a fifteen-knot southerly wind driving scattered cumulus clouds with bases at 3,000 feet.

Shortly after 6:00, Air Group 90's night fighters were headed back to their roost. They had been spreading "the big blue blanket" over enemy airfields, keeping Japanese bombers and suicide planes grounded. The Hellcats had downed three more bandits in the previous five hours—a real boost for McCullough's eager pilots, who had notched a dozen kills in three days.

But some airfields were beyond the range of carrier aircraft. Literally and figuratively rising with the sun, airplanes bearing the rust-red *Hinomaru* insignia lifted off Kyushu runways and winged seaward. Shipboard radar operators tallied them as they registered on green-tinted scopes: formations and singles flying different altitudes and courses. There was a calculated method behind the seeming disjointedness. The kamikaze masters wanted to present as confusing a radar picture as possible to the Americans.

Enterprise's homing Hellcats were flying a racetrack pattern around the ship, lining up to land, when the radar illuminated a gaggle of inbound raiders. The fighter direction officer keyed his microphone and ordered some of the waiting planes to take up defensive positions. Pilots sucked up their wheels and flaps, added power, and began climbing to the northwest.

Radar had tracked twenty-six raiders inbound from the coast. When the hostiles met the task group's Hellcat umbrella, some sixteen Japanese fell in widespread interceptions. Six more got close enough to succumb to shipboard antiaircraft gunners. Others turned away, seeking better prospects.

The 26th intended to die gloriously.

At 6:23 radar plotted more bandits at twenty miles and closing. Three times in the next seventeen minutes, lookouts trained their binoculars to the southwest. Smoky tendrils rose into the morning air, testament to the lethal efficiency of the combat air patrols.

Ten minutes later the destroyer *Hunt* was detached to retrieve the body of a Japanese pilot while Hellcats hunted for cagey Zekes playing three-dimensional cat and mouse. One in particular proved elusive. He ducked in and out of clouds, tracked by radar and occasionally by optical gun directors, but the Hellcats could not corner him. He was unusually persistent, obviously biding his time while making good use of the low clouds.

The intruder was Lieutenant (jg) Shunsuke Tomiyasu of the 306th Squadron, 721st Naval Air Group. The 306th was deadly good at its job. Ensign Kioyoshi Ogawa had expended his life against the *Bunker Hill* three days before.

Like his squadron mate Ogawa, Tomiyasu was twenty-two years old. His relatives remembered him as a cheerful young man, fond of sports and music, who dabbled in painting. He urged his family to "live with great enthusiasm," but that morning his skills were applied in another direction, leading twenty-one other Zekes on a one-way sortie against the enemy. Shunsuke Tomiyasu was equally capable of dying with great enthusiasm.

Now, seeing an opportunity, at 6:53 Tomiyasu pointed his Mitsubishi's nose at the American carrier group and initiated a run, broad on the starboard beam.

The sailors were alert. Almost immediately the lone attacker was taken under antiaircraft fire. Brown-black splotches erupted beneath the puffy white clouds, radar-directed shells with fuses containing miniature radio transmitters that detonated when they sensed an aircraft nearby.

Recognizing a no-win setup, Tomiyasu hauled back on his stick and popped up into the clouds again. Frequently he dropped out of the cloud deck to assess the situation, each time banking and turning to deny the Yankees a clear shot at him.

He edged ever closer, now about two miles out on the same heading as *Enterprise*. Then he reversed course and flew back another mile or so. Apparently he never considered changing to another target. It was as if he knew the Big E's reputation as the worst enemy of Imperial Japan.

It took less than three minutes for Shunsuke Tomiyasu to find his opportunity to die.

As the Zeke sprinted from the clouds at 1,500 feet, Captain Hall ordered a hard port turn. By swinging the stern to starboard as the bow came left, Hall unmasked more antiaircraft guns and forced the pilot to make a correction to avoid an overshoot.

Enterprise sailors now got a good look at Shunsuke Tomiyasu. His

Zeke was painted dark green on the upper surfaces, and suspended from the fuselage was a large bomb. At 6:57 he came straight on, in a thirty-degree dive, not jinking to avoid the flak and tracers that flashed and flared around him. "Everybody unloaded on him," said Marine gunner Jack Maroney.

It seemed incredible that an airplane could survive such gunfire. By one reckoning, the Zeke was subjected to fifty-five barrels, ranging from 20mm and 40mm to five-inch.

Near the bottom of his dive, Tomiyasu recognized that he would overshoot to starboard. Two hundred yards out, in the final seconds of life, he snap-rolled left to inverted and tugged the stick back, performing the first quarter of a split-ess maneuver.

It was a beautiful piece of flying.

On the flag bridge, Mitscher's operations officer stepped out to get a better view. Instantly he was back inside, flinging himself prone. Jim Flatley shouted, "Hit the deck!"

On escorting ships, men watched incredulously as the suicide pilot performed an inverted forty-five-degree dive into Big E's Douglas fir flight deck, splintering it just aft of the number one elevator. The hull trembled with the violence of the ensuing explosion; men felt it throughout the ship.

The explosion—first red, then black and gray, turning white at the top—lofted a large section of the fifteen-ton elevator some 400 feet into the air; the rest flipped over and fell upside down into the elevator well. In a forward gun group, normally disciplined crews left their mount to look over the side, gaping at the huge piece of elevator that careened into the sea.

Pounding along to starboard was battleship *Washington* whose photographer recorded the scene—more than half the elevator momentarily perched atop a huge smoke plume.

Lieutenant (jg) Albert Stephan was intelligence officer in the fighter squadron. He recalled, "When we saw the Jap diving in, we hit the deck . . . and not a minute too soon, for the blast sheared off an armor plate from a nearby gun and it whistled through the room over our heads."

The bulkhead between the pilots' staterooms was obliterated, leaving a ballroom-sized pile of rubble. The flight deck was bulged upward nearly five feet, and twenty-five aircraft were destroyed.

Among those who barely escaped death was the hangar deck officer, Lieutenant (jg) Charles B. Wilkinson. Like the previous exec, Tom Hamilton, he possessed exceptional athletic credentials, having played football on

Minnesota's three national championship teams in the 1930s. That reputation only increased in the decade after the war—as coach Bud Wilkinson of Oklahoma. Standing behind a girder when the Zeke exploded, he reckoned that he would have been killed if he had stood three feet nearer the elevator.

Lieutenant Commander John Munro already was one of the most experienced damage control officers in the U.S. Navy. He had been aboard since 1943, and his ship had been hit on March 18, March 20, and April 11—now four times in seven weeks. But the latest was the worst—more so than Eastern Solomons or Santa Cruz.

By word of mouth and sound-powered phone the information poured into Damage Control Central: a serious fire in the forward hangar bay, threatening ammunition lockers; the aviation fuel system was ruined, lines severed and tanks leaking high-test gasoline. Seawater was streaming in unchecked through breaches in the hull, and three- and six-inch water mains were broken, aggravating the flooding. Any one of those was serious; together they posed a catastrophic threat.

Yet *Enterprise* responded as she had off Guadalcanal. Individually and corporately the men, the crew—the ship—fought back. Up forward where the situation was worst, damage repair teams rushed to work. Hull technicians, carpenters, and bosun's mates gathered their gangs, shouted orders over roaring flames, directed firefighters, and began fighting the fire. Some sailors picked up five-inch shells and powder bags, passing them hand to hand until the last man in line pitched the explosives overboard. Others sought the maimed, dead, or dying and pulled, carried, or tugged them out of the way.

Enterprise won her fight in seventeen minutes. The worst of the flames were suppressed and the rest finally extinguished in two hours.

Eight men had been blown overboard or jumped, including Marine PFC Walter Keil, who was forced off his 20mm mount. He swam to a large piece of debris—remnant of the aircraft elevator—where two men had taken refuge. Then Keil saw another man in the water but the sailors on the wreckage thought he was too badly hurt to retrieve. Keil left the elevator and stroked to the wounded man, Machinist's Mate Robert F. Riessland, who said, "I'm going to die anyway. Go ahead . . . and let me drown." Walter Keil couldn't do that. He remained with his unknown shipmate for hours, keeping his body and his morale afloat until picked up. The next day both were transferred from a destroyer to *Enterprise* where Riessland recovered. The story was not known for nearly sixty years, but in 2004 Keil received the Navy and Marine Corps Medal for lifesaving.

Meanwhile, power to forward guns was interrupted or destroyed but other batteries remained in the fight. While the residue still smoldered, Big E gunners splashed two more bloodsuckers in the next hour or so.

Then it was time to count the cost. Fourteen men including three junior officers were dead. About sixty were wounded, half of them seriously. The toll was small compared to the sixty-six crewmen *Enterprise* had lost at Eastern Solomons and forty-four at Santa Cruz—let alone *Franklin*'s and *Bunker Hill*'s hundreds. But shipmates are special in the sea services, and three of the Big E's dead sailors had been aboard since 1942.

One other casualty was tended to. When the flooded elevator well was drained, sailors recovered the remains of the lethal Zeke and its pilot. Tomiyasu's body was largely intact, and intelligence officers retrieved his papers including identification and some folding money.

Much has been made of the racial aspects of the Pacific war—genuine and perceived bigotry on both sides. But generally the U.S. Navy accorded proper if not Christian burial to dead Japanese: two instances involved the battleship *Missouri* and escort carrier *Sargent Bay*. So it was in *Enterprise*. That afternoon the medical department sutured the enemy pilot's wounds. His body was enshrouded in a mattress cover, then committed to the ocean off the stern.

The kamikaze's name was improperly translated as "Tomi Zai," and remained so for decades. But assiduous research on both sides of the Pacific finally solved the riddle, and some of Tomiyasu's personal effects with pieces of his airplane were delivered to his family in 2003.

It was a time for reckoning. In the nearly five months that Night Air Group 90 was aboard, thirty-two pilots and aircrewmen were killed. It was a heavy toll but could have been worse, considering the normal dangers of flying high-performance aircraft off a straight-deck carrier at night. The two squadrons wrote off eighty-five planes to all causes, but significantly thirty-one had been destroyed on deck by Japanese bombs or kamikazes. Subsequently the threat diminished considerably: the next night flying unit, *Bon Homme Richard*'s Air Group 91, suffered ten fatalities in nine weeks of combat.

The morning of May 15, Vice Admiral Mitscher and his remaining staff transferred to the new carrier *Randolph,* their third flagship in five days.

The day after, *Enterprise* was eastbound. Though she retained twenty-five aircraft, she could not launch them from her ruined flight deck so she set course for Ulithi, Bremerton, and points east. Her war—from Pearl Harbor to Midway, Guadalcanal, Hollandia, Truk, the Marianas, Leyte, Iwo Jima, Okinawa, and Japan itself—was over.

12

★ ★ ★

"The *Enterprise* Has a Soul"

Four first to last *Enterprise* men who served aboard from 1938 through 1945. L–R: pay clerk Stanley W. Carter, Chief James M. Martin, Lts. (jg) Sam H. Brewer and Ralph E. Tucker. (Enterprise Assn.)

Two weeks after Lieutenant Tomiyasu ended his life and *Enterprise*'s combat career, she received a tumultuous reception at Pearl Harbor. On May 30 some people there still remembered the Big E arriving in the smoke-and-oil darkness of December 8, 1941, and her return to a hero's reception after the Marshalls raid two months later. Now the locals sought to outdo themselves. At least two bands blared a lusty welcome while ships' sirens wailed and—best of all—busloads of WAVES smiled sweetly-saucily at the men of the Big E, who ganged the catwalk for a better look.

Enterprise's damage was obvious, with the gaping hole in the forward elevator well and the warped, buckled flight deck. Nobody knew it, of course, but they were seeing the last fast carrier ever hit by a kamikaze. However, there was precious little time for commiseration;

in less than forty-eight hours Captain Hall got her under way again, course northeast.

The ship was five days en route, 2,645 miles to Bremerton where she received another boisterous reception on June 7. She sported a 578-foot pennant suspended by balloons, reportedly representing each day since leaving Bremerton on November 1, 1943.

By 1945 the Puget Sound Navy Yard was vastly experienced in ship repair. Bremerton's workers were fast and efficient, mending the repairable, and replacing components destroyed or damaged beyond repair. Unknown to most, the invasion of Japan was scheduled to begin in November, and *Enterprise*'s next air group—her fifth—was waiting for her in Hawaii. But on August 14 *Enterprise* was still laid up in dry dock, ringing with the clatter of rivet guns, aglow with arc welders, and redolent of the tangy odor of acetylene, when the word flashed from WestPac, the oceanic battleground of the western Pacific: following the atomic bombings that destroyed two Japanese cities, and the Soviet Union's declaration of war, Emperor Hirohito had interceded. Overriding his hard-line war cabinet, he announced acceptance of the Allies' surrender terms. The next day the Second World War was over.

Horns honked; sirens wailed; people laughed, cried, and prayed. Confetti showered from office buildings. Twenty-five miles across Puget Sound, reporters described downtown Seattle as "a rooting, tooting, honking mass" of celebrants. Streets overflowed with people, many from the navy yard. Sailors climbed lamp posts and secretaries blew kisses from second-story windows. Men in uniform could not buy a drink among patriotic citizens. People who had never met before, and likely never would meet again, exchanged heartfelt hugs, kisses, solicitations, and body fluids. That Northwest summer day it was just incredibly wonderful to be young and alive and to have a future.

Briefly amid the joyous noise, *Enterprise* men paused to remember absent friends—nearly 150 from the ship's company over the previous four years. But the world-historic import of the moment demanded attention. The *Bremerton Sun* headlined the news, simultaneously noting that the Navy had canceled $6 billion of contracts and predicted that seven million people were about to lose their jobs. But that did not include anyone on USS *Enterprise*. Fully repaired, in mid-September she again nosed into the Strait of Juan de Fuca, headed for the familiar Pacific, on a final mission to Hawaii.

PEARL HARBOR FAREWELL

Postwar Pearl Harbor was a different world than *Enterprise* had known. Three months previously she had steamed in, her topsides wrecked and blackened, a warship vitally in need of repair to return to combat. But wartime June had melted into peaceful September, shortly after the formal surrender ceremony in Tokyo Bay. *Enterprise* embarked Commander William W. Soverel's Night Air Group 55 plus hundreds of repatriated POWs and released hospital patients joyously bound for "Uncle Sugar." It was the first of the Big E's four Operation Magic Carpet trips returning soldiers from overseas.

That summer, *Enterprise* learned about some of her missing, as twelve men had fallen into captivity and eight survived Japanese prisons. The first captured were Dale Hilton and his radioman, Jack Leaming, downed at Marcus Island three and a half long years before.

Four fliers survived the turmoil of Santa Cruz. Fighting 10's Dusty Rhodes and Al Mead were picked up by Japanese ships, as were Torpedo 10 crewmen Mick Glasser and Tom Nelson. Glasser was unusually fortunate: in 1944 the Navy told his family that he was alive, and he heard from them via the Red Cross that October. But Nelson had been thought dead: after sufficient time had passed, his parents held a memorial service, and the mayor of his hometown named a street in his honor.

At Edenton, North Carolina, Air Group 20 rejoiced at the survival of fighter pilot Fred Turnbull and torpedo pilot Bill Ross, captured after the October 1944 strikes on Formosa. But Ross's crewmen, Harry Aldro and Charles McVay, had been murdered with a dozen other American POWs in June 1945.

More time passed before the accounting was complete, but eventually Big E veterans learned the fate of the Dauntless crew of Frank O'Flaherty and Bruno Gaido, missing after Midway. They had been picked up by a Japanese destroyer, largely resisted interrogation, and were thrown overboard about ten days later. Apparently none of the murderers was ever prosecuted.

Among plankowners, the story of a prewar sailor was especially bittersweet. During 1939 maneuvers, *Enterprise* received a request from the base on Guam for a chief machinist "soonest." Baldy Pownall loaned his best, Chief Michael Krump, who had portrayed King Neptune during the crossing the line ritual. The assignment proved so pleasant that Krump sent for his wife, who remained until September 1941 when international tensions dictated evacuation of civilians. Mrs. Krump, then pregnant, joined the chief's family in Kansas, where she delivered a boy.

Three months later the Japanese overwhelmed Guam's meager defenses but Krump and five others escaped into the hills. They remained at large until September 1942 when the invaders caught Krump and two others. The Japanese beheaded the captives but Guamanians gave the Americans a Christian burial. Despite Japanese torture and death penalties, no Chamorro islander betrayed surviving Radioman George Tweed.

The story came full circle when Krump's son joined the Navy and became a chief petty officer who retired to his native Kansas.

Once the missing were accounted for, a final reckoning was possible. During the war at least 384 *Enterprise* men lost their lives, including fliers and sailors. The greatest loss was sustained by the original Enterprise Air Group, which became Air Group Six, with 105 fatalities from 1941 through 1943. *Enterprise*'s was the third-highest toll among all American carriers, exceeded only by *Franklin*'s 800-plus and *Bunker Hill*'s 529, though both of those figures were mainly due to single catastrophic attacks.

On September 25 Captain William L. Rees relieved Grover Hall, severing another link with the Big E's years of combat. *Enterprise* then laid on the knots southeasterly for a change, in a direction she had not taken since before the war. With two light carriers and two battleships, the Big E had a date in the Big Apple.

NEW YORK AND A PARADE

When *Enterprise* entered the west end of the Panama Canal on October 11, she left behind the greatest of oceans and the stage of her role in history's greatest drama. Emerging from the east end, she returned to the Caribbean, where she made her shakedown cruise, and again breasted the Atlantic. She had steamed 275,000 nautical miles during the war—the equivalent of eleven times around the earth at the equator—and now she was headed home.

On October 17 the globe-trotting *Enterprise* felt unfamiliar water on her hull as she entered the Hudson. Embarking Vice Admiral Frederick C. Sherman, who had the old *Lexington* sunk beneath him at Coral Sea, she was flagship of a contingent of Pacific Fleet veterans, gliding between the light carriers *Monterey* ahead and *Bataan* astern. With a blimp hovering overhead, the three flattops were trailed by five destroyers, all of which had survived man-made and natural storms—the Divine Wind of the kamikazes and both of "Halsey's hurricanes" when Third Fleet had ignored the worsening weather that killed three ships and pummeled many more.

Navy Day actually was October 27, Teddy Roosevelt's birthday, but the celebration began prematurely with 101 aircraft launched from the three flattops. Night Air Group 55 contributed forty-four planes droning above the Manhattan skyscrapers before landing at nearby Floyd Bennett Field in Brooklyn. The naval assembly finally totaled more than fifty ships or submarines. *Time* magazine called the armada "the people's fleet, 90% manned by civilians in uniform."

Thus began ten days of festivities which *Enterprise* sailors enjoyed to the fullest. If any felt it was only their due, so it was. Moored pierside on the Hudson, the Big E received more than a quarter million visitors anxious to see "the fightingest ship" in the U.S. Navy. Perhaps one percent of the throng that crowded aboard could associate more than two or three names with the Big E. Bull Halsey easily would have led the list, though his direct affiliation with the ship had ended more than three years before, and probably Butch O'Hare came next. Perhaps one in 1,000 could conjure a name like Lindsey or Strong or Vejtasa.

But small wonder. The war had been fought and won on an industrial scale, and a Navy that absorbed four million people and lost 62,000 was easier envisioned in a machine than in a man. So it was that fall: *Enterprise* the ship represented the human institution of the Big E, just as battleship *Arizona* became at once the setstone and tombstone for the visceral rage attending Pearl Harbor's 2,400 dead. Even better remembered were the five Sullivan brothers who died with their cruiser off Guadalcanal—subject of a well-received 1944 movie.

On Navy Day, President Harry Truman watched the naval review from battleship *Missouri,* fresh from her historic role in the surrender ceremony in Tokyo Bay. Then 50,000 people jammed into Central Park to hear him honor the naval services, no one imagining that in the coming year he would begin an ill-fated campaign to dismantle naval aviation.

Thereafter, *Enterprise* was accorded pride of place in the formal celebration ashore. By then the city was familiar with ticker-tape parades: the previous one for Nimitz occurred two weeks before and another for Halsey on December 14.

The ship had three bands through most of the war, one each for military events, concerts, and dances, with overlap among the members. Battleships, carriers, and heavy cruisers normally had twenty-three-piece bands sent to the fleet as complete organizations. In 1945 the Big E's primary band was "Number 51," denoting its graduation sequence from the Navy music school in Washington, D.C. Musicians were assigned to R Division, cross-trained in damage control and first-aid.

A parade band needed a drum major, and the Big E's only prior parade probably was the Puerto Rico event in 1938. However, bugler Arlond Banks—a two-year *Enterprise* veteran—had performed as a drum major in high school and volunteered for the position. After two days of practice on the flight deck, chief musician James "Swede" Lundgren reckoned that Band 51 was ship-shape for New York.

That Friday afternoon, with "Jack" Banks strutting his stuff, *Enterprise*'s band headed the victory parade down Sixth Avenue, just renamed Avenue of the Americas. Preceding droves of military men and New York police, the band blared out "Anchors Aweigh" as well as "The Marines' Hymn" and other eminently marchable tunes as sailors in white, marines in khaki, and cops in blue stepped out in time to the brisk four-four beat.

The show continued after dark when Air Group 55's Hellcats and Avengers flew overhead, running lights aglow.

THE FINAL RECORD

Enterprise received enormous publicity that fall. Navy Department news releases from 1945 have been taken at face value for six decades, crediting *Enterprise* aircrews with downing 911 Japanese aircraft and sinking seventy-one ships. In truth, the eighteen squadrons or detachments that served aboard the Big E were credited with 404 aerial victories, the balance being 507 "grounders." The top-scoring squadrons were VF-20 with 135 and VF-10 which counted 121 kills during its two deployments.

With seventeen aces (seventh-highest among twenty-six fast carriers), *Enterprise* was paced by Fighting 20's Doug Baker with a dozen kills. He disappeared while flying from *Lexington* in December 1944, after running his string to sixteen. The other leaders included Don Runyon of VF-6 with nine, plus Rod Devine and Swede Vejtasa of the Grim Reapers with eight each.

It's unknown how many of the seventy-one ships actually were sunk or how many, such as *Musashi,* were shared with other air groups.

MAGIC CARPET RIDES

Amid the publicity, adoration, and acclaim, *Enterprise* basked in the rosy glow of victory. Then suddenly it ended as the nation rushed to embrace peace once more. But *Enterprise,* though without airplanes, still had a mission. Modified with thousands of bunks and expanded galley services, she was deployed on more Magic Carpet rides, returning troops from Europe.

In November *Enterprise* raised steam and departed the States, sailors savoring the memory of girls loved and left. Late that month she called at Southampton, where the First Sea Lord, Sir Albert V. Alexander, headed an Admiralty delegation—the first such assembly on a foreign warship. The Admiralty Board's pennant was hoisted to mark the presence of three or more sea lords, and Mrs. Alexander presented it to *Enterprise,* saying, "The Board of the Admiralty would be proud if you would accept the gift of this flag to *Enterprise* as a token of respect for her gallant record, and as a sincere tribute from a great and historic navy to the prowess of the comrades in arms in the United States fleet."

For decades thereafter, *Enterprise* sailors regarded the pennant as an award comparable to the Presidential Unit Citation, but the Big E did not "win" the flag—it was bestowed as a memento between allies.

Sir Albert added that "it would be a great thing" if *Enterprise* would be preserved as Lord Nelson's HMS *Victory* was in England.

Buoyed by the prospects of preserving their historic ship, *Enterprise* men loaded some 4,400 passengers and resumed her role as a high-speed, flat-roofed transport. That Christmas would be the first at peace in four years, and all hands earnestly wished for leave. But Poseidon had his own blustery agenda. *Enterprise* clashed with four North Atlantic storms, warping part of her bow and slowing her progress before she arrived at Bayonne on December 24. Passengers and crew were off-loaded as fast as possible, all but a fortunate few with local families seeking the best way to spend the holiday.

On Christmas morning the phone rang in the chaplain's office. The call came from a New Jersey home for orphan boys who lacked any chance of a traditional Christmas. The home's administrator asked if *Enterprise* might possibly help.

The world knew that the Big E possessed guts; now it learned she possessed a heart. With most of the crew still aboard, all hands were called upon to lay to and help prepare a Christmas party. Some still nursed hangovers but all responded, organizing a party, and providing a tree, small presents, and the holiday meal that the orphans' home could not provide.

Some 140 foundlings were treated to *Enterprise* hospitality, thoroughly spoiled by men far from home who ensured that the boys departed the ship with candy bars and Dixie cup sailor hats sporting a symbolic *E*. Radar operator Richard Kenyon spoke for all when he said, "It was a tossup as to who had the best Christmas—the boys or the crusty old crew."

As 1945 fell astern, men inevitably reflected upon the recent past. Not long ago the Big E had steamed in the front rank of America's national defense, even before the war. In December 1941 the Navy counted 383,000 personnel for 790 ships and vessels, including seven fast carriers. Four years later the numbers had leapt almost an order of magnitude: 3,400,000 personnel to support 6,768 vessels including ninety-nine carriers of all types.

Amid the drastic postwar reductions, still *Enterprise* had a purpose. On January 1, 1946, *Enterprise* again turned her bow eastward, steaming to the Azores, fetching back 3,345 men and 212 Army women. Sixteen days after departing, Captain Rees eased her alongside the Bayonne, New Jersey, pier. In all, *Enterprise*'s four Magic Carpet rides returned 13,779 personnel to that most wonderful destination: home.

HELD IN RESERVE

Once secured at Bayonne, *Enterprise*'s boilers were shut down and her steam plant fell idle. The subsequent three skippers served in caretaker status with a minimal crew to perform routine maintenance. In May 1946 she entered dry dock to begin cocooning for reserve status—a process that lasted into the new year. She never again moved under her own power.

Yet some trace of *Enterprise*'s origins still served among the diminishing crew. In 1946 four plankowners remained among the original 2,100 from 1938: Lieutenant (jg) Sam H. Brewer, acting pay clerk Stanley W. Carter, chief yeoman James M. Martin, Jr., and Lieutenant (jg) Ralph E. Tucker. Carter was the last to depart. At a farewell dinner late that year the skipper, Commander Conrad Craven, presented him a memorial watch and asked "Nick" to say something. He had to sit down. Eight and a half years aboard the Big E could not be put into words.

At the end of January 1947 Commander Lewis E. Davis took over caretaker status, her fifteenth and last commanding officer and the only non–Annapolis graduate. Seventeen days later he presided over the final official act, when her white-starred commissioning pennant was lowered. *Enterprise* had served less than nine years. In half that time she had more than fulfilled her purpose presaged by Lucy Swanson in her 1936 christening with Shakespeare's words, "I have done the State some service."

★   ★   ★

Once *Enterprise* had been first among equals; now she entered the reserve fleet, inactive at Bayonne. She was in good company, as that year the Navy had shrunk to 529,000 personnel, one sixth of the wartime high.

For all her unmatched success and enduring fame, *Enterprise* faced at best an uncertain future. Though fully repaired, she had become naval driftwood, cast ashore between the rising tide of progress and the ebb tide of history. Smaller and less capable than her newer teammates, she could not economically be upgraded, and with twenty-four Essex class carriers in service or on order, there was no need. Moreover, the next generation of flattops was already afloat with the first two of the even larger Midway class.

But it wasn't merely about ship size or design. In January 1945, when Air Group 90 had just entered combat, the faint sound of aviation's future had been heard in the United States. Anemic turbojet engines had propelled the Navy's first all-jet aircraft—McDonnell's FH-1 Phantom—in its first flight. Though still two years from fleet service, the twin-engine jet clearly showed the way ahead. Bigger, heavier jets would follow close astern, with higher landing speeds that the Big E's deck could not easily accommodate.

If she were to deploy again it would have to be with propeller aircraft, so *Enterprise* was assigned a role that she could perform. In 1953 she was redesignated CVS-6, an antisubmarine carrier. She could have flown Avengers modified for that role, but the call never came. She remained part of the huge reserve fleet that not even the Korean War required.

THE LAST BATTLE

Early on, veterans and the public endorsed preserving *Enterprise*. Clearly unusable in the fleet, she was proposed as a museum with early suggestions centering on New York and San Francisco. In 1946 the Navy, cash-strapped in the immediate postwar era, said that it could not afford to move her, let alone provide maintenance.

In 1954 the Big E's men formed the USS Enterprise Association. Former Ordnanceman Mike Cochrane was the first president whose successors included the enormously popular B. H. "Bulkhead" Beams, champion gambler and, contrarily, master at arms.

The association's concept of a floating museum generated top-end support. The most noteworthy proponent was retired Fleet Admiral Halsey, who proclaimed the importance of preserving his former flagship. A congressional resolution was passed, endorsing the ship as a museum in the nation's capital. However, the chilly political winds blowing off the Potomac glazed the warm reception. In 1956 the government insisted that the association provide for the ship's movement and upkeep, with only six months to raise $2 million.

Recognizing a no-win situation, the *Enterprise* men struck a bargain with the Navy. In exchange for a $10,000 donation, the Annapolis athletic stadium would erect "the Enterprise tower" featuring the ship's unique tripod mast, and other parts would be available for displays around the country. Additionally, the Navy agreed that the first nuclear-powered carrier would be christened *Enterprise.*

The Navy delivered on most of the bargain, but the mast was never provided to the Naval Academy.

USS *Enterprise* was dropped from the naval register in October 1956. It was a death sentence. Though the association knew what was coming, the final announcement hit hard. Pedro Sandoval, a Big E shipfitter from 1942 to 1946, said, "When I heard she'd be sold for scrap, I cried." Electrician's Mate Ed Suto considered the news "heartbreaking." Scrapping began in 1958.

LEGACY

Despite the loss of the ship, *Enterprise*'s legacy endured. Commander Edward P. Stafford, an active-duty naval officer encouraged by Ernest Hemingway, spent five years writing *The Big E,* published in 1962. Stafford's engaging, literate style set the standard for every ship's history to follow. Yet surprisingly few *Enterprise* books followed over the next four decades. The association issued a memorial volume and historian Steve Ewing produced a pictorial history in 1982, but otherwise no additional publications emerged.

But new media emerged. In 2008 the History Channel produced a ten-part series about the ship, titled *Battle 360.* Featuring computer graphics and comments by *Enterprise* veterans and historians, the programs introduced the Big E to a new generation. Among younger viewers (and perhaps some not so young), the series provided context for those who assumed that USS *Enterprise* referred to *Star Trek*'s legendary space ship.

Enterprise is honored with museum exhibits at the Naval and Maritime Museum at Patriots Point, South Carolina; the National Museum of Naval Aviation in Pensacola; USS Lexington Museum in Corpus Christi; the EAA World War II Museum in Oshkosh, Wisconsin; and the Planes of Fame air museum at Chino, California. She's also represented by the incomplete Annapolis tower.

Other carriers have been preserved as museums, with varying degrees of success. The Essex class ships *Yorktown* (CV-10), *Intrepid* (CV-11), *Hornet* (CV-12), and *Lexington* (CV-16)—veterans of the 1943–45 campaigns—remain pierside in Charleston, New York, Alameda, and Corpus Christi, respectively. The first of her class, *Midway* (CV-41), is moored in San Diego. All had honorable careers far longer than *Enterprise*'s, but none mattered nearly as much. That statement in no way denigrates any of them, nor their sisters and follow-on members of the Forrestal and Nimitz classes. It's simply a fact. After November 1942, no individual ship of any kind could exert the war-winning influence of the Big E.

Furthermore, a ship turned into a static museum cannot retain its character. Just as airplanes are craft of the air, ships are creatures of the sea, and both lose something of their essence when tethered to the ground. But apart from the enormous expense and effort of upkeep, ships must be altered to comply with a daunting variety of concerns including environmental regulations, handicapped access, and commercial outlets. Preserved ships pay rare tribute to those who served aboard in war or peace, but their very immobility represents the difference between a taxidermist's shop and a zoo.

The ambience lacking in many museums—the emotional component—is reverence. It's a concern often expressed among *Enterprise* men. Alvin Kernan, who flew that last mission with Butch O'Hare, said, "Kids running about screaming, selling of candy and ice cream . . . it always seemed degrading. I always felt the *Enterprise* was truly noble and I didn't want to see her tied up."

The greatest loss in scrapping *Enterprise* was to future generations. In the twenty-first century, conventional naval and air forces play a secondary role in war fighting. Once the World War II generation passes away, only the equipment will remain as a tangible connection with that era. A largely intact aircraft carrier, unmodified beyond its 1946 configuration, would be a priceless historical asset. *Franklin* and *Bunker Hill*, both fully repaired, were the only other candidates, and they were discarded in 1964 and 1973, respectively.

REBIRTH

But there are other ways of honoring men of war. Just as the Big E was the eighth U.S. Navy vessel to bear the name, the ninth *Enterprise* (CVN-65) continued the line. She represented a historic step: the world's first nuclear-powered carrier, fueled by eight reactors. But there was more continuity than simply the name. Her first skipper was Captain Vincent P. De Poix, who, as Lieutenant De Poix, had flown with Fighting Six at Guadalcanal.

Vince De Poix took his responsibility seriously. In an action perhaps unique in U.S. Navy history, he arranged for five of his old ship's portholes to be installed in "E-65's" hull. The silver service presented by Mrs. White, widow of the Big E's first captain, also transferred to the new ship.

The second Big E was commissioned in 1961, at 83,000 tons more than four times the size of her predecessor. Over the next five decades "the 65 boat" made more than two dozen deployments, mainly to the Mediterranean, western Pacific, and Arabian Gulf, including two world cruises and six off Vietnam. Her eight reactors proved extraordinarily expensive, however, and none of her planned five sisters were laid down. She left on her penultimate scheduled deployment in December 2010 with decommissioning planned for 2013.

Ship naming remains a sore subject among naval purists. Sailors quip that the U.S. Navy is extremely consistent in christening some types of ships, as submarines are named for cities, states, politicians, and fish. During the 1970s the Navy began pandering to Congress for new carriers by naming the most important warships afloat for politicians. (Two previous carriers were named for FDR and JFK.) Every carrier purchased since 1970 has been named for presidents ranging from Washington (CVN-73) to Reagan (CVN-76) and big-Navy congressman Carl Vinson (CVN-70). The list also includes politicians such as Truman (CVN-75), who tried to dismantle naval aviation after World War II, and G. H. W. Bush (CVN-77), who presided over the Tailhook witch hunt in the 1990s, following allegations of sexual harassment by aviators attending a symposium. Eventually enough Navy supporters made their voices heard over the political clamoring to get *Enterprise* considered again. At one point CVN-78 was due for the honor, but Republican partisans preferred Gerald R. Ford, scheduled for commissioning in 2015.

An online petition was established by Big E boosters, with some heartfelt comments. "Naming carriers for politicians is the height of demeaning silliness," wrote one poster. Another noted, "History shows that those honored in the present day often prove to be unworthy, and that those who are ignored in their life are found to be most honorable in the future. Remember that we are a country of ideals, not men, and name our ships that way."

The second Gerald R. Ford class carrier, CVN-78, offered a prospect for reviving the Enterprise name, but the Navy defaulted to its political setting.

In 2011 the newly authorized CVN-79 was named *John F. Kennedy* even though the previous JFK (CV-67) had only been decommissioned in 2007.

Forty-four other ships have been named for *Enterprise* men, two being twice named, honoring Lieutenant (jg) Randolph M. Holder and Ensign James A. Shelton, who both died at Midway. The most recent was a guided missile destroyer named for William Pinckney, the heroic cook who rescued an unconscious shipmate from the choking, superheated boiler room at Santa Cruz. He passed away in 1975; the ship bearing his name was commissioned in 2004.

THE LEADERSHIP FACTORY

Enterprise was about leadership. Amoebalike, she spawned cell after new cell of leaders at every level, men who absorbed the lessons of their mentors and passed those values to the next generation like naval DNA. Her veterans continued contributing to the Navy and the nation for decades. At least two prewar aviators rose to full admiral, including Thomas H. Moorer, chairman of the Joint Chiefs of Staff, 1970–74, and John Hyland, who commanded the Pacific Fleet, 1967–70.

Vice admirals included Bill Martin, who eventually commanded the Sixth Fleet in the Mediterranean. His record of some 400 night carrier landings stood for forty years and propelled naval aviation into an all-weather, round-the-clock weapon. Jim Flatley also rose to three stars and founded the naval aviation safety center. He died of cancer soon after retiring in 1958, having established a four-generation aviation dynasty. Killer Kane commanded the light carrier *Saipan* and continued flying despite his poor vision, dying in a jet accident in 1957.

Wade McClusky of Midway fame received an honorary retirement of rear admiral, as did his successor, Max Leslie. Dick Best, medically retired as a lieutenant commander in 1944, never fully got over the bitter disappointment of leaving the war prematurely. Later he worked with the RAND Corporation as a security specialist.

The outspoken Jig Dog Ramage astonished everyone—including himself—by achieving rear admiral. His career ended during the 1970s purges of Chief of Naval Operations Elmo Zumwalt, as did Red Carmody's.

Stockton Birney Strong, recommended for the Medal of Honor after Santa Cruz, continued his stellar ways. A subordinate remembered him as "the most obnoxious little bastard you ever met—but good, really good." He commanded *Lexington* in 1960–61 and retired as a rear admiral.

Swede Vejtasa led his own air group, commanded the super-carrier *Constellation,* and retired a captain, having influenced fighter design and training. The Navy's famed Top Gun weapon school was established under his aegis in 1969.

Dog Smith also retired an admiral and died in 1971.

Probably the most aggressive aviator who ever launched from *Enterprise* was Charles English Henderson III. The dedicated night attack pilot found the peacetime Navy far too dull and entered business in the Far East. He married an Australian woman and was grooming one of his daughters for the world aerobatic championship when he died in 1986.

Enterprise pilots practically invented the Blue Angels flight demonstration team in 1946. The team's first skipper was Roy "Butch" Voris, and other early members were Fighting 10 alumni including Maurice "Wick" Wickendoll, Dusty Rhodes, and Whitey Feightner.

Then there was John Crommelin.

In 1947 Uncle John was a captain in the Pentagon when the Navy's battle was joined with the newly independent Air Force, which posed a serious threat to naval aviation. When, in 1950, he was identified as the source of leaked letters from admirals opposing the Air Force, the *New York Times* deemed him "a stormy petrel who wouldn't shut up." His career effectively over, Crommelin retired that year, receiving a tombstone promotion to rear admiral, based on combat decorations. Subsequently Crommelin was active in right-wing politics, running unsuccessfully for gubernatorial and senatorial seats, often on segregationist platforms.

However, nearly every man who served with Commander Crommelin aboard the Big E held him in reverence. Long after he left the ship, former *Enterprise* sailors knew they could take personal or professional problems to Captain or Admiral Crommelin as if he were still their exec. Which, in a real sense, he was.

The ship's last living combat captain was Cato Glover, skipper in the second half of 1944, who passed away in 1988.

Admiral Bull Halsey, who rode *Enterprise* to glory in 1942 and soured many sailors with his performance as a fleet commander, remained loyal to the Big E. Even after his losing battle to save her, he kept her close to his heart until his death in 1959.

Despite having nine full-time captains between commissioning and VJ

Day, none of the skippers exerted as much influence as John Crommelin, Tom Hamilton, damage control officer John Munro, and long-term non-commissioned personnel such as Jim Martin and Bulkhead Beams. They represented the sinews that bound the Big E together, the corporate knowledge and bottom-up leadership that turned a Yorktown class aircraft carrier into an essential strategic asset. Every successful warship produces such men; nowhere did it matter so much as in CV-6.

Enterprise exec Tom Hamilton died in 1994, aged eighty-eight. Looking back, he spoke for all Big E men in the crucial period. "During the first year or year and a half, there was a heck of a lot of doubt from the people that were out there . . . particularly when the *Enterprise* was all alone down there in '42 and '43. It was kind of *Enterprise* against the world. People felt pretty lonely. I figured we were going to win, but I knew it was going to take forever. The motto was, 'The Golden Gate by '48,' but we got back three years early!"

Probably every man who ever reported aboard *Enterprise* shared the sentiment and the satisfaction of belonging not just to a ship but to an institution. Bill Norberg, yeoman for every wartime captain, said, "I still think the *Enterprise* has a personality living today . . . it's gone to the scrap heap but it lives in the hearts and minds of those of us who are still living. I truly love USS *Enterprise* CV-6."

Bomber aircrewman Arthur Kropp reflected, "I didn't see any glamour in it at all. All I saw was a lot of destruction, a lot of bad things. There's nothing glamorous about war. But the country's worth fighting for. That's why we do it."

Among the Big E's most successful alumni is Jack C. Taylor, the VF-20 pilot who founded Enterprise Rent-A-Car. He says, "I was a callow youth when I joined the Navy, and I came out of it with more confidence and feeling that I was going to live a happy life and do the right thing."

Perhaps more than anyone, an anonymous sailor spoke for thousands when he insisted, "I wouldn't take any other ship in the fleet. The *Enterprise* has a soul."

As of 2011, some 450 veterans remained active in the Enterprise Association. A tradition was established at one of the early reunions when association business was concluded with time remaining. Some members suggested that they end the meeting as they had opened it—by reciting the Pledge of Allegiance. So they did. And so they still do.

REQUIEM AND RECKONING

The Big E's contribution to victory in 1942 cannot be denied. At Midway her squadrons sank three of the four enemy carriers, forever depriving Japan of its strategic initiative. In the Guadalcanal campaign she was essential to defending the Marines ashore. The presence of Air Group 10 during the November climax at Cactus was, at the very least, a major contribution to that crucial victory.

But for another perspective, consider how the Pacific war would have progressed had *Enterprise* been sunk or severely damaged any number of times. Had she not been delayed reaching Pearl in December 1941, she likely would have been destroyed in port. Her loss there or at Midway probably would have prevented the Guadalcanal landings and much that followed. If she had been more seriously crippled or lost at Eastern Solomons or Santa Cruz, her vital support of the Cactus Air Force would have been diminished. Any one of those prospects would have affected the U.S. Navy's ability to take the offensive when it was running out of flight decks almost monthly.

Would America have lost the Pacific without *Enterprise*? For a time in 1942, perhaps. Eventually the nation's immense industrial capacity and burning anger would have made good the deficit, and American warships would have dropped anchor in Tokyo Bay. But absent the Big E, that may not have occurred until 1947, with additional thousands of lives lost during the interim.

Thus passed into history USS *Enterprise* (CV-6), America's ship—the most decorated naval vessel in the nation's history. Pioneering, enduring, victorious, indispensable, she proved to be all that and more. But above all, when the odds were longest and the stakes the greatest, she ever proved herself master of the Pacific.

Appendix 1

AMERICAN AIRCRAFT

Dates are year the plane entered service.

Avenger: Grumman TBF carrier-based three-seat torpedo plane, 1942.

Catalina: Consolidated PBY twin-engine patrol plane, 1936.

Corsair: Vought F4U carrier-based fighter, 1943.

Curtiss SBC: carrier-based two-seat scout-bomber biplane, 1938.

Dauntless: Douglas SBD carrier-based two-seat dive-bomber, 1941.

Devastator: Douglas TBD carrier-based three-seat torpedo plane, 1937.

Grumman F3F: single-seat biplane carrier fighter, 1936.

Hellcat: Grumman F6F carrier-based fighter, 1943.

Helldiver: Curtiss SB2C carrier-based two-seat dive-bomber, 1943.

Kingfisher: Vought OS2U two-seat floatplane, 1940.

Northrop BT: two-seat carrier dive-bomber, 1938.

Seagull: Curtiss SOC two-seat float biplane, 1935.

Wildcat: Grumman F4F carrier-based fighter, 1941.

Appendix 2

JAPANESE AIRCRAFT

Betty: Mitsubishi G4M twin-engine, navy land-based bomber.

Claude: Mitsubishi A5M single-seat navy fighter; fixed landing gear.

Dave: Nakajima E8N float biplane reconnaissance aircraft.

Dinah: Mitsubishi Ki. 46 twin-engine army reconnaissance plane.

Emily: Kawanishi H8K four-engine seaplane, navy patrol bomber.

George: Kawanishi N1K1 single-engine naval land-based fighter.

Jake: Aichi E13A monoplane twin-float reconnaissance plane.

Judy: Yokosuka D4Y carrier dive-bomber.

Kate: Nakajima B5N single-engine, three-seat carrier torpedo plane.

Mavis: Kawanishi H6K four-engine seaplane, navy patrol bomber.

Nell: Mitsubishi G3M twin-engine, navy land-based bomber.

Oscar: Nakajima Ki. 43 single-engine army fighter.

Pete: Mitsubishi F1M two-seat float biplane.

Rufe: Nakajima A6M2N floatplane fighter based on the Zero.

Tabby: Nakajima L2D copy of the Douglas DC-2 airliner.

Tojo: Nakajima Ki. 44 single-engine army fighter.

Tony: Kawasaki Ki. 61 single-engine army fighter.

Val: Aichi D3A single-engine, two-seat navy dive-bomber; fixed landing
gear.

Zeke/Zero: Mitsubishi A6M single-engine navy fighter.

Acknowledgments

History is like antifreeze: you cannot add it too early; you can only add it too late. *Enterprise* began as a last-minute grab at history. When I started writing it in 2009, only four of *Enterprise*'s original 2,100 officers and men from the 1938 roster were known living. Nearly half of the Big E veterans I had consulted for previous books were already deceased, and more contributors have died as of manuscript completion. Thus, authors of World War II history are increasingly aware that each book likely will be the last ever compiled with direct contribution of those who lived the events described.

My teammates in bringing the *Enterprise* story to fruition were the same ones who produced *Whirlwind* (Simon & Schuster, 2010). Agent Jim Hornfischer—himself a top-rank naval historian—and editor Roger Labrie saw the project from inception to completion.

Support of the USS Enterprise Association was unstinting from the start. My friend Arnold Olson provided invaluable support and contact with other Big E veterans, many of whom otherwise would have been difficult to track down. Additionally, Joel Shepherd serves as the association's webmaster, maintaining one of the finest ship sites on the Internet.

I owe a debt to Navy veteran Ron Russell, moderator of the Battle of Midway Internet roundtable, and a superior manuscript editor and fact-checker. Exceptional support also came from historians Dr. Steve Ewing and Chuck Haberlein.

A special thank-you to Edward P. Stafford, author of the Big E's 1962 biography, who provided early encouragement.

Barrett Tillman
May 2011

ENTERPRISE MEN

James C. Barnhill	S Division, 1941–44 (d. 2010)
Richard H. Best	CO VB-6, 1941–42 (d. 2001)
Martin D. Carmody	VS-10, 1942–43 (d. 2008)
David Cawley	VS, VB-10, 1942–44
James G. Daniels	VF-6, LSO 1941–42 (d. 2004)
Jack Glass	VB-10, V-4 Division, 1942–44
Donald Gordon	VF-10, 1942–44 (d. 2010)
Ron Graetz	VT-6, 1941–42
James S. Gray	CO VF-6, 1939–42 (d. 1998)
Lester E. Gray	VF-10, 1943–44
Richard E. Harmer	CO VFN-101, 1944 (d. 1999)
Charles E. Henderson	VT-10, VTN-90, 1942–45 (d. 1986)
Alvin B. Kernan	VT-6, 1942–44
Norman Jack Kleiss	VS-6, 1941–42
Joseph T. Lawler	VF-20, 1944 (d. 2008)
James R. Lee	CO VS-10, 1942 (d. 2000)
Maxwell F. Leslie	Air group commander, 1942 (d.1985)
Robin M. Lindsey	VF-6, LSO, 1941–43 (d. 1994)
Lee Paul Mankin	VF-6, 1942 (d. 2011)
Carl J. Marble	S Division, 1938–41
William I. Martin	CO VT-10, CAG-90 (d. 1996)
Richard H. May	VF-10, 1943 (d. 2011)
Robert S. Nelson	VT-10, 1943–44
Bill Norberg	K Division, 1941–45
Arnold W. Olson	VFN-90, 1945
James D. Ramage	CO VB-10, 1943–44
Russell Reiserer	VF-10, 1942–43 (d. 2009)
Wilton Syckes	R Division, 1944–45
Stanley W. Vejtasa	VF-10, 1942–43
Charles C. Wheeler	Fifth Division, 1941–44

CONTRIBUTORS

David Baker III (special thanks); Jim Bresnahan (special thanks); Laura Clark Brown; CDR Pete Clayton; Paul Clegg; Michael J. Crawford; Robert C. Cressman; Mrs. Cleo J. Dobson; Robert F. Dorr; James H. Farmer; RADM James H. Flatley, Jr.; Kevin Flynn; Richard B. Frank; Jock Gardner; Reagan Grau; Jon Guttman; Janis Jorgensen; Donald M. Kehn, Jr.; Sander Kingsepp; Loraine Koski; Richard Latture; Rich Leonard; Leslie N. Long; Joseph E. Low; John B. Lundstrom; Helen McDonald; Owen Miller; Rick Morgan; Seth Paridon (special thanks); Norman Polmar;

CDR Robert R. Powell; Jonty Powis; David Reid; Mary Ripley; Henry Sakaida; Joel Shepherd; William J. Shinneman; CDR Doug Siegfried (special thanks); Joseph A. Springer; Paul Stillwell; Randy Stone; Kan Sugahara (special thanks); Osamu Tagaya; Bill Vickrey; Michael Weeks; Ron Werneth; Tracy White; CDR Jack Woodul; Jenny Wraight.

Beuhler Library at the National Museum of Naval Aviation
J-aircraft.com
National Museum of the Pacific War
National World War II Museum
Naval History and Heritage Command
Naval History magazine
Newton White Mansion, Maryland-National Capital Park
Royal Navy Historical Branch
The Tailhook Association
University of North Carolina, Chapel Hill
U.S. Naval Institute
USS Enterprise Association

Notes

PROLOGUE: KEARNY, NEW JERSEY, 1958

3 *Disposal of the ship:* Details from Richard F. Dempewolff, "The Big E Dies with Her Boots On," *Popular Mechanics,* May 1960.

4 Enterprise *was involved:* For a full list of battle stars, see http://ibiblio.net/hy perwar/USN/ships/dafs/BattleStars.html#partIII. Frequently the Pacific total is given as twenty-two, but how that number was derived remains unknown.

1. "I HAVE DONE THE STATE SOME SERVICE"

8 *"I should welcome":* PBS, "Timeline," http://www.pbs.org/crucible/t17.html, December 7, 2009.

10 *But every ship is a compromise:* Norman Friedman, *U.S. Aircraft Carriers* (Annapolis: Naval Institute Press, 1983), 90–91.

11 *"the sun broke through":* Bureau of Aeronautics Newsletter, June 15, 1938.

13 *"What'd I do* now?*":* Phone interviews with Carl Marble, November 2009.

13 *"I was nineteen":* Ibid.

14 *"They're shooting":* Ibid.

14 *"like a sack":* Ibid.

14 *"What damn poor":* Life, August 8, 1938, 36.

14 *"I'd been in":* Marble, phone interviews.

16   *The bombing and scouting squadrons:* Navy aircraft were identified by a series of letters or alphanumerics: the first letters denoted the mission such as B for bomber, SB for scout bomber, TB for torpedo bomber, and F for fighter. The manufacturer's letter came last: C for Curtiss, D for Douglas, F for Grumman, and T for Northrop. Thus, the BT-1 was Northrop's first bomber, while F3F was the third fighter from Grumman.

17   *"Charlie, how would":* Vice Admiral Charles A. Pownall, USN (Ret), U.S. Naval Institute oral history, 1970, 92–93.

17   *"Norfolk Navy Yard was":* Ibid., 95.

18   *"The workmen":* Ibid., 96.

18   *religious aspect:* Clark G. Reynolds, *The Fast Carriers* (New York: McGraw-Hill, 1968), xvi; interview with Rear Admiral James D. Ramage, USN (Ret), October 2009.

18   *"Captain Pownall":* Marble, phone interviews.

19   *"Sir, I've sounded":* Pownall, Naval Institute oral history, 97.

20   *"She was a beauty":* Rear Admiral James D. Ramage, USN (Ret), U.S. Naval Institute oral history, 1999, 26.

20   *"None of you ensigns":* Ibid., 26–27.

21   *"We didn't particularly":* Ibid., 31.

21   *"It was obvious":* Ronald W. Graetz emails, October 2009.

22   *"It was hate":* Ramage, Naval Institute oral history, 38.

22   *"Those goddam":* Ibid., 39–40.

23   *"the big outriggers":* Edward P. Stafford, *The Big E: The Story of the USS Enterprise* (Annapolis: Naval Institute Press, 2002), 10.

23   *Some ships required:* http://www.ussarizona.org/survivors/ballard/index.html.

24   *"Mr. Secretary":* Barrett Tillman and Robert L. Lawson, *Carrier Air War: In Original WWII Color* (Osceola, Wis.: Motorbooks International, 1996), 7.

24   *"the best":* MGM trailer on TCM.com, December 7, 2009.

25   *"Fred MacMurray":* Joseph Springer email, October 2009.

25   *"Toomey said":* James H. Farmer email, December 7, 2009.

26   *"a wonderful ship":* Pownall, Naval Institute oral history, 93.

26   *"Young man":* Ramage, Naval Institute oral history, 27–28.

27   *"If you will put":* Graetz email, October 2009.

28   *"There was never":* Ramage, Naval Institute oral history, 29.

28   *"Always be":* Ibid.

28   *"where I spent":* Graetz email, October 2009.

28   *"We got along":* Ibid.

29   *"the best":* Peter C. Smith, *Midway: Dauntless Victory* (Barnsley, U.K.: Pen & Sword, 2007), 130.

29   *"This is my first":* Captain N. J. Kleiss, USN (Ret), Battle of Midway circular, April 2009.

29   *"Officers and enlisted"*: Smith, *Midway,* 131.

29   *"Few enlisted men"*: Alvin Kernan, *The Unknown Battle of Midway* (New Haven, Conn.: Yale University Press, 2005), 57.

30   *"We were"*: Kleiss, Battle of Midway circular.

30   *"Don't worry"*: Ronald W. Russell, *No Right to Win: A Continuing Dialogue with Veterans of the Battle of Midway* (New York: iUniverse, 2006), 236.

30   *the figures alone lack context*: http://www.thepeoplehistory.com/1940s.html.

31   *"To chip it all off"*: Alvin Kernan, *Crossing the Line: A Bluejacket's Odyssey* (New Haven, Conn.: Yale University Press, 2007), 37–38.

32   *pilots logged nearly forty hours*: Copy of Richard H. Best's logbook in author's collection.

32   *Ashworth was killed*: Ibid.

32   *"I do not recall"*: Graetz email, June 2010.

2. "KEEP COOL, KEEP YOUR HEADS, AND FIGHT"

PAGE

33   *"Mr. Dickinson"*: Lieutenant Clarence E. Dickinson, *The Flying Guns* (New York: Charles Scribner's Sons, 1942), 1–2.

34   *"If anything"*: USS *Enterprise,* Battle Order Number One, November 28, 1942, http://www.cv6.org/1941/btlord1/btlord1.htm.

34   *"We in the"*: W. W. Norberg email, June 2010.

34   *"The worse"*: William F. Halsey and J. Bryan III, *Admiral Halsey's Story* (New York: McGraw-Hill, 1947), 56.

35   *"one of those fresh"*: Robert C. Cressman, "Steady Nerves and Stout Hearts," *The Hook,* August 1991, 13.

35   *"The plane"*: USS *Enterprise* action report, December 15, 1941, http://www.cv6.org/ship/logs/ph/eag-action19411207.htm.

36   *"Admiral, there's"*: Halsey, *Admiral Halsey's Story,* 77.

36   *"Pearl Harbor is under"*: Rear Admiral W. Earl Gallaher (Ret), radio interview by Jim Bresnahan, 1980, courtesy Jim Bresnahan.

36   *"We're at war"*: Interview with James Barnhill, November 2009.

37   *"When I reached"*: Claude Clegg, undated letter, 1941, courtesy Paul Clegg, 2009.

37   *"It was the most"*: Barrett Tillman, "Where Are They Now? Dick Best," *The Hook,* Spring 1996, 15.

37   *"This is 6-B-3"*: Robert C. Cressman and J. Michael Wenger, "This Is No Drill!" *Naval Aviation News,* November–December 1991, 22.

39   *"low-wing monoplanes"*: *Enterprise* action report, December 15, 1941.

39   *"a real dive-bomber's wife"*: Interview with Mrs. C. J. Dobson, San Diego, 1990.

42   *"Moments later"*: Steve Ewing, *USS* Enterprise *(CV-6): A Pictorial History* (Missoula, Mont.: Pictorial Histories, 1982), 17.

42   *"very, very angry"*: Gallaher interview by Bresnahan, 1980.

43   *"Before we're through"*: Halsey, *Admiral Halsey's Story,* 81.

43   *"the personal conviction"*: Bobby Oglesby, www.cv6.org.

44   *"an extremely reliable"*: Dickinson, *The Flying Guns,* 55.

44   *"a great big"*: Ibid., 57–58, 61.

45   *"In the first"*: Commander T. F. Caldwell, Jr., Bureau of Aeronautics interview, March 1945.

46   *"I was"*: Robert Trumbull, *The Raft* (Annapolis: Naval Institute Press, 1992), 6.

47   An eye: John B. Lundstrom, *The First Team: Pacific Naval Air Combat from Pearl Harbor to Midway* (Annapolis: Naval Institute Press, 1984), 63.

47   *"That piece"*: Dickinson, *The Flying Guns,* 72.

47   *"I really"*: Ronald W. Graetz, unpublished memoir.

49   *"Hal went"*: Gallaher interview by Bresnahan, 1980.

49   *"He must have"*: Graetz, unpublished memoir.

50   *"a pretty sight"*: Tillman, "Where Are They Now? Dick Best," 15.

50   *"The other forty-plus"*: Ibid.

51   *"Action starboard!"*: Narrative, Commander E. B. Mott, Office of Naval Records, March 22, 1944, 6.

52   *"Bingo!"*: Lundstrom, *The First Team,* 75.

53   *"I want"*: Halsey, *Admiral Halsey's Story,* 97.

53   *"a rolling fire"*: Gallaher interview by Bresnahan, 1980.

54   *"We'll take him"*: Lundstrom, *The First Team,* 115.

54   *"We launched"*: Gallaher interview by Bresnahan, 1980.

55   *"a clear"*: *The 1936 Lucky Bag,* U.S. Naval Academy, 227.

55   *"a swell lot"*: Jack Leaming, http://www.cv6.org/company/accounts/jleaming/.

56   *"This task force"*: "The Doolittle Raid," www.cv6.org/1942/doolittle.htm.

57   To Colonel Doolittle: Ibid.

58   *"That was"*: Ron Graetz email, January 2010.

58   *"bloodthirsty bunch"*: Lundstrom, *The First Team,* 150.

3. "REVENGE, SWEET REVENGE"

PAGE

61   *"Expedite return"*: Edward P. Stafford, *The Big E: The Story of the USS Enterprise* (Annapolis: Naval Institute Press, 2002), 87.

62   *"We must have this ship"*: Walter Lord, *Incredible Victory* (New York: Pocket Books, 1967), 29.

64   *"His brow"*: *The 1930 Lucky Bag,* U.S. Naval Academy.

65   *"If presence"*: John B. Lundstrom, *The First Team: Pacific Naval Air Combat from Pearl Harbor to Midway* (Annapolis: Naval Institute Press, 1984), 322.

65 *"I was one"*: Rear Admiral Clarence E. Dickinson (Ret), radio interview by Jim Bresnahan, 1980, courtesy Jim Bresnahan.

66 *"The Japanese fleet"*: Alvin Kernan, *Crossing the Line: A Bluejacket's Odyssey* (New Haven, Conn.: Yale University Press, 2007), 261.

66 *"I thought"*: Barrett Tillman, "Where Are They Now? Dick Best," *The Hook,* Spring 1996, 17.

67 *"slept like a baby"*: Ibid.

67 *"More than any"*: Rear Admiral W. Earl Gallaher (Ret), radio interview by Jim Bresnahan, 1980, courtesy Jim Bresnahan.

67 *"If one of our"*: Captain James S. Gray, USN, "Decision at Midway," http://www.midway42.org/aa-reports/vf-6.html.

67 *"This is"*: Lord, *Incredible Victory,* 82.

67 *"It was scary"*: Ronald W. Graetz, unpublished memoir.

67 *"Come on down"*: Lundstrom, *The First Team,* 343.

68 *"As he climbed"*: Commander James F. Murray (Ret), "Midway: The View from a Rear Seat," *The Hook,* Spring 1989, 41.

68 *"Proceed on mission assigned"*: Lundstrom, *The First Team,* 335.

70 *"We were at"*: Captain James S. Gray (Ret), at National Museum of Naval Aviation, 1988, http://home.comcast.net/~r2russ/midway//Backissues/2010-01.htm.

70 *"The fighter's job"*: Lieutenant Commander Richard H. Best (Ret) to author, 1993.

71 *"The fact that"*: Dickinson interview by Bresnahan, 1980.

73 *"We knew"*: Gallaher interview by Bresnahan, 1980.

73 *"and at that distance"*: Battle of Midway circular, June 24, 2002.

74 *"Earl, follow me down!"*: Scouting Six action report, USS *Enterprise* site, http://www.cv6.org/1942/midway/midway_3.htm.

75 *"It was just"*: Gallaher interview by Bresnahan, 1980.

76 *"I do not know"*: Battle of Midway circular, June 24, 2002.

76 Kaga's losses: Jonathan Parshall and Anthony Tully, *Shattered Sword: The Untold Story of the Battle of Midway* (Dulles, Va.: Potomac Books, 2005), 476.

76 *"It forces you"*: Tillman, "Where Are They Now? Dick Best," 16.

77 *"Nobody pushed"*: Parshall and Tully, 242.

77 *"I wanted to see"*: Tillman, "Where Are They Now? Dick Best," 16.

77 *"Arizona, I remember you!"* John Toland, *The Rising Sun: The Decline and Fall of the Japanese Empire* (New York: Random House, 1970), 335.

78 *"We all"*: Dickinson interview by Bresnahan, 1980.

78 *"Suddenly a burst"*: Rear Admiral C. W. McClusky, "Historical Commentary," http://www.centuryinter.net/midway/durling/sbd4618_mcclusky.html.

78 *"The tracer display"*: Robert C. Cressman, "Charlie Ware and the Battle of Midway," *The Hook,* Spring 1996, 28.

79 *"in good shape"*: Ibid., 29.

80 *"I was a"*: Tillman, "Where Are They Now? Dick Best," 16.

80 *"My god"*: Lord, *Incredible Victory,* 170.

80 *"like firecrackers"*: Commander E. B. Mott, Narrative, Office of Naval Records, March 22, 1944, 12.

82 *"Everyone and his brother"*: Peter C. Smith, *Midway: Dauntless Victory* (Barnsley, U.K.: Pen & Sword, 2007), 208.

84 *"a knock-down"*: Ibid., 222.

84 *"I'll do what"*: Ibid.

85 *"Of course we"*: Graetz, unpublished memoir.

86 *"I'll lose"*: Tillman, "Where Are They Now? Dick Best," 17.

87 *substantial losses: Enterprise*'s action report says twenty-four pilots and twenty-five gunners were lost but several were recovered after the report was compiled.

87 *"sincere wish"*: VT-6 action report, June 1942, http://www.cv6.org/ship/logs/action19420604-vt6.htm.

87 *Yet in 2009:* http://www.navy.mil/navydata/people/cno/Roughead/Speech/6.4.09_Battle%20of%20Midway%20Remarks%20(2)-%20LT%20Gandy%20final.doc.

87 *"Revenge, sweet revenge"*: Tillman, "Where Are They Now? Dick Best," 16.

4. "WE DIDN'T KNOW A DAMNED THING"

PAGE

89 *"Oh, don't listen"*: James D. Ramage to author; Steve Ewing to author, 2010.

92 *Jack London had written:* Jack London, *Cruise of the Snark* (New York: Macmillan, 1918), 166.

92 *"the tollgate"*: Samuel Eliot Morison, *The Two Ocean War* (Annapolis: Naval Institute Press, 2007), 165.

93 *"Now I know"*: Sadamu Komachi at Pensacola, Florida, May 1992, related to author by John B. Lundstrom.

94 *"We didn't know"*: Barrett Tillman, "Where Are They Now? Lou Bauer," *The Hook,* Fall 1994, 15.

94 *"My Navy mentor"*: Vice Admiral David Richardson, USN (Ret), to author, 2009.

96 *"I could see"*: Henry Sakaida, *Winged Samurai* (Mesa, Ariz.: Champlin Museum Press, 1985), 78.

96 *"My seat"*: Robert D. Gibson, unpublished memoir, 2001.

97 *"Pilots are"*: Captain Henry A. Rowe to author, 1978.

98 *One was gunnery officer Benny Mott:* Interview with Dr. Steve Ewing, August 28, 2010. Later Mott revised his opinion. See Navy Library interview, March 1946.

98 *"We had done"*: Bill Norberg email, September 2, 2010.

99 I-175: http://www.combinedfleet.com/I-175.htm.

99 *About half of the enemy boats:* "Imperial Submarines," http://www.combined fleet.com/I-121.htm.

101 *"Keeping the sun"*: Gibson, unpublished memoir.

102 *"The Japs"*: Eugene Burns, *Then There Was One* (New York: Harcourt, Brace, 1944), 74.

102 *"Many bogeys"*: John B. Lundstrom, *The First Team and the Guadalcanal Campaign: Naval Fighter Combat from August to November 1942* (Annapolis: Naval Institute Press, 1994), 128.

103 *"sweating like a Turk"*: Ibid., 133.

103 *top-scoring F4F pilot:* The leading Eastern Aircraft FM-2 Wildcat pilot downed nine enemy planes.

103 *"The* Enterprise's *elevators"*: Commander Lee Paul Mankin to author, 1990.

104 *"I dived"*: Barrett Tillman, *TBF-TBM Avenger Units of WW2* (Oxford, U.K.: Osprey, 1999), 14.

104 *"late afternoon"*: Commander E. B. Mott, Narrative, Office of Naval Records, March 22, 1944, 14.

104 *"Here come"*: Burns, *Then There Was One*, 76.

105 *"The dives"*: USS *Enterprise* action report, August 24, 1942, http://www.cv6 .org/ship/logs/action19420824.htm#action.

105 *14,000 rounds:* USS *Enterprise* gunnery report, September 1, 1942, http://www .cv6.org/ship/logs/gunnery19420824.htm.

106 *"Only because"*: Crommelin quoted by Dr. Steve Ewing to author, June 4, 2010. Photographer's Mate Marion Riley filmed the third hit, losing his movie camera in the process, but still images were widely published.

107 *"I kept"*: Burns, *Then There Was One*, 82.

108 *"I'll go"*: Ibid., 83.

108 *"Well, I did"*: Ibid., 86.

109 *"There's a point"*: Richard Tregaskis, *Guadalcanal Diary* (New York: Random House, 1943), 250.

109 *"Max, keep coming"*: Tillman, *TBF-TBM Avenger Units of WW2*, 18.

110 *seventy-eight killed:* The action report lists seventy-four fatalities but missing aircrew raised the toll. Full accounting from the Enterprise Association, courtesy of Arnold W. Olson.

110 *"I'll never"*: Interview with James Barnhill, November 2009.

110 *"that damned island"*: Lieutenant Colonel Kerry Lane, USMC (Ret), *Guadalcanal Marine* (Jackson: University Press of Mississippi, 2004), 107.

5. "A FIGHTING CHANCE"

112   *twenty-six-year career:* Some sources say that Hardison commanded the presidential yacht *Mayflower* in the 1920s but no documentation has arisen.

112   *"in a daze":* Bill Norberg emails, May 2010.

113   *"A fine bunch":* Stanley W. Vejtasa interview, American Airpower Foundation, 113, Texas, 2000.

113   *"He asked me":* Captain Donald Gordon to author, 2009.

113   *"raring to go":* Lieutenant Commander James R. Lee, Bureau of Aeronautics interview, April 1943.

113   *"I did night qual":* Gordon to author, 2009.

114   *"Kill Japs":* Samuel Eliot Morison, *History of United States Naval Operations in WW II,* Vol. V: *The Struggle for Guadalcanal* (Edison, N.J.: Castle, 2001), 187.

114   *"the hottest potato":* William F. Halsey and J. Bryan III, *Admiral Halsey's Story* (New York: McGraw-Hill, 1947), 120.

114   *"Carrier power":* Ibid.

114   *American airpower at Guadalcanal:* John B. Lundstrom, *The First Team and the Guadalcanal Campaign* (Annapolis: Naval Institute Press, 1994), 329.

114   *STRIKE REPEAT STRIKE!:* Ibid., 349, 580 note 31.

116   *"You men":* Edward P. Stafford, *The Big E: The Story of the USS Enterprise* (Annapolis: Naval Institute Press, 2002), 175.

116   *"We are on":* Eugene Burns, *Then There Was One* (New York: Harcourt, Brace, 1944), 111–13.

117   *"Things happened":* Lee to author, January 1973.

118   *"His good common sense":* The 1937 *Lucky Bag,* U.S. Naval Academy, 253.

120   *"had the satisfying":* Stephen L. Moore et al., *The Buzzard Brigade: Torpedo Squadron Ten at War* (Missoula, Mont.: Pictorial Histories, 1996), 43.

122   *"one of the most":* Polmar, *Aircraft Carriers,* Vol. I, 1909–1945 (Washington, D.C.: Potomac Books, 2006), 299.

123   *"Burns, you're the":* Burns, *Then There Was One,* 122.

123   *"a solid citizen":* Vejtasa interview, American Airpower Foundation, Midland, Texas, 2000.

123   *"I was able":* Ibid.

123   *"Looking up":* E. G. Johnston to the Director of Naval History, February 20, 1968.

124   *"I felt":* Ibid.

125   *"When the first guy":* http://www.pinckney.navy.mil/site%20pages/History.aspx.

125   *"I had some":* Elias B. Mott interview, Naval Records and Library, March 5, 1946, 17.

126   *"Gosh no":* Stanley J. Vejtasa interview, *Dogfights,* The History Channel, 2006.

127 *"3.0 in academics"*: The 1923 *Lucky Bag*, U.S. Naval Academy, .

127 *"That's good shooting"*: Hardison papers, University of North Carolina, Chapel Hill, collection.

128 *"If thee"*: Burns, *Then There Was One*, 130.

129 *"I don't want"*: Interview with Robin Lindsey, 1985.

129 *"like it was"*: Phone interview with Stanley W. Vejtasa, July 12, 2010.

130 *"I was looking"*: Ibid.

130 *Imperial Navy lost more aircrew*: Probably 110 at Midway and 145 at Santa Cruz: Jonathan Parshall and Anthony Tully, *Shattered Sword: The Untold Story of the Battle of Midway* (Dulles, Va.: Potomac Books, 2005), 476; Lundstrom, *The First Team and the Guadalcanal Campaign*, 454.

131 *"I know"*: Captain Elias B. Mott, "The Battles of Santa Cruz and Guadalcanal," *The Hook*, August 1990, 45.

131 *"God in His"*: Steve Ewing, *Reaper Leader: The Life of Jimmy Flatley* (Annapolis: Naval Institute Press, 2002), 143.

6. "THE MOST EXCITING PART OF YOUR DAY"

PAGE

134 *"When aroused"*: The 1934 *Lucky Bag*, U.S. Naval Academy, 168.

136 *"My God"*: John B. Lundstrom, *The First Team and the Guadalcanal Campaign* (Annapolis: Naval Institute Press, 1994), 480.

137 *"afire and"*: Stephen L. Moore et al., *The Buzzard Brigade: Torpedo Squadron Ten at War* (Missoula, Mont.: Pictorial Histories, 1996), 72.

137 *"Being heavily shelled"*: William F. Halsey and J. Bryan III, *Admiral Halsey's Story* (New York: McGraw-Hill, 1947), 129.

138 *"When you're jinking"*: Robert D. Gibson, "An Average American at Guadalcanal," unpublished memoir.

139 *"Okay everybody"*: Steve Ewing, *Reaper Leader: The Life of Jimmy Flatley* (Annapolis: Naval Institute Press, 2002), 152.

139 *"In combat"*: Ibid.

140 *Some pilots logged*: Logbook of Martin D. Carmody, in author's collection.

140 *"a prince"*: Vejtasa to author, July 2010.

142 *"after the beating"*: Lundstrom, *The First Team*, 521.

144 *"the crud"*: Vejtasa to author, July 2010.

144 *"Pass the word"*: J. W. Shepherd letter, November 11, 1942, http://www.cv6.org/company/accounts/jshepherd/.

145 *"You're a fighting fool"*: Ewing, *Reaper Leader*, 167.

146 *the Japanese lost*: Richard B. Frank, *Guadalcanal: The Definitive Account* (New York: Random House, 1990), 581.

146 *"Take care"*: Ewing, *Reaper Leader*, 168.

146 *"The whole campaign"*: Richard Frank email, April 10, 2010.

7. "A LONG AND TEEDJUS JOURNEY"

148 *"He was built"*: Richard May phone interview, January 2010.

149 *"Stay on"*: Ibid.

149 *"The fact that"*: Ibid.

150 *"our genial"*: Stephen L. Moore et al., *The Buzzard Brigade: Torpedo Squadron Ten at War* (Missoula, Mont.: Pictorial Histories, 1996), 109.

150 *"For a group"*: Ibid., 108.

151 *six sets of brothers:* Email from Arnold Olson, USS Enterprise Association, November 2010.

151 *"Ramage, I am going"*: James D. Ramage to author, January 2010.

151 *"I'll get you aboard"*: Rear Admiral James D. Ramage, USN (Ret), U.S. Naval Institute oral history, 1985, 65.

153 *"For consistently"*: "Presidential Unit Citation," www.cv6.org/decoration/puc/puc.htm.

153 *"got into a little discussion"*: Admiral Charles D. Griffin, USN (Ret), U.S. Naval Institute oral history, 1970, 101.

153 *"It took half"*: Ibid.

154 *he dealt the cards:* Bill Shinneman email, January 2010.

154 *"Money meant"*: Ronald W. Graetz email, January 2010.

154 *"He tore up the cards"*: Bill Shinneman email, January 2010.

155 *"What's the ante?"*: Bill Norberg email, January 2010.

155 *"a truly great officer"*: Rear Admiral Thomas J. Hamilton, USN (Ret), U.S. Naval Institute oral history, 1978.

156 *Big E had been made over:* Details on 1943 refit from Norman Friedman, *U.S. Aircraft Carriers: An Illustrated Design History* (Annapolis: Naval Institute Press, 1983), 97–99.

157 *"it was a long"*: Martin, c. 1978.

158 *"a cold-blooded will"*: In Hamilton's Naval Institute oral history, Hamilton to Captain Radford, director of aviation training, December 1941, "Tentative Proposed Physical Training Program."

158 *"a soft"*: Hamilton, Naval Institute oral history.

158 *"It was"*: Ibid.

159 *"a stern disciplinarian"*: Bill Norberg email, January 2010.

161 *"There isn't"*: Steve Ewing and John B. Lundstrom, *Fateful Rendezvous: The Life of Butch O'Hare* (Annapolis: Naval Institute Press, 1997), 229–30.

163 *"If you see"*: Ibid., 239.

166 *"I have them in sight"*: Ibid., 274.

167 *"Oh, I'm hit"*: Hamilton, Naval Institute oral history.

167 *"The fighters were over"*: Ramage, Naval Institute oral history, 79.

167 *"We took off"*: Interview of Commander W. I. Martin, USN Air Intelligence Division, October 1944, 4.

167 *"The low escort"*: Ramage, Naval Institute oral history, 79.

168 *"most visible"*: Bill Norberg, http://www.cv6.org/company/accounts/gflynn/; http://www.everestconfessions.com/Excerpt/chapter32.html.

8. "IF ANY OF THEM LIVED, IT WASN'T OUR FAULT"

PAGE

171 *"Tom Hamilton was"*: Rear Admiral James D. Ramage, USN (Ret), U.S. Naval Institute oral history, 1999.

171 *"If the Essex class"*: Rear Admiral Thomas J. Hamilton, USN (Ret), U.S. Naval Institute oral history, 1978/1983.

175 *"a Hollywood war"*: Barrett Tillman, *Hellcat: The F6F in WW II* (Annapolis: Naval Institute Press, 1979), 57.

175 *"It was a good day"*: Ramage, Naval Institute oral history, 88.

176 *"They had"*: Ibid., 88.

176 *"with its head"*: Interview of Commander W. I. Martin, USN Air Intelligence Division, October 1944, 8.

176 *"When the target"*: William I. Martin to author, 1978.

176 *"The tunnel"*: Barrett Tillman, *Avenger at War* (Surrey, U.K.: Ian Allan, 1979), 40.

178 *"We even"*: Harmer to author, various dates, 1977–78.

180 *"Before that"*: Ramage, Naval Institute oral history.

180 *"Our world"*: Ramage to author, 2010.

180 *"He certainly was"*: Jack Glass email, January 2010.

180 *"Killer was just great"*: Interview with Rear Admiral James D. Ramage, USN (Ret), January 2010.

180 *"A fifth of booze"*: Interview with Commander Lester Gray, November 2010.

180 *"Mr. Flynn"*: Hamilton, Naval Institute oral history.

182 *"We really wanted"*: Ramage interview, January 2010.

9. "VECTOR TWO-SEVEN-ZERO"

PAGE

184 *Eleven Japanese naval air groups*: Barrett Tillman, *Carrier Battle in the Philippine Sea* (St. Paul: Phalanx, 1994), 45.

186 *"On the count"*: Stephen L. Moore et al., *The Buzzard Brigade: Torpedo Squadron Ten at War* (Missoula, Mont.: Pictorial Histories, 1996), 103.

187 *"a drink of something"*: Ibid., 197.

189 *"I didn't think"*: http://www.cv6.org/1944/marianas/marianas_2.htm.

190 *"They got"*: VF-10 action report, June 19, 1944.

191   *Shinya Ozaki*: http://www.pacificwrecks.com/people/visitors/wiggs.html.

192   *"more credit"*: Tillman, *Avenger at War* (Surrey, U.K.: Ian Allan, 1979), 116.

192   *"Enemy fleet"*: Ibid.

192   *"leaving a circular wake"*: Ibid., 96.

192   *"We're going to be"*: Ramage to author.

193   *"The carrier below"*: Ramage, Naval Institute oral history, 108.

195   *"my old hero"*: Ibid., 120.

196   *"How much ice cream"*: Hamilton, Naval Institute oral history, 84–85.

197   *"You never saw"*: Ibid.

10. "ONLY HUMAN"

PAGE

201   *"The embodiment"*: *The 1934 Lucky Bag*, U.S. Naval Academy, 112.

202   *"We went aboard"*: "VT-20 Sea Stories," http://www.cv6.org/ship/logs/ag20/vt20.htm.

202   *"a very aggressive"*: Hamilton, Naval Institute oral history, 18.

204   *"Koror Island was"*: Captain Joe Lawler, USN (Ret), "VF-20—Making History," *The Hook,* Spring 1983, 10.

206   Enterprise *bombers found*: "The Official Chronology of the U.S. Navy in World War II," http://ibiblio.org/hyperwar/USN/USN-Chron/USN-Chron-1944.html.

207   *"a lonely aviator"*: Lawler, "VF-20—Making History," 11.

208   *"Bail out, Shorty!"*: "Accounts—Bob Barnes," www.cv6.org/company/accounts/bbarnes/.

210   *"apparently going"*: VB-20 action report, October 24, 1944, http://www.cv6.org/ship/logs/ag20/vb20.htm.

211   *"something you dream"*: Robert J. Barnes, "Helldivers of the Big E," http://www.cv6.org/company/accounts/bbarnes/.

212   *"enemy bullets"*: Anthony Tully, *Battle of Surigao Strait* (Bloomington: Indiana University Press, 2009), 68.

212   *"outstanding"*: Bombing 20 action report, October 24, 1944.

214   *"From about 17,000"*: Lawler, "VF-20—Making History," 14.

214   *At least three*: Details of *Musashi* damage from an analysis by Sander Kingsepp, email, 2010.

216   *"The last report"*: Hamilton, Naval Institute oral history.

217   *"looked like"*: Barnes, "Helldivers of the Big E."

217   *"the most intense"*: Ibid.

219   *Battle of Leyte Gulf*: For the definitive account of the Battle off Samar, part of the Battle of Leyte Gulf, see James D. Hornfischer, *Last Stand of the Tin Can Sailors* (New York: Bantam, 2004).

219 *"For the Imperial Japanese Navy"*: Evan Thomas, *Sea of Thunder: Four Commanders and the Last Great Naval Campaign* (New York: Simon & Schuster, 2007), 5.

221 *"His physical condition"*: USS *Hardhead* report of second war patrol, http://issuu.com/hnsa/docs/ss-365_hardhead?mode=a_p.

222 *"The Big E is only human"*: *Enterprise* document, November 22, 1944, http://www.cv6.org/ship/logs/ag20/loose-gear.htm.

11. "LIVE WITH GREAT ENTHUSIASM"

PAGE

225 *"We're going"*: Interview with Arnold W. Olson, January 2010.

225 *"That was the first"*: Olson interview, January 2011.

225 *Air Group 90 contained*: John W. MacGlashing, *Batmen: Night Air Group 90 in World War II* (St. Paul: Phalanx, 1995), 43–45.

226 *"Everyone tried"*: Ibid., 11.

226 *"he drove that ship"*: Olson interview, January 2010.

230 *"intense to incredible"*: USS *Hancock* pilot William E. Tobin to author, 1990.

231 *"Many of us"*: VT(N)-90 Squadron History, http://www.cv6.org/ship/logs/vtn90/vtn90-4501.htm.

234 *fifty American vessels*: Compiled from http://ibiblio.org/hyperwar/USN/USN-Chron/USN-Chron-1945.html.

234 *"all over the Western Pacific"*: MacGlashing, *Batmen*, 22.

235 *"The Jap roared"*: Arnold Olson emails, February 2009.

237 *The kamikazes came*: Japanese records indicate no Judys taking off from Kyushu on April 11. The kamikazes undoubtedly were Zekes flown by Flight Petty Officers Takashi Sokabe and Hisao Miyazaki. Kan Sugahara, emails July 2011.

238 *"Wearing of mourning"*: USS *Enterprise* plan of the day, April 14, 1945.

239 *"A blue funk"*: VT(N)-90 Squadron History.

242 *"live with great enthusiasm"*: Kan Sugahara, "Who Knocked the *Enterprise* Out of the War?" *Naval History*, April 2008.

243 *"Everybody unloaded on him"*: *Battle 360*, Episode 10, "The Empire's Last Stand," The History Channel, 2008.

243 *"When we saw"*: Erwin Below, *Cincinnati Post*, August 1945, http://www.cv6.org/news/45-07.htm.

244 *"I'm going to die"*: *Battle 360*, http://www.youtube.com/watch?v=REYJYpwjdeA&feature=related.

245 *But assiduous research*: Kan Sugahara, "Who Knocked the *Enterprise* Out of the War?" *Naval History*, 2008.

12. "THE *ENTERPRISE* HAS A SOUL"

PAGE

248 *578-foot pennant:* Actually, November 2, 1943, to June 5, 1945, was 582 days.

248 *"a rooting, tooting":* http://content.lib.washington.edu/cgi-bin/viewer.exe?CISO ROOT=/imlsmohai&CISOPTR=458&CISORESTMP=&CISOVIEWTMP=& CISOMODE=grid; *Bremerton Sun* article, http://web.kitsapsun.com/bremerton centennial/waryears/wecandoit.html.

249 *Chief Michael Krump:* His fate related in Arnold Olson 2009 emails and http:// www.nps.gov/archive/wapa/indepth/extContent/Lib/liberation5.htm.

250 *a final reckoning:* The National Memorial to Naval Aviation in Charleston, South Carolina, lists 359 *Enterprise* men lost in World War II. However, that figure was based on incomplete records and omits aircrew temporarily attached to the ship and some who died while flying ashore. Full data from the USS Enterprise Association, January 2010.

251 *"the people's fleet":* "Navy Day, 1945," *Time,* October 29, 1945, http:// www.time.com/time/magazine/article/0,9171,776313-1,00.html. In October the ships at New York included thirty-one destroyers, five cruisers, nine submarines, two battleships, and two auxiliaries plus the carriers *Enterprise, Bataan, Monterey,* and *Midway.* Some ships left New York before Navy Day the 27th, http://www.uscs.org/collectingtopics/navyday/MasterFileNavy Day.pdf.

252 *aerial victories:* Derived from Frank Olynyk, *USN Credits for the Destruction of Enemy Aircraft in Air-to-Air Combat, World War 2* (privately published, 1982).

253 *"The Board":* Associated Press wire story, November 23, 1945.

254 *"It was a tossup":* http://www.cv6.org/company/accounts/rkenyon/.

254 *As 1945 fell astern:* Navy personnel and ships, 1941–45: http://www.history .navy.mil/branches/org9-4.htm#1938.

254 *four plankowners:* Martin died September 2010.

256 *"When I heard":* Battle 360.

256 *"heartbreaking":* Ibid.

257 *"Kids running about":* Ibid.

258 *"Naming carriers for politicians":* http://ussntrprs.epetitions.net/signatures .php?petition_id=784.

259 *"the most obnoxious":* Interview with James D. Ramage, January 2010.

260 *"a stormy petrel":* *New York Times* obituary, November 12, 1996.

261 *"During the first":* Hamilton, Naval Institute oral history.

261 *"I still think":* Battle 360.

261 *"I didn't see":* Ibid.

261 *"I was a callow":* http://www.veteransadvantage.com/cms/content/jack-taylor.

261 *"I wouldn't take"*: http://webcache.googleusercontent.com/search?q=cache:1
      oYzWg64mJUJ:byng.vsb.bc.ca/eyuen/yuen/social%2520studies%252011%25
      20block%2520e/Claire%2520Boucher/Kamikaze.ppt+Cincinnati+%22erwin+
      below%22&cd=6&hl=en&ct=cInk&gl=us.

INDEX

Page numbers in *italics* refer to illustrations and maps.

About the Author

BARRET TILLMAN is a widely recognized authority on air warfare in World War II and the author of more than forty nonfiction and fiction books on military topics. The former managing editor of *The Hook* (the magazine of the Tailhook Association), Tillman has appeared in many television documentaries. He has received six awards for history and literature, including the Admiral Arthur Radford Award for Naval History and Literature. He lives in Mesa, Arizona.